The Valley of

Edith Wharton

Alpha Editions

This edition published in 2024

ISBN : 9789362095299

Design and Setting By
Alpha Editions
www.alphaedis.com
Email - info@alphaedis.com

Contents

BOOK I.
THE OLD ORDER.

Prima che incontro alla festosa fronte
I lugubri suoi lampi il ver baleni.

1.1.

It was very still in the small neglected chapel. The noises of the farm came faintly through closed doors—voices shouting at the oxen in the lower fields, the querulous bark of the old house-dog, and Filomena's angry calls to the little white-faced foundling in the kitchen.

The February day was closing, and a ray of sunshine, slanting through a slit in the chapel wall, brought out the vision of a pale haloed head floating against the dusky background of the chancel like a water-lily on its leaf. The face was that of the saint of Assisi—a sunken ravaged countenance, lit with an ecstasy of suffering that seemed not so much to reflect the anguish of the Christ at whose feet the saint knelt, as the mute pain of all poor down-trodden folk on earth.

When the small Odo Valsecca—the only frequenter of the chapel—had been taunted by the farmer's wife for being a beggar's brat, or when his ears were tingling from the heavy hand of the farmer's son, he found a melancholy kinship in that suffering face; but since he had fighting blood in him too, coming on the mother's side of the rude Piedmontese stock of the Marquesses di Donnaz, there were other moods when he turned instead to the stout Saint George in gold armour, just discernible through the grime and dust of the opposite wall.

The chapel of Pontesordo was indeed as wonderful a storybook as fate ever unrolled before the eyes of a neglected and solitary child. For a hundred years or more Pontesordo, a fortified manor of the Dukes of Pianura, had been used as a farmhouse; and the chapel was never opened save when, on Easter Sunday, a priest came from the town to say mass. At other times it stood abandoned, cobwebs curtaining the narrow windows, farm tools leaning against the walls, and the dust deep on the sea-gods and acanthus volutes of the altar. The manor of Pontesordo was very old. The country people said that the great warlock Virgil, whose dwelling-place was at Mantua, had once shut himself up for a year in the topmost chamber of the keep, engaged in unholy researches; and another legend related that Alda, wife of an early lord of Pianura, had thrown herself from its battlements to escape the pursuit of the terrible Ezzelino. The chapel adjoined this keep, and Filomena, the farmer's wife, told Odo that it was even older than the tower and that the walls had been painted by early martyrs who had concealed themselves there from the persecutions of the pagan emperors.

On such questions a child of Odo's age could obviously have no pronounced opinion, the less so as Filomena's facts varied according to the seasons or her mood, so that on a day of east wind or when the worms were not hatching well, she had been known to affirm that the pagans had painted the chapel under Virgil's instruction, to commemorate the Christians they had tortured. In spite of the distance to which these conflicting statements seemed to relegate them, Odo somehow felt as though these pale strange people—youths with ardent faces under their small round caps, damsels with wheat-coloured hair and boys no bigger than himself, holding spotted dogs in leash—were younger and nearer to him than the dwellers on the farm: Jacopone the farmer, the shrill Filomena, who was Odo's foster-mother, the hulking bully their son and the abate who once a week came out from Pianura to give Odo religious instruction and who dismissed his questions with the invariable exhortation not to pry into matters that were beyond his years. Odo had loved the pictures in the chapel all the better since the abate, with a shrug, had told him they were nothing but old rubbish, the work of the barbarians.

Life at Pontesordo was in truth not very pleasant for an ardent and sensitive little boy of nine, whose remote connection with the reigning line of Pianura did not preserve him from wearing torn clothes and eating black bread and beans out of an earthen bowl on the kitchen doorstep.

"Go ask your mother for new clothes!" Filomena would snap at him, when his toes came through his shoes and the rents in his jacket-sleeves had spread beyond darning. "These you are wearing are my Giannozzo's, as you well know, and every rag on your back is mine, if there were any law for poor folk, for not a copper of pay for your keep or a stitch of clothing for your body have we had these two years come Assumption—. What's that? You can't ask your mother, you say, because she never comes here? True enough—fine ladies let their brats live in cow-dung, but they must have Indian carpets under their own feet. Well, ask the abate, then—he has lace ruffles to his coat and a naked woman painted on his snuff box—What? He only holds his hands up when you ask? Well, then, go ask your friends on the chapel-walls—maybe they'll give you a pair of shoes—though Saint Francis, for that matter, was the father of the discalced, and would doubtless tell you to go without!" And she would add with a coarse laugh: "Don't you know that the discalced are shod with gold?"

It was after such a scene that the beggar-noble, as they called him at Pontesordo, would steal away to the chapel and, seating himself on an upturned basket or a heap of pumpkins, gaze long into the face of the mournful saint.

There was nothing unusual in Odo's lot. It was that of many children in the eighteenth century, especially those whose parents were cadets of noble houses, with an appanage barely sufficient to keep their wives and themselves in court finery, much less to pay their debts and clothe and educate their children. All over Italy at that moment, had Odo Valsecca but known it, were lads whose ancestors, like his own, had been dukes and crusaders, but who, none the less, were faring, as he fared, on black bread and hard blows, and the half-comprehended taunts of unpaid foster-parents. Many, doubtless, there were who cared little enough, as long as they might play morro with the farmer's lads and ride the colt bare-back through the pasture and go bird-netting and frog-hunting with the village children; but some perhaps, like Odo, suffered in a dumb animal way, without understanding why life was so hard on little boys.

Odo, for his part, had small taste for the sports in which Gianozzo and the village lads took pleasure. He shrank from any amusement associated with the frightening or hurting of animals, and his bosom swelled with the fine gentleman's scorn of the clowns who got their fun in so coarse a way. Now and then he found a moment's glee in a sharp tussle with one of the younger children who had been tormenting a frog or a beetle; but he was still too young for real fighting, and could only hang on the outskirts when the bigger boys closed, and think how some day he would be at them and break their lubberly heads. There were thus many hours when he turned to the silent consolations of the chapel. So familiar had he grown with the images on its walls that he had a name for every one: the King, the Knight, the Lady, the children with guinea-pigs, basilisks and leopards, and lastly the Friend, as he called Saint Francis. An almond-faced lady on a white palfrey with gold trappings represented his mother, whom he had seen too seldom for any distinct image to interfere with the illusion; a knight in damascened armour and scarlet cloak was the valiant captain, his father, who held a commission in the ducal army; and a proud young man in diadem and ermine, attended by a retinue of pages, stood for his cousin, the reigning Duke of Pianura.

A mist, as usual at that hour, was rising from the marshes between Pontesordo and Pianura, and the light soon ebbed from the saint's face, leaving the chapel in obscurity. Odo had crept there that afternoon with a keener sense than usual of the fact that life was hard on little boys; and though he was cold and hungry and half afraid, the solitude in which he cowered seemed more endurable than the noisy kitchen where, at that hour, the farm hands were gathering for their polenta, and Filomena was screaming at the frightened orphan who carried the dishes to the table. He knew, of course, that life at Pontesordo would not last for ever—that in time he would grow up and be mysteriously transformed into a young gentleman with a sword and laced coat, who would go to court and perhaps be an officer in the Duke's army or in that of some neighbouring prince; but, viewed from the lowliness of his nine years, that dazzling prospect was too remote to yield much solace for the cuffs and sneers, the ragged shoes and sour bread of the present. The fog outside had thickened, and the face of Odo's friend was now discernible only as a spot of pallor in the surrounding dimness. Even he seemed farther away than usual, withdrawn into the fog as into that mist of indifference which lay all about Odo's hot and eager spirit. The child sat down among the gourds and medlars on the muddy floor and hid his face against his knees.

He had sat there a long time when the noise of wheels and the crack of a postillion's whip roused the dogs chained in the stable. Odo's heart began to beat. What could the sounds mean? It was as though the flood-tide of the unknown were rising about him and bursting open the chapel door to pour in on his loneliness. It was, in fact, Filomena who opened the door, crying out to him in an odd Easter Sunday voice, the voice she used when she had on her silk neckerchief and gold chain or when she was talking to the bailiff.

Odo sprang up and hid his face in her lap. She seemed, of a sudden, nearer to him than any one else—a last barrier between himself and the mystery that awaited him outside.

"Come, you poor sparrow," she said, dragging him across the threshold of the chapel, "the abate is here asking for you;" and she crossed herself, as though she had named a saint.

Odo pulled away from her with a last wistful glance at Saint Francis, who looked back at him in an ecstasy of commiseration.

"Come, come," Filomena repeated, dropping to her ordinary key as she felt the resistance of the little boy's hand. "Have you no heart, you wicked child? But, to be sure, the poor innocent doesn't know! Come cavaliere, your illustrious mother waits."

"My mother?" The blood rushed to his face; and she had called him "cavaliere"!

"Not here, my poor lamb! The abate is here; don't you see the lights of the carriage? There, there, go to him. I haven't told him, your reverence; it's my silly tender-heartedness that won't let me. He's always been like one of my own creatures to me—" and she confounded Odo by bursting into tears.

The abate stood on the doorstep. He was a tall stout man with a hooked nose and lace ruffles. His nostrils were stained with snuff and he took a pinch from a tortoise-shell box set with the miniature of a lady; then he looked down at Odo and shrugged his shoulders.

Odo was growing sick with apprehension. It was two days before the appointed time for his weekly instruction and he had not prepared his catechism. He had not even thought of it—and the abate could use the cane. Odo stood silent and envied girls, who are not disgraced by crying. The tears were in his throat, but he had fixed principles about crying. It was his opinion that a little boy who was a cavaliere might weep when he was angry or sorry, but never when he was afraid; so he held his head high and put his hand to his side, as though to rest it on his sword.

The abate sneezed and tapped his snuff-box.

"Come, come, cavaliere, you must be brave—you must be a man; you have duties, you have responsibilities. It's your duty to console your mother—the poor lady is plunged in despair. Eh? What's that? You haven't told him? Cavaliere, your illustrious father is no more."

Odo stared a moment without understanding; then his grief burst from him in a great sob, and he hid himself against Filomena's apron, weeping for the father in damascened armour and scarlet cloak.

"Come, come," said the abate impatiently. "Is supper laid? for we must be gone as soon as the mist rises." He took the little boy by the hand. "Would it not distract your mind to recite the catechism?" he inquired.

"No, no!" cried Odo with redoubled sobs.

"Well, then, as you will. What a madman!" he exclaimed to Filomena. "I warrant it hasn't seen its father three times in its life. Come in, cavaliere; come to supper."

Filomena had laid a table in the stone chamber known as the bailiff's parlour, and thither the abate dragged his charge and set him down before the coarse tablecloth covered with earthen platters. A tallow dip threw its flare on the abate's big aquiline face as he sat opposite Odo, gulping the hastily prepared frittura and the thick purple wine in its wicker flask. Odo could eat nothing. The tears still ran down his cheeks and his whole soul was possessed by the longing to steal back and see whether the figure of the knight in the scarlet cloak had vanished from the chapel wall. The abate sat in silence, gobbling his food like the old black pig in the yard. When he had finished he stood up, exclaiming: "Death comes to us all, as the hawk said to the chicken. You must be a man, cavaliere." Then he stepped into the kitchen, and called out for the horses to be put to.

The farm hands had slunk away to one of the outhouses, and Filomena and Jacopone stood bowing and curtseying as the carriage drew up at the kitchen door. In a corner of the big vaulted room the little foundling was washing the dishes, heaping the scraps in a bowl for herself and the fowls. Odo ran back and touched her arm. She gave a start and looked at him with frightened eyes. He had nothing to give her, but he said: "Good-bye, Momola"; and he thought to himself that when he was grown up and had a sword he would surely come back and bring her a pair of shoes and a panettone. The abate was calling him, and the next moment he found himself lifted into the carriage, amid the blessings and lamentations of his foster-parents; and with a great baying of dogs and clacking of whipcord the horses clattered out of the farmyard, and turned their heads toward Pianura.

The mist had rolled back and fields and vineyards lay bare to the winter moon. The way was lonely, for it skirted the marsh, where no one lived; and only here and there the tall black shadow of a crucifix ate into the whiteness of the road. Shreds of vapour still hung about the hollows, but beyond these fold on fold of translucent hills melted into a sky dewy with stars. Odo cowered in his corner, staring out awestruck at the unrolling of the strange white landscape. He had seldom been out at night, and never in a carriage; and there was something terrifying to him in this flight through the silent moon-washed fields, where no oxen moved in the furrows, no peasants pruned the mulberries, and not a goat's bell tinkled among the oaks. He felt himself alone in a ghostly world from which even the animals had vanished, and at last he averted his eyes from the dreadful scene and sat watching the abate, who had fixed a reading-lamp at his back, and whose hooked-nosed shadow, as the springs jolted him up and down, danced overhead like the huge Pulcinella at the fair of Pontesordo.

1.2.

The gleam of a lantern woke Odo. The horses had stopped at the gates of Pianura, and the abate giving the pass-word, the carriage rolled under the gatehouse and continued its way over the loud cobble-stones of the ducal streets. These streets were so dark, being lit but by some lantern projecting here and there from the angle of a wall, or by the flare of an oil-lamp under a shrine, that Odo, leaning eagerly out, could only now and then catch a sculptured palace-window, the grinning mask on the keystone of an archway, or the gleaming yellowish facade of a church inlaid with marbles. Once or twice an uncurtained window showed a group of men drinking about a wineshop table, or an artisan bending over his work by the light of a tallow dip; but for the most part doors and windows were barred and the streets disturbed only by the watchman's cry or by a flash of light and noise as a sedan chair passed with its escort of linkmen and servants. All this was amazing enough to the sleepy eyes of the little boy so unexpectedly translated from the solitude of Pontesordo; but when the carriage turned under another arch and drew up before the doorway of a great building ablaze with lights, the pressure of accumulated emotions made him fling his arms about his preceptor's neck.

"Courage, cavaliere, courage! You have duties, you have responsibilities," the abate admonished him; and Odo, choking back his fright, suffered himself to be lifted out by one of the lacqueys grouped about the door. The abate, who carried a much lower crest than at Pontesordo, and seemed far more anxious to please the servants than they to oblige him, led the way up a shining marble staircase where beggars whined on the landings and powdered footmen in the ducal livery were running to and fro with trays of refreshments. Odo, who knew that his mother lived in the Duke's palace, had vaguely imagined that his father's death must have plunged its huge precincts into silence and mourning; but as he followed the abate up successive flights of stairs and down long corridors full of shadow he heard a sound of dance music below and caught the flash of girandoles through the antechamber doors. The thought that his father's death had made no difference to any one in the palace was to the child so much more astonishing than any of the other impressions crowding his brain, that these were scarcely felt, and he passed as in a dream through rooms where servants were quarrelling over cards and waiting-women rummaged in wardrobes full of perfumed finery, to a bedchamber in which a lady dressed in weeds sat disconsolately at supper.

"Mamma! Mamma!" he cried, springing forward in a passion of tears.

The lady, who was young, pale and handsome, pushed back her chair with a warning hand.

"Child," she exclaimed, "your shoes are covered with mud; and, good heavens, how you smell of the stable! Abate, is it thus you teach your pupil to approach me?"

"Madam, I am abashed by the cavaliere's temerity. But in truth I believe excessive grief has clouded his wits—'tis inconceivable how he mourns his father!"

Donna Laura's eyebrows rose in a faint smile. "May he never have worse to grieve for!" said she in French; then, extending her scented hand to the little boy, she added solemnly: "My son, we have suffered an irreparable loss."

Odo, abashed by her rebuke and the abate's apology, had drawn his heels together in a rustic version of the low bow with which the children of that day were taught to approach their parents.

"Holy Virgin!" said his mother with a laugh, "I perceive they have no dancing-master at Pontesordo. Cavaliere, you may kiss my hand. So—that's better; we shall make a gentleman of you yet. But what makes your face so wet? Ah, crying, to be sure. Mother of God! as for crying, there's enough to cry about." She put the child aside and turned to the preceptor. "The Duke refuses to pay," she said with a shrug of despair.

"Good heavens!" lamented the abate, raising his hands. "And Don Lelio?" he faltered.

She shrugged again, impatiently. "As great a gambler as my husband. They're all alike, abate: six times since last Easter has the bill been sent to me for that trifle of a turquoise buckle he made such a to-do about giving me." She rose and began to pace the room in disorder. "I'm a ruined woman," she cried, "and it's a disgrace for the Duke to refuse me."

The abate raised an admonishing finger. "Excellency...excellency..."

She glanced over her shoulder.

"Eh? You're right. Everything is heard here. But who's to pay for my mourning the saints alone know! I sent an express this morning to my father, but you know my brothers bleed him like leeches. I could have got this easily enough from the Duke a year ago—it's his marriage has made him so stiff. That little white-faced fool—she hates me because Lelio won't look at her, and she thinks it's my fault. As if I cared whom he looks at! Sometimes I think he has money put away...all I want is two hundred ducats...a woman of my rank!" She turned suddenly on Odo, who stood, very small and frightened, in the corner to which she had pushed him. "What are you staring at, child? Eh! the monkey is dropping with sleep. Look at his eyes, abate! Here, Vanna, Tonina, to bed with him; he may sleep with you in my dressing-closet, Tonina. Go with her, child, go; but for God's sake wake him if he snores. I'm too ill to have my rest disturbed." And she lifted a pomander to her nostrils.

The next few days dwelt in Odo's memory as a blur of strange sights and sounds. The super-acute state of his perceptions was succeeded after a night's sleep by the natural passivity with which children accept the improbable, so that he passed from one novel impression to another as easily and with the same exhilaration as if he had been listening to a fairy tale. Solitude and neglect had no surprises for him, and it seemed natural enough that his mother and her maids should be too busy to remember his presence.

For the first day or two he sat unnoticed on his little stool in a corner of his mother's room, while packing-chests were dragged in, wardrobes emptied, mantua-makers and milliners consulted, and troublesome creditors dismissed with abuse, or even blows, by the servants lounging in the ante-chamber.

Donna Laura continued to show the liveliest symptoms of concern, but the child perceived her distress to be but indirectly connected with the loss she had suffered, and he had seen enough of poverty at the farm to guess that the need of money was somehow at the bottom of her troubles. How any one could be in want, who slept between damask curtains and lived on sweet cakes and chocolate, it exceeded his fancy to conceive; yet there were times when his mother's voice had the same frightened angry sound as Filomena's on the days when the bailiff went over the accounts at Pontesordo.

Her excellency's rooms, during these days, were always crowded, for besides the dressmakers and other merchants there was the hairdresser, or French Monsu—a loud, important figure, with a bag full of cosmetics and curling-irons—the abate, always running in and out with messages and letters, and taking no more notice of Odo than if he had never seen him, and a succession of ladies brimming with condolences, and each followed by a servant who swelled the noisy crowd of card-playing lacqueys in the ante-chamber.

Through all these figures came and went another, to Odo the most noticeable,—that of a handsome young man with a high manner, dressed always in black, but with an excess of lace ruffles and jewels, a clouded amber head to his cane, and red heels to his shoes. This young gentleman, whose age could not have been more than twenty, and who had the coldest insolent air, was treated with profound respect by all but Donna Laura, who was for ever quarrelling with him when he was present, yet could not support his absence without lamentations and alarm. The abate appeared to act as messenger between the two, and when he came to say that the Count rode with the court, or was engaged to sup with the Prime Minister, or had business on his father's estate in the country, the lady would openly yield to her distress, crying out that she knew well enough what his excuses meant: that she was the most cruelly outraged of women, and that he treated her no better than a husband.

For two days Odo languished in his corner, whisked by the women's skirts, smothered under the hoops and falbalas which the dressmakers unpacked from their cases, fed at irregular hours, and faring on the whole no better than at Pontesordo. The third morning, Vanna, who seemed the most good-natured of the women, cried out on his pale looks when she brought him his cup of chocolate. "I declare," she exclaimed, "the child has had no air since he came in from the farm. What does your excellency say? Shall the hunchback take him for a walk in the gardens?"

To this her excellency, who sat at her toilet under the hair-dresser's hands, irritably replied that she had not slept all night and was in no state to be tormented about such trifles, but that the child might go where he pleased.

Odo, who was very weary of his corner, sprang up readily enough when Vanna, at this, beckoned him to the inner ante-chamber. Here, where persons of a certain condition waited (the outer being given over to servants and tradesmen), they found a lean humpbacked boy, shabbily dressed in darned stockings and a faded coat, but with an extraordinary keen pale face that at once attracted and frightened the child.

"There, go with him; he won't eat you," said Vanna, giving him a push as she hurried away; and Odo, trembling a little, laid his hand in the boy's. "Where do you come from?" he faltered, looking up into his companion's face.

The boy laughed and the blood rose to his high cheekbones. "I?—From the Innocenti, if your Excellency knows where that is," said he.

Odo's face lit up. "Of course I do," he cried, reassured. "I know a girl who comes from there—the Momola at Pontesordo."

"Ah, indeed?" said the boy with a queer look. "Well, she's my sister, then. Give her my compliments when you see her, cavaliere. Oh, we're a large family, we are!"

Odo's perplexity was returning. "Are you really Momola's brother?" he asked.

"Eh, in a way—we're children of the same house."

"But you live in the palace, don't you?" Odo persisted, his curiosity surmounting his fear. "Are you a servant of my mother's?"

"I'm the servant of your illustrious mother's servants; the abatino of the waiting-women. I write their love-letters, do you see, cavaliere, I carry their rubbish to the pawnbroker's when their sweethearts have bled them of their savings; I clean the birdcages and feed the monkeys, and do the steward's accounts when he's drunk, and sleep on a bench in the portico and steal my food from the pantry...and my father very likely goes in velvet and carries a sword at his side."

The boy's voice had grown shrill, and his eyes blazed like an owl's in the dark. Odo would have given the world to be back in his corner, but he was ashamed to betray his lack of heart; and to give himself courage he asked haughtily: "And what is your name, boy?"

The hunchback gave him a gleaming look. "Call me Brutus," he cried, "for Brutus killed a tyrant." He gave Odo's hand a pull. "Come along," said he, "and I'll show you his statue in the garden—Brutus's statue in a prince's garden, mind you!" And as the little boy trotted at his side down the long corridors he kept repeating under his breath in a kind of angry sing-song, "For Brutus killed a tyrant."

The sense of strangeness inspired by his odd companion soon gave way in Odo's mind to emotions of delight and wonder. He was, even at that age, unusually sensitive to external impressions, and when the hunchback, after descending many stairs and winding through endless back-passages, at length led him out on a terrace above the gardens, the beauty of the sight swelled his little heart to bursting.

A Duke of Pianura had, some hundred years earlier, caused a great wing to be added to his palace by the eminent architect Carlo Borromini, and this accomplished designer had at the same time replanted and enlarged the ducal gardens. To Odo, who had never seen plantations more artful than the vineyards and mulberry orchards about Pontesordo, these perspectives of clipped beech and yew, these knots of box filled in with multi-coloured sand, appeared, with the fountains, colonnades and trellised arbours surmounted by globes of glass, to represent the very pattern and Paradise of gardens. It seemed indeed too beautiful to be real, and he trembled, as he sometimes did at the music of the Easter mass, when the hunchback, laughing at his amazement, led him down the terrace steps.

It was Odo's lot in after years to walk the alleys of many a splendid garden, and to pace, often wearily enough, the paths along which he was now led; but never after did he renew the first enchanted impression of mystery and brightness that remained with him as the most vivid emotion of his childhood.

Though it was February the season was so soft that the orange and lemon trees had been put out in their earthen vases before the lemon-house, and the beds in the parterres were full of violets, daffodils and auriculas; but the scent of the orange-blossoms and the bright colours of the flowers moved Odo less than the noble ordonnance of the pleached alleys, each terminated by a statue or a marble seat; and when he came to the grotto where, amid rearing sea-horses and Tritons, a cascade poured from the grove above, his wonder passed into such delicious awe as hung him speechless on the hunchback's hand.

"Eh," said the latter with a sneer, "it's a finer garden than we have at our family palace. Do you know what's planted there?" he asked, turning suddenly on the little boy. "Dead bodies, cavaliere! Rows and rows of them; the bodies of my brothers and sisters, the Innocents who die like flies every year of the cholera and the measles and the putrid fever." He saw the terror in Odo's face and added in a gentler tone: "Eh, don't cry, cavaliere; they sleep better in those beds than in any others they're like to lie on. Come, come, and I'll show your excellency the aviaries."

From the aviaries they passed to the Chinese pavilion, where the Duke supped on summer evenings, and thence to the bowling-alley, the fish-stew and the fruit-garden. At every step some fresh surprise arrested Odo; but the terrible vision of that other garden planted with the dead bodies of the Innocents robbed the spectacle of its brightness, dulled the plumage of the birds behind their gilt wires and cast a deeper shade over the beech-grove, where figures of goat-faced men lurked balefully in the twilight. Odo was glad when they left the blackness of this grove for the open walks, where gardeners were working and he had the reassurance of the sky. The hunchback, who seemed sorry that he had frightened him, told him many curious stories about the marble images that adorned the walks; and pausing suddenly before one of a naked man with a knife in his hand, cried out in a frenzy: "This is my namesake, Brutus!" But when Odo would have asked if the naked man was a kinsman, the boy hurried him on, saying only: "You'll read of him some day in Plutarch."

1.3.

Odo, next morning, under the hunchback's guidance, continued his exploration of the palace. His mother seemed glad to be rid of him, and Vanna packing him off early, with the warning that he was not to fall into the fishponds or get himself trampled by the horses, he guessed, with a thrill, that he had leave to visit the stables. Here in fact the two boys were soon making their way among the crowd of grooms and strappers in the yard, seeing the Duke's carriage-horses groomed, and the Duchess's cream-coloured hackney saddled for her ride in the chase; and at length, after much lingering and gazing, going on to the harness-rooms and coach-house. The state-carriages, with their carved and gilt wheels, their panels gay with flushed divinities and their stupendous velvet hammer-cloths edged with bullion, held Odo spellbound. He had a born taste for splendour, and the thought that he might one day sit in one of these glittering vehicles puffed his breast with pride and made him address the hunchback with sudden condescension. "When I'm a man I shall ride in these carriages," he said; whereat the other laughed and returned good-humouredly: "Eh, that's not so much to boast of, cavaliere; I shall ride in a carriage one of these days myself." Odo stared, not over-pleased, and the boy added: "When I'm carried to the churchyard, I mean," with a chuckle of relish at the joke.

From the stables they passed to the riding-school, with its open galleries supported on twisted columns, where the duke's gentlemen managed their horses and took their exercise in bad weather. Several rode there that morning; and among them, on a fine Arab, Odo recognised the young man in black velvet who was so often in Donna Laura's apartments.

"Who's that?" he whispered, pulling the hunchback's sleeve, as the gentleman, just below them, made his horse execute a brilliant balotade.

"That? Bless the innocent! Why, the Count Lelio Trescorre, your illustrious mother's cavaliere servente."

Odo was puzzled, but some instinct of reserve withheld him from further questions. The hunchback, however, had no such scruples. "They do say, though," he went on, "that her Highness has her eye on him, and in that case I'll wager your illustrious mamma has no more chance than a sparrow against a hawk."

The boy's words were incomprehensible, but the vague sense that some danger might be threatening his mother's friend made Odo whisper: "What would her Highness do to him?"

"Make him a prime-minister, cavaliere," the hunchback laughed.

Odo's guide, it appeared, was not privileged to conduct him through the state apartments of the palace, and the little boy had now been four days under the ducal roof without catching so much as a glimpse of his sovereign and cousin. The very next morning, however, Vanna swept him from his trundle-bed with the announcement that he was to be received by the Duke that day, and that the tailor was now waiting to try on his court dress. He found his mother propped against her pillows, drinking chocolate, feeding her pet monkey and giving agitated directions to the maidservants on their knees before the open carriage-trunks. Her excellency informed Odo that she had that moment received an express from his grandfather, the old Marquess di Donnaz; that they were to start next morning for the castle of Donnaz, and that he was to be presented to the Duke as soon as his Highness had risen from dinner. A plump purse lay on the coverlet, and her countenance wore an air of kindness and animation which, together with the prospect of wearing a court dress and travelling to his grandfather's castle in the mountains, so worked on Odo's spirits that, forgetting the abate's instructions, he sprang to her with an eager caress.

"Child, child," was her only rebuke; and she added, with a tap on his cheek: "It is lucky I shall have a sword to protect me."

Long before the hour Odo was buttoned into his embroidered coat and waistcoat. He would have on the sword at once, and when they sat down to dinner, though his mother pressed him to eat with more concern than she had before shown, it went hard with him to put his weapon aside, and he cast longing eyes at the corner where it lay. At length a chamberlain summoned them and they set out down the corridors, attended by two servants. Odo held his head high, with one hand leading Donna Laura (for he would not appear to be led by her) while the other fingered his sword. The deformed beggars who always lurked about the great staircase fawned on them as they passed, and on a landing they crossed the humpbacked boy, who grinned mockingly at Odo; but the latter, with his chin up, would not so much as glance at him.

A master of ceremonies in short black cloak and gold chain received them in the antechamber of the Duchess's apartments, where the court played lansquenet after dinner; the doors of her Highness's closet were thrown open, and Odo, now glad enough to cling to his mother's hand, found himself in a tall room, with gods and goddesses in the clouds overhead and personages as supra-terrestrial seated in gilt armchairs about a smoking brazier. Before one of these, to whom Donna Laura swept successive curtsies in advancing, the frightened cavaliere found himself dragged with his sword between his legs. He ducked his head like the old drake diving for worms in the puddle at the farm, and when at last he dared look up, it was to see an odd sallow face, half-smothered in an immense wig, bowing back at him with infinite ceremony—and Odo's heart sank to think that this was his sovereign.

The Duke was in fact a sickly narrow-faced young man with thick obstinate lips and a slight lameness that made his walk ungainly; but though no way resembling the ermine-cloaked king of the chapel at Pontesordo, he yet knew how to put on a certain majesty with his state wig and his orders. As for the newly married Duchess, who sat at the other end of the cabinet caressing a toy spaniel, she was scant fourteen and looked a mere child in her great hoop and jewelled stomacher. Her wonderful fair hair, drawn over a cushion and lightly powdered, was twisted with pearls and roses, and her cheeks excessively rouged, in the French fashion; so that as she arose on the approach of the visitors she looked to Odo for all the world like the wooden Virgin hung with votive offerings in the parish church at Pontesordo. Though they were but three months married the Duke, it was rumoured, was never with her, preferring the company of the young Marquess of Cerveno, his cousin and heir-presumptive, a pale boy scented with musk and painted like a comedian, whom his Highness would never suffer away from him and who now leaned with an impertinent air against the back of the ducal armchair.

On the other side of the brazier sat the dowager Duchess, the Duke's grandmother, an old lady so high and forbidding of aspect that Odo cast but one look at her face, which was yellow and wrinkled as a medlar, and surmounted, in the Spanish style, with black veils and a high coif. What these alarming personages said and did, the child could never recall; nor were his own actions clear to him, except for a furtive caress that he remembered giving the spaniel as he kissed the Duchess's hand; whereupon her Highness snatched up the pampered animal and walked away with a pout of anger. Odo noticed that her angry look followed him as he and Donna Laura withdrew; but the next moment he heard the Duke's voice and saw his Highness limping after them.

"You must have a furred cloak for your journey, cousin," said he awkwardly, pressing something in the hand of Odo's mother, who broke into fresh compliments and curtsies, while the Duke, with a finger on his thick lip, withdrew hastily into the closet.

The next morning early they set out on their journey. There had been frost in the night and a cold sun sparkled on the palace windows and on the marble church-fronts as their carriage lumbered through the streets, now full of noise and animation. It was Odo's first glimpse of the town by daylight, and he clapped his hands with delight at sight of the people picking their way across the reeking gutters, the asses laden with milk and vegetables, the servant-girls bargaining at the provision-stalls, the shop-keepers' wives going to mass in pattens and hoods, with scaldini in their muffs, the dark recessed openings in the palace basements, where fruit sellers, wine-merchants and coppersmiths displayed their wares, the pedlars hawking books and toys, and here and there a gentleman in a sedan chair returning flushed and disordered from a night at bassett or faro. The travelling-carriage was escorted by half-a-dozen of the Duke's troopers and Don Lelio rode at the door followed by two grooms. He wore a furred coat and boots, and never, to Odo, had he appeared more proud and splendid; but Donna Laura had hardly a word for him, and he rode with the set air of a man who acquits himself of a troublesome duty.

Outside the gates the spectacle seemed tame in comparison; for the road bent toward Pontesordo, and Odo was familiar enough with the look of the bare fields, set here and there with oak-copses to which the leaves still clung. As the carriage skirted the marsh his mother raised the windows, exclaiming that they must not expose themselves to the pestilent air; and though Odo was not yet addicted to general reflections, he could not but wonder that she should display such dread of an atmosphere she had let him breathe since his birth. He knew of course that the sunset vapours on the marsh were unhealthy: everybody on the farm had a touch of the ague, and it was a saying in the village that no one lived at Pontesordo who could buy an ass to carry him away; but that Donna Laura, in skirting the place on a clear morning of frost, should show such fear of infection, gave a sinister emphasis to the ill-repute of the region.

The thought, he knew not why, turned his mind to Momola, who often on damp evenings sat shaking and burning in the kitchen corner. He reflected with a pang that he might never see her again, and leaning forward he strained his eyes for a glimpse of Pontesordo. They were passing through a patch of oaks; but where these ended the country opened, and beyond a belt of osiers and the mottled faded stretches of the marsh the keep stood up like a beckoning finger. Odo cried out as though in answer to its call; but that moment the road turned a knoll and bent across rising ground toward an unfamiliar region.

"Thank God!" cried his mother, lowering the window, "we're rid of that poison and can breath the air."

As the keep vanished Odo reproached himself for not having begged a pair of shoes for Momola. He had felt very sorry for her since the hunchback had spoken so strangely of life at the foundling hospital; and he had a sudden vision of her bare feet, pinched with cold and cut with the pebbles of the yard, perpetually running across the damp stone floors, with Filomena crying after her: "Hasten then, child of iniquity! You are slower than a day without bread!" He had almost resolved to speak of the foundling to his mother, who still seemed in a condescending humour; but his attention was unexpectedly distracted by a troop of Egyptians, who came along the road leading a dancing bear; and hardly had these passed when the chariot of an itinerant dentist engaged him. The whole way, indeed, was alive with such surprises; and at Valsecca, where they dined, they found the yard of the inn crowded with the sumpter-mules and servants of a cardinal travelling to Rome, who was to lie there that night and whose bedstead and saucepans had preceded him.

Here, after dinner, Don Lelio took leave of Odo's mother, with small show of regret on either side; the lady high and sarcastic, the gentleman sullen and polite; and both, as it seemed, easier when the business was despatched and the Count's foot in the stirrup. He had so far taken little notice of Odo, but he now bent from the saddle and tapped the boy's cheek, saying in his cold way: "In a few years I shall see you at court;" and with that rode away toward Pianura.

1.4.

Lying that night at Pavia, the travellers set forward next morning for the city of Vercelli. The road, though it ran for the most part through flat mulberry orchards and rice-fields reflecting the pale blue sky in their sodden channels, would yet have appeared diverting enough to Odo, had his mother been in the mood to reply to his questions; for whether their carriage overtook a party of strolling jugglers, travelling in a roofed-in waggon, with the younger children of the company running alongside in threadbare tights and trunkhose decked with tinsel; or whether they drove through a village market-place, where yellow earthen crocks and gaudy Indian cottons, brass pails and braziers and platters of bluish pewter, filled the stalls with a medley of colour—at every turn was something that excited the boy's wonder; but Donna Laura, who had fallen into a depression of spirits, lamenting the cold, her misfortunes and the discomfort of the journey, was at no more pains than the abate to satisfy the promptings of his curiosity.

Odo had indeed met but one person who cared to listen to him, and that was the strange hunchback who had called himself Brutus. Remembering how entertainingly this odd guide had explained all the wonders of the ducal grounds, Odo began to regret that he had not asked his mother to let him have Brutus for a body-servant. Meanwhile no one attended to his questions and the hours were beginning to seem long when, on the third day, they set out from Vercelli toward the hills. The cold increased as they rose; and Odo, though he had often wished to see the mountains, was yet dismayed at the gloomy and menacing aspect of the region on which they were entering. Leafless woods, prodigious boulders and white torrents foaming and roaring seemed a poor exchange for the pleasantly-ordered gardens of Pianura. Here were no violets and cowslips in bloom; hardly a green blade pierced the sodden roadside, and snowdrifts lingered in the shaded hollows.

Donna Laura's loudly expressed fear of robbers seemed to increase the loneliness of the way, which now traversed tracts of naked moorland, now plunged again into forest, with no sign of habitation but here and there a cowherd's hut under the trees or a chapel standing apart on some grassy eminence. When night fell the waters grew louder, a stinging wind swept the woods, and the carriage, staggering from rut to rut, seemed every moment about to land them in some invisible ravine. Fear and cold at last benumbed the little boy, and when he woke he was being lifted from his seat and torches were flashing on a high escutcheoned doorway set in battlemented walls. He was carried into a hall lit with smoky oil-lamps and hung with armour and torn banners.

Here, among a group of rough-looking servants, a tall old man in a nightcap and furred gown was giving orders in a loud passionate voice. This personage, who was of a choleric complexion, with a face like mottled red marble, seized Odo by the wrist and led him up a flight of stairs so worn and slippery that he tripped at every step; thence down a corridor and into a gloomy apartment where three ladies shivered about a table set with candles. Bidden by the old gentleman to salute his grandmother and great-aunts, Odo bowed over three wrinkled hands, one fat and soft as a toad's stomach, the others yellow and dry as lemon-skins. His mother embraced the ladies in the same humble manner, and the Marquess, first furiously calling for supper, thrust Odo down on a stool in the ingle.

From this point of observation the child, now vividly awake, noted the hangings of faded tapestry that heaved in the draught, the ceiling of beams and the stone floor strewn with rushes. The candle-light flickering on the faces of his aged relatives showed his grandmother to be a pale heavycheeked person with little watchful black eyes which she dropped at her husband's approach; while the two great-aunts, seated side by side in high-backed chairs with their feet on braziers, reminded Odo of the narrow elongated saints squeezed into the niches of a church-door. The old Marchioness wore the high coif and veil of the previous century; the aunts, who, as Odo afterwards learned, were canonesses of a noble order, were habited in a semi-conventual dress, with crosses hanging on their bosoms; and none spoke but when the Marquess addressed them.

Their timidity appeared to infect Odo's mother, who, from her habitual volubility of temper, sank to a mood of like submissiveness. A supper of venison and goat's cheese was not designed to restore her spirits, and when at length she and Odo had withdrawn to their cavernous bedchamber, she flung herself weeping on the bed and declared she must die if she remained long in this prison.

Falling asleep under such influences, it was the more wonderful to Odo to wake with the sun on his counterpane, a sweet noise of streams through the casement and the joyous barking of hounds in the castle court. From the window-seat he looked out on a scene extraordinarily novel to his lowland eyes. The chamber commanded the wooded steep below the castle, with a stream looping its base; beyond, the pastures sloped pleasantly under walnut trees, with here and there a clearing ploughed for the spring crops and a sunny ledge or two planted with vines. Above this pastoral landscape, bare crags upheld a snowpeak; and, as if to lend a human interest to the scene, the old Marquess, his flintlock on his shoulder, his dogs and beaters at his heels, now rode across the valley.

Wonder succeeded to wonder that first morning; for there was the castle to be seen, with the kennels and stables roughly kept, but full of dogs and horses; and Odo, in the Marquess's absence, was left free to visit every nook of his new home. Pontesordo, though perhaps as ancient as Donnaz, was but a fortified manor in the plain; but here was the turreted border castle, bristling at the head of the gorge like the fangs in a boar's throat: its walls overhung by machicolations, its portcullis still dropped at nightfall, and the loud stream forming a natural moat at its base. Through the desert spaces of this great structure Odo wandered at will, losing himself in its network of bare chambers, some now put to domestic uses, with smoked meats hanging from the rafters, cheeses ranged on shelves and farmer's implements stacked on the floor; others abandoned to bats and spiders, with slit-like openings choked by a growth of wild cherries, and little animals scurrying into their holes as Odo opened the unused doors. At the next turn he mounted by a winding stair to the platform behind the battlements, whence he could look down on the inner court, where horses were being groomed, dogs fed, harnesses mended, and platters of smoking food carried from the kitchen to the pantry; or, leaning another way, discovered, between the cliff and the rampart a tiny walled garden with fruit-trees and a sundial.

The ladies kept to themselves in a corner of the castle, where the rooms were hung with tapestry and a few straight-backed chairs stood about the hearth; but even here no fires were suffered till nightfall, nor was there so much as a carpet in the castle. Odo's grandmother, the old Marchioness, a heavy woman who would doubtless have enjoyed her ease in a cushioned seat, was afoot all day attending to her household; for besides the dairy and the bakehouse and the stillroom where fruits were stewed and pastes prepared, there was the great spinning-room full of distaffs and looms, where the women spun and wove all the linen used in the castle and the coarse stuffs worn by its inmates; with workshops for the cobbler and tailor who clothed and shod the Marquess and his household. All these the Marchioness must visit, and attend to her devotions between; the ladies being governed by a dark-faced priest, their chaplain and director, who kept them perpetually running along the cold stone corridors to the chapel in a distant wing, where they knelt without so much as a brazier to warm them or a cushion to their knees. As to the chapel, though larger and loftier than that of Pontesordo, with a fine carved and painted tabernacle and many silver candlesticks, it seemed to Odo, by reason of its bare walls, much less beautiful than that deserted oratory; nor did he, amid all the novelty of his surroundings, cease to regret the companionship of his familiar images.

His delight was the greater, therefore, when, exploring a part of the castle now quite abandoned, he came one day on a vaulted chamber used as a kind of granary, where, under layers of dirt and cobwebs, lovely countenances flowered from the walls. The scenes depicted differed indeed from those of Pontesordo, being less animated and homely and more difficult for a child to interpret; for here were naked laurel-crowned knights on prancing horses, nimble goat-faced creatures grouped in adoration round a smoking altar and youths piping to saffron-haired damsels on grass-banks set with poplars. The very strangeness of the fable set forth perhaps engaged the child's fancy; or the benignant mildness of the countenances, so unlike the eager individual faces of the earlier artist; for he returned again and again to gaze unweariedly on the inhabitants of that tranquil grassy world, studying every inch of the walls and with much awe and fruitless speculation deciphering on the hem of a floating drapery the inscription: Bernardinus Lovinus pinxit.

His impatience to know more of the history of these paintings led him to question an old man, half house-servant, half huntsman, now too infirm for service and often to be found sunning himself in the court with an old hound's chin on his knee. The old man, whose name was Bruno, told him the room in question had been painted for the Marquess Gualberto di Donnaz, who had fought under the Duke of Milan hundreds of years before:

a splendid and hospitable noble, patron of learning and the arts, who had brought the great Milanese painter to Donnaz and kept him there a whole summer adorning the banqueting-room. "But I advise you, little master," Bruno added, "not to talk too loudly of your discovery; for we live in changed days, do you see, and it seems those are pagan sorcerers and witches painted on the wall, and because of that, and their nakedness, the chaplain has forbidden all the young boys and wenches about the place to set foot there; and the Marchioness herself, I'm told, doesn't enter without leave."

This was the more puzzling to Odo that he had seen so many naked pagans, in colours and marble, at his cousin's palace of Pianura, where they were praised as the chief ornament of that sumptuous fabric; but he kept Bruno's warning in mind and so timed his visits that they escaped the chaplain's observation. Whether this touch of mystery added charm to the paintings; or whether there was already forming in him what afterward became an instinctive resistance to many of the dictates of his age; certain it is that, even after he had been privileged to admire the stupendous works of the Caracci at Parma and of the immortal Giulio Romano at Mantua, Odo's fancy always turned with peculiar fondness to the clear-limbed youths moving in that world of untroubled beauty.

Odo, the day after his arrival at Donnaz, learned that the chaplain was to be his governor; and he was not long in discovering that the system of that ecclesiastic bore no resemblance to the desultory methods of his former pedagogue. It was not that Don Gervaso was a man of superior acquirements: in writing, ciphering and the rudiments of Latin he seemed little likely to carry Odo farther than the other; but in religious instruction he suffered no negligence or inattention. His piety was of a stamp so different from the abate's that it vivified the theological abstractions over which Odo had formerly languished, infusing a passionate meaning into the formulas of the textbooks. His discourse breathed the same spirit, and had his religion been warmed by imagination or tempered by charity the child had been a ductile substance in his hands; but the shadow of the Council of Trent still hung over the Church in Savoy, making its approach almost as sombre and forbidding as that of the Calvinist heresy. As it was, the fascination that drew Odo to the divine teachings was counteracted by a depressing awe: he trembled in God's presence almost as much as in his grandfather's, and with the same despair of discovering what course of action was most likely to call down the impending wrath. The beauty of the Church's offices, now for the first time revealed to him in the well-ordered services of the chapel, was doubly moving in contrast with the rude life at Donnaz; but his confessions tortured him and the penances which the chaplain inflicted abased without reforming his spirit.

Next to the mass, the books Don Gervaso lent him were his chief pleasure: the Lives of the Saints, Cardinal Bellarmine's Fables and The Mirror of true Penitence. The Lives of the Saints fed at once his imagination and his heart, and over the story of Saint Francis, now first made known to him, he trembled with delicious sympathy. The longing to found a hermitage like the Portiuncula among the savage rocks of Donnaz, and live there in gentle communion with plants and animals, alternated in him with the martial ambition to ride forth against the Church's enemies, as his ancestors had ridden against the bloody and pestilent Waldenses; but whether his piety took the passive or the aggressive form, it always shrank from the subtleties of doctrine. To live like the saints, rather than to reason like the fathers, was his ideal of Christian conduct; if indeed a vague pity for suffering creatures and animals was not the source of his monastic yearnings, and a desire to see strange countries the secret of his zeal against the infidel.

The chaplain, though reproving his lukewarmness in matters of dogma, could not but commend his devotion to the saints; and one day his grandmother, to reward him for some act of piety, informed him with tears of joy that he was destined for holy orders, and that she had good hopes of living to see him a bishop. This news had hardly the intended effect; for Odo's dream was of the saint's halo rather than the bishop's mitre; and throwing himself on his knees before the old Marquess, who was present, he besought that he might be allowed to join the Franciscan order. The Marquess at this flew into so furious a rage, cursing the meddlesomeness of women and the chaplain's bigotry, that the ladies burst into tears and Odo's swelling zeal turned small. There was indeed but one person in the castle who seemed not to regard its master's violences, and that was the dark-faced chaplain, who, when the Marquess had paused out of breath, tranquilly returned that nothing could make him repent of having brought a soul to Christ, and that, as to the cavaliere Odo, if his maker designed him for a religious, the Pope himself could not cross his vocation.

"Ay, ay! vocation," snarled the Marquess. "You and the women here shut the child up between you and stuff his ears full of monkish stories and miracles and the Lord knows what, and then talk of the simpleton's vocation. His vocation, nom de Dieu, is to be an abbot first, and then a monsignore, and then a bishop, if he can—and to the devil with your cowls and cloisters!" And he gave orders that Odo should hunt with him next morning.

The chaplain smiled. "Hubert was a huntsman," said he, "and yet he died a saint."

From that time forth the old Marquess kept Odo oftener at his side, making his grandson ride with him about his estates and on such hunting-parties as were not beyond the boy's strength. The domain of Donnaz included many a mile of vine and forest, over which, till the fifteenth century, its lords had ruled as sovereign Marquesses. They still retained a part of their feudal privileges, and Odo's grandfather, tenacious of these dwindling rights, was for ever engaged in vain contests with his peasantry. To see these poor creatures cursed and brow-beaten, their least offences punished, their few claims disputed, must have turned Odo's fear of his grandfather to hatred, had he not observed that the old man gave with one hand what he took with the other, so that, in his dealings with his people, he resembled one of those torrents which now devastate and now enrich their banks. The Marquess, in fact, while he held obstinately to his fishing rights, prosecuted poachers, enforced the corvee and took toll at every ford, yet laboured to improve his lands, exterminated the wild beasts that preyed on them, helped his peasants in sickness, nourished them in old age and governed them with a paternal tyranny doubtless less insufferable than the negligence of the great land-owners who lived at court.

To Odo, however, these rides among the tenantry were less agreeable than the hunting-expeditions which carried them up the mountain in the solitude of morning. Here the wild freshness of the scene and the exhilaration of pursuit roused the fighting strain in the boy's blood, and so stirred his memory with tales of prowess that sometimes, as they climbed the stony defiles in the clear shadow before sunrise, he fancied himself riding forth to exterminate the Waldenses who, according to the chaplain, still lurked like basilisks and dragons in the recesses of the mountains. Certain it is that his rides with the old Marquess, if they inflamed his zeal against heresy, cooled the ardour of his monastic vocation; and if he pondered on his future, it was to reflect that doubtless he would some day be a bishop, and that bishops were territorial lords, we might hunt the wolf and boar in their own domains.

1.5.

Reluctantly, every year about the Epiphany, the old Marquess rode down from Donnaz to spend two months in Turin. It was a service exacted by King Charles Emanuel, who viewed with a jealous eye those of his nobles inclined to absent themselves from court and rewarded their presence with privileges and preferments. At the same time the two canonesses descended to their abbey in the plain, and thus with the closing in of winter the old Marchioness, Odo and his mother were left alone in the castle.

To the Marchioness this was an agreeable period of spiritual compunction and bodily repose; but to Donna Laura a season of despair. The poor lady, who had been early removed from the rough life at Donnaz to the luxurious court of Pianura, and was yet in the fulness of youth and vivacity, could not resign herself to an existence no better, as she declared, than that of any herdsman's wife upon the mountains. Here was neither music nor cards, scandal nor love-making; no news of the fashions, no visits from silk-mercers or jewellers, no Monsu to curl her hair and tempt her with new lotions, or so much as a strolling soothsayer or juggler to lighten the dullness of the long afternoons. The only visitors to the castle were the mendicant friars drawn thither by the Marchioness's pious repute; and though Donna Laura disdained not to call these to her chamber and question them for news, yet their country-side scandals were no more to her fancy than the two-penny wares of the chapmen who unpacked their baubles on the kitchen hearth.

She pined for some word of Pianura; but when a young abate, who had touched there on his way from Tuscany, called for a night at the castle to pay his duty to Don Gervaso, the word he brought with him of the birth of an heir to the duchy was so little to Donna Laura's humour that she sprang up from the supper-table, and crying out to the astonished Odo, "Ah, now you are for the Church indeed," withdrew in disorder to her chamber. The abate, who ascribed her commotion to a sudden seizure, continued to retail the news of Pianura, and Odo, listening with his elders, learned that Count Lelio Trescorre had been appointed Master of the Horse, to the indignation of the Bishop, who desired the place for his nephew, Don Serafino; that the Duke and Duchess were never together; that the Duchess was suspected of being in secret correspondence with the Austrians, and that the young Marquess of Cerveno was gone to the baths of Lucca to recover from an attack of tertian fever contracted the previous autumn at the Duke's hunting-lodge near Pontesordo. Odo listened for some mention of his humpbacked friend, or of Momola the foundling; but the abate's talk kept a higher level and no one less than a cavaliere figured on his lips. He was the only visitor of quality who came that winter to Donnaz, and after his departure a fixed gloom settled on Donna Laura's spirits. Dusk at that season fell early in the gorge, fierce winds blew off the glaciers, and Donna Laura sat shivering and lamenting on one side of the hearth, while the old Marchioness, on the other, strained her eyes over an embroidery in which the pattern repeated itself like the invocations of a litany, and Don Gervaso, near the smoking oil-lamp, read aloud from the Glories of Mary or the Way of Perfection of Saint Theresa.

On such evenings Odo, stealing from the tapestry parlour, would seek out Bruno, who sat by the kitchen hearth with the old hound's nose at his feet. The kitchen, indeed, on winter nights, was the pleasantest place in the castle. The fire-light from its great stone chimney shone on the strings of maize and bunches of dried vegetables that hung from the roof and on the copper kettles and saucepans ranged along the wall. The wind raged against the shutters of the unglazed windows, and the maid-servants, distaff in hand, crowded closer to the blaze, listening to the songs of some wandering fiddler or to the stories of a ruddy-nosed Capuchin monk who was being regaled, by the steward's orders, on a supper of tripe and mulled wine. The Capuchin's tales, told in the Piedmontese jargon, and seasoned with strange allusions and boisterous laughter, were of little interest to Odo, who would creep into the ingle beside Bruno and beg for some story of his ancestors. The old man was never weary of rehearsing the feats and gestures of the lords of Donnaz, and Odo heard again and again how they had fought the savage Switzers north of the Alps and the Dauphin's men in the west; how they had marched with Savoy against Montferrat and with France against the Republic of Genoa. Better still he liked to hear of the Marquess Gualberto, who had been the Duke of Milan's ally and had brought home the great Milanese painter to adorn his banqueting-room at Donnaz. The lords of Donnaz had never been noted for learning, and Odo's grandfather was fond of declaring that a nobleman need not be a scholar; but the great Marquess Gualberto, if himself unlettered, had been the patron of poets and painters and had kept learned clerks to write down the annals of his house on parchment painted by the monks. These annals were locked in the archives, under Don Gervaso's care; but Odo learned from the old servant that some of the great Marquess's books had lain for years on an upper shelf in the vestry off the chapel; and here one day, with Bruno's aid, the little boy dislodged from a corner behind the missals and altar-books certain sheepskin volumes clasped in blackened silver. The comeliest of these, which bore on their title-page a dolphin curled about an anchor, were printed in unknown characters; but on opening the smaller volumes Odo felt the same joyous catching of the breath as when he had stepped out on the garden-terrace at Pianura. For here indeed were gates leading to a land of delectation: the country of the giant Morgante, the enchanted island of Avillion, the court of the Soldan and the King's palace at Camelot.

In this region Odo spent many blissful hours. His fancy ranged in the wake of heroes and adventurers who, for all he knew, might still be feasting and fighting north of the Alps, or might any day with a blast of their magic horns summon the porter to the gates of Donnaz. Foremost among them, a figure towering above even Rinaldo, Arthur and the Emperor Frederic, was that Conrad, father of Conradin, whose sayings are set down in the old story-book of the Cento Novelle, "the flower of gentle speech." There was one tale of King Conrad that the boy never forgot: how the King, in his youth, had always about him a company of twelve lads of his own age; how when Conrad did wrong, his governors, instead of punishing him, beat his twelve companions; and how, on the young King's asking what the lads were being punished for, the pedagogues replied:

"For your Majesty's offences."

"And why do you punish my companions instead of me?"

"Because you are our lord and master," he was told.

At this the King fell to thinking, and thereafter, it is said, in pity for those who must suffer in his stead he set close watch on himself, lest his sinning should work harm to others. This was the story of King Conrad; and much as Odo loved the clash of arms and joyous feats of paladins rescuing fair maids in battle, yet Conrad's seemed to him, even then, a braver deed than these.

In March of the second year the old Marquess, returning from Turin, was accompanied, to the surprise of all, by the fantastical figure of an elderly gentleman in the richest travelling dress, with one of the new French toupets, a thin wrinkled painted face, and emitting with every movement a prodigious odour of millefleurs. This visitor, who was attended by his French barber and two or three liveried servants, the Marquess introduced as the lord of Valdù, a neighbouring seigneurie of no great account. Though his lands marched with the Marquess's, it was years since the Count had visited Donnaz, being one of the King's chamberlains and always in attendance on his Majesty; and it was amazing to see with what smirks and grimaces, and ejaculations in Piedmontese French, he complimented the Marchioness on her appearance, and exclaimed at the magnificence of the castle, which must doubtless have appeared to him little better than a cattle-grange. His talk was unintelligible to Odo, but there was no mistaking the nature of the glances he fixed on Donna Laura, who, having fled to her room on his approach, presently descended in a ravishing new sacque, with an air of extreme surprise, and her hair curled (as Odo afterward learned) by the Count's own barber.

Odo had never seen his mother look handsomer. She sparkled at the Count's compliments, embraced her father, playfully readjusted her mother's coif, and in the prettiest way made their excuses to the Count for the cold draughts and bare floors of the castle. "For having lived at court myself," said she, "I know to what your excellency is accustomed, and can the better value your condescension in exposing yourself, at this rigorous season, to the hardships of our mountain-top."

The Marquess at this began to look black, but seeing the Count's pleasure in the compliment, contented himself with calling out for dinner, which, said he, with all respect to their visitor, would stay his stomach better than the French kick-shaws at his Majesty's table. Whether the Count was of the same mind, it was impossible to say, though Odo could not help observing that the stewed venison and spiced boar's flesh seemed to present certain obstacles either to his jaws or his palate, and that his appetite lingered on the fried chicken-livers and tunny-fish in oil; but he cast such looks at Donna Laura as seemed to declare that for her sake he would willingly have risked his teeth on the very cobblestones of the court. Knowing how she pined for company, Odo was not surprised at his mother's complaisance; yet wondered to see the smile with which she presently received the Count's half-bantering disparagement of Pianura. For the duchy, by his showing, was a place of small consequence, an asylum of superannuated fashions; whereas no Frenchman of quality ever visited Turin without exclaiming on its resemblance to Paris, and vowing that none who had the entree of Stupinigi need cross the Alps to see Versailles. As to the Marquess's depriving the court of Donna Laura's presence, their guest protested against it as an act of overt disloyalty to the sovereign; and what most surprised Odo, who had often heard his grandfather declaim against the Count as a cheap jackanapes that hung about the court for what he could make at play, was the indulgence with which the Marquess received his visitor's sallies. Father and daughter in fact vied in amenities to the Count. The fire was kept alight all day in his rooms, his Monsu waited on with singular civility by the steward, and Donna Laura's own woman sent down by her mistress to prepare his morning chocolate.

Next day it was agreed the gentlemen should ride to Valdu; but its lord being as stiff-jointed as a marionette, Donna Laura, with charming tact, begged to be of the party, and thus enabled him to attend her in her litter. The Marquess thereupon called on Odo to ride with him; and setting forth across the mountain they descended by a long defile to the half-ruined village of Valdu. Here, for the first time, Odo saw the spectacle of a neglected estate, its last penny wrung from it for the absent master's pleasure by a bailiff who was expected to extract his pay from the sale of clandestine concessions to the tenants. Riding beside the Marquess, who swore under his breath at the ravages of the undyked stream and the sight of good arable land run wild and choked with underbrush, the little boy obtained a precocious insight into the evils of a system which had long outlived its purpose, and the idea of feudalism was ever afterward embodied for him in his glimpse of the peasants of Valdu looking up sullenly from their work as their suzerain and protector thrust an unfamiliar painted smile between the curtains of his litter.

What his grandfather thought of Valdu (to which the Count on the way home referred with smirking apologies as the mountain-lair of his barbarous ancestors) was patent enough even to Odo's undeveloped perceptions; but it would have required a more experienced understanding to detect the motive that led the Marquess, scarce two days after their visit, to accord his daughter's hand to the Count. Odo felt a shock of dismay on learning that his beautiful mother was to become the property of an old gentleman whom he guessed to be of his grandfather's age, and whose enamoured grimaces recalled the antics of her favourite monkey, and the boy's face reflected the blush of embarrassment with which Donna Laura imparted the news; but the children of that day were trained to a passive acquiescence, and had she informed him that she was to be chained in the keep on bread and water, Odo would have accepted the fact with equal philosophy. Three weeks afterward his mother and the old Count were married in the chapel of Donnaz, and Donna Laura, with many tears and embraces, set out for Turin, taking her monkey but leaving her son behind. It was not till later that Odo learned of the social usage which compelled young widows to choose between remarriage and the cloister; and his subsequent views were unconsciously tinged by the remembrance of his mother's melancholy bridal.

Her departure left no traces but were speedily repaired by the coming of spring. The sun growing warmer, and the close season putting an end to the Marquess's hunting, it was now Odo's chief pleasure to carry his books to the walled garden between the castle and the southern face of the cliff. This small enclosure, probably a survival of medieval horticulture, had along the upper ledge of its wall a grass walk commanding the flow of the stream, and an angle turret that turned one slit to the valley, the other to the garden lying below like a tranquil well of scent and brightness: its box trees clipped to the shape of peacocks and lions, its clove pinks and simples set in a border of thrift, and a pear tree basking on its sunny wall. These pleasant spaces, which Odo had to himself save when the canonesses walked there to recite their rosary, he peopled with the knights and ladies of the novelle, and the fantastic beings of Pulci's epic: there walked the Fay Morgana, Regulus the loyal knight, the giant Morgante, Trajan the just Emperor and the proud figure of King Conrad; so that, escaping thither from the after-dinner dullness of the tapestry parlour, the boy seemed to pass from the most oppressive solitude to a world of warmth and fellowship.

1.6.

Odo, who, like all neglected children, was quick to note in the demeanour of his elders any hint of a change in his own condition, had been keenly conscious of the effect produced at Donnaz by the news of the Duchess of Pianura's deliverance. Guided perhaps by his mother's exclamation, he noticed an added zeal in Don Gervaso's teachings and an unction in the manner of his aunts and grandmother, who embraced him as though they were handling a relic; while the old Marquess, though he took his grandson seldomer on his rides, would sit staring at him with a frowning tenderness that once found vent in the growl—"Morbleu, but he's too good for the tonsure!" All this made it clear to Odo that he was indeed meant for the Church, and he learned without surprise that the following spring he was to be sent to the seminary at Asti.

With a view to prepare him for this change, the canonesses suggested his attending them that year on their annual pilgrimage to the sanctuary of Oropa. Thither, for every feast of the Assumption, these pious ladies travelled in their litter; and Odo had heard from them many tales of the miraculous Black Virgin who drew thousands to her shrine among the mountains. They set forth in August, two days before the feast, ascending through chestnut groves to the region of bare rocks; thence downward across torrents hung with white acacia and along park-like grassy levels deep in shade. The lively air, the murmur of verdure, the perfume of mown grass in the meadows and the sweet call of the cuckoos from every thicket made an enchantment of the way; but Odo's pleasure redoubled when, gaining the high-road to Oropa, they mingled with the long train of devotees ascending from the plain. Here were pilgrims of every condition, from the noble lady of Turin or Asti (for it was the favourite pilgrimage of the Sardinian court), attended by her physician and her cicisbeo, to the half-naked goatherd of Val Sesia or Salluzzo; the cheerful farmers of the Milanese, with their wives, in silver necklaces and hairpins, riding pillion on plump white asses; sick persons travelling in closed litters or carried on hand-stretchers; crippled beggars obtruding their deformities; confraternities of hooded penitents, Franciscans, Capuchins and Poor Clares in dusty companies; jugglers, pedlars, Egyptians and sellers of drugs and amulets. From among these, as the canonesses' litter jogged along, an odd figure advanced toward Odo, who had obtained leave to do the last mile of the journey on foot. This was a plump abate in tattered ecclesiastical dress, his shoes white as a miller's and the perspiration streaking his face as he laboured along in the dust. He accosted Odo in a soft shrill voice, begging leave to walk beside the young cavaliere, whom he had more than once had the honour of seeing at Pianura; and, in reply to the boy's surprised glance, added, with a swelling of the chest and an absurd gesture of self-introduction, "But perhaps the cavaliere is not too young to have heard of the illustrious Cantapresto, late primo soprano of the ducal theatre of Pianura?"

Odo being obliged to avow his ignorance, the fat creature mopped his brow and continued with a gasp—"Ah, your excellency, what is fame? From glory to obscurity is no farther than from one milestone to another! Not eight years ago, cavaliere, I was followed through the streets of Pianura by a greater crowd than the Duke ever drew after him! But what then? The voice goes—it lasts no longer than the bloom of a flower—and with it goes everything: fortune, credit, consideration, friends and parasites! Not eight years ago, sir—would you believe me?—I was supping nightly in private with the Bishop, who had nearly quarrelled with his late Highness for carrying me off by force one evening to his casino; I was heaped with dignities and favours; all the poets in the town composed sonnets in my honour; the Marquess of Trescorre fought a duel about me with the Bishop's nephew, Don Serafino;

I attended his lordship to Rome; I spent the villeggiatura at his villa, where I sat at play with the highest nobles in the land; yet when my voice went, cavaliere, it was on my knees I had to beg of my heartless patron the paltry favour of the minor orders!" Tears were running down the abate's cheeks, and he paused to wipe them with a corner of tattered bands.

Though Odo had been bred in an abhorrence of the theatre, the strange creature's aspect so pricked his compassion that he asked him what he was now engaged in; at which Cantapresto piteously cried, "Alas, what am I not engaged in, if the occasion offers? For whatever a man's habit, he will not wear it long if it cover an empty belly; and he that respects his calling must find food enough to continue in it. But as for me, sir, I have put a hand to every trade, from composing scenarios for the ducal company of Pianura, to writing satirical sonnets for noblemen that desire to pass for wits. I've a pretty taste, too, in compiling almanacks, and when nothing else served I have played the public scrivener at the street corner; nay, sir, necessity has even driven me to hold the candle in one or two transactions I would not more actively have mixed in; and it was to efface the remembrance of one of these—for my conscience is still over-nice for my condition—that I set out on this laborious pilgrimage."

Much of this was unintelligible to Odo; but he was moved by any mention of Pianura, and in the abate's first pause he risked the question—"Do you know the hump-backed boy Brutus?"

His companion stared and pursed his soft lips.

"Brutus?" says he. "Brutus? Is he about the Duke's person?"

"He lives in the palace," said Odo doubtfully.

The fat ecclesiastic clapped a hand to his thigh.

"Can it be your excellency has in mind the foundling boy Carlo Gamba? Does the jackanapes call himself Brutus now? He was always full of his classical allusions! Why, sir, I think I know him very well; he is even rumoured to be a brother of Don Lelio Trescorre's, and I believe the Duke has lately given him to the Marquess of Cerveno, for I saw him not long since in the Marquess's livery at Pontesordo."

"Pontesordo?" cried Odo. "It was there I lived."

"Did you indeed, cavaliere? But I think you will have been at the Duke's manor of that name; and it was the hunting-lodge on the edge of the chase that I had in mind. The Marquess uses it, I believe, as a kind of casino; though not without risk of a distemper. Indeed, there is much wonder at his frequenting it, and 'tis said he does so against the Duke's wishes."

The name of Pontesordo had set Odo's memories humming like a hive of bees, and without heeding his companion's allusions he asked—"And did you see the Momola?"

The other looked his perplexity.

"She's an Innocent too," Odo hastened to explain. "She is Filomena's servant at the farm."

The abate at this, standing still in the road, screwed up his eyelids and protruded a relishing lip. "Eh, eh," said he, "the girl from the farm, you say?" And he gave a chuckle. "You've an eye, cavaliere, you've an eye," he cried, his soft body shaking with enjoyment; but before Odo could make a guess at his meaning their conversation was interrupted by a sharp call from the litter. The abate at once disappeared in the crowd, and a moment later the litter had debouched on the grassy quadrangle before the outer gates of the monastery. This space was set in beech-woods, amid which gleamed the white-pillared chapels of the Way of the Cross; and the devouter pilgrims, dispersed beneath the trees, were ascending from one chapel to another, preparatory to entering the church.

The quadrangle itself was crowded with people, and the sellers of votive offerings, in their booths roofed with acacia-boughs, were driving a noisy trade in scapulars and Agnus Deis, images of the Black Virgin of Oropa, silver hearts and crosses, and phials of Jordan water warranted to effect the immediate conversion of Jews and heretics. In one corner a Carmelite missionary had set up his portable pulpit, and, crucifix in hand, was exhorting the crowd; in another, an improvisatore intoned canticles to the miraculous Virgin; a barefoot friar sat selling indulgences at the monastery gate, and pedlars with trays of rosaries and religious prints pushed their way among the pilgrims. Young women of less pious aspect solicited the attention of the better-dressed travellers, and jugglers, mountebanks and quacks of every description hung on the outskirts of the square. The sight speedily turned Odo's thought from his late companion, and the litter coming to a halt he was leaning forward to observe the antics of a tumbler who had spread his carpet beneath the trees, when the abate's face suddenly rose to the surface of the throng and his hand thrust a crumpled paper between the curtains of the litter. Odo was quick-witted enough to capture this missive without attracting the notice of his grand-aunts, and stealing a glance at it, he read— "Cavaliere, I starve. When the illustrious ladies descend, for Christ's sake beg a scudo of them for the unhappy Cantapresto."

By this the litter had disengaged itself and was moving toward the outer gates. Odo, aware of the disfavour with which the theatre was viewed at Donnaz, and unable to guess how far the soprano's present habit would be held to palliate the scandal of his former connection, was perplexed how to communicate his petition to the canonesses. A moment later, however, the question solved itself; for as the aunts descended at the door of the rector's lodging, the porter, running to meet them, stumbled on a black mass under the arcade, and raised the cry that here was a man dropped dead. A crowd gathering, some one called out that it was an ecclesiastic had fallen; whereat the great-aunts were hurrying forward when Odo whispered the eldest, Donna Livia, that the sick man was indeed an abate from Pianura. Donna Livia immediately bid her servants lift him into the porter's lodge, where, with the administering of spirits, the poor soprano presently revived and cast a drowning glance about the chamber.

"Eight years ago, illustrious ladies," he gurgled, "I had nearly died one night of a surfeit of ortolans; and now it is of a surfeit of emptiness that I am perishing."

The ladies at this, with exclamations of pity, called on the lay-brothers for broth and cordials, and bidding the porter enquire more particularly into the history of the unhappy ecclesiastic, hastened away with Odo to the rector's parlour.

Next morning betimes all were afoot for the procession, which the canonesses were to witness from the monastery windows. The apothecary had brought word that the abate, whose seizure was indeed the result of hunger, was still too weak to rise; and Donna Livia, eager to open her devotions with an act of pity, pressed a sequin in the man's hand, and bid him spare no care for the sufferer's comfort.

This sent Odo in a cheerful mood to the red-hung windows, whence, peering between the folds of his aunts' gala habits, he admired the great court enclosed in nobly-ordered cloisters and strewn with fresh herbs and flowers. Thence one of the rector's chaplains conducted them to the church, placing them, in company with the monastery's other noble guests, in a tribune constructed above the choir. It was Odo's first sight of a great religious ceremony, and as he looked down on the church glimmering with votive offerings and gold-fringed draperies, and seen through rolling incense in which the altar-candles swam like stars reflected in a river, he felt an almost sensual thrill of pleasure at the thought that his life was to be passed amid scenes of such mystic beauty. The sweet singing of the choir raised his spirit to a higher view of the scene; and the sight of the huddled misery on the floor of the church revived in him the old longing for the Franciscan cowl.

From these raptures he was speedily diverted by the sight awaiting him at the conclusion of the mass. Hardly had the spectators returned to the rector's windows when, the doors of the church swinging open, a procession headed by the rector himself descended the steps and began to make the circuit of the court. Odo's eyes swam with the splendour of this burst of banners, images and jewelled reliquaries, surmounting the long train of tonsured heads and bathed in a light almost blinding after the mild penumbra of the church. As the monks advanced, the pilgrims, pouring after them, filled the court with a dark undulating mass through which the procession wound like a ray of sunlight down the brown bosom of a torrent. Branches of oleander swung in the air, devout cries hailed the approach of the Black Madonna's canopy, and hoarse voices swelled to a roar the measured litanies of the friars.

The ceremonies over, Odo, with the canonesses, set out to visit the chapels studding the beech-knoll above the monastic buildings. Passing out of Juvara's great portico they stood a moment above the grassy common, which presented a scene in curious contrast to that they had just quitted. Here refreshment-booths had been set up, musicians were fiddling, jugglers unrolling their carpets, dentists shouting out the merits of their panaceas, and light women drinking with the liveried servants of the nobility. The very cripples who had groaned the loudest in church now rollicked with the mountebanks and dancers; and no trace remained of the celebration just concluded but the medals and relics strung about the necks of those engaged in these gross diversions.

It was strange to pass from this scene to the solitude of the grove, where, in a twilight rustling with streams, the chapels lifted their white porches. Peering through the grated door of each little edifice, Odo beheld within a group of terra-cotta figures representing some scene of the Passion—here a Last Supper, with a tigerish Judas and a Saint John resting his yellow curls on his Master's bosom, there an Entombment or a group of stricken Maries. These figures, though rudely modelled and daubed with bright colours, yet, by a vivacity of attitude and gesture which the mystery of their setting enhanced, conveyed a thrilling impression of the sacred scenes set forth; and Odo was yet at an age when the distinction between flesh-and-blood and its plastic counterfeits is not clearly defined, or when at least the sculptured image is still a mysterious half-sentient thing, denizen of some strange borderland between art and life. It seemed to him, as he gazed through the chapel gratings, that those long-distant episodes of the divine tragedy had been here preserved in some miraculous state of suspended animation, and as he climbed from one shrine to another he had the sense of treading the actual stones of Gethsemane and Calvary.

As was usual with him, the impressions of the moment had effaced those preceding it, and it was almost with surprise that, at the rector's door, he beheld the primo soprano of Pianura totter forth to the litter and offer his knee as a step for the canonesses. The charitable ladies cried out on him for this imprudence, and his pallor still giving evidence of distress, he was bidden to wait on them after supper with his story. He presented himself promptly in the parlour, and being questioned as to his condition at once rashly proclaimed his former connection with the ducal theatre of Pianura. No avowal could have been more disastrous to his cause. The canonesses crossed themselves with horror, and the abate, seeing his mistake, hastened to repair it by exclaiming—"What, ladies, would you punish me for following a vocation to which my frivolous parents condemned me when I was too young to resist their purpose? And have not my subsequent sufferings, my penances and pilgrimages, and the state to which they have reduced me, sufficiently effaced the record of an involuntary error?"

Seeing the effect of this appeal the abate made haste to follow up his advantage. "Ah, illustrious ladies," he cried, "am I not a living example of the fate of those who leave all to follow righteousness? For while I remained on the stage, among the most dissolute surroundings, fortune showered me with every benefit she heaps on her favourites. I had my seat at every table in Pianura; the Duke's chair to carry me to the theatre; and more money than I could devise how to spend; while now that I have resigned my calling to embrace the religious life, you see me reduced to begging a crust from the very mendicants I formerly nourished. For," said he, moved to tears by his own recital, "my superfluity was always spent in buying the prayers of the unfortunate, and to judge how I was esteemed by those acquainted with my private behaviour you need only learn that, on my renouncing the stage, 'twas the Bishop of Pianura who himself accorded me the tonsure."

This discourse, which Odo admired for its adroitness, visibly excited the commiseration of the ladies; but at mention of the Bishop, Donna Livia exchanged a glance with her sister, who enquired, with a quaint air of astuteness, "But how comes it, abate, that with so powerful a protector you have been exposed to such incredible reverses?"

Cantapresto rolled a meaning eye.

"Alas, madam, it was through my protector that misfortune attacked me; for his lordship having appointed me secretary to his favourite nephew, Don Serafino, that imprudent nobleman required of me services so incompatible with my cloth that disobedience became a duty; whereupon, not satisfied with dismissing me in disgrace, he punished me by blackening my character to his uncle. To defend myself was to traduce Don Serafino; and rather than reveal his courses to the Bishop I sank to the state in which you see me; a state," he added with emotion, "that I have travelled this long way to commend to the adorable pity of Her whose Son had not where to lay His head."

This stroke visibly touched the canonesses, still soft from the macerations of the morning; and Donna Livia compassionately asked how he had subsisted since his rupture with the Bishop.

"Madam, by the sale of my talents in any service not at odds with my calling: as the compiling of pious almanacks, the inditing of rhymed litanies and canticles, and even the construction of theatrical pieces"—the ladies lifted hands of reprobation—"of theatrical pieces," Cantapresto impressively repeated, "for the use of the Carmelite nuns of Pianura. But," said he with a deprecating smile, "the wages of virtue are less liberal than those of sin, and spite of a versatility I think I may honestly claim, I have often had to subsist on the gifts of the pious, and sometimes, madam, to starve on their compassion."

This ready discourse, and the soprano's evident distress, so worked on the canonesses that, having little money at their disposal, it was fixed, after some private consultation, that he should attend them to Donnaz, where Don Gervaso, in consideration of his edifying conduct in renouncing the stage, might be interested in helping him to a situation; and when the little party set forth from Oropa, the abate Cantapresto closed the procession on one of the baggage-mules, with Odo riding pillion at his back. Good fortune loosened the poor soprano's tongue, and as soon as the canonesses' litter was a safe distance ahead he began to beguile the way with fragments of reminiscence and adventure. Though few of his allusions were clear to Odo, the glimpse they gave of the motley theatrical life of the north Italian cities—the quarrels between Goldoni and the supporters of the expiring commedia dell' arte—the rivalries of the prime donne and the arrogance of the popular comedians—all these peeps into a tinsel world of mirth, cabal and folly, enlivened by the recurring names of the Four Masks, those lingering gods of the older dispensation, so lured the boy's fancy and set free his vagrant wonder, that he was almost sorry to see the keep of Donnaz reddening in the second evening's sunset.

Such regrets, however, their arrival at the castle soon effaced; for in the doorway stood the old Marquess, a letter in hand, who springing forward caught his grandson by the shoulders, and cried with his great boar-hunting shout, "Cavaliere, you are heir-presumptive of Pianura!"

1.7.

The Marquess of Cerveno had succumbed to the tertian ague contracted at the hunting-lodge of Pontesordo; and this unforeseen calamity left but one life, that of the sickly ducal infant, between Odo and the succession to the throne of Pianura. Such was the news conveyed post-haste from Turin by Donna Laura; who added the Duke's express wish that his young kinsman should be fitted for the secular career, and the information that Count Valdu had already entered his stepson's name at the Royal Academy of Turin.

The Duke of Pianura being young and in good health, and his wife having already given him an heir, the most sanguine imagination could hardly view Odo as being brought much nearer the succession; yet the change in his condition was striking enough to excuse the fancy of those about him for shaping the future to their liking. The priestling was to turn courtier and perhaps soldier; Asti was to be exchanged for Turin, the seminary for the academy; and even the old chief of Donnaz betrayed in his grumbling counsels to the boy a sense of the exalted future in which they might some day serve him.

The preparations of departure and the wonder of his new state left Odo little space wherein to store his thought with impressions of what he was leaving; and it was only in after years, when the accretion of superficial incident had dropped from his past, that those last days at Donnaz gained their full distinctness. He saw them then, heavy with the warmth of the long summer, from the topmost pine-belt to the bronzed vineyards turning their metallic clusters to the sun; and in the midst his small bewildered figure, netted in a web of association, and seeming, as he broke away, to leave a shred of himself in every corner of the castle.

Sharpest of all, there remained with him the vision of his last hour with Don Gervaso. The news of Odo's changed condition had been received in silence by the chaplain. He was not the man to waste words and he knew the futility of asserting the Church's claim to the heir-presumptive of a reigning house. Therefore if he showed no enthusiasm he betrayed no resentment; but, the evening before the boy's departure, led him, still in silence, to the chapel. Here the priest knelt with Odo; then, raising him, sat on one of the benches facing the high altar, and spoke a few grave words.

"You are setting out," said he, "on a way far different from that in which it has been my care to guide you; yet the high road and the mountain path may, by diverse windings, lead to the same point; and whatever walk a man chooses, it will surely carry him to the end that God has appointed. If you are called to serve Him in the world, the journey on which you are now starting may lead you to the throne of Pianura; but even so," he went on, "there is this I would have you remember: that should this dignity come to you it may come as a calamity rather than a joy; for when God confers earthly honours on a child of His predilection, He sometimes deigns to render them as innocuous as misfortune; and my chief prayer for you is that you should be raised to this eminence, it may be at a moment when such advancement seems to thrust you in the dust."

The words burned themselves into Odo's heart like some mystic writing on the walls of memory, long afterward to start into fiery meaning. At the time he felt only that the priest spoke with a power and dignity no human authority could give; and for a moment all the stored influences of his faith reached out to him from the dimly-gleaming altar.

The next sun rose on a new world. He was to set out at daylight, and dawn found him at the casement, footing it in thought down the road as yet undistinguishable in a dying glimmer of stars. Bruno was to attend him to Turin; but one of the women presently brought word that the old huntsman's rheumatism had caught him in the knee, and that the Marquess, resolved not to delay his grandson's departure, had chosen Cantapresto as the boy's companion. The courtyard, when Odo descended, fairly bubbled with the voluble joy of the fat soprano, who was giving directions to the servants, receiving commissions and instructions from the aunts, assuring everybody of his undying devotion to the heir-presumptive of Pianura, and citing impressive instances of the responsibilities with which the great of the earth had formerly entrusted him.

As a companion for Odo the abate was clearly not to Don Gervaso's taste; but he stood silent, turning the comment of a cool eye on the soprano's protestations, and saying only, as Cantapresto swept the company into the circle of an obsequious farewell:—"Remember, signor abate, it is to your cloth this business is entrusted." The abate's answer was a rush of purple to the forehead; but Don Gervaso imperturbably added, "And you lie but one night on the road."

Meanwhile the old Marquess, visibly moved, was charging Odo to respect his elders and superiors, while in the same breath warning him not to take up with the Frenchified notions of the court, but to remember that for a lad of his condition the chief virtues were a tight seat in the saddle, a quick hand on the sword and a slow tongue in counsel. "Mind your own business," he concluded, "and see that others mind theirs."

The Marchioness thereupon, with many tears, hung a scapular about Odo's neck, bidding him shun the theatre and be regular at confession; one of the canonesses reminded him not to omit a visit to the chapel of the Holy Winding-sheet, while the other begged him to burn a candle for her at the Consolata; and the servants pressed forward to embrace and bless their little master.

Day was high by this, and as the Marquess's travelling-chariot rumbled down the valley the shadows seemed to fly before it. Odo at first lay numb; but presently his senses woke to the call of the brightening landscape. The scene was such as Salvator might have painted: wild blocks of stone heaped under walnut-shade; here the white plunge of water down a wall of granite, and there, in bluer depths, a charcoal burner's hut sending up its spiral of smoke to the dark raftering of branches. Though it was but a few hours since Odo had travelled from Oropa, years seemed to have passed over him, and he saw the world with a new eye. Each sound and scent plucked at him in passing: the roadside started into detail like the foreground of some minute Dutch painter; every pendent mass of fern, dark dripping rock, late tuft of harebell called out to him: "Look well, for this is your last sight of us!" His first sight too, it seemed: since he had lived through twelve Italian summers without sense of the sun-steeped quality of atmosphere that, even in shade, gives each object a golden salience. He was conscious of it now only as it suggested fingering a missal stiff with gold-leaf and edged with a swarming diversity of buds and insects. The carriage moved so slowly that he was in no haste to turn the pages; and each spike of yellow foxglove, each clouding of butterflies about a patch of speedwell, each quiver of grass over a hidden thread of moisture, became a marvel to be thumbed and treasured.

From this mood he was detached by the next bend of the road. The way, hitherto winding through narrow glens, now swung to a ledge overhanging the last escarpment of the mountains; and far below, the Piedmontese plain unrolled to the southward its interminable blue-green distances mottled with forest. A sight to lift the heart; for on those sunny reaches Ivrea, Novara, Vercelli lay like sea-birds on a summer sea. It was the future unfolding itself to the boy; dark forests, wide rivers, strange cities and a new horizon: all the mystery of the coming years figured to him in that great plain stretching away to the greater mystery of heaven.

To all this Cantapresto turned a snoring countenance. The lively air of the hills, the good fare of Donnaz, and the satisfaction, above all, of rolling on cushions over a road he had thought to trudge on foot, had lapped the abate in Capuan slumber. The midday halt aroused him. The travellers rested at an inn on the edge of the hills, and here Cantapresto proved to his charge that, as he phrased it, his belly had as short a memory for food as his heart for injuries. A flask of Asti put him in the talking mood, and as they drove on he regaled Odo with a lively picture of the life on which he was to enter.

"You are going," said he, "to one of the first cities of Europe; one that has all the beauty and elegance of the French capital without its follies and excesses. Turin is blessed with a court where good manners and a fine tone are more highly prized than the extravagances of genius; and I have heard it said of his Majesty that he was delighted to see his courtiers wearing the French fashions outside their heads, provided they didn't carry the French ideas within. You are too young, doubtless, cavaliere, to have heard of the philosophers who are raising such a pother north of the Alps: a set of madmen that, because their birth doesn't give them the entree of Versailles, are preaching that men should return to a state of nature, great ladies suckle their young like animals, and the peasantry own their land like nobles. Luckily you'll hear little of this infectious talk in Turin: the King stamps out the philosophers like vermin or packs them off to splutter their heresies in Milan or Venice. But to a nobleman mindful of the privileges of his condition there is no more agreeable sojourn in Europe. The wines are delicious, the women—er—accomplished—and though the sbirri may hug one a trifle close now and then, why, with money and discretion, a friend or two in the right quarters, and the wit to stand well with the Church, there's no city in Europe where a man may have pleasanter sins to confess."

The carriage, by this, was descending the last curves above the valley, and before them, in a hollow of the hills, blinked the warm shimmer of maize and vine, like some bright vintage brimming its cup. The soprano waved a convivial hand.

"Look," he cried, "what Nature has done for this happy region! Where herself has spread the table so bountifully, should her children hang back from the feast? I vow, cavaliere, if the mountains were built for hermits and ascetics, then the plain was made level for dancing, banqueting and the pleasures of the villeggiatura. If God had meant us to break our teeth on nuts and roots, why did He hang the vine with fruit and draw three crops of wheat from this indulgent soil? I protest when I look on such a scene as this, it is sufficient incentive to lowliness to remember that the meek shall inherit the earth!"

This mood held Cantapresto till his after-dinner sleep overtook him; and when he woke again the chariot was clattering across the bridge of Chivasso. The Po rolled its sunset crimson between flats that seemed dull and featureless after the broken scenery of the hills; but beyond the bridge rose the towers and roofs of the town, with its cathedral-front catching the last slant of light. In the streets dusk had fallen and a lamp flared under the arch of the inn before which the travellers halted. Odo's head was heavy, and he hardly noticed the figures thronging the caffe into which they were led; but presently there rose a shout of "Cantapresto!" and a ring of waving arms and flashing teeth encircled his companion.

These appendages belonged to a troop of men and women, some masked and in motley, others in discoloured travel-stained garments, who pressed about the soprano with cries of joyous recognition. He was evidently an old favourite of the band, for a duenna in tattered velvet fell on his neck with genial unreserve, a pert soubrette caught him by the arm the duenna left free, and a terrific Matamor with a nose like a scimitar slapped him on the back with a tin sword.

Odo's glimpse of the square at Oropa told him that here was a band of strolling players such as Cantapresto had talked of on the ride back to Donnaz. Don Gervaso's instructions and the old Marchioness's warning against the theatre were present enough in the boy's mind to add a touch of awe to the curiosity with which he observed these strange objects of the Church's reprobation. They struck him, it must be owned, as more pitiable than alarming, for the duenna's toes were coming through her shoes, and one or two of the children who hung on the outskirts of the group looked as lean and hungry under their spangles as the foundling-girl of Pontesordo. Spite of this they seemed a jolly crew, and ready (at Cantapresto's expense) to celebrate their encounter with the ex-soprano in unlimited libations of Asti and Val Pulicello. The singer, however, hung back with protesting gestures.

"Gently, then, gently, dear friends—dear companions! When was it we parted? In the spring of the year—and we meet now in the late summer. As the seasons change so do our conditions: if the spring is a season of folly, then is the harvest-time the period for reflection. When we last met I was a strolling poet, glad to serve your gifted company within the scope of my talents—now, ladies and gentlemen, now"—he drew himself up with pride—"now you behold in me the governor and friend of the heir-presumptive of Pianura."

Cries of incredulity and derision greeted this announcement, and one of the girls called out laughingly, "Yet you have the same old cassock to your back!"

"And the same old passage from your mouth to your belly," added an elastic Harlequin, reaching an arm across the women's shoulders. "Come, Cantapresto, we'll help you line it with good wine, to the health of his most superlatively serene Highness, the heir-presumptive of Pianura; and where is that fabulous personage, by the way?"

Odo at this retreated hastily behind the soprano; but a pretty girl catching sight of him, he found himself dragged into the centre of the company, who hailed him with fantastic obeisances. Supper meanwhile was being laid on the greasy table down the middle of the room. The Matamor, who seemed the director of the troupe, thundered out his orders for maccaroni, fried eels and sausages; the inn-servants flanked the plates with wine-flasks and lumps of black bread, and in a moment the hungry comedians, thrusting Odo into a high seat at the head of the table, were falling on the repast with a prodigious clatter of cutlery.

Of the subsequent incidents of the feast—the banter of the younger women, the duenna's lachrymose confidences, the incessant interchange of theatrical jargon and coarse pleasantry—there remained to Odo but a confused image, obscured by the smoke of guttering candles, the fumes of wine and the stifling air of the low-ceilinged tavern. Even the face of the pretty girl who had dragged him from his concealment, and who now sat at his side, plying him with sweets from her own plate, began to fade into the general blur; and his last impression was of Cantapresto's figure dilating to immense proportions at the other end of the table, as the soprano rose with shaking wine-glass to favour the company with a song. The chorus, bursting forth in response, surged over Odo's drowning senses, and he was barely aware, in the tumult of noise and lights, of an arm slipped about him, a softly-heaving pillow beneath his head, and the gradual subsidence into dark delicious peace.

So, on the first night of his new life, the heir-presumptive of Pianura fell asleep with his head in a dancing-girl's breast.

1.8.

The travellers were to journey by Vettura from Chivasso to Turin; and when Odo woke next morning the carriage stood ready in the courtyard.

Cantapresto, mottled and shamefaced, with his bands awry and an air of tottering dignity, was gathering their possessions together, and the pretty girl who had pillowed Odo's slumbers now knelt by his bed and laughingly drew on his stockings. She was a slim brown morsel, not much above his age, with a glance that flitted like a bird, and round shoulders slipping out of her kerchief. A wave of shyness bathed Odo to the forehead as their eyes met: he hung his head stupidly and turned away when she fetched the comb to dress his hair.

His toilet completed, she called out to the abate to go below and see that the cavaliere's chocolate was ready; and as the door closed she turned and kissed Odo on the lips.

"Oh, how red you are!" she cried laughing. "Is that the first kiss you've ever had? Then you'll remember me when you're Duke of Pianura—Mirandolina of Chioggia, the first girl you ever kissed!" She was pulling his collar straight while she talked, so that he could not get away from her. "You will remember me, won't you?" she persisted. "I shall be a great actress by that time, and you'll appoint me prima amorosa to the ducal theatre of Pianura, and throw me a diamond bracelet from your Highness's box and make all the court ladies ready to poison me for rage!" She released his collar and dropped away from him. "Ah, no, I shall be a poor strolling player, and you a great prince," she sighed, "and you'll never, never think of me again; but I shall always remember that I was the first girl you ever kissed!"

She hung back in a dazzle of tears, looking so bright and tender that Odo's bashfulness melted like a spring frost.

"I shall never be Duke," he cried, "and I shall never forget you!" And with that he turned and kissed her boldly and then bolted down the stairs like a hare. And all that day he scorched and froze with the thought that perhaps she had been laughing at him.

Cantapresto was torpid after the feast, and Odo detected in him an air of guilty constraint. The boy was glad enough to keep silence, and they rolled on without speaking through the wide glowing landscape. Already the nearness of a great city began to make itself felt. The bright champaign was scattered over with farm-houses, their red-tiled pigeon-cots and their granges latticed with openwork terra-cotta pleasantly breaking the expanse of maize and mulberry; villages lay along the banks of the canals intersecting the plain; and the hills beyond the Po were planted with villas and monasteries.

All the afternoon they drove between umbrageous parks and under the walls of terraced vineyards. It was a region of delectable shade, with glimpses here and there of gardens flashing with fountains and villa roofs decked with statues and vases; and at length, toward sunset, a bend of the road brought them out on a fair-spreading city, so flourishing in buildings, so beset with smiling hills, that Odo, springing from his seat, cried out in sheer joy of the spectacle.

They had still the suburbs to traverse; and darkness was falling when they entered the gates of Turin. This brought the fresh amazement of wide lamplit streets, clean and bright as a ball-room, lined with palaces and filled with well-dressed loungers: officers in the brilliant Sardinian uniforms, fine gentlemen in French tie-wigs and narrow-sleeved coats, merchants hurrying home from business, ecclesiastics in high-swung carriages, and young bloods dashing by in their curricles. The tables before the coffee-houses were thronged with idlers taking their chocolate and reading the gazettes; and here and there the arched doorway of a palace showed some gay party supping al fresco in a garden hung with lamps.

The flashing of lights and the noise of the streets roused Cantapresto, who sat up with a sudden assumption of dignity.

"Ah, cavaliere," said he, "you now see a great city, a famous city, a city aptly called 'the Paris of Italy.' Nowhere else shall you find such well-lit streets, such fair pavements, shops so full of Parisian wares, promenades so crowded with fine carriages and horses. What a life a young gentleman may lead here! The court is hospitable, society amiable, the theatres are the best-appointed in Italy."

Here Cantapresto paused with a deprecating cough.

"Only one thing is necessary," he went on, "to complete enjoyment of the fruits of this garden of Eden; and that is"—he coughed again—"discretion. His Majesty, cavaliere, is a father to his subjects; the Church is their zealous mother; and between two such parents, and the innumerable delegates of their authority, why, you may fancy, sir, that a man has to wear his eyes on all sides of his head. Discretion is a virtue the Church herself commends; it is natural, then, that she should afford her children full opportunity to practise it. And look you, cavaliere, it is like gymnastics: the younger you acquire it, the less effort it costs. Our Maker Himself has taught us the value of silence by putting us speechless into the world: if we learn to talk later we do it at our own risk! But for your own part, cavaliere—since the habit cannot too early be exercised—I would humbly counsel you to say nothing to your illustrious parents of our little diversion of last evening."

The Countess Valdu lived on the upper floor of a rococo palace near the Piazza San Carlo; and here Odo, led by Cantapresto, presently found himself shown into an apartment where several ladies and gentlemen sat at cards. His mother, detaching herself from the group, embraced him with unusual warmth, and the old Count, more painted and perfumed than ever, hurried up with an obsequious greeting. Odo for the first time found himself of consequence in the world; and as he was passed from guest to guest, questioned about his journey, praised for his good colour and stout looks, complimented on his high prospects, and laughingly entreated not to forget his old friends when fortune should advance him to the duchy, he began to feel himself a reigning potentate already.

His mother, as he soon learned, had sunk into a life almost as dull and restricted as that she had left Donnaz to escape. Count Valdu's position at court was more ornamental than remunerative, the income from his estates was growing annually smaller, and he was involved in costly litigation over the sale of some entailed property. Such conditions were little to the Countess's humour, and the society to which her narrow means confined her offered few distractions to her vanity. The frequenters of the house were chiefly poor relations and hangers-on of the Count's, the parasites who in those days were glad to subsist on the crumbs of the slenderest larder. Half-a-dozen hungry Countesses, their lean admirers, a superannuated abate or two, and a flock of threadbare ecclesiastics, made up Donna Laura's circle; and even her cicisbeo, selected in family council under the direction of her confessor, was an austere gentleman of middle age, who collected ancient coins and was engaged in composing an essay on the Martellian verse.

This company, which devoted hours to the new French diversion of the parfilage, and spent the evenings in drinking lemonade and playing basset for small stakes, found its chief topic of conversation in the only two subjects safely discussed in Turin at that day—the doings of the aristocracy and of the clergy. The fashion of the Queen's headdress at the last circle, the marked manner in which his Majesty had lately distinguished the brilliant young cavalry officer, Count Roberto di Tournanches, the third marriage of the Countess Alfieri of Asti, the incredibility of the rumour that the court ladies of Versailles had taken to white muslin and Leghorn hats, the probable significance of the Vicar-general's visit to Rome, the subject of the next sacred representation to be given by the nuns of Santa Croce—such were the questions that engaged the noble frequenters of Casa Valdu.

This was the only society that Donna Laura saw; for she was too poor to dress to her taste and too proud to show herself in public without the appointments becoming her station. Her sole distraction consisted in visits to the various shrines—the Sudario, the Consolata, the Corpus Domini—at which the feminine aristocracy offered up its devotions and implored absolution for sins it had often no opportunity to commit: for though fashion accorded cicisbei to the fine ladies of Turin, the Church usually restricted their intercourse to the exchange of the most harmless amenities.

Meanwhile the antechamber was as full of duns as the approach to Donna Laura's apartment at Pianura; and Odo guessed that the warmth of the maternal welcome sprang less from natural affection than from the hope of using his expectations as a sop to her creditors. The pittance which the ducal treasury allowed for his education was scarce large enough to be worth diverting to other ends; but a potential prince is a shield to the most vulnerable fortunes. In this character Odo for the first time found himself flattered, indulged, and made the centre of the company. The contrast to his life of subjection at Donnaz; the precocious initiation into motives that tainted the very fount of filial piety; the taste of this mingled draught of adulation and disillusionment, might have perverted a nature more self-centred than his. From this perversion, and from many subsequent perils he was saved by a kind of imaginative sympathy, a wondering joy in the mere spectacle of life, that tinged his most personal impressions with a streak of the philosophic temper. If this trait did not save him from sorrow, it at least lifted him above pettiness; if it could not solve the difficulties of life it could arm him to endure them. It was the best gift of the past from which he sprang; but it was blent with another quality, a deep moral curiosity that ennobled his sensuous enjoyment of the outward show of life; and these elements were already tending in him, as in countless youths of his generation, to the formation of a new spirit, the spirit that was to destroy one world without surviving to create another.

Of all this none could have been less conscious than the lad just preparing to enter on his studies at the Royal Academy of Turin. That institution, adjoining the royal palace, was a kind of nursery or forcing-house for the budding nobility of Savoy. In one division of the sumptuous building were housed his Majesty's pages, a corps of luxurious indolent young fops; another wing accommodated the regular students of the Academy, sons of noblemen and gentlemen destined for the secular life, while a third was set aside for the "forestieri" or students from foreign countries and from the other Italian states. To this quarter Odo Valsecca was allotted; though it was understood that on leaving the Academy he was to enter the Sardinian service.

It was customary for a young gentleman of Odo's rank to be attended at the Academy not only by a body-servant but by a private governor or pedant, whose business it was to overlook his studies, attend him abroad, and have an eye to the society he frequented. The old Marquess of Donnaz had sent his daughter, by Odo's hand, a letter recommending her to select her son's governor with particular care, choosing rather a person of grave behaviour and assured morality than one of your glib ink-spatterers who may know the inside of all the folios in the King's library without being the better qualified for the direction of a young gentleman's conduct; and to this letter Don Gervaso appended the terse postcript: "Your excellency is especially warned against according this or any other position of trust to the merry-andrew who calls himself the abate Cantapresto."

Donna Laura, with a shrug, handed the letter to her husband; Count Valdu, adjusting his glasses, observed it was notorious that people living in the depths of the country thought themselves qualified to instruct their city relatives on all points connected with the social usages; and the cicisbeo suggested that he could recommend an abate who was proficient in the construction of the Martellian verse, and who would made no extra charge for that accomplishment.

"Charges!" the Countess cried. "There's a matter my father doesn't deign to consider. It's not enough, nowadays, to give the lads a governor, but they must maintain their servants too, an idle gluttonous crew that prey on their pockets and get a commission off every tradesman's bill."

Count Valdu lifted a deprecating hand.

"My dear, nothing could be more offensive to his Majesty than any attempt to reduce the way of living of the pupils of the Academy."

"Of course," she shrugged—"But who's to pay? The Duke's beggarly pittance hardly clothes him."

The cicisbeo suggested that the cavaliere Odo had expectations; at which Donna Laura flushed and turned uneasy; while the Count, part of whose marital duty it was to intervene discreetly between his lady and her knight, now put forth the remark that the abate Cantapresto seemed a shrewd serviceable fellow.

"Nor do I like to turn him adrift," cried the Countess instantly, "after he has obliged us by attending my son on his journey."

"And I understand," added the Count, "that he would be glad to serve the cavaliere in any capacity you might designate."

"Why not in all?" said the cicisbeo thoughtfully. "There would be undoubted advantages to the cavaliere in possessing a servant who would explain the globes while powdering his hair and not be above calling his chair when he attended him to a lecture."

And the upshot of it was that when Odo, a few days later, entered on his first term at the Academy, he was accompanied by the abate Cantapresto, who had agreed, for a minimum of pay, to serve him faithfully in the double capacity of pedagogue and lacquey.

The considerable liberty accorded the foreign students made Odo's first year at the Academy at once pleasanter and less profitable than had he been one of the regular pupils. The companions among whom he found himself were a set of lively undisciplined young gentlemen, chiefly from England, Russia and the German principalities; all in possession of more or less pocket-money and attended by governors either pedantic and self-engrossed or vulgarly subservient. These young sprigs, whose ambition it was to ape the dress and manners of the royal pages, led a life of dissipation barely interrupted by a few hours of attendance at the academic classes. From the ill-effects of such surroundings Odo was preserved by an intellectual curiosity that flung him ravening on his studies. It was not that he was of a bookish habit, or that the drudgery of the classes was less irksome to him than to the other pupils; but not even the pedantic methods then prevailing, or the distractions of his new life, could dull the flush of his first encounter with the past. His imagination took fire over the dry pages of Cornelius Nepos, glowed with the mild pastoral warmth of the Georgics and burst into flame at the first hexameters of the Aeneid. He caught but a fragment of meaning here and there, but the sumptuous imagery, the stirring names, the glimpses into a past where Roman senators were mingled with the gods of a gold-pillared Olympus, filled his mind with a misty pageant of immortals. These moments of high emotion were interspersed with hours of plodding over the Latin grammar and the textbooks of philosophy and logic. Books were unknown ground to Cantapresto, and among masters and pupils there was not one who could help Odo to the meaning of his task, or who seemed aware that it might have a meaning. To most of the lads about him the purpose of the Academy was to fit young gentlemen for the army or the court; to give them the chance of sweating a shirt every morning with the fencing-master and of learning to thread the intricacies of the court minuet. They modelled themselves on the dress and bearing of the pages, who were always ruffling it about the quadrangle in court dress and sword, or booted and spurred for a day's hunting at the King's chase of Stupinigi. To receive a nod or a word from one of these young demigods on his way to the King's opera-box or just back from a pleasure-party at her Majesty's villa above the Po—to hear of their tremendous exploits and thrilling escapades—seemed to put the whole school in touch with the fine gentleman's world of intrigue, cards and duelling: the world in which ladies were subjugated, fortunes lost, adversaries run through and tradesmen ruined with that imperturbable grace which distinguished the man of quality from the plebeian.

Among the privileges of the foreign pupils were frequent visits to the royal theatre; and here was to Odo a source of unimagined joys. His superstitious dread of the stage (a sentiment, he soon discovered, that not even his mother's director shared) made his heart beat oppressively as he first set foot in the theatre. It was a gala night, boxes and stalls were thronged, and the audience-hall unfolded its glittering curves like some poisonous flower enveloping him in rich malignant fragrance. This impression was dispelled by the rising of the curtain on a scene of such Claude-like loveliness as it would have been impossible to associate with the bug-bear tales of Donnaz or with the coarse antics of the comedians at Chivasso. A temple girt with mysterious shade, lifting its colonnade above a sunlit harbour; and before the temple, vine-wreathed nymphs waving their thyrsi through the turns of a melodious dance—such was the vision that caught up Odo and swept him leagues away from the rouged and starred assemblage gathered in the boxes to gossip, flirt, eat ices and chocolates, and incidentally, in the pauses of their talk, to listen for a moment to the ravishing airs of Metastasio's Achilles in Scyros.

The distance between such performances—magic evocations of light and colour and melody—and the gross buffoonery of the popular stage, still tainted with the obscenities of the old commedia dell' arte, in a measure explains the different points from which at that period the stage was viewed in Italy: a period when in such cities as Milan, Venice, Turin, actors and singers were praised to the skies and loaded with wealth and favours, while the tatterdemalion players who set up their boards in the small towns at market-time or on feast-days were despised by the people and flung like carrion into unconsecrated graves. The impression Odo had gathered from Don Gervaso's talk was of the provincial stage in all its pothouse license; but here was a spectacle as lofty and harmonious as some great religious pageant. As the action developed and the beauty of the verse was borne to Odo on the light hurrying ripples of Caldara's music he turned instinctively to share his pleasure with those about him. Cantapresto, in a new black coat and ruffles, was conspicuously taking snuff from the tortoiseshell box which the Countess's cicisbeo had given him; but Odo saw that he took less pleasure in the spectacle than in the fact of accompanying the heir-presumptive of Pianura to a gala performance at the royal theatre; and the lads about them were for the most part engaged either with their own dress and appearance, or in exchanging greetings with the royal pages and the older students. A few of these sat near Odo, disdainfully superior in their fob-chains and queues; and as the boy glanced about him he met the fixed stare of one of the number, a tall youth seated at his elbow, and conspicuous, even in that modish company, for the exaggerated elegance of his dress. This young man, whose awkward bearing and long lava-hued face crowned with flamboyant hair contrasted oddly with his finical apparel, returned Odo's look with a gaze of eager comprehension. He too, it was clear, felt the thrill and wonder, or at least re-lived them in the younger lad's emotion; and from that moment Odo felt himself in mute communion with his neighbour.

The quick movement of the story—the succession of devices by which the wily Ulysses lures Achilles to throw off his disguise, while Deidamia strives to conceal his identity; the scenic beauties of the background, shifting from sculpture-gallery to pleasance, from pleasance to banquet-hall; the pomp and glitter of the royal train, the melting graces of Deidamia and her maidens; seemed, in their multiple appeal, to develop in Odo new faculties of perception. It was his first initiation into Italian poetry, and the numbers, now broken, harsh and passionate, now flowing into liquid sweetness, were so blent with sound and colour that he scarce knew through which sense they reached him. Deidamia's strophes thrilled him like the singing-girl's kiss, and at the young hero's cry—

Ma lo so ch' io sono Achille,
E mi sento Achille in sen—

his fists tightened and the blood hummed in his ears.

In the scene of the banquet-hall, where the followers of Ulysses lay before Lycomedes the offerings of the Greek chieftains, and, while the King and Deidamia are marvelling at the jewels and the Tyrian robes, Achilles, unmindful of his disguise, bursts out

Ah, chi vide finora armi piu belle?

—at this supreme point Odo again turned to his neighbour. They exchanged another look, and at the close of the act the youth leaned forward to ask with an air of condescension: "Is this your first acquaintance with the divine Metastasio?"

"I have never been in a play-house before," said Odo reddening.

The other smiled. "You are fortunate in having so worthy an introduction to the stage. Many of our operas are merely vulgar and ridiculous; but Metastasio is a great poet." Odo nodded a breathless assent. "A great poet," his new acquaintance resumed, "and handling a great theme. But do you not suffer from the silly songs that perpetually interrupt the flow of the verse? To me they are intolerable. Metastasio might have been a great tragic dramatist if Italy would have let him. But Italy does not want tragedies—she wishes to be sung to, danced to, made eyes at, flattered and amused! Give her anything, anything that shall help her to forget her own abasement. Panem et circenses! that is always her cry. And who can wonder that her sovereigns and statesmen are willing to humour her, when even her poets stoop to play the mountebank for her diversion?" The speaker, ruffling his locks with a hand that scattered the powder, turned on the brilliant audience his strange corrugated frown. "Fools! simpletons!" he cried, "not to see that in applauding the Achilles of Metastasio they are smiling at the allegory of their own abasement! What are the Italians of today but men tricked out in women's finery, when they should be waiting full-armed to rally at the first signal of revolt? Oh, for the day when a poet shall arise who dares tell them the truth, not disguised in sentimental frippery, not ending in a maudlin reconciliation of love and glory—but the whole truth, naked, cold and fatal as a patriot's blade; a poet who dares show these bedizened courtiers they are no freer than the peasants they oppress, and tell the peasants they are entitled to the same privileges as their masters!" He paused and drew back with a supercilious smile. "But doubtless, sir," said he, "I offend you in thus arraigning your sacred caste; for unless I mistake you belong to the race of demi-gods—the Titans whose downfall is at hand?" He swept the boxes with a contemptuous eye.

Little of this tirade was clear to Odo; but something in the speaker's tone moved him to answer, with a quick lifting of his head: "My name is Odo Valsecca, of the Dukes of Pianura;" when, fearing he had seemed to parade his birth before one evidently of inferior station, he at once added with a touch of shyness: "And you, sir, are perhaps a poet, since you speak so beautifully?"

At which, with a stare and a straightening of his long awkward body, the other haughtily returned: "A poet, sir? I am the Count Vittorio Alfieri of Asti."

1.9.

The singular being with whom chance had thus brought him acquainted was to have a lasting influence on the formation of Odo's character.

Vittorio Alfieri, then just concluding, at the age of sixteen, his desultory years of academic schooling, was probably the most extraordinary youth in Charles Emmanuel's dominion. Of the future student, of the tragic poet who was to prepare the liberation of Italy by raising the political ideals of his generation, this moody boy with his craze for dress and horses, his pride of birth and contempt for his own class, his liberal theories and insolently aristocratic practice, must have given small promise to the most discerning observer. It seems indeed probable that none thought him worth observing and that he passed among his townsmen merely as one of the most idle and extravagant young noblemen in a society where idleness and extravagance were held to be the natural attributes of the great. But in the growth of character the light on the road to Damascus is apt to be preceded by faint premonitory gleams;

and even in his frivolous days at the Academy Alfieri carried a Virgil in his pocket and wept and trembled over Ariosto's verse.

It was the instant response of Odo's imagination that drew the two together. Odo, as one of the foreign pupils, was quartered in the same wing of the Academy with the students of Alfieri's class, and enjoyed an almost equal freedom. Thus, despite the difference of age, the lads found themselves allied by taste and circumstances. Among the youth of their class they were perhaps the only two who already felt, however obscurely, the stirring of unborn ideals, the pressure of that tide of renovation that was to sweep them, on widely-sundered currents, to the same uncharted deep. Alfieri, at any rate, represented to the younger lad the seer who held in his hands the keys of knowledge and beauty. Odo could never forget the youth who first leant him Annibale Caro's Aeneid and Metastasio's opera libretti, Voltaire's Zaire and the comedies of Goldoni; while Alfieri perhaps found in his companion's sympathy with his own half-dormant tastes the first incentive to a nobler activity. Certain it is that, in the interchange of their daily comradeship, the elder gave his friend much that he was himself unconscious of possessing, and perhaps first saw reflected in Odo's more vivid sensibility an outline of the formless ideals coiled in the depths of his own sluggish nature.

The difference in age, and the possession of an independent fortune, which the laws of Savoy had left Alfieri free to enjoy since his fifteenth year, gave him an obvious superiority over Odo; but if Alfieri's amusements separated him from his young friend, his tastes were always drawing them together; and Odo was happily of those who are more engaged in profiting by what comes their way than in pining for what escapes them. Much as he admired Alfieri, it was somehow impossible for the latter to condescend to him; and the equality of intercourse between the two was perhaps its chief attraction to a youth surfeited with adulation.

Of the opportunities his new friendship brought him, none became in after years a pleasanter memory to Odo than his visits with Vittorio to the latter's uncle, the illustrious architect Count Benedetto Alfieri. This accomplished and amiable man, who had for many years devoted his talents to the King's service, was lodged in a palace adjoining the Academy; and thither, one holiday afternoon, Vittorio conducted his young friend.

Ignorant as Odo was of all the arts, he felt on the very threshold the new quality of his surroundings. These tall bare rooms, where busts and sarcophagi were ranged as in the twilight of a temple, diffused an influence that lowered the voice and hushed the step. In the semi-Parisian capital where French architects designed the King's pleasure-houses and the nobility imported their boudoir-panellings from Paris and their damask hangings from Lyons, Benedetto Alfieri represented the old classic tradition, the tradition of the "grand manner," which had held its own through all later variations of taste, running parallel with the barocchismo of the seventeenth century and the effeminate caprices of the rococo period. He had lived much in Rome, in the company of men like Winckelmann and Maffei, in that society where the revival of classical research was being forwarded by the liberality of Princes and Cardinals and by the indefatigable zeal of the scholars in their pay. From this centre of aesthetic reaction Alfieri had returned to the Gallicized Turin, with its preference for the graceful and ingenious rather than for the large, the noble, the restrained; bringing to bear on the taste of his native city the influence of a view raised but perhaps narrowed by close study of the past: the view of a generation of architects in whom archeological curiosity had stifled the artistic instinct, and who, instead of assimilating the spirit of the past like their great predecessors, were engrossed in a sterile restoration of the letter. It may be said of this school of architects that they were of more service to posterity than to their contemporaries; for while they opened the way to modern antiquarian research, their pedantry checked the natural development of a style which, if left to itself, might in time have found new and more vigorous forms of expression.

To Odo, happily, Count Benedetto's surroundings spoke more forcibly than his theories. Every object in the calm severe rooms appealed to the boy with the pure eloquence of form. Casts of the Vatican busts stood against the walls and a niche at one end of the library contained a marble copy of the Apollo Belvedere. The sarcophagi with their winged genii, their garlands and bucranes, and porphyry tazzas, the fragments of Roman mosaic and Pompeian fresco-painting, roused Odo's curiosity as if they had been the scattered letters of a new alphabet; and he saw with astonishment his friend Vittorio's indifference to these wonders. Count Benedetto, it was clear, was resigned to his nephew's lack of interest. The old man doubtless knew that he represented to the youth only the rich uncle whose crotchets must be humoured for the sake of what his pocket may procure; and such kindly tolerance made Odo regret that Vittorio should not at least affect an interest in his uncle's pursuits.

Odo's eagerness to see and learn filled Count Benedetto with a simple joy. He brought forth all his treasures for the boy's instruction and the two spent many an afternoon poring over Piranesi's Roman etchings, Maffei's Verona Illustrata, and Count Benedetto's own elegant pencil-drawings of classical remains. Like all students of his day he had also his cabinet of antique gems and coins, from which Odo obtained more intimate glimpses of that buried life so marvellously exhumed before him: hints of traffic in far-off market-places and familiar gestures of hands on which those very jewels might have sparkled. Nor did the Count restrict the boy's enquiries to that distant past;

and for the first time Odo heard of the masters who had maintained the great classical tradition on Latin soil: Sanmichele, Vignola, Sansovino, and the divine Michael Angelo, whom the old architect never named without baring his head. From the works of these architects Odo formed his first conception of the earlier, more virile manner which the first contact with Graeco-Roman antiquity had produced. The Count told him, too, of the great painters whose popularity had been lessened, if their fame had not been dimmed, by the more recent achievements of Correggio, Guido, Guercino, and the Bolognese school. The splendour of the stanze of the Vatican, the dreadful majesty of the Sistine ceiling, revealed to Odo the beauty of that unmatched moment before grandeur broke into bombast. His early association with the expressive homely art of the chapel at Pontesordo and with the half-pagan beauty of Luini's compositions had formed his taste on soberer lines than the fashion of the day affected; and his imagination breathed freely on the heights of the Latin Parnassus. Thus, while his friend Vittorio stormed up and down the quiet rooms, chattering about his horses, boasting of his escapades, or ranting against the tyranny of the Sardinian government, Odo, at the old Count's side, was entering on the great inheritance of the past.

Such an initiation was the more precious to him from the indifference of those about him to all forms of liberal culture. Among the greater Italian cities, Turin was at that period the least open to new influences, the most rigidly bound up in the formulas of the past. While Milan, under the Austrian rule, was becoming a centre of philosophic thought; while Naples was producing a group of economists such as Galiani, Gravina and Filangieri; while ecclesiastical Rome was dedicating herself to the investigation of ancient art and polity, and even flighty Venice had her little set of "liberals," who read Voltaire and Hume and wept over the rights of man, the old Piedmontese capital lay in the grasp of a bigoted clergy and of a reigning house which was already preparing to superimpose Prussian militarism on the old feudal discipline of the border. Generations of hard fighting and rigorous living had developed in the nobles the qualities which were preparing them for the great part their country was to play; and contact with the Waldensian and Calvinist heresies had stiffened Piedmontese piety into a sombre hatred of schism and a minute observance of the mechanical rules of the faith. Such qualities could be produced only at the expense of intellectual freedom; and if Piedmont could show a few nobles like Massimo d'Azeglio's father, who "made the education of his children his first and gravest thought" and supplemented the deficiencies of his wife's conventual training by "consecrating to her daily four hours of reading, translating and other suitable exercises," the commoner view was that of Alfieri's own parents, who frequently repeated in their son's hearing "the old maxim of the Piedmontese nobility" that there is no need for a gentleman to be a scholar. Such at any rate was the opinion of the old Marquess of Donnaz, and of all the frequenters of Casa Valdu. Odo's stepfather was engrossed in the fulfilment of his duties about the court, and Donna Laura, under the influence of poverty and ennui, had sunk into a state of rigid pietism; so that the lad, on his visits to his mother, found himself in a world where art was represented by the latest pastel-portrait of a court beauty, literature by Liguori's Glories of Mary or the blessed Battista's Mental Sorrows of Christ, and history by the conviction that Piedmont's efforts to stamp out the enemies of the Church had distinguished her above every other country of Europe. Donna Laura's cicisbeo was indeed a member of the local Arcadia, and given to celebrating in verse every incident in the noble household of Valdu, from its lady's name-day to the death of a pet canary; but his own tastes inclined to the elegant Bettinelli, whose Lettere Virgiliane had so conclusively shown Dante to be a writer of barbarous doggerel; and among the dilettanti of the day one heard less of Raphael than of Carlo Maratta, less of Ariosto and Petrarch than of the Jesuit poet Padre Cevo, author of the sublime "heroico-comic" poem on the infancy of Jesus.

It was in fact mainly to the Jesuits that Italy, in the early part of the eighteenth century, owed her literature and her art, as well as the direction of her religious life. Though the reaction against the order was everywhere making itself felt, though one Italian sovereign after another had been constrained to purchase popularity or even security by banishing the Society from his dominions, the Jesuits maintained their hold on the aristocracy, whose pretentions they flattered, whose tastes they affected, and to whom they represented the spirit of religious and political conservatism, against which invisible forces were already felt to be moving. For the use of their noble supporters, the Jesuits had devised a religion as elaborate and ceremonious as the social usages of the aristocracy: a religion which decked its chapels in imitation of great ladies' boudoirs and prescribed observances in keeping with the vapid and gossiping existence of their inmates.

To Odo, fresh from the pure air of Donnaz, where the faith of his kinsfolk expressed itself in charity, self-denial and a noble decency of life, there was something stifling in the atmosphere of languishing pietism in which his mother's friends veiled the emptiness of their days. Under the instruction of the Countess's director the boy's conscience was enervated by the casuistries of Liguorianism and his devotion dulled by the imposition of interminable "pious practices." It was in his nature to grudge no sacrifice to his ideals, and he might have accomplished without question the monotonous observances his confessor exacted, but for the changed aspect of the Deity in whose name they were imposed.

As with most thoughtful natures, Odo's first disillusionment was to come from discovering not what his God condemned, but what He condoned. Between Cantapresto's coarse philosophy of pleasure and the refined complaisances of his new confessor he felt the distinction to be one rather of taste than of principle; and it seemed to him that the religion of the aristocracy might not unfairly be summed up in the ex-soprano's cynical aphorism: "As respectful children of our Heavenly Father it behoves us not to speak till we are spoken to."

Even the religious ceremonies he witnessed did not console him for that chill hour of dawn, when, in the chapel at Donnaz, he had served the mass for Don Gervaso, with a heart trembling at its own unworthiness yet uplifted by the sense of the Divine Presence. In the churches adorned like aristocratic drawing-rooms, of which some Madonna, wreathed in artificial flowers, seemed the amiable and indulgent hostess, and where the florid passionate music of the mass was rendered by the King's opera singers before a throng of chattering cavaliers and ladies, Odo prayed in vain for a reawakening of the old emotion. The sense of sonship was gone. He felt himself an alien in the temple of this affable divinity, and his heart echoed no more than the cry which had once lifted him on wings of praise to the very threshold of the hidden glory—

Domine, dilexi decorem domus tuae et locum habitationis gloriae tuae!

It was in the first reaction from this dimly felt loss that he lit one day on a volume which Alfieri had smuggled into the Academy—the Lettres Philosophiques of Francois Arouet de Voltaire.

BOOK II.
THE NEW LIGHT.

Zu neuen Ufern lockt ein neuer Tag.

2.1.

One afternoon of April in the year 1774, Odo Valsecca, riding down the hillside below the church of the Superga, had reined in his horse at a point where a group of Spanish chestnuts overhung the way. The air was light and pure, the shady turf invited him, and dismounting he bid his servant lead the horses to the wayside inn half way down the slope.

The spot he had chosen, though secluded as some nook above the gorge of Donnaz, commanded a view of the Po rolling at his feet like a flood of yellowish metal, and beyond, outspread in clear spring sunshine, the great city in the bosom of the plain. The spectacle was fair enough to touch any fancy: brown domes and facades set in new-leaved gardens and surrounded by vineyards extending to the nearest acclivities; country-houses glancing through the fresh green of planes and willows; monastery-walls cresting the higher ridges; and westward the Po winding in sunlit curves toward the Alps.

Odo had lost none of his sensitiveness to such impressions; but the sway of another mood turned his eye from the outstretched beauty of the city to the vernal solitude about him. It was the season when old memories of Donnaz worked in his blood; when the banks and hedges of the fresh hill-country about Turin cheated him with a breath of budding beech-groves and the fragrance of crushed fern in the glens of the high Pennine valleys. It was a mere waft, perhaps, from some clod of loosened earth, or the touch of cool elastic moss as he flung himself face downward under the trees; but the savour, the contact filled his nostrils with mountain air and his eyes with dim-branched distances. At Donnaz the slow motions of the northern spring had endeared to him all those sweet incipiencies preceding the full choral burst of leaf and flower: the mauve mist over bare woodlands, the wet black gleams in frost-bound hollows, the thrust of fronds through withered bracken, the primrose-patches spreading like pale sunshine along wintry lanes. He had always felt a sympathy for these delicate unnoted changes; but the feeling which had formerly been like the blind stir of sap in a plant was now a conscious sensation that groped for speech and understanding.

He had grown up among people to whom such emotions were unknown. The old Marquess's passion for his fields and woods was the love of the agriculturist and the hunter, not that of the naturalist or the poet; and the aristocracy of the cities regarded the country merely as so much soil from which to draw their maintenance. The gentlefolk never absented themselves from town but for a few weeks of autumn, when they went to their villas for the vintage, transporting thither all the diversions of city life and venturing no farther afield than the pleasure-grounds that were but so many open-air card-rooms, concert-halls and theatres. Odo's tenderness for every sylvan function of renewal and decay, every shifting of light and colour on the flying surface of the year, would have been met with the same stare with which a certain enchanting Countess had received the handful of wind-flowers that, fresh from a sunrise on the hills, he had laid one morning among her toilet-boxes. The Countess Clarice had stared and laughed, and every one of his acquaintance, Alfieri even, would have echoed her laugh; but one man at least had felt the divine commotion of nature's touch, had felt and interpreted it, in words as fresh as spring verdure, in the pages of a volume that Odo now drew from his pocket.

"I longed to dream, but some unexpected spectacle continually distracted me from my musings. Here immense rocks hung their ruinous masses above my head; there the thick mist of roaring waterfalls enveloped me; or some unceasing torrent tore open at my very feet an abyss into which the gaze feared to plunge. Sometimes I was lost in the twilight of a thick wood; sometimes, on emerging from a dark ravine, my eyes were charmed by the sight of an open meadow...Nature seemed to revel in unwonted contrasts; such varieties of aspect had she united in one spot. Here was an eastern prospect bright with spring flowers, while autumn fruits ripened to the south and the northern face of the scene was still locked in wintry frosts...Add to this the different angles at which the peaks took the light, the chiaroscuro of sun and shade, and the variations of light resulting from it at morning and evening...sum up the impressions I have tried to describe and you will be able to form an idea of the enchanting situation in which I found myself...The scene has indeed a magical, a supernatural quality, which so ravishes the spirit and senses that one seems to lose all exact notion of one's surroundings and identity."

This was a new language to eighteenth-century readers. Already it had swept through the length and breadth of France, like a spring storm-wind bursting open doors and windows, and filling close candle-lit rooms with wet gusts and the scent of beaten blossoms; but south of the Alps the new ideas travelled slowly, and the Piedmontese were as yet scarce aware of the man who had written thus of their own mountains. It was true that, some thirty years earlier, in one of the very monasteries on which Odo now looked down, a Swiss vagrant called Rousseau had embraced the true faith with the most moving signs of edification; but the rescue of Helvetian heretics was a favourite occupation of the Turinese nobility and it is doubtful if any recalled the name of the strange proselyte who had hastened to signalise his conversion by robbing his employers and slandering an innocent maid-servant. Odo in fact owed his first acquaintance with the French writers to Alfieri, who, in the intervals of his wandering over Europe, now and then reappeared in Turin laden with the latest novelties in Transalpine literature and haberdashery. What his eccentric friend failed to provide, Odo had little difficulty in obtaining for himself; for though most of the new writers were on the Index, and the Sardinian censorship was notoriously severe, there was never yet a barrier that could keep out books, and Cantapresto was a skilled purveyor of contraband dainties. Odo had thus acquainted himself with the lighter literature of England and France; and though he had read but few philosophical treatises, was yet dimly aware of the new standpoint from which, north of the Alps, men were beginning to test the accepted forms of thought. The first disturbance of his childish faith, and the coincident reading of the Lettres Philosophiques, had been followed by a period of moral perturbation, during which he suffered from that sense of bewilderment, of inability to classify the phenomena of life, that is one of the keenest trials of inexperience. Youth and nature had their way with him, however, and a wholesome reaction of indifference set in. The invisible world of thought and conduct had been the frequent subject of his musings; but the other, tangible world was close to him too, spreading like a rich populous plain between himself and the distant heights of speculation. The old doubts, the old dissatisfactions, hung on the edge of consciousness; but he was too profoundly Italian not to linger awhile in that atmosphere of careless acquiescence that is so pleasant a medium for the unhampered enjoyment of life. Some day, no doubt, the intellectual curiosity and the moral disquietude would revive; but what he wanted now were books which appealed not to his reason but to his emotions, which reflected as in a mirror the rich and varied life of the senses: books that were warm to the touch, like the little volume in his hand.

For it was not only of nature that the book spoke. Amid scenes of such rustic freshness were set human passions as fresh and natural: a great romantic love, subdued to duty, yet breaking forth again and again as young shoots spring from the root of a felled tree. To eighteenth-century readers such a picture of life was as new as its setting. Duty, in that day, to people of quality, meant the observance of certain fixed conventions: the correct stepping of a moral minuet; as an inner obligation, as a voluntary tribute to Diderot's "divinity on earth," it had hardly yet drawn breath. To depict a personal relation so much purer and more profound than any form of sentiment then in fashion, and then to subordinate it, unflinchingly, to the ideal of those larger relations that link the individual to the group—this was a stroke of originality for which it would be hard to find a parallel in modern fiction. Here at last was an answer to the blind impulses agrope in Odo's breast—the loosening of those springs of emotion that gushed forth in such fresh contrast to the stagnant rills of the sentimental pleasure-garden. To renounce a Julie would be more thrilling than—

Odo, with a sigh, thrust the book in his pocket and rose to his feet. It was the hour of the promenade at the Valentino and he had promised the Countess Clarice to attend her. The old high-roofed palace of the French princess lay below him, in its gardens along the river: he could figure, as he looked down on it, the throng of carriages and chairs, the modishly dressed riders, the pedestrians crowding the footpath to watch the quality go by. The vision of all that noise and glitter deepened the sweetness of the woodland hush. He sighed again. Suddenly voices sounded in the road below—a man's speech flecked with girlish laughter. Odo hung back listening: the girl's voice rang like a bird-call through his rustling fancies. Presently she came in sight: a slender black-mantled figure hung on the arm of an elderly man in the sober dress of one of the learned professions—a physician or a lawyer, Odo guessed. Their being afoot, and the style of the man's dress, showed that they were of the middle class; their demeanour, that they were father and daughter. The girl moved with a light forward flowing of her whole body that seemed the pledge of grace in every limb: of her face Odo had but a bright glimpse in the eclipse of her flapping hat-brim. She stood under his tree unheeded; but as they rose abreast of him the girl paused and dropped her companion's arm.

"Look! The cherry flowers!" she cried, and stretched her arms to a white gush of blossoms above the wall across the road. The movement tilted back her hat, and Odo caught her small fine profile, wide-browed as the head on some Sicilian coin, with a little harp-shaped ear bedded in dark ripples.

"Oh," she wailed, straining on tiptoe, "I can't reach them!"

Her father smiled. "May temptation," said he philosophically, "always hang as far out of your reach."

"Temptation?" she echoed.

"Is it not theft you're bent on?"

"Theft? This is a monk's orchard, not a peasant's plot."

"Confiscation, then," he humorously conceded.

"Since they pay no taxes on their cherries they might at least," she argued, "spare a few to us poor taxpayers."

"Ah," said her father, "I want to tax their cherries, not to gather them." He slipped a hand through her arm. "Come, child," said he, "does not the philosopher tell us that he who enjoys a thing possesses it? The flowers are yours already!"

"Oh, are they?" she retorted. "Then why doesn't the loaf in the baker's window feed the beggar that looks in at it?"

"Casuist!" he cried and drew her up the bend of the road.

Odo stood gazing after them. Their words, their aspect, seemed an echo of his reading. The father in his plain broadcloth and square-buckled shoes, the daughter with her unpowdered hair and spreading hat, might have stepped from the pages of the romance. What a breath of freshness they brought with them! The girl's cheek was clear as the cherry-blossoms, and with what lovely freedom did she move! Thus Julie might have led Saint Preux through her "Elysium." Odo crossed the road and, breaking one of the blossoming twigs, thrust it in the breast of his uniform. Then he walked down the hill to the inn where the horses waited. Half an hour later he rode up to the house where he lodged in the Piazza San Carlo.

In the archway Cantapresto, heavy with a nine years' accretion of fat, laid an admonishing hand on his bridle.

"Cavaliere, the Countess's black boy—"

"Well?"

"Three several times has battered the door down with a missive."

"Well?"

"The last time, I shook him off with the message that you would be there before him."

"Be where?"

"At the Valentino; but that was an hour ago!"

Odo slipped from the saddle.

"I must dress first. Call a chair; or no—write a letter for me first. Let Antonio carry it."

The ex-soprano, wheezing under the double burden of flesh and consequence, had painfully laboured after Odo up the high stone flights to that young gentleman's modest lodgings, and they stood together in a study lined with books and hung with prints and casts from the antique. Odo threw off his dusty coat and called the servant to remove his boots.

"Will you read the lady's letters, cavaliere?" Cantapresto asked, obsequiously offering them on a lacquered tray.

"No—no: write first. Begin 'My angelic lady'—"

"You began the last letter in those terms, cavaliere," his scribe reminded him with suspended pen.

"The devil! Well, then—wait. 'Throned goddess'—"

"You ended the last letter with 'throned goddess.'"

"Curse the last letter! Why did you send it?" Odo sprang up and slipped his arms into the dress-tunic his servant had brought him. "Write anything. Say that I am suddenly summoned by—"

"By the Count Alfieri?" Cantapresto suggested.

"Count Alfieri? Is he here? He has returned?"

"He arrived an hour ago, cavaliere. He sent you this Moorish scimitar with his compliments. I understand he comes recently from Spain."

"Imbecile, not to have told me before! Quick, Antonio—my gloves, my sword." Odo, flushed and animated, buckled his sword-belt with impatient hands. "Write anything—anything to free my evening. Tomorrow morning—tomorrow morning I shall wait on the lady. Let Antonio carry her a nosegay with my compliments. Did you see him Cantapresto? Was he in good health? Does he sup at home? He left no message? Quick, Antonio, a chair!" he cried with his hand on the door.

Odo had acquired, at twenty-two, a nobility of carriage not incompatible with the boyish candour of his gaze, and becomingly set off by the brilliant dress-uniform of a lieutenant in one of the provincial regiments. He was tall and fair, and a certain languor of complexion, inherited from his father's house, was corrected in him by the vivacity of the Donnaz blood. This now sparkled in his grey eye, and gave a glow to his cheek, as he stepped across the threshold, treading on a sprig of cherry-blossom that had dropped unnoticed to the floor.

Cantapresto, looking after him, caught sight of the flowers and kicked them aside with a contemptuous toe. "I sometimes think he botanises," he murmured with a shrug. "The Lord knows what queer notions he gets out of all these books!"

2.2.

As an infusion of fresh blood to Odo were Alfieri's meteoric returns to Turin. Life moved languidly in the strait-laced city, even to a young gentleman a-tiptoe for adventure and framed to elicit it as the hazel-wand draws water. Not that vulgar distractions were lacking. The town, as Cantapresto had long since advised him, had its secret leniencies, its posterns opening on clandestine pleasure; but there was that in Odo which early turned him from such cheap counterfeits of living. He accepted the diversions of his age, but with a clear sense of their worth; and the youth who calls his pleasures by their true name has learned the secret of resisting them.

Alfieri's coming set deeper springs in motion. His follies and extravagances were on a less provincial scale than those of Odo's daily associates. The breath of a freer life clung to him and his allusions were so many glimpses into a larger world. His political theories were but the enlargement of his private grievances, but the mere play of criticism on accepted institutions was an exercise more novel and exhilirating than the wildest ride on one of his half-tamed thorough-breds. Still chiefly a man of pleasure, and the slave, as always, of some rash infatuation, Alfieri was already shaking off the intellectual torpor of his youth; and the first stirrings of his curiosity roused an answering passion in Odo. Their tastes were indeed divergent, for to that external beauty which was to Odo the very bloom of life, Alfieri remained insensible; while of its imaginative counterpart, its prolongation in the realm of thought and emotion, he had but the most limited conception. But his love of ringing deeds woke the chivalrous strain in Odo, and his vague celebration of Liberty, that unknown goddess to whom altars were everywhere building, chimed with the other's scorn of oppression and injustice. So far, it is true, their companionship had been mainly one of pleasure; but the temper of both gave their follies that provisional character which saves them from vulgarity.

Odo, who had slept late on the morning after his friend's return, was waked by the pompous mouthing of certain lines just then on every lip in Italy:—

Meet was it that, its ancient seats forsaking,
An Empire should set forth with dauntless sail,
And braving tempests and the deep's betrayal,
Break down the barriers of inviolate worlds—
That Cortez and Pizarro should esteem
The blood of man a trivial sacrifice
When, flinging down from their ancestral thrones
Incas and Mexicans of royal line,
They wrecked two kingdoms to refresh thy palate—

They were the verses in which the abate Parini, in his satire of The Morning, apostrophizes the cup of chocolate which the lacquey presents to his master. Cantapresto had in fact just entered with a cup of this beverage, and Alfieri, who stood at his friend's bedside with unpowdered locks and a fashionable undress of Parisian cut, snatching the tray from the soprano's hands presented it to Odo in an attitude of mock servility.

The young man sprang up laughing. It was the fashion to applaud Parini's verse in the circles at which his satire was aimed, and none recited his mock heroics with greater zest than the young gentlemen whose fopperies he ridiculed. Odo's toilet was indeed a rite almost as elaborate as that of Parini's hero; and this accomplished, he was on his way to fulfil the very duty the poet most unsparingly derides: the morning visit of the cicisbeo to his lady; but meanwhile he liked to show himself above the follies of his class by joining in the laugh against them. When he issued from the powder-room in his gold-laced uniform, with scented gloves and carefully-adjusted queue, he presented the image of a young gentleman so clearly equal to the most flattering emergencies that Alfieri broke into a smile of half-ironical approval. "I see, my dear cavaliere, that it were idle to invite you to try one of the new Arabs I have brought with me from Spain, since it is plain other duties engage you; but I come to lay claim to your evening."

Odo hesitated. "The Queen holds a circle this evening," he said.

"And her lady-in-waiting is in attendance?" returned Alfieri. "And the lady-in-waiting's gentleman-in-waiting also?"

Odo made an impatient movement. "What inducements do you offer?" said he carelessly.

Alfieri stepped close and tapped him on the sleeve. "Meet me at ten o'clock at the turn of the lane behind the Corpus Domini. Wear a cloak and a mask, and leave this gentleman at home with a flask of Asti." He glanced at Cantapresto.

Odo hesitated a moment. He knew well enough where such midnight turnings led, and across the vision evoked by his friend's words a girl's face flitted suddenly.

"Is that all?" he said with a shrug. "You find me, I fear, in no humour for such exploits."

Alfieri smiled. "And if I say that I have promised to bring you?"

"Promised—?"

"To one as chary of exacting such pledges as I of giving them. If I say that you stake your life on the adventure, and that the stake is not too great for the reward—?"

His sallow face had reddened with excitement, and Odo's forehead reflected the flush. Was it possible—? But the thought set him tingling with disgust.

"Why, you say little," he cried lightly, "at the rate at which I value my life."

Alfieri turned on him. "If your life is worthless; make it worth something!" he exclaimed. "I offer you the opportunity tonight."

"What opportunity?"

"The sight of a face that men have laid down their lives to see."

Odo laughed and buckled on his sword. "If you answer for the risk, I agree to take it," said he. "At ten o'clock then, behind the Corpus Domini."

If the ladies whom gallant gentlemen delight to serve could guess what secret touchstones of worth these same gentlemen sometimes carry into the adored presence, many a handsome head would be carried with less assurance, and many a fond exaction less confidently imposed. If, for instance, the Countess Clarice di Tournanches, whose high-coloured image reflected itself so complacently in her Venetian toilet-glass, could have known that the Cavaliere Odo Valsecca's devoted glance saw her through the medium of a countenance compared to which her own revealed the most unexpected shortcomings, she might have received him with less airy petulance of manner. But how could so accomplished a mistress doubt the permanence of her rule? The Countess Clarice, in singling out young Odo Valsecca (to the despair of a score of more experienced cavaliers) had done him an honour that she could no more imagine his resigning than an adventurer a throne to which he is unexpectedly raised. She was a finished example of the pretty woman who views the universe as planned for her convenience. What could go wrong in a world where noble ladies lived in palaces hung with tapestry and damask, with powdered lacqueys to wait on them, a turbaned blackamoor to tend their parrots and monkeys, a coronet-coach at the door to carry them to mass or the ridotto, and a handsome cicisbeo to display on the promenade? Everything had combined to strengthen the Countess Clarice's faith in the existing order of things. Her husband, Count Roberto di Tournanches, was one of the King's equerries and distinguished for his brilliant career as an officer of the Piedmontese army—a man marked for the highest favours in a society where military influences were paramount. Passing at sixteen from an aristocratic convent to the dreary magnificence of the Palazzo Tournanches, Clarice had found herself a lady-in-waiting at the dullest court in Europe and the wife of an army officer engrossed in his profession, and pledged by etiquette to the service of another lady. Odo Valsecca represented her escape from this bondage—the dash of romance and folly in a life of elegant formalities; and the Countess, who would not have sacrificed to him one of her rights as a court-lady or a nobil donna of the Golden Book, regarded him as the reward which Providence accords to a well-regulated conduct.

Her room, when Odo entered it on taking leave of Alfieri, was crowded, as usual at that hour, with the hangers-on of the noble lady's lever: the abatino in lace ruffles, handing about his latest rhymed acrostic, the jeweller displaying a set of enamelled buckles newly imported from Paris, and the black-breeched doctor with white bands who concocted remedies for the Countess's vapours and megrims. These personages, grouped about the toilet-table where the Countess sat under the hands of a Parisian hairdresser, were picturesquely relieved against the stucco panelling and narrow mirrors of the apartment, with its windows looking on a garden set with mossy statues. To Odo, however, the scene suggested the most tedious part of his day's routine. The compliments to be exchanged, the silly verses to be praised, the gewgaws from Paris to be admired, were all contrasted in his mind with the vision of that other life which had come to him on the hillside of the Superga. On this mood the Countess Clarice's sarcasms fell without effect. To be pouted at because he had failed to attend the promenade of the Valentino was to Odo but a convenient pretext for excusing himself from the Queen's circle that evening. He had engaged with little ardour to join Alfieri in what he guessed to be a sufficiently commonplace adventure; but as he listened to the Countess's chatter about the last minuet-step, and the relative merits of sanspareil water and oil-of-lilies, of gloves from Blois and Vendome, his impatience hailed any alternative as a release. Meanwhile, however, long hours of servitude intervened. The lady's toilet completed, to the adjusting of the last patch, he must attend her to dinner, where, placed at her side, he was awarded the honour of carving the roast; must sit through two hours of biribi in company with the abatino, the doctor, and half-a-dozen parasites of the noble table; and for two hours more must ride in her gilt coach up and down the promenade of the Valentino.

Escaping from this ceremonial, with the consciousness that it must be repeated on the morrow, Odo was seized with that longing for freedom that makes the first street-corner an invitation to flight. How he envied Alfieri, whose travelling-carriage stood at the beck of such moods! Odo's scant means forbade evasion, even had his military duties not kept him in Turin. He felt himself no more than a puppet dancing to the tune of Parini's satire, a puny doll condemned, as the strings of custom pulled, to feign the gestures of immortal passions.

2.3.

The night was moonless, with cold dashes of rain, and though the streets of Turin were well-lit no lantern-ray reached the windings of the lane behind the Corpus Domini.

As Odo, alone under the wall of the church, awaited his friend's arrival, he wondered what risk had constrained the reckless Alfieri to such unwonted caution. Italy was at that time a vast network of espionage, and the

Piedmontese capital passed for one of the best-policed cities in Europe; but even on a moonless night the law distinguished between the noble pleasure-seeker and the obscure delinquent whose fate it was to pay the other's shot. Odo knew that he would probably be followed and his movements reported to the authorities; but he was almost equally certain that there would be no active interference in his affairs. What chiefly puzzled him was Alfieri's insistence that Cantapresto should not be privy to the adventure. The soprano had long been the confidant of his pupil's escapades, and his adroitness had often been of service in intrigues such as that on which Odo now fancied himself engaged. The place, again, perplexed him: a sober quarter of convents and private dwellings, in the very eye of the royal palace, scarce seeming the theatre for a light adventure. These incongruities revived his former wonder; nor was this dispelled by Alfieri's approach.

The poet, masked and unattended, rejoined his friend without a word; and Odo guessed in him an eye and ear alert for pursuit. Guided by the pressure of his arm, Odo was hurried round the bend of the lane, up a transverse alley and across a little square lost between high shuttered buildings. Alfieri, at his first word, gripped his arm with a backward glance; then urged him on under the denser blackness of an arched passage-way, at the end of which an oil-light glimmered. Here a gate in a wall confronted them. It opened at Alfieri's tap and Odo scented wet box-borders and felt the gravel of a path under foot. The gate was at once locked behind them and they entered the ground-floor of a house as dark as the garden. Here a maid-servant of close aspect met them with a lamp and preceded them upstairs to a bare landing hung with charts and portulani. On Odo's flushed anticipations this antechamber, which seemed the approach to some pedant's cabinet, had an effect undeniably chilling; but Alfieri, heedless of his surprise, had cast off cloak and mask, and now led the way into a long conventual-looking room lined with book-shelves. A knot of middle-aged gentlemen of sober dress and manner, gathered about a cabinet of fossils in the centre of this apartment, looked up at the entrance of the two friends; then the group divided, and Odo with a start recognised the girl he had seen on the road to the Superga.

She bowed gravely to the young men. "My father," said she, in a clear voice without trace of diffidence, "has gone to his study for a book, but will be with you in a moment."

She wore a dress in keeping with her manner, its black stuff folds and the lawn kerchief crossed on her bosom giving height and authority to her slight figure. The dark unpowdered hair drawn back over a cushion made a severer setting for her face than the fluctuating brim of her shade-hat; and this perhaps added to the sense of estrangement with which Odo gazed at her; but she met his look with a smile, and instantly the rosy girl flashed through her grave exterior.

"Here is my father," said she; and her companion of the previous day stepped into the room with several folios under his arm.

Alfieri turned to Odo. "This, my dear Odo," said he, "is my distinguished friend, Professor Vivaldi, who has done us the honour of inviting us to his house." He took the Professor's hand. "I have brought you," he continued, "the friend you were kind enough to include in your invitation—the Cavaliere Odo Valsecca."

Vivaldi bowed. "Count Alfieri's friends," said he, "are always welcome to my house; though I fear there is here little to interest a young gentleman of the Cavaliere Valsecca's years." And Odo detected a shade of doubt in his glance.

"The Cavaliere Valsecca," Alfieri smilingly rejoined, "is above his years in wit and learning, and I answer for his interest as I do for his discretion."

The Professor bowed again. "Count Alfieri, sir," he said, "has doubtless explained to you the necessity that obliges me to be so private in receiving my friends; and now perhaps you will join these gentlemen in examining some rare fossil fish newly sent me from the Monte Bolca."

Odo murmured a civil rejoinder; but the wonder into which the sight of the young girl had thrown him was fast verging on stupefaction. What mystery was here? What necessity compelled an elderly professor to receive his scientific friends like a band of political conspirators? How above all, in the light of the girl's presence, was Odo to interpret Alfieri's extravagant allusions to the nature of their visit?

The company having returned to the cabinet of fossils, none seemed to observe his disorder but the young lady who was its cause; and seeing him stand apart she advanced with a smile, saying, "Perhaps you would rather look at some of my father's other curiosities."

Simple as the words were, they failed to restore Odo's self-possession, and for a moment he made no answer. Perhaps she partly guessed the cause of his commotion; yet it was not so much her beauty that silenced him, as the spirit that seemed to inhabit it. Nature, in general so chary of her gifts, so prone to use one good feature as the palliation of a dozen deficiencies, to wed the eloquent lip with the ineffectual eye, had indeed compounded her of all fine meanings, making each grace the complement of another and every outward charm expressive of some inward quality. Here was as little of the convent-bred miss as of the flippant and vapourish fine lady; and any suggestion of a less fair alternative vanished before such candid graces. Odo's confusion had in truth sprung from Alfieri's ambiguous hints; and these shrivelling to nought in the gaze that encountered his, constraint gave way to a sense of wondering pleasure.

"I should like to see whatever you will show me," said he, as simply as one child speaking to another; and she answered in the same tone, "Then we'll glance at my father's collections before the serious business of the evening begins."

With these words she began to lead him about the room, pointing out and explaining the curiosities it contained. It was clear that, like many scholars of his day, Professor Vivaldi was something of an eclectic in his studies, for while one table held a fine orrery, a cabinet of coins stood near, and the bookshelves were surmounted by specimens of coral and petrified wood. Of all these rarities his daughter had a word to say, and though her explanations were brief and without affectation of pedantry, they put her companion's ignorance to the blush. It must be owned, however, that had his learning been a match for hers it would have stood him in poor stead at the moment; his faculties being lost in the wonder of hearing such discourse from such lips. To his compliments on her erudition she returned with a smile that what learning she had was no merit, since she had been bred in a library; to which she suddenly added:—"You are not unknown to me, Cavaliere; but I never thought to see you here."

The words renewed her hearer's surprise; but giving him no time to reply, she went on in a lower tone:—"You are young and the world is fair before you. Have you considered that before risking yourself among us?"

She coloured under Odo's wondering gaze, and at his random rejoinder that it was a risk any man would gladly take without considering, she turned from him with a gesture in which he fancied a shade of disappointment.

By this they had reached the cabinet of fossils, about which the interest of the other guests still seemed to centre. Alfieri, indeed, paced the farther end of the room with the air of awaiting the despatch of some tedious business; but the others were engaged in an animated discussion necessitating frequent reference to the folios Vivaldi had brought from his study.

The latter turned to Odo as though to include him in the group. "I do not know, sir," said he, "whether you have found leisure to study these enigmas of that mysterious Sphinx, the earth; for though Count Alfieri has spoken to me of your unusual acquirements, I understand your tastes have hitherto lain rather in the direction of philosophy and letters;" and on Odo's prompt admission of ignorance, he courteously continued: "The physical sciences seem, indeed, less likely to appeal to the imaginative and poetical faculty in man, and, on the other hand, religion has appeared to prohibit their too close investigation; yet I question if any thoughtful mind can enter on the study of these curious phenomena without feeling, as it were, an affinity between such investigations and the most abstract forms of thought. For whether we regard these figured stones as of terriginous origin, either mere lusus naturae, or mineral formations produced by a plastic virtue latent in the earth, or whether as in fact organic substances lapidified by the action of water; in either case, what speculations must their origin excite, leading us back into that dark and unexplored period of time when the breath of Creation was yet moving on the face of the waters!"

Odo had listened but confusedly to the first words of this discourse; but his intellectual curiosity was too great not to respond to such an appeal, and all his perplexities slipped from him in the pursuit of the Professor's thought.

One of the other guests seemed struck by his look of attention. "My dear Vivaldi," said this gentleman, laying down a fossil, and fixing his gaze on Odo while he addressed the Professor, "why use such superannuated formulas in introducing a neophyte to a study designed to subvert the very foundations of the Mosaic cosmogony? I take it the Cavaliere is one of us, since he is here this evening: why, then, permit him to stray even for a moment in the labyrinth of theological error?"

The Professor's deprecating murmur was cut short by an outburst from another of the learned group, a red-faced spectacled personage in a doctor's gown.

"Pardon me for suggesting," he exclaimed, "that the conditional terms in which our host was careful to present his hypotheses are better suited to the instruction of the neophyte than our learned friend's positive assertions. But if the Vulcanists are to claim the Cavaliere Valsecca, may not the Diluvials also have a hearing? How often must it be repeated that theology as well as physical science is satisfied by the Diluvial explanation of the origin of petrified organisms, whereas inexorable logic compels the Vulcanists to own that their thesis is subversive of all dogmatic belief?"

The first speaker answered with a gesture of disdain. "My dear doctor, you occupy a chair in our venerated University. From that exalted cathedra the Mosaic theory of Creation must still be expounded; but in the security of these surroundings—the catacombs of the new faith—why keep up the forms of an obsolete creed? As long ago as Pythagoras, man was taught that all things were in a state of flux, without end as without beginning, and must we still, after more than two thousand years, pretend to regard the universe as some gigantic toy manufactured in six days by a Superhuman Artisan, who is presently to destroy it at his pleasure?"

"Sir," cried the other, flushing from red to purple at this assault, "I know not on what ground you insinuate that my private convictions differ from my public doctrine—"

But here, with a firmness tempered by the most scrupulous courtesy, Professor Vivaldi intervened.

"Gentlemen," said he, "the discussion in which you are engaged, interesting as it is, must, I fear, distract us from the true purpose of our meeting. I am happy to offer my house as the asylum of all free research; but you must remember that the first object of these reunions is, not the special study of any one branch of modern science, but the application of physical investigation to the origin and destiny of man. In other words, we ask the study of nature to lead us to the knowledge of ourselves; and it is because we approach this great problem from a point as yet unsanctioned by dogmatic authority, that I am reluctantly obliged"—and here he turned to Odo with a smile—"to throw a veil of privacy over these inoffensive meetings."

Here at last was the key to the enigma. The gentlemen assembled in Professor Vivaldi's rooms were met there to discuss questions not safely aired in public. They were conspirators indeed, but the liberation they planned was intellectual rather than political; though the acuter among them doubtless saw whither such innovations tended. Meanwhile they were content to linger in that wide field of speculation which the development of the physical sciences had recently opened to philosophic thought. As, at the Revival of Learning, the thinker imprisoned in mediaeval dialectics suddenly felt under his feet the firm ground of classic argument, so, in the eighteenth century, philosophy, long suspended in the void of metaphysic, touched earth again and, Antaeus-like, drew fresh life from the contact. It was clear that Professor Vivaldi, whose very name had been unknown to Odo, was an important figure in the learned world, and one uniting the tact and firmness necessary to control those dissensions from which philosophy itself does not preserve its disciples. His words calmed the two disputants who were preparing to do battle over Odo's unborn scientific creed, and the talk growing more general, the Professor turned to his daughter, saying, "My Fulvia, is the study prepared?"

She signed her assent, and her father led the way to an inner cabinet, where seats were drawn about a table scattered with pamphlets, gazettes and dictionaries, and set out with modest refreshments. Here began a conversation ranging from chemistry to taxation, and from the perfectibility of man to the secondary origin of the earth's surface. It was evident to Odo that, though the Professor's guests represented all shades of opinion, some being clearly loth to leave the safe anchorage of orthodoxy, while others already braved the seas of free enquiry, yet all were at one as to the need of unhampered action and discussion. Odo's dormant curiosity woke with a start at the summons of fresh knowledge. Here were worlds to explore, or rather the actual world about him, a region then stranger and more unfamiliar than the lost Atlantis of fable. Liberty was the word on every lip, and if to some it represented the right to doubt the Diluvial origin of fossils, to others that of reforming the penal code, to a third (as to Alfieri) merely personal independence and relief from civil restrictions; yet these fragmentary conceptions seemed, to Odo's excited fancy, to blend in the vision of a New Light encircling the whole horizon of thought. He understood at last Alfieri's allusion to a face for the sight of which men were ready to lay down their lives; and if, as he walked home before dawn, those heavenly lineaments were blent in memory with features of a mortal cast, yet these were pure and grave enough to stand for the image of the goddess.

2.4.

Professor Orazio Vivaldi, after filling with distinction the chair of Philosophy at the University of Turin, had lately resigned his office that he might have leisure to complete a long-contemplated work on the Origin of Civilisation. His house was the meeting-place of a society calling itself of the Honey-Bees and ostensibly devoted to the study of the classical poets, from whose pages the members were supposed to cull mellifluous nourishment; but under this guise the so-called literati had for some time indulged in free discussion of religious and scientific questions. The Academy of the Honey-Bees comprised among its members all the independent thinkers of Turin: doctors of law, of philosophy and medicine, chemists, philologists and naturalists, with one or two members of the nobility, who, like Alfieri, felt, or affected, an interest in the graver problems of life, and could be trusted not to betray the true character of the association.

These details Odo learned the next day from Alfieri; who went on to say that, owing to the increased vigilance of the government, and to the banishment of several distinguished men accused by the Church of heretical or seditious opinions, the Honey-Bees had of late been obliged to hold their meetings secretly, it being even rumoured that Vivaldi, who was their president, had resigned his professorship and withdrawn behind the shelter of literary employment in order to elude the observation of the authorities. Men had not yet forgotten the fate of the Neapolitan historian, Pietro Giannone, who for daring to attack the censorship and the growth of the temporal power had been driven from Naples to Vienna, from Vienna back to Venice, and at length, at the prompting of the Holy See, lured across the Piedmontese frontier by Charles Emmanuel of Savoy, and imprisoned for life in the citadel of Turin. The memory of his tragic history—most of all, perhaps, of his recantation and the "devout ending" to which solitude and persecution had forced the freest spirit of his day—hovered like a warning on the horizon of thought and constrained political speculation to hide itself behind the study of fashionable trifles. Alfieri had lately joined the association of the Honey-Bees, and the Professor, at his suggestion, had invited Odo, for whose discretion his friend declared himself ready to answer. The Honey-Bees were in fact desirous of attracting young men of rank who felt an interest in scientific or economic problems; for it was hoped that in this manner the new ideas might imperceptibly permeate the class whose privileges and traditions presented the chief obstacle to reform. In France, it was whispered, free-thinkers and political agitators were the honoured guests of the nobility, who eagerly embraced their theories and applied them to the remedy of social abuses. Only by similar means could the ideals of the Piedmontese reformers be realised; and in those early days of universal illusion none appeared to suspect the danger of arming inexperienced hands with untried weapons. Utopia was already in sight; and all the world was setting out for it as for some heavenly picnic ground.

Of Vivaldi himself, Alfieri spoke with extravagant admiration. His affable exterior was said to conceal the moral courage of one of Plutarch's heroes. He was a man after the antique pattern, ready to lay down fortune, credit and freedom in the defence of his convictions. "An Agamemnon," Alfieri exclaimed, "who would not hesitate to sacrifice his daughter to obtain a favourable wind for his enterprise!"

The metaphor was perhaps scarcely to Odo's taste; but at least it gave him the chance for which he had waited. "And the daughter?" he asked.

"The lovely doctoress?" said Alfieri carelessly. "Oh, she's one of your prodigies of female learning, such as our topsy-turvy land produces: an incipient Laura Bassi or Gaetana Agnesi, to name the most distinguished of their tribe; though I believe that hitherto her father's good sense or her own has kept her from aspiring to academic honours. The beautiful Fulvia is a good daughter, and devotes herself, I'm told, to helping Vivaldi in his work; a far more becoming employment for one of her age and sex than defending Latin theses before a crew of ribald students."

In this Odo was of one mind with him; for though Italy was used to the spectacle of the Improvisatrice and the female doctor of philosophy, it is doubtful if the character was one in which any admirer cared to see his divinity figure. Odo, at any rate, felt a distinct satisfaction in learning that Fulvia Vivaldi had thus far made no public display of her learning. How much pleasanter to picture her as her father's aid, perhaps a sharer in his dreams: a vestal cherishing the flame of Liberty in the secret sanctuary of the goddess! He scarce knew as yet of what his feeling for the girl was compounded. The sentiment she had roused was one for which his experience had no name: an emotion in which awe mingled with an almost boyish sense of fellowship, sex as yet lurking out of sight as in some hidden ambush. It was perhaps her association with a world so unfamiliar and alluring that lent her for the moment her greatest charm. Odo's imagination had been profoundly stirred by what he had heard and seen at the meeting of the Honey-Bees. That impatience with the vanity of his own pursuits and with the injustice of existing conditions, which hovered like a phantom at the feast of life, had at last found form and utterance. Parini's satires and the bitter mockery of the "Frusta Letteraria" were but instruments of demolition; but the arguments of the Professor's friends had that constructive quality so appealing to the urgent temper of youth. Was the world in ruins? Then here was a plan to rebuild it. Was humanity in chains? Behold the angel on the threshold of the prison!

Odo, too impatient to await the next reunion of the Honey-Bees, sought out and frequented those among the members whose conversation had chiefly attracted him. They were grave men, of studious and retiring habit, leading the frugal life of the Italian middle-class, a life in dignified contrast to the wasteful and aimless existence of the nobility. Odo's sensitiveness to outward impressions made him peculiarly alive to this contrast. None was more open than he to the seducements of luxurious living, the polish of manners, the tacit exclusion of all that is ugly or distressing; but it seemed to him that fine living should be but the flower of fine feeling, and that such external graces, when they adorned a dull and vapid society, were as incongruous as the royal purple on a clown. Among certain of his new friends he found a clumsiness of manner somewhat absurdly allied with an attempt at Roman austerity; but he was fair-minded enough to see that the middle-class doctor or lawyer who tries to play the Cicero is, after all, a more respectable figure than the Marquess who apes Caligula or Commodus. Still, his lurking dilettantism made him doubly alive to the elegance of the Palazzo Tournanches when he went thither from a coarse meal in the stuffy dining-parlour of one of his new acquaintances; as he never relished the discourse of the latter more than after an afternoon in the society of the Countess's parasites.

Alfieri's allusions to the learned ladies for whom Italy was noted made Odo curious to meet the wives and daughters of his new friends; for he knew it was only in their class that women received something more than the ordinary conventual education; and he felt a secret desire to compare Fulvia Vivaldi with other young girls of her kind. Learned ladies he met, indeed; for though the women-folk of some of the philosophers were content to cook and darn for them (and perhaps secretly burn a candle in their behalf to Saint Thomas Aquinas or Saint Dominick, refuters of heresy), there were others who aspired to all the honours of scholarship, and would order about their servant-girls in Tuscan, and scold their babies in Ciceronian Latin. Among these fair grammarians, however, he met none that wore her learning lightly. They were forever tripping in the folds of their doctors' gowns, and delivering their most trivial views ex cathedra; and too often the poor philosophers, their lords and fathers, cowered under their harangues like frightened boys under the tongue of a schoolmaster.

It was in fact only in the household of Orazio Vivaldi that Odo found the simplicity and grace of living for which he longed. Alfieri had warned him not to visit the Professor too often, since the latter, being under observation, might be compromised by the assiduity of his friends. Odo therefore waited for some days before presenting himself, and when he did so it was at the angelus, when the streets were crowded and a man's comings and goings the less likely to be marked. He found Vivaldi reading with his daughter in the long library where the Honey-Bees held their meetings; but Fulvia at once withdrew, nor did she show herself again during Odo's visit. It was clear that, proud of her as Vivaldi was, he had no wish to parade her attainments, and that in her daily life she maintained the Italian habit of seclusion; but to Odo she was everywhere present in the quiet room with its well-ordered books and curiosities, and the scent of flowers rising through the shuttered windows. He was sensible of an influence permeating even the inanimate objects about him, so that they seemed to reflect the spirit of those who dwelt there. No room had given him this sense of companionship since he had spent his boyish holidays in the old Count Benedetto's apartments; but it was of another, intangible world that his present surroundings spoke. Vivaldi received him kindly and asked him to repeat his visit; and Odo returned as often as he thought prudent.

The Professor's conversation engaged him deeply. Vivaldi's familiarity with French speculative literature, and with its sources in the experiential philosophy of the English school, gave Odo his first clear conception of the origin and tendency of the new movement. This coordination of scattered ideas was aided by his readings in the Encyclopaedia, which, though placed on the Index in Piedmont, was to be found behind the concealed panels of more than one private library. From his talks with Alfieri, and from the pages of Plutarch, he had gained a certain insight into the Stoical view of reason as the measure of conduct, and of the inherent sufficiency of virtue as its own end. He now learned that all about him men were endeavouring to restore the human spirit to that lost conception of its dignity; and he longed to join the band of new crusaders who had set out to recover the tomb of truth from the forces of superstition. The distinguishing mark of eighteenth-century philosophy was its eagerness to convert its acquisitions in every branch of knowledge into instruments of practical beneficence; and this quality appealed peculiarly to Odo, who had ever been moved by abstract theories only as they explained or modified the destiny of man. Vivaldi, pleased by his new pupil's eagerness to learn, took pains to set before him this aspect of the struggle.

"You will now see," he said, after one of their long talks about the Encyclopaedists, "why we who have at heart the mental and social regeneration of our countrymen are so desirous of making a concerted effort against the established system. It is only by united action that we can prevail. The bravest mob of independent fighters has little chance against a handful of disciplined soldiers, and the Church is perfectly logical in seeing her chief danger in the Encyclopaedia's systematised marshalling of scattered truths. As long as the attacks on her authority were isolated, and as it were sporadic, she had little to fear even from the assaults of genius; but the most ordinary intellect may find a use and become a power in the ranks of an organised opposition. Seneca tells us the slaves in ancient Rome were at one time so numerous that the government prohibited their wearing a distinctive dress lest they should learn their strength and discover that the city was in their power; and the Church knows that when the countless spirits she has enslaved without subduing have once learned their number and efficiency they will hold her doctrines at their mercy.—The Church again," he continued, "has proved her astuteness in making faith the gift of grace and not the result of reason. By so doing she placed herself in a position which was well-nigh impregnable till the school of Newton substituted observation for intuition and his followers showed with increasing clearness the inability of the human mind to apprehend anything outside the range of experience. The ultimate claim of the Church rests on the hypothesis of an intuitive faculty in man. Disprove the existence of this faculty, and reason must remain the supreme test of truth. Against reason the fabric of theological doctrine cannot long hold out, and the Church's doctrinal authority once shaken, men will no longer fear to test by ordinary rules the practical results of her teaching. We have not joined the great army of truth to waste our time in vain disputations over metaphysical subtleties. Our aim is, by freeing the mind of man from superstition to relieve him from the practical abuses it entails. As it is impossible to examine any fiscal or industrial problem without discovering that the chief obstacle to improvement lies in the Church's countless privileges and exemptions, so in every department of human activity we find some inveterate wrong taking shelter under the claim of a divinely-revealed authority. This claim demolished, the stagnant current of human progress will soon burst its barriers and set with a mighty rush toward the wide ocean of truth and freedom..."

That general belief in the perfectibility of man which cheered the eighteenth-century thinkers in their struggle for intellectual liberty coloured with a delightful brightness this vision of a renewed humanity. It threw its beams on every branch of research, and shone like an aureole round those who laid down fortune and advancement to purchase the new redemption of mankind. Foremost among these, as Odo now learned, were many of his own countrymen. In his talks with Vivaldi he first explored the course of Italian thought and heard the names of the great jurists, Vico and Gravina, and of his own contemporaries, Filangieri, Verri and Beccaria. Vivaldi lent him Beccaria's famous volume and several numbers of the "Caffe," the brilliant gazette which Verri and his associates were then publishing in Milan, and in which all the questions of the day, theological, economic and literary, were discussed with a freedom possible only under the lenient Austrian rule.

"Ah," Vivaldi cried, "Milan is indeed the home of the free spirit, and were I not persuaded that a man's first duty is to improve the condition of his own city and state, I should long ago have left this unhappy kingdom; indeed I sometimes fancy I may yet serve my own people better by proclaiming the truth openly at a distance than by whispering it in their midst."

It was a surprise to Odo to learn that the new ideas had already taken such hold in Italy, and that some of the foremost thinkers on scientific and economic subjects were among his own countrymen. Like all eighteenth-century Italians of his class he had been taught to look to France as the source of all culture, intellectual and social; and he was amazed to find that in jurisprudence, and in some of the natural sciences, Italy led the learning of Europe.

Once or twice Fulvia showed herself for a moment; but her manner was retiring and almost constrained, and her father always contrived an excuse for dismissing her. This was the more noticeable as she continued to appear at the meetings of the Honey-Bees, where she joined freely in the conversation, and sometimes diverted the guests by playing on the harpsichord or by recitations from the poets; all with such art and grace, and withal so much simplicity, that it was clear she was accustomed to the part. Odo was thus driven to the not unflattering conclusion that she had been instructed to avoid his company; and after the first disappointment he was too honest to regret it. He was deeply drawn to the girl; but what part could she play in the life of a man of his rank? The cadet of an impoverished house, it was unlikely that he would marry; and should he do so, custom forbade even the thought of taking a wife outside of his class. Had he been admitted to free intercourse with Fulvia, love might have routed such prudent counsels; but in the society of her father's associates, where she moved, as in a halo of learning, amid the respectful admiration of middle-aged philosophers and jurists, she seemed as inaccessible as a young Minerva.

Odo, at first, had been careful not to visit Vivaldi too often; but the Professor's conversation was so instructive, and his library so inviting, that inclination got the better of prudence, and the young man fell into the habit of turning almost daily down the lane behind the Corpus Domini. Vivaldi, too proud to betray any concern for his personal safety, showed no sign of resenting the frequency of these visits; indeed, he received Odo with an increasing cordiality that, to an older observer, might have betokened an effort to hide his apprehension.

One afternoon, escaping later than usual from the Valentino, Odo had again bent toward the quiet quarter behind the palace. He was afoot, with a cloak over his laced coat, and the day being Easter Monday the streets were filled with a throng of pleasure-seekers amid whom it seemed easy enough for a man to pass unnoticed. Odo, as he crossed the Piazza Castello, thought it had never presented a gayer scene. Booths with brightly-striped awnings had been set up under the arcades, which were thronged with idlers of all classes; court-coaches dashed across the square or rolled in and out of the palace-gates; and the Palazzo Madama, lifting against the sunset its ivory-tinted columns and statues, seemed rather some pictured fabric of Claude's or Bibbiena's than an actual building of brick and marble. The turn of a corner carried him from this spectacle into the solitude of a by-street where his own tread was the only sound. He walked on carelessly; but suddenly he heard what seemed an echo of his step. He stopped and faced about. No one was in sight but a blind beggar crouching at the side-door of the Corpus Domini. Odo walked on, listening, and again he heard the step, and again turned to find himself alone. He tried to fancy that his ear had tricked him; but he knew too much of the subtle methods of Italian espionage not to feel a secret uneasiness. His better judgment warned him back; but the desire to spend a pleasant hour prevailed. He took a turn through the neighbouring streets, in the hope of diverting suspicion, and ten minutes later was at the Professor's gate.

It opened at once, and to his amazement Fulvia stood before him. She had thrown a black mantle over her head, and her face looked pale and vivid in the fading light. Surprise for a moment silenced Odo, and before he could speak the girl, without pausing to close the gate, had drawn him toward her and flung her arms about his neck. In the first disorder of his senses he was conscious only of seeking her lips; but an instant later he knew it was no kiss of love that met his own, and he felt her tremble violently in his arms. He saw in a flash that he was on unknown ground; but his one thought was that Fulvia was in trouble and looked to him for aid. He gently freed himself from her hold and tried to shape a soothing question; but she caught his arm and, laying a hand over his mouth, drew him across the garden and into the house. The lower floor stood dark and empty. He followed Fulvia up the stairs and into the library, which was also empty. The shutters stood wide, admitting the evening freshness and a drowsy scent of jasmine from the garden.

Odo could not control a thrill of strange anticipation as he found himself alone in this silent room with the girl whose heart had so lately beat against his own. She had sunk into a chair, with her face hidden, and for a moment or two he stood before her without speaking. Then he knelt at her side and took her hands with a murmur of endearment.

At his touch she started up. "And it was I," she cried, "who persuaded my father that he might trust you!" And she sank back sobbing.

Odo rose and moved away, waiting for her overwrought emotion to subside. At length he gently asked, "Do you wish me to leave you?"

She raised her head. "No," she said firmly, though her lip still trembled; "you must first hear an explanation of my conduct; though it is scarce possible," she added, flushing to the brow, "that you have not already guessed the purpose of this lamentable comedy."

"I guess nothing," he replied, "save that perhaps I may in some way serve you."

"Serve me?" she cried, with a flash of anger through her tears. "It is a late hour to speak of service, after what you have brought on this house!"

Odo turned pale. "Here indeed, madam," said he, "are words that need an explanation."

"Oh," she broke forth, "and you shall have it; though I think to any other it must be writ large upon my countenance." She rose and paced the floor impetuously. "Is it possible," she began again, "you do not yet perceive the sense of that execrable scene? Or do you think, by feigning ignorance, to prolong my humiliation? Oh," she said, pausing before him, her breast in a tumult, her eyes alight, "it was I who persuaded my father of your discretion and prudence, it was through my influence that he opened himself to you so freely; and is this the return you make? Alas, why did you leave your fashionable friends and a world in which you are so fitted to shine, to bring unhappiness on an obscure household that never dreamed of courting your notice?"

As she stood before him in her radiant anger, it went hard with Odo not to silence with a kiss a resentment that he guessed to be mainly directed against herself; but he controlled himself and said quietly: "Madam, I were a dolt not to perceive that I have had the misfortune to offend; but when or how, I swear to heaven I know not; and till you enlighten me I can neither excuse nor defend myself."

She turned pale, but instantly recovered her composure. "You are right," she said; "I rave like a foolish girl; but indeed I scarce know if I am in my waking senses"—She paused, as if to check a fresh rush of emotion. "Oh, sir," she cried, "can you not guess what has happened? You were warned, I believe, not to frequent this house too openly; but of late you have been an almost daily visitor, and you never come here but you are followed. My father's doctrines have long been under suspicion, and to be accused of perverting a man of your rank must be his ruin. He was too proud to tell you this, and profiting today by his absence, and knowing that if you came the spies would be at your heels, I resolved to meet you at the gate, and welcome you in such a way that our enemies should be deceived as to the true cause of your visits."

Her voice wavered on the last words, but she faced him proudly, and it was Odo whose gaze fell. Never perhaps had he been conscious of cutting a meaner figure; yet shame was so blent in him with admiration for the girl's nobility and courage, that compunction was swept away in the impulse that flung him at her feet.

"Ah," he cried, "I have been blind indeed, and what you say abases me to earth. Yes, I was warned that my visits might compromise your father; nor had I any pretext for returning so often but my own selfish pleasure in his discourse; or so at least," he added in a lower voice, "I chose to fancy—but when we met just now at the gate, if you acted a comedy, believe me, I did not; and if I have come day after day to this house, it is because, unknowingly, I came for you."

The words had escaped him unawares, and he was too sensible of their untimeliness not to be prepared for the gesture with which she cut him short.

"Oh," said she, in a tone of the liveliest reproach, "spare me this last affront if you wish me to think the harm you have already done was done unknowingly!"

Odo rose to his feet, tingling under the rebuke. "If respect and admiration be an affront, madam," he said, "I cannot remain in your presence without offending, and nothing is left me but to withdraw; but before going I would at least ask if there is no way of repairing the harm that my over-assiduity has caused."

She flushed high at the question. "Why, that," she said, "is in part, I trust, already accomplished; indeed," she went on with an effort, "it was when I learned the authorities suspected you of coming here on a gallant adventure that I devised the idea of meeting you at the gate; and for the rest, sir, the best reparation you can make is one that will naturally suggest itself to a gentleman whose time must already be so fully engaged."

And with that she made him a deep reverence, and withdrew to the inner room.

2.5.

When the Professor's gate closed on Odo night was already falling and the oil-lamp at the end of the arched passage-way shed its weak circle of light on the pavement. This light, as Odo emerged, fell on a retreating figure which resembled that of the blind beggar he had seen crouching on the steps of the Corpus Domini. He ran forward, but the man hurried across the little square and disappeared in the darkness. Odo had not seen his face; but though his dress was tattered, and he leaned on a beggar's staff, something about his broad rolling back recalled the well-filled outline of Cantapresto's cassock.

Sick at heart, Odo rambled on from one street to another, avoiding the more crowded quarters, and losing himself more than once in the districts near the river, where young gentlemen of his figure seldom showed themselves unattended. The populace, however, was all abroad, and he passed as unregarded as though his sombre thoughts had enveloped him in actual darkness.

It was late when at length he turned again into the Piazza Castello, which was brightly lit and still thronged with pleasure-seekers. As he approached, the crowd divided to make way for three or four handsome travelling-carriages, preceded by linkmen and liveried out-riders and followed by a dozen mounted equerries. The people, evidently in the humour to greet every incident of the streets as part of a show prepared for their diversion, cheered lustily as the carriages dashed across the square; and Odo, turning to a man at his elbow, asked who the distinguished visitors might be.

"Why, sir," said the other laughing, "I understand it is only an Embassage from some neighbouring state; but when our good people are in their Easter mood they are ready to take a mail-coach for Elijah's chariot and their wives' scolding for the Gift of Tongues."

Odo spent a restless night face to face with his first humiliation. Though the girl's rebuff had cut him to the quick, it was the vision of the havoc his folly had wrought that stood between him and sleep. To have endangered the liberty, the very life, perhaps, of a man he loved and venerated, and who had welcomed him without heed of personal risk, this indeed was bitter to his youthful self-sufficiency. The thought of Giannone's fate was like a cold clutch at his heart; nor was there any balm in knowing that it was at Fulvia's request he had been so freely welcomed; for he was persuaded that, whatever her previous feeling might have been, the scene just enacted must render him forever odious to her. Turn whither it would, his tossing vanity found no repose; and dawn rose for him on a thorny waste of disillusionment.

Cantapresto broke in early on this vigil, flushed with the importance of a letter from the Countess Valdù. The lady summoned her son to dinner, "to meet an old friend and distinguished visitor"; and a verbal message bade Odo come early and wear his new uniform. He was too well acquainted with his mother's exaggerations to attach much importance to the summons; but being glad of an excuse to escape his daily visit at the Palazzo Tournanches, he sent Donna Laura word that he would wait on her at two.

On the very threshold of Casa Valdù, Odo perceived that unwonted preparations were afoot. The shabby liveries of the servants had been refurbished and the marble floor newly scoured; and he found his mother seated in the drawing-room, an apartment never unshrouded save on the most ceremonious occasions. As to Donna Laura, she had undergone the same process of renovation, and with more striking results. It seemed to Odo, when she met him sparkling under her rouge and powder, as though some withered flower had been dipped in water, regaining for the moment a languid semblance of its freshness. Her eyes shone, her hand trembled under his lips, and the diamonds rose and fell on her eager bosom.

"You are late!" she tenderly reproached him; and before he had time to reply, the double doors were thrown open, and the major-domo announced in an awed voice: "His excellency Count Lelio Trescorre."

Odo turned with a start. To his mind, already crowded with a confusion of thoughts, the name summoned a throng of memories. He saw again his mother's apartments at Pianura, and the handsome youth with lace ruffles and a clouded amber cane, who came and went among her other visitors with an air of such superiority, and who rode beside the travelling-carriage on the first stage of their journey to Donnaz. To that handsome youth the gentleman just announced bore the likeness of the finished portrait to the sketch. He was a man of about two-and-thirty, of the middle height, with a delicate dark face and an air of arrogance not unbecomingly allied to an insinuating courtesy of address. His dress of sombre velvet, with a star on the breast, and a profusion of the finest lace, suggested the desire to add dignity and weight to his appearance without renouncing the softer ambitions of his age.

He received with a smile Donna Laura's agitated phrases of welcome. "I come," said he kissing her hand, "in my private character, not as the Envoy of Pianura, but as the friend and servant of the Countess Valdù; and I trust," he added turning to Odo, "of the Cavaliere Valsecca also."

Odo bowed in silence.

"You may have heard," Trescorre continued, addressing him in the same engaging tone, "that I am come to Turin on a mission from his Highness to the court of Savoy: a trifling matter of boundary-lines and customs, which I undertook at the Duke's desire, the more readily, it must be owned, since it gave me the opportunity to renew my acquaintance with friends whom absence has not taught me to forget." He smiled again at Donna Laura, who blushed like a girl.

The curiosity which Trescorre's words excited was lost to Odo in the painful impression produced by his mother's agitation. To see her, a woman already past her youth, and aged by her very efforts to preserve it, trembling and bridling under the cool eye of masculine indifference, was a spectacle the more humiliating that he was too young to be moved by its human and pathetic side. He recalled once seeing a memento mori of delicately-tinted ivory, which represented a girl's head, one side all dewy freshness, the other touched with death; and it seemed to him that his mother's face resembled this tragic toy, the side her mirror reflected being still rosy with youth, while that which others saw was already a ruin. His heart burned with disgust as he followed Donna Laura and Trescorre into the dining-room, which had been set out with all the family plate, and decked with rare fruits and flowers. The Countess had excused her husband on the plea of his official duties, and the three sat down alone to a meal composed of the costliest delicacies.

Their guest, who ate little and drank less, entertained them with the latest news of Pianura, touching discreetly on the growing estrangement between the Duke and Duchess, and speaking with becoming gravity of the heir's weak health. It was clear that the speaker, without filling an official position at the court, was already deep in the Duke's counsels, and perhaps also in the Duchess's; and Odo guessed under his smiling indiscretions the cool aim of the man who never wastes a shot.

Toward the close of the meal, when the servants had withdrawn, he turned to Odo with a graver manner. "You have perhaps guessed, cavaliere," he said, "that in venturing to claim the Countess's hospitality in so private a manner, I had in mind the wish to open myself to you more freely than would be possible at court." He paused a moment, as though to emphasise his words; and Odo fancied he cultivated the trick of deliberate speaking to counteract his natural arrogance of manner. "The time has come," he went on, "when it seems desirable that you should be more familiar with the state of affairs at Pianura. For some years it seemed likely that the Duchess would give his Highness another son; but circumstances now appear to preclude that hope; and it is the general opinion of the court physicians that the young prince has not many years to live." He paused again, fixing his eyes on Odo's flushed face. "The Duke," he continued, "has shown a natural reluctance to face a situation so painful both to his heart and his ambitions; but his feelings as a parent have yielded to his duty as a sovereign, and he recognises the fact that you should have an early opportunity of acquainting yourself more nearly with the affairs of the duchy, and also of seeing something of the other courts of Italy. I am persuaded," he added, "that, young as you are, I need not point out to you on what slight contingencies all human fortunes hang, and how completely the heir's recovery or the birth of another prince must change the aspect of your future. You have, I am sure, the heart to face such chances with becoming equanimity, and to carry the weight of conditional honours without any undue faith in their permanence."

The admonition was so lightly uttered that it seemed rather a tribute to Odo's good sense than a warning to his inexperience; and indeed it was difficult for him, in spite of an instinctive aversion to the man, to quarrel with anything in his address or language. Trescorre in fact possessed the art of putting younger men at their ease, while appearing as an equal among his elders: a gift doubtless developed by the circumstances of court life, and the need of at once commanding respect and disarming diffidence.

He took leave upon his last words, declaring, in reply to the Countess's protests, that he had promised to accompany the court that afternoon to Stupinigi. "But I hope," he added, turning to Odo, "to continue our talk at greater length, if you will favour me with a visit tomorrow at my lodgings."

No sooner was the door closed on her illustrious visitor than Donna Laura flung herself on Odo's bosom.

"I always knew it," she cried, "my dearest; but, oh, that I should live to see the day!" and she wept and clung to him with a thousand endearments, from the nature of which he gathered that she already beheld him on the throne of Pianura. To his laughing reminder of the distance that still separated him from that dizzy eminence, she made answer that there was far more than he knew, that the Duke had fallen into all manner of excesses which had already gravely impaired his health, and that for her part she only hoped her son, when raised to a station so far above her own, would not forget the tenderness with which she had ever cherished him, or the fact that Count Valdu's financial situation was one quite unworthy the stepfather of a reigning prince.

Escaping at length from this parody of his own sensations, Odo found himself in a tumult of mind that solitude served only to increase. Events had so pressed upon him within the last few days that at times he was reduced to a passive sense of spectatorship, an inability to regard himself as the centre of so many converging purposes. It was clear that Trescorre's mission was mainly a pretext for seeing the Duke's young kinsman; and that some special motive must have impelled the Duke to show such sudden concern for his cousin's welfare. Trescorre need hardly have cautioned Odo against fixing his hopes on the succession. The Duke himself was a man not above five-and-thirty, and more than one chance stood between Odo and the duchy; nor was it this contingency that set his pulses beating, but rather the promise of an immediate change in his condition. The Duke wished him to travel, to visit the different courts of Italy: what was the prospect of ruling over a stagnant principality to this near vision of the world and the glories thereof, suddenly discovered from the golden height of opportunity? Save for a few weeks of autumn villeggiatura at some neighbouring chase or vineyard, Odo had not left Turin for nine years. He had come there a child and had grown to manhood among the same narrow influences and surroundings. To be turned loose on the world at two-and-twenty, with such an arrears of experience to his credit, was to enter on a richer inheritance than any duchy; and in Odo's case the joy of the adventure was doubled by its timeliness. That fate should thus break at a stroke the meshes of habit, should stoop to play the advocate of his secret inclinations, seemed to promise him the complicity of the gods. Once in a lifetime, chance will thus snap the toils of a man's making; and it is instructive to see the poor puppet adore the power that connives at his evasion...

Trescorre remained a week in Turin; and Odo saw him daily at court, at his lodgings, or in company. The little sovereignty of Pianura being an important factor in the game of political equilibrium, her envoy was sure of a flattering reception from the neighbouring powers; and Trescorre's person and address must have commended him to the most fastidious company. He continued to pay particular attention to Odo, and the rumour was soon abroad that the Cavaliere Valsecca had been sent for to visit his cousin, the reigning Duke; a rumour which, combined with Donna Laura's confidential hints, made Odo the centre of much feminine solicitude, and roused the Countess Clarice to a vivid sense of her rights. These circumstances, and his own tendency to drift on the current of sensation, had carried Odo more easily than he could have hoped past the painful episode of the Professor's garden. He was still tormented by the sense of his inability to right so grave a wrong; but he found solace in the thought that his absence was after all the best reparation he could make.

Trescorre, though distinguishing Odo by his favours, had not again referred to the subject of their former conversation; but on the last day of his visit he sent for Odo to his lodgings and at once entered upon the subject.

"His Highness," said he, "does not for the present recommend your resigning your commission in the Sardinian army; but as he desires you to visit him at Pianura, and to see something of the neighbouring courts, he has charged me to obtain for you a two years' leave of absence from his Majesty's service: a favour the King has already been pleased to accord. The Duke has moreover resolved to double your present allowance and has entrusted me with the sum of two hundred ducats, which he desires you to spend in the purchase of a travelling-carriage, and such other appointments as are suitable to a gentleman of your rank and expectations." As he spoke, he unlocked his despatch-box and handed a purse to Odo. "His Highness," he continued, "is impatient to see you; and once your preparations are completed, I should advise you to set out without delay; that is," he added, after one of his characteristic pauses, "if I am right in supposing that there is no obstacle to your departure."

Odo, inferring an allusion to the Countess Clarice, smiled and coloured slightly. "I know of none," he said.

Trescorre bowed. "I am glad to hear it," he said, "for I know that a man of your age and appearance may have other inclinations than his own to consider. Indeed, I have had reports of a connection that I should not take the liberty of mentioning, were it not that your interest demands it." He waited a moment, but Odo remained silent. "I am sure," he went on, "you will do me the justice of believing that I mean no reflection on the lady, when I warn you against being seen too often in the quarter behind the Corpus Domini. Such attachments, though engaging at the outset to a fastidious taste, are often more troublesome than a young man of your age can foresee; and in this case the situation is complicated by the fact that the girl's father is in ill odour with the authorities, so that, should the motive of your visits be mistaken, you might find yourself inconveniently involved in the proceedings of the Holy Office."

Odo, who had turned pale, controlled himself sufficiently to listen in silence, and with as much pretence of indifference as he could assume. It was the peculiar misery of his situation that he could not defend Fulvia without betraying her father, and that of the two alternatives prudence bade him reject the one that chivalry would have chosen. It flashed across him, however, that he might in some degree repair the harm he had done by finding out what measures were to be taken against Vivaldi; and to this end he carelessly asked:—"Is it possible that the Professor has done anything to give offence in such quarters?"

His assumption of carelessness was perhaps overdone; for Trescorre's face grew as blank as a shuttered house-front.

"I have heard rumours of the kind," he rejoined; "but they would scarcely have attracted my notice had I not learned of your honouring the young lady with your favours." He glanced at Odo with a smile. "Were I a father," he added, "with a son of your age, my first advice to him would be to form no sentimental ties but in his own society or in the world of pleasure—the only two classes where the rules of the game are understood."

2.6.

Odo had appointed to leave Turin some two weeks after Trescorre's departure; but the preparations for a young gentleman's travels were in those days a momentous business, and one not to be discharged without vexatious postponements. The travelling-carriage must be purchased and fitted out, the gold-mounted dressing-case selected and engraved with the owner's arms, servants engaged and provided with liveries, and the noble tourist's own wardrobe stocked with an assortment of costumes suited to the vicissitudes of travel and the requirements of court life.

Odo's impatience to be gone increased with every delay, and at length he determined to go forward at all adventure, leaving Cantapresto to conclude the preparations and overtake him later. It had been agreed with Trescorre that Odo, on his way to Pianura, should visit his grandfather, the old Marquess, whose increasing infirmities had for some years past imprisoned him on his estates, and accordingly about the Ascension he set out in the saddle for Donnaz, attended only by one servant, and having appointed that Cantapresto should meet him with the carriage at Ivrea.

The morning broke cloudy as he rode out of the gates. Beyond the suburbs a few drops fell, and as he pressed forward the country lay before him in the emerald freshness of a spring rain, vivid strips of vineyard alternating with silvery bands of oats, the domes of the walnut-trees dripping above the roadside, and the poplars along the water-courses all slanting one way in the soft continuous downpour. He had left Turin in that mood of clinging melancholy which waits on the most hopeful departures, and the landscape seemed an image of anticipations clouded with regret. He had had a stormy but tender parting with Clarice, whose efforts to act the forsaken Ariadne were somewhat marred by her irrepressible pride in her lover's prospects, and whose last word had charged him to bring her back one of the rare lap-dogs bred by the monks of Bologna. Seen down the lengthening vista of separation even Clarice seemed regrettable; and Odo would have been glad to let his mind linger on their farewells. But another thought importuned him. He had left Turin without news of Vivaldi or Fulvia, and without having done anything to conjure the peril to which his rashness had exposed them. More than once he had been about to reveal his trouble to Alfieri; but shame restrained him when he remembered that it was Alfieri who had vouched for his discretion. After his conversation with Trescorre he had tried to find some way of sending a word of warning to Vivaldi; but he had no messenger whom he could trust; and would not Vivaldi justly resent a warning from such a source? He felt himself the prisoner of his own folly, and as he rode along the wet country roads an invisible gaoler seemed to spur beside him.

The clouds lifted at noon; and leaving the plain he mounted into a world sparkling with sunshine and quivering with new-fed streams. The first breath of mountain-air lifted the mist from his spirit, and he began to feel himself a boy again as he entered the high gorges in the cold light after sunset. It was about the full of the moon, and in his impatience to reach Donnaz he resolved to push on after nightfall. The forest was still thinly-leaved, and the rustle of wind in the branches and the noise of the torrents recalled his first approach to the castle, in the wild winter twilight. The way lay in darkness till the moon rose, and once or twice he took a wrong turn and found himself engaged in some overgrown woodland track; but he soon regained the high-road, and his servant, a young fellow of indomitable cheerfulness, took the edge off their solitude by frequent snatches of song. At length the moon rose, and toward midnight Odo, spurring out of a dark glen, found himself at the opening of the valley of Donnaz. A cold radiance bathed the familiar pastures, the houses of the village along the stream, and the turrets and crenellations of the castle at the head of the gorge. The air was bitter, and the horses' hoofs struck sharply on the road as they trotted past the slumbering houses and halted at the gateway through which Odo had first been carried as a sleepy child. It was long before the travellers' knock was answered, but a bewildered porter at length admitted them, and Odo cried out when he recognised in the man's face the features of one of the lads who had taught him to play pallone in the castle court.

Within doors all were abed; but the cavaliere was expected, and supper laid for him in the very chamber where he had slept as a lad. The sight of so much that was strange and yet familiar—of the old stone walls, the banners, the flaring lamps and worn slippery stairs—all so much barer, smaller, more dilapidated than he had remembered—stirred the deep springs of his piety for inanimate things, and he was seized with a fancy to snatch up a light and explore the recesses of the castle. But he had been in the saddle since dawn, and the keen air and the long hours of riding were in his blood. They weighted his lids, relaxed his limbs, and gently divesting him of his hopes and fears, pressed him down in the deep sepulchre of a dreamless sleep...

Odo remained a month at Donnaz. His grandfather's happiness in his presence would in itself have sufficed to detain him, apart from his natural tenderness for old scenes and associations. It was one of the compensations of his rapidly travelling imagination that the past, from each new vantage-ground of sensation, acquired a fascination which to the more sober-footed fancy only the perspective of years can give. Life, in childhood, is a picture-book of which the text is undecipherable; and the youth now revisiting the unchanged setting of his boyhood was spelling out for the first time the legend beneath the picture.

The old Marquess, though broken in body, still ruled his household from his seat beside the hearth. The failure of bodily activity seemed to have doubled his moral vigour, and the walls shook with the vehemence of his commands. The Marchioness was sunk in a state of placid apathy from which only her husband's outbursts roused her; one of the canonesses was dead, and the other, drier and more shrivelled than ever, pined in her corner like a statue whose mate is broken. Bruno was dead too; his old dog's bones had long since enriched a corner of the vineyard; and some of the younger lads that Odo had known about the place were grown to sober-faced men with wives and children.

Don Gervaso was still chaplain of Donnaz; and Odo saw with surprise that the grave ecclesiastic who had formerly seemed an old man to him was in fact scarce past the middle age. In general aspect he was unchanged; but his countenance had darkened, and what Odo had once taken for harshness of manner he now perceived to be a natural melancholy. The young man had not been long at Donnaz without discovering that in that little world of crystallised traditions the chaplain was the only person conscious of the new forces abroad. It had never occurred to the Marquess that anything short of a cataclysm such as it would be blasphemy to predict could change the divinely established order whereby the territorial lord took tithes from his peasantry and pastured his game on their crops. The hierarchy which rested on the bowed back of the toiling serf and culminated in the figure of the heaven-sent King seemed to him as immutable as the everlasting hills. The men of his generation had not learned that it was built on a human foundation and that a sudden movement of the underlying mass might shake the structure to its pinnacle. The Marquess, who, like Donna Laura, already beheld Odo on the throne of Pianura, was prodigal of counsels which showed a touching inability to discern the new aspect under which old difficulties were likely to present themselves. That a ruler should be brave, prudent, personally abstemious, and nobly lavish in his official display; that he should repress any attempts on the privileges of the Church, while at the same time protecting his authority from the encroachments of the Holy See; these axioms seemed to the old man to sum up the sovereign's duty to the state. The relation, to his mind, remained a distinctly personal and paternal one; and Odo's attempts to put before him the new theory of government, as a service performed by the ruler in the interest of the ruled, resulted only in stirring up the old sediment of absolutism which generations of feudal power had deposited in the Donnaz blood.

Only the chaplain perceived what new agencies were at work; but even he looked on as a watcher from a distant tower, who sees opposing armies far below him in the night, without being able to follow their movements or guess which way the battle goes.

"The days," he said to Odo, "are evil. The Church's enemies, the basilisks and dragons of unbelief and license, are stirring in their old lairs, the dark places of the human spirit. It is time that a fresh purification by blood should cleanse the earth of its sins. That hour has already come in France, where the blood of heretics has lately fertilised the soil of faith; it will come here, as surely as I now stand before you; and till it comes the faithful can only weary heaven with their entreaties, if haply thereby they may mitigate the evil. I shall remain here," he continued, "while the Marquess needs me; but that task discharged, I intend to retire to one of the contemplative orders, and with my soul perpetually uplifted like the arms of Moses, wear out my life in prayer for those whom the latter days shall overtake."

Odo had listened in silence; but after a moment he said: "My father, among those who have called in to question the old order of things there are many animated by no mere desire for change, no idle inclination to pry into the divine mysteries, but who earnestly long to ease the burden of mankind and let light into what you have called the dark places of the spirit. How is it, they ask, that though Christ came to save the poor and the humble, it is on them that life presses most heavily after eighteen hundred years of His rule? All cannot be well in a world where such contradictions exist, and what if some of the worst abuses of the age have found lodgment in the very ramparts that faith has built against them?"

Don Gervaso's face grew stern and his eyes rested sadly on Odo. "You speak," said he, "of bringing light into dark places; but what light is there on earth save that which is shed by the Cross, and where shall they find guidance who close their eyes to that divine illumination?"

"But is there not," Odo rejoined, "a divine illumination within each of us, the light of truth which we must follow at any cost—or have the worst evils and abuses only to take refuge in the Church to find sanctuary there, as malefactors find it?"

The chaplain shook his head. "It is as I feared," he said, "and Satan has spread his subtlest snare for you; for if he tempts some in the guise of sensual pleasure, or of dark fears and spiritual abandonment, it is said that to those he most thirsts to destroy he appears in the likeness of their Saviour. You tell me it is to right the wrongs of the poor and the humble that your new friends, the philosophers, have assailed the authority of Christ. I have only one answer to make: Christ, as you said just now, died for the poor—how many of your philosophers would do as much? Because men hunger and thirst, is that a sign that He has forsaken them? And since when have earthly privileges been the token of His favour? May He not rather have designed that, by continual sufferings and privations, they shall lay up for themselves treasures in Heaven such as your eyes and mine shall never see or our ears hear? And how dare you assume that any temporal advantages could atone for that of which your teachings must deprive them—the heavenly consolations of the love of Christ?"

Odo listened with a sense of deepening discouragement. "But is it necessary," he urged, "to confound Christ with His ministers, the law with its exponents? May not men preserve their hope of heaven and yet lead more endurable lives on earth?"

"Ah, my child, beware, for this is the heresy of private judgment, which has already drawn down thousands into the pit. It is one of the most insidious errors in which the spirit of evil has ever masqueraded; for it is based on the fallacy that we, blind creatures of a day, and ourselves in the meshes of sin, can penetrate the counsels of the Eternal, and test the balances of the heavenly Justice. I tremble to think into what an abyss your noblest impulses may fling you, if you abandon yourself to such illusions; and more especially if it pleases God to place in your hands a small measure of that authority of which He is the supreme repository.—When I took leave of you here nine years since," Don Gervaso continued in a gentler tone, "we prayed together in the chapel; and I ask you, before setting out on your new life, to return there with me and lay your doubts and difficulties before Him who alone is able to still the stormy waves of the soul."

Odo, touched by the appeal, accompanied him to the chapel, and knelt on the steps whence his young spirit had once soared upward on the heavenly pleadings of the Mass. The chapel was as carefully tended as ever; and amid the comely appointments of the altar shone forth that Presence which speaks to men of an act of love perpetually renewed. But to Odo the voice was mute, the divinity wrapped in darkness; and he remembered reading in some Latin author that the ancient oracles had ceased to speak when their questioners lost faith in them. He knew not whether his own faith was lost; he felt only that it had put forth on a sea of difficulties across which he saw the light of no divine command.

In this mood there was no more help to be obtained from Don Gervaso than from the Marquess. Odo's last days at Donnaz were clouded by a sense of the deep estrangement between himself and that life of which the outward aspect was so curiously unchanged. His past seemed to look at him with unrecognising eyes, to bar the door against his knock; and he rode away saddened by that sense of isolation which follows the first encounter with a forgotten self.

At Ivrea the sight of Cantapresto and the travelling-carriage roused him as from a waking dream. Here, at his beck were the genial realities of life, embodied, humorously enough, in the bustling figure which for so many years had played a kind of comic accompaniment to his experiences. Cantapresto was in a fever of expectation. To set forth on the road again, after nine years of well-fed monotony, and under conditions so favourable to his physical well-being, was to drink the wine of romance from a golden cup. Odo was at the age when the spirit lies as naturally open to the variations of mood as a lake to the shifting of the breeze; and Cantapresto's exuberant humour, and the novel details of their travelling equipment, had soon effaced the graver influences of Donnaz. Life stretched before him alluring and various as the open road; and his pulses danced to the tune of the postillion's whip as the carriage rattled out of the gates.

It was a bright morning and the plain lay beneath them like a planted garden, in all the flourish and verdure of June; but the roads being deep in mire, and unrepaired after the ravages of the winter, it was past noon before they reached the foot of the hills. Here matters were little better, for the highway was ploughed deep by the wheels of the numberless vans and coaches journeying from one town to another during the Whitsun holidays, so that even a young gentleman travelling post must resign himself to a plebeian rate of progression. Odo at first was too much pleased with the novelty of the scene to quarrel with any incidental annoyances; but as the afternoon wore on the way began to seem long, and he was just giving utterance to his impatience when Cantapresto, putting his head out of the window, announced in a tone of pious satisfaction that just ahead of them were a party of travellers in far worse case than themselves. Odo, leaning out, saw that, a dozen yards ahead, a modest chaise of antique pattern had in fact come to grief by the roadside. He called to his postillion to hurry forward, and they were soon abreast of the wreck, about which several people were grouped in anxious colloquy. Odo sprang out to offer his services; but as he alit he felt Cantapresto's hand on his sleeve.

"Cavaliere," the soprano whispered, "these are plainly people of no condition, and we have yet a good seven miles to Vercelli, where all the inns will be crowded for the Whitsun fair. Believe me, it were better to go forward."

Odo advanced without heeding this admonition; but a moment later he had almost regretted his action; for in the centre of the group about the chaise stood the two persons whom, of all the world, he was at that moment least wishful of meeting.

2.7.

It was in fact Vivaldi who, putting aside the knot of idlers about the chaise, stepped forward at Odo's approach. The philosopher's countenance was perturbed, his travelling-coat spattered with mud, and his daughter, hooded and veiled, clung to him with an air of apprehension that smote Odo to the heart. He caught a blush of recognition beneath her veil; and as he drew near she raised a finger to her lip and faintly shook her head.

The mute signal reassured him. "I see, sir," said he, turning courteously to Vivaldi, "that you are in a bad plight, and I hope that I or my carriage may be of service to you." He ventured a second glance at Fulvia, but she had turned aside and was inspecting the wheel of the chaise with an air of the most disheartening detachment.

Vivaldi, who had returned Odo's greeting without any sign of ill-will, bowed slightly and seemed to hesitate a moment. "Our plight, as you see," he said, "is indeed a grave one; for the wheel has come off our carriage and my driver here tells me there is no smithy this side Vercelli, where it is imperative we should lie tonight. I hope, however," he added, glancing down the road, "that with all the traffic now coming and going we may soon be overtaken by some vehicle that will carry us to our destination."

He spoke calmly, but it was plain some pressing fear underlay his composure, and the nature of the emergency was but too clear to Odo.

"Will not my carriage serve you?" he hastily rejoined. "I am for Vercelli, and if you will honour me with your company we can go forward at once."

Fulvia, during this exchange of words, had affected to be engaged with the luggage, which lay in a heap beside the chaise; but at this point she lifted her head and shot a glance at her father from under her black travelling-hood.

Vivaldi's constraint increased. "This, sir," said he, "is a handsome offer, and one for which I thank you; but I fear our presence may incommode you and the additional weight of our luggage perhaps delay your progress. I have little fear but some van or waggon will overtake us before nightfall; and should it chance otherwise," he added with a touch of irresistible pedantry, "why, it behoves us to remember that we shall be none the worse off, since the sage is independent of circumstances."

Odo could hardly repress a smile. "Such philosophy, sir, is admirable in principle, but in practice hardly applicable to a lady unused to passing her nights in a rice-field. The region about here is notoriously unhealthy and you will surely not expose your daughter to the risk of remaining by the roadside or of finding a lodging in some peasant's hut."

Vivaldi drew himself up. "My daughter," said he, "has been trained to face graver emergencies with an equanimity I have no fear of putting to the touch—'the calm of a mind blest in the consciousness of its virtue'; and were it not that circumstances are somewhat pressing—" he broke off and glanced at Cantapresto, who was fidgeting about Odo's carriage or talking in undertones with the driver of the chaise.

"Come, sir," said Odo urgently, "Let my servants put your luggage up and we'll continue this argument on the road."

Vivaldi again paused. "Sir," he said at length, "will you first step aside with me a moment?" he led Odo a few paces down the road. "I make no pretence," he went on when they were out of Cantapresto's hearing, "of concealing from you that this offer comes very opportune to our needs, for it is urgent we should be out of Piedmont by tomorrow. But before accepting a seat in your carriage, I must tell you that you offer it to a proscribed man; since I have little reason to doubt that by this time the sbirri are on my track."

It was impossible to guess from Vivaldi's manner whether he suspected Odo of being the cause of his misadventure; and the young man, though flushing to the forehead, took refuge in the thought of Fulvia's signal and maintained a self-possessed silence.

"The motive of my persecution," Vivaldi continued, "I need hardly explain to one acquainted with my house and with the aims and opinions of those who frequent it. We live, alas, in an age when it is a moral offence to seek enlightenment, a political crime to share it with others. I have long foreseen that any attempt to raise the condition of my countrymen must end in imprisonment or flight; and though perhaps to have suffered the former had been a more impressive vindication of my views, why, sir, the father at the last moment overruled the philosopher, and thinking of my poor girl there, who but for me stands alone in the world, I resolved to take refuge in a state where a man may work for the liberty of others without endangering his own."

Odo had listened with rising eagerness. Was not here an opportunity, if not to atone, at least to give practical evidence of his contrition?

"What you tell me sir," he exclaimed, "cannot but increase my zeal to serve you. Here is no time to palter. I am on my way to Lombardy, which, from what you say, I take to be your destination also; and if you and your daughter will give me your company across the border I think you need fear no farther annoyance from the police, since my passports, as the Duke of Pianura's cousin, cover any friends I choose to take in my company."

"Why, sir," said Vivaldi, visibly moved by the readiness of the response, "here is a generosity so far in excess of our present needs that it encourages me to accept the smaller favour of travelling with you to Vercelli. There we have friends with whom we shall be safe for the night, and soon after sunrise I hope we may be across the border."

Odo at once followed up his advantage by pointing out that it was on the border that difficulties were most likely to arise; but after a few moments of debate Vivaldi declared he must first take counsel with his daughter, who still hung like a mute interrogation on the outskirts of their talk.

After a few words with her, he returned to Odo. "My daughter," said he, "whose good sense puts my wisdom to the blush, wishes me first to enquire if you purpose returning to Turin; since in that case, as she points out, your kindness might result in annoyances to which we have no right to expose you."

Odo coloured. "Such considerations, I beg your daughter to believe, would not weigh with me an instant; but as I am leaving Piedmont for two years I am not so happy as to risk anything by serving you."

Vivaldi on this assurance at once consented to accept a seat in his carriage as far as Boffalora, the first village beyond the Sardinian frontier. It was agreed that at Vercelli Odo was to set down his companions at an inn whence, alone and privately, they might gain their friend's house; that on the morrow at daybreak he was to take them up at a point near the convent of the Umiliati, and that thence they were to push forward without a halt for Boffalora.

This agreement reached, Odo was about to offer Fulvia a hand to the carriage when an unwelcome thought arrested him.

"I hope, sir," said he, again turning to Vivaldi, and blushing furiously as he spoke, "that you feel assured of my discretion; but I ought perhaps to warn you that my companion yonder, though the good-naturedest fellow alive, is not one to live long on good terms with a secret, whether his own or another's."

"I am obliged to you," said Vivaldi, "for the hint; but my daughter and I are like those messengers who, in time of war, learn to carry their despatches beneath their tongues. You may trust us not to betray ourselves; and your friend may, if he chooses, suppose me to be travelling to Milan to act as governor to a young gentleman of quality."

The Professor's luggage had by this been put on Odo's carriage, and the latter advanced to Fulvia. He had drawn a favourable inference from the concern she had shown for his welfare; but to his mortification she merely laid two reluctant finger tips in his hand and took her seat without a word of thanks or so much as a glance at her rescuer. This unmerited repulse, and the constraint occasioned by Cantapresto's presence, made the remainder of the drive interminable. Even the Professor's apposite reflections on rice-growing and the culture of the mulberry did little to shorten the way; and when at length the bell-towers of Vercelli rose in sight Odo felt the relief of a man who has acquitted himself of a tedious duty. He had looked forward with the most romantic anticipations to the outcome of this chance encounter with Fulvia; but the unforgiving humour which had lent her a transitory charm now became as disfiguring as some physical defect; and his heart swelled with the defiance of youthful disappointment.

It was near the angelus when they entered the city. Just within the gates Odo set down his companions, who took leave of him, the one with the heartiest expressions of gratitude, the other with a hurried inclination of her veiled head. Thence he drove on to the Three Crowns, where he designed to lie. The streets were still crowded with holiday-makers and decked out with festal hangings. Tapestries and silken draperies adorned the balconies of the houses, innumerable tiny lamps framed the doors and windows, and the street-shrines were dressed with a profusion of flowers; while every square and open space in the city was crowded with booths, with the tents of ambulant comedians and dentists, and with the outspread carpets of snake-charmers, posture-makers and jugglers. Among this mob of quacks and pedlars circulated other fantastic figures, the camp-followers of the army of hucksters: dwarfs and cripples, mendicant friars, gypsy fortune-tellers, and the itinerant reciters of Ariosto and Tasso. With these mingled the towns-people in holiday dress, the well-to-do farmers and their wives, and a throng of nondescript idlers, ranging from the servants of the nobility pushing their way insolently through the crowd, to those sinister vagabonds who lurk, as it were, in the interstices of every concourse of people.

It was not long before the noise and animation about him had dispelled Odo's ill-humour. The world was too fair to be darkened by a girl's disdain, and a reaction of feeling putting him in tune with the humours of the market-place, he at once set forth on foot to view the city. It was now near sunset and the day's decline irradiated the stately front of the Cathedral, the walls of the ancient Hospital that faced it, and the groups gathered about the stalls and platforms obstructing the square. Even in his travelling-dress Odo was not a figure to pass unnoticed, and he was soon assailed by laughing compliments on his looks and invitations to visit the various shows concealed behind the flapping curtains of the tents. There were enough pretty faces in the crowd to justify such familiarities, and even so modest a success was not without solace to his vanity. He lingered for some time in the square, answering the banter of the blooming market-women, inspecting the filigree-ornaments from Genoa, and watching a little yellow bitch in a hooped petticoat and lappets dance the furlana to the music of an armless fiddler who held the bow in his teeth. As he turned from this show Odo's eye was caught by a handsome girl who, on the arm of a dashing cavalier in somewhat shabby velvet, was cheapening a pair of gloves at a neighbouring stall. The girl, who was masked, shot a dark glance at Odo from under her three-cornered Venetian hat; then, tossing down a coin, she gathered up the gloves and drew her companion away. The manoeuvre was almost a challenge, and Odo was about to take it up when a pretty boy in a Scaramouch habit, waylaying him with various graceful antics, thrust a play-bill in his hand; and on looking round he found the girl and her gallant had disappeared. The play-bill, with a wealth of theatrical rhetoric, invited Odo to attend the Performance to be given that evening at the Philodramatic Academy by the celebrated Capo Comico Tartaglia of Rimini and his world-renowned company of Comedians, who, in the presence of the aristocracy of Vercelli, were to present a new comedy entitled "Le Gelosie di Milord Zambo," with an Intermezzo of singing and dancing by the best Performers of their kind.

Dusk was already falling, and Odo, who had brought no letters to the gentry of Vercelli, where he intended to stay but a night, began to wonder how he should employ his evening. He had hoped to spend it in Vivaldi's company, but the Professor not having invited him, he saw no prospect but to return to the inn and sup alone with Cantapresto. In the doorway of the Three Crowns he found the soprano awaiting him. Cantapresto, who had been as mute as a fish during the afternoon's drive, now bustled forward with a great show of eagerness.

"What poet was it," he cried, "that paragoned youth to the Easter sunshine, which, wherever it touches, causes a flower to spring up? Here we are scarce alit in a strange city, and already a messenger finds the way to our inn with a most particular word from his lady to the Cavaliere Odo Valsecca." And he held out a perfumed billet sealed with a flaming dart.

Odo's heart gave a leap at the thought that the letter might be from Fulvia; but on breaking the seal he read these words, scrawled in an unformed hand:—

"Will the Cavaliere Valsecca accept from an old friend, who desires to renew her acquaintance with him, the trifling gift of a side-box at Don Tartaglia's entertainment this evening?"

Vexed at his credulity, Odo tossed the invitation to Cantapresto; but a moment later, recalling the glance of the pretty girl in the market-place, he began to wonder if the billet might not be the prelude to a sufficiently diverting adventure. It at least offered a way of passing the evening; and after a hurried supper he set out with Cantapresto for the Philodramatic Academy. It was late when they entered their box, and several masks were already capering before the footlights, exchanging lazzi with the townsfolk in the pit, and addressing burlesque compliments to the quality in the boxes. The theatre seemed small and shabby after those of Turin, and there was little in the old-fashioned fopperies of a provincial audience to interest a young gentleman fresh from the capital. Odo looked about for any one resembling the masked beauty of the market-place; but he beheld only ill-dressed dowagers and matrons, or ladies of the town more conspicuous for their effrontery than for their charms.

The main diversion of the evening was by this begun. It was a comedy in the style of Goldoni's early pieces, representing the actual life of the day, but interspersed with the antics of the masks, to whose improvised drolleries the people still clung. A terrific Don Spavento in cloak and sword played the jealous English nobleman, Milord Zambo, and the part of Tartaglia was taken by the manager, one of the best-known interpreters of the character in Italy. Tartaglia was the guardian of the prima amorosa, whom the enamoured Briton pursued; and in the Columbine, when she sprang upon the stage with a pirouette that showed her slender ankles and embroidered clocks, Odo instantly recognised the graceful figure and killing glance of his masked beauty. Her face, which was now uncovered, more than fulfilled the promise of her eyes, being indeed as arch and engaging a countenance as ever flashed distraction across the foot-lights. She was greeted with an outburst of delight that cost her a sour glance from the prima amorosa, and presently the theatre was ringing with her improvised sallies, uttered in the gay staccato of the Venetian dialect. There was to Odo something perplexingly familiar in this accent and in the light darting movements of her little head framed in a Columbine's ruff, with a red rose thrust behind one ear; but after a rapid glance about the house she appeared to take no notice of him and he began to think it must be to some one else he owed his invitation.

From this question he was soon diverted by his increasing enjoyment of the play. It was not indeed a remarkable example of its kind, being crudely enough put together, and turning on a series of ridiculous and disconnected incidents; but to a taste formed on the frigid elegancies of Metastasio and the French stage there was something refreshing in this plunge into the coarse homely atmosphere of the old popular theatre. Extemporaneous comedies were no longer played in the great cities, and Odo listened with surprise to the swift thrust and parry, the inexhaustible flow of jest and repartee, the readiness with which the comedians caught up each other's leads, like dancers whirling without a false step through the mazes of some rapid contradance.

So engaged was he that he no longer observed the Columbine save as a figure in this flying reel; but presently a burst of laughter fixed his attention and he saw that she was darting across the stage pursued by Milord Zambo, who, furious at the coquetries of his betrothed, was avenging himself by his attentions to the Columbine. Half way across, her foot caught and she fell on one knee. Zambo rushed to the rescue; but springing up instantly, and feigning to treat his advance as a part of the play, she cried out with a delicious assumption of outraged dignity:—

"Not a step farther, villain! Know that it is sacrilege for a common mortal to embrace one who has been kissed by his most illustrious Highness the Heir-presumptive of Pianura!"

"Mirandolina of Chioggia!" sprang to Odo's lips. At the same instant the Columbine turned about and swept him a deep curtsey, to the delight of the audience, who had no notion of what was going forward, but were in the humour to clap any whim of their favourite's; then she turned and darted off the stage, and the curtain fell on a tumult of applause.

Odo had hardly recovered from his confusion when the door of the box opened and the young Scaramouch he had seen in the market-place peeped in and beckoned to Cantapresto. The soprano rose with alacrity, leaving Odo alone in the dimly-lit box, his mind agrope in a labyrinth of memories. A moment later Cantapresto returned with that air of furtive relish that always proclaimed him the bearer of a tender message. The one he now brought was to the effect that the Signorina Miranda Malmocco, justly renowned as one of the first Columbines of Italy, had charged him to lay at the Cavaliere Valsecca's feet her excuses for the liberty she had taken with his illustrious name, and to entreat that he would show his magnanimity by supping with her after the play in her room at the Three Crowns—a request she was emboldened to make by the fact that she was lately from Pianura, and could give him the last news of the court.

The message chimed with Odo's mood, and the play over he hastened back to the inn with Cantapresto, and bid the landlord send to the Signorina Miranda's room whatever delicacies the town could provide. Odo on arriving that afternoon had himself given orders that his carriage should be at the door the next morning an hour before sunrise; and he now repeated these instructions to Cantapresto, charging him on his life to see that nothing interfered with their fulfilment. The soprano objected that the hour was already late, and that they could easily perform the day's journey without curtailing their rest; but on Odo's reiteration of the order he resigned himself, with the remark that it was a pity old age had no savings-bank for the sleep that youth squandered.

2.8.

It was something of a disappointment to Odo, on entering the Signorina Miranda's room, to find that she was not alone. Engaged in feeding her pet monkey with sugar-plums was the young man who had given her his arm in the Piazza. This gentleman, whom she introduced to Odo as her cousin and travelling companion, the Count of Castelrovinato, had the same air of tarnished elegance as his richly-laced coat and discoloured ruffles. He seemed, however, of a lively and obliging humour, and Mirandolina observed with a smile that she could give no better notion of his amiability than by mentioning that he was known among her friends as the Cavaliere Frattanto. This praise, Odo thought, seemed scarcely to the cousin's liking; but he carried it off with the philosophic remark that it is the mortar between the bricks that holds the building together.

"At present," said Mirandolina laughing, "he is engaged in propping up a ruin; for he has fallen desperately in love with our prima amorosa, a lady who lost her virtue under the Pharaohs, but whom, for his sake, I have been obliged to include in our little supper."

This, it was clear, was merely a way of palliating the Count's infatuation for herself; but he took the second thrust as good-naturedly as the first, remarking that he had been bred for an archeologist and had never lost his taste for the antique.

Odo's servants now appearing with a pasty of beccafichi, some bottles of old Malaga and a tray of ices and fruits, the three seated themselves at the table, which Mirandolina had decorated with a number of wax candles stuck in the cut-glass bottles of the Count's dressing-case. Here they were speedily joined by the actress's monkey and parrot, who had soon spread devastation among the dishes. While Miranda was restoring order by boxing the monkey's ears and feeding the shrieking bird from her lips, the door opened to admit the prima amorosa, a lady whose mature charms and mellifluous manner suggested a fine fruit preserved in syrup. The newcomer was clearly engrossed in captivating the Count, and the latter amply justified his nick-name by the cynical complaisance with which he cleared the way for Odo by responding to her advances.

The tete-a-tete thus established, Miranda at once began to excuse herself for the means she had taken to attract Odo's attention at the theatre. She had heard from the innkeeper that the Duke of Pianura's cousin, the Cavaliere Valsecca, was expected that day in Vercelli; and seeing in the Piazza a young gentleman in travelling-dress and French toupet, had at once guessed him to be the distinguished stranger from Turin. At the theatre she had been much amused by the air of apprehension with which Odo had appeared to seek, among the dowdy or vulgar inmates of the boxes, the sender of the mysterious billet; and the contrast between the elegant gentleman in embroidered coat and gold-hilted sword, and the sleepy bewildered little boy of the midnight feast at Chivasso, had seized her with such comic effect that she could not resist a playful allusion to their former meeting. All this was set forth with so sprightly an air of mock-contrition that, had Odo felt the least resentment, it must instantly have vanished. He was, however, in the humour to be pleased by whatever took his mind off his own affairs, and none could be more skilled than Mirandolina in profiting by such a mood.

He pressed her to tell him something of what had befallen her since they had met, but she replied by questioning him about his own experiences, and on learning that he had been called to Pianura on account of the heir's ill-health she declared it was notorious that the little prince had not long to live, and that the Duke could not hope for another son.

"The Duke's life, however," said Odo, "is as good as mine, and in truth I am far less moved by my remote hopes of the succession than by the near prospect of visiting so many famous cities and seeing so much that is novel and entertaining."

Miranda shrugged her pretty shoulders. "Why, as to the Duke's life," said she, "there are some that would not give a counterfeit penny for it; but indeed his Highness lives so secluded from the world, and is surrounded by persons so jealous to conceal his true condition even from the court, that the reports of his health are no more to be trusted than the other strange rumours about him. I was told in Pianura that but four persons are admitted to his familiarity: his confessor, his mistress, Count Trescorre, who is already comptroller of finance and will soon be prime-minister, and a strange German doctor or astrologer that is lately come to the court. As to the Duchess, she never sees him; and were it not for Trescorre, who has had the wit to stand well with both sides, I doubt if she would know more of what goes on about her husband than any scullion in the ducal kitchens."

She spoke with the air of one well-acquainted with the subject, and Odo, curious to learn more, asked her how she came to have such an insight into the intrigues of the court.

"Why," said she, "in the oddest way imaginable—by being the guest of his lordship the Bishop of Pianura; and since you asked me just now to tell you something of my adventures, I will, if you please, begin by relating the occurrences that procured me this extraordinary honour. But first," she added with a smile, "would it not be well to open another bottle of Malaga?"

MIRANDOLINA'S STORY.

You must know, she continued, when Odo had complied with her request, that soon after our parting at Chivasso the company with which I was travelling came to grief through the dishonesty of the Harlequin, who ran away with the Capo Comico's wife, carrying with him, besides the lady, the far more irretrievable treasure of our modest earnings. This brought us to destitution, and the troop was disbanded. I had nothing but the spangled frock on my back, and thinking to make some use of my sole possession I set out as a dancer with the flute-player of the company, a good-natured fellow that had a performing marmozet from the Indies. We three wandered from one town to another, spreading our carpet wherever there was a fair or a cattle-market, going hungry in bad seasons, and in our luckier days attaching ourselves to some band of strolling posture-makers or comedians.

One day, after about a year of this life, I had the good fortune, in the market-place of Parma, to attract the notice of a rich English nobleman who was engaged in writing a book on the dances of the ancients. This gentleman, though no longer young, and afflicted with that strange English malady that obliges a man to wrap his feet in swaddling-clothes like a new-born infant, was of a generous and paternal disposition, and offered, if I would accompany him to Florence, to give me a home and a genteel education. I remained with him about two years, during which time he had me carefully instructed in music, French and the art of the needle. In return for this, my principal duties were to perform in antique dances before the friends of my benefactor—whose name I could never learn to pronounce—and to read aloud to him the works of the modern historians and philosophers.

We lived in a large palace with exceedingly high-ceilinged rooms, which my friend would never have warmed on account of his plethoric habit, and as I had to dance at all seasons in the light draperies worn by the classical goddesses, I suffered terribly from chilblains and contracted a cruel cough. To this, however, I might have resigned myself; but when I learned from a young abate who frequented the house that the books I was compelled to read were condemned by the Church, and could not be perused without deadly peril to the soul, I at once resolved to fly from such contaminating influences. Knowing that his lordship would not consent to my leaving him, I took the matter out of his hands by slipping out one day during the carnival, carrying with me from that accursed house nothing but the few jewels that my benefactor had expressed the intention of leaving me in his will. At the nearest church I confessed my involuntary sin in reading the prohibited books, and having received absolution and the sacrament, I joined my friend the abate at Cafaggiolo, whence we travelled to Modena, where he was acquainted with a theatrical manager just then in search of a Columbine. My dancing and posturing at Florence had given me something of a name among the dilettanti, and I was at once engaged by the manager, who took me to Venice, where I subsequently joined the company of the excellent Tartaglia with whom I am now acting. Since then I have been attended by continued success, which I cannot but ascribe to my virtuous resolve to face poverty and distress rather than profit a moment longer by the beneficence of an atheist.

All this I have related to show you how the poor ignorant girl you met at Chivasso was able to acquire something of the arts and usages of good company; but I will now pass on to the incident of my visit to Pianura. Our manager, then, had engaged some time since to give a series of performances at Pianura during the last carnival. The Bishop's nephew, Don Serafino, who has a pronounced taste for the theatre, had been instrumental in making the arrangement; but at the last moment he wrote us that, owing to the influence of the Duke's confessor, the Bishop had been obliged to prohibit the appearance of women on the stage of Pianura. This was a cruel blow, as we had prepared a number of comedies in which I was to act the leading part; and Don Serafino was equally vexed, since he did me the honour of regarding me as the chief ornament of the company. At length it was agreed that, to overcome the difficulty, it should be given out that the celebrated Tartaglia of Rimini would present himself at Pianura with his company of comedians, among whom was the popular favourite, Mirandolino of Chioggia, twin brother of the Signorina Miranda Malmocco, and trained by that actress to play in all her principal parts.

This satisfied the scruples and interests of all concerned, and soon afterward I made my first appearance in Pianura. My success was greater than we had foreseen; for I threw myself into the part with such zest that every one was taken in, and even Don Serafino required the most categorical demonstration to convince him that I was not my own brother. The illusion I produced was, however, not without its inconveniences; for, among the ladies who thronged to see the young Mirandolino, were several who desired a closer acquaintance with him; and one of these, as it happened, was the Duke's mistress, the Countess Belverde. You will see the embarrassment of my situation. If I failed to respond to her advances, her influence was sufficient to drive us from the town at the opening of a prosperous season; if I discovered my sex to her, she might more cruelly avenge herself by throwing the whole company into prison, to be dealt with by the Holy Office. Under these circumstances, I decided to appeal to the Bishop, but without, of course, revealing to him that I was, so to speak, my own sister. His lordship, who is never sorry to do the Belverde a bad turn, received me with the utmost indulgence, and declared that, to protect my innocence from the designs of this new Potiphar's wife, he would not only give me a lodging in the Episcopal palace, but confer on me the additional protection of the minor orders. This was rather more than I had bargained for, but he that wants the melon is a fool to refuse the rind, and I thanked the Bishop for his kindness and allowed him to give out that, my heart having been touched by grace, I had resolved, at the end of the season, to withdraw from the stage and prepare to enter the Church.

I now fancied myself safe; for I knew the Countess could not attempt my removal without risk of having her passion denounced to the Duke. I spent several days very agreeably in the Episcopal palace, entertained at his lordship's own table, and favoured with private conversations during which he told me many curious and interesting things about the Duke and the court, and delicately abstained from all allusion to my coming change of vocation. The Countess, however, had not been idle. One day I received notice that the Holy Office disapproved of the appearance on the stage of a young man about to enter the Church, and requested me to withdraw at once to the Barnabite monastery, where I was to remain till I received the minor orders.

Now the Abbot of the Barnabites was the Belverde's brother, and I saw at once that to obey his order would place me in that lady's power. I again addressed myself to the Bishop, but to my despair he declared himself unable to aid me farther, saying that he dared not offend the Holy Office, and that he had already run considerable risk in protecting me from the Countess.

I was accordingly transferred to the monastery, in spite of my own entreaties and those of the good Tartaglia, who moved heaven and earth to save his Columbine from sequestration. You may imagine my despair. My fear of doing Tartaglia an injury kept me from revealing my sex, and for twenty-four hours I languished in my cell, refusing food and air, and resisting the repeated attempts of the good monks to alleviate my distress. At length however I bethought me that the Countess would soon appear; and it flashed across me that the one person who could protect me from her was her brother. I at once sought an interview with the Abbot, who received me with great indulgence. I explained to him that the distress I suffered was occasioned by the loss that my sequestration was causing my excellent manager, and begged him to use his influence to have me released from the monastery. The Abbot listened attentively, and after a pause replied that there was but one person who could arrange the matter, and that was his sister the Countess Belverde, whose well-known piety gave her considerable influence in such matters. I now saw that no alternative remained but to confess the truth; and with tears of agitation I avowed my sex, and threw myself on his mercy.

I was not disappointed in the result. The Abbot listened with the greatest benevolence to all the details of my adventure. He laughed heartily at his sister's delusion, but said I had done right in not undeceiving her, as her dread of ridicule might have led to unpleasant reprisals. He declared that for the present he could not on any account consent to let me out of his protection; but he promised if I submitted myself implicitly to his guidance, not only to preserve me from the Belverde's machinations, but to ensure my reappearing on the stage within two days at the latest. Knowing him to be a very powerful personage I thought it best to accept these conditions, which in any case it would have been difficult to resist; and the next day he informed me that the Holy Office had consented to the Signorina Miranda Malmocco's appearing on the stage of Pianura during the remainder of the season, in consideration of the financial injury caused to the manager of the company by the edifying conversion of her twin-brother.

"In this way," the Abbot was pleased to explain, "you will be quite safe from my sister, who is a woman of the most unexceptionable morals, and at the same time you will not expose our excellent Bishop to the charge of having been a party to a grave infraction of ecclesiastical discipline.—My only condition," he added with a truly paternal smile, "is that, after the Signorina Miranda's performance at the theatre her twin-brother the Signor

Mirandolino shall return every evening to the monastery: a condition which seems necessary to the preservation of our secret, and which I trust you will not regard as too onerous, in view of the service I have been happy enough to render you."

It would have ill become me to dispute the excellent ecclesiastic's wishes, and Tartaglia and the rest of the company having been sworn to secrecy, I reappeared that very evening in one of my favourite parts, and was afterward carried back to the monastery in the most private manner. The Signorina Malmocco's successes soon repaired the loss occasioned by her brother's withdrawal, and if any suspected their identity all were interested to conceal their suspicions.

Thus it came about that my visit to Pianura, having begun under the roof of a Bishop, ended in a monastery of Barnabites—nor have I any cause to complain of the hospitality of either of my hosts...

Odo, charmed by the vivacity with which this artless narrative was related, pressed Miranda to continue the history of her adventures. The actress laughingly protested that she must first refresh herself with one of the ices he had so handsomely provided; and meanwhile she begged the Count to favour them with a song.

This gentleman, who seemed glad of any pretext for detaching himself from his elderly flame, rescued Mirandolina's lute from the inquisitive fingering of the monkey, and striking a few melancholy chords, sang the following words, which he said he had learned from a peasant of the Abruzzi:—

Flower of the thyme!
She draws me as your fragrance draws the bees,
She draws me as the cold moon draws the seas,
And summer winter-time.

Flower of the broom!
Like you she blossoms over dark abysses,
And close to ruin bloom her sweetest kisses,
And on the brink of doom.

Flower of the rue!
She wore you on her breast when first we met.
I begged your blossom and I wear it yet—
Flower of regret!

The song ended, the prima amorosa, overcome by what she visibly deemed an appeal to her feelings, declared with some agitation that the hour was late and she must withdraw. Miranda wished the actress an affectionate goodnight and asked the Count to light her to her room, which was on the farther side of the gallery surrounding the courtyard of the inn. Castelrovinato complied with his usual air of resignation, and the door closing on the couple, Odo and Miranda found themselves alone.

"And now," said the good-natured girl, placing herself on the sofa and turning to her guest with a smile, "if you will take a seat at my side I will gladly continue the history of my adventures"...

2.9.

Odo woke with a start. He had been trying to break down a great gold-barred gate, behind which Fulvia, pale and disordered, struggled in the clutch of the blind beggar of the Corpus Domini...

He sat up and looked about him. The gate was still there; but as he gazed it resolved itself into his shuttered window, barred with wide lines of sunlight. It was day, then! He sprang out of bed and flung open the shutters. Beneath him lay the piazza of Vercelli, bathed in the vertical brightness of a summer noon; and as he stared out on this inexorable scene, the clock over the Hospital struck twelve.

Twelve o'clock! And he had promised to meet Vivaldi at dawn behind the Umiliati! As the truth forced itself on Odo he dropped into a chair and hid his face with a groan. He had failed them again, then—and this time how cruelly and basely! He felt himself the victim of a conspiracy which in some occult manner was forever forcing him to outrage and betray the two beings he most longed to serve. The idea of a conspiracy flashed a sudden light on his evening's diversion, and he sprang up with a cry. Yes! It was a plot, and any but a dolt must have traced the soprano's hand in this vulgar assault upon his senses. He choked with anger at the thought of having played the dupe when two lives he cherished were staked upon his vigilance...

To his furious summons Cantapresto presented a blank wall of ignorance. Yes, the Cavaliere had given orders that the carriage should be ready before daybreak; but who was authorised to wake the cavaliere? After keeping the carriage two hours at the door Cantapresto had ventured to send it back to the stable; but the horses should instantly be put to, and within an hour they would be well forward on their journey. Meanwhile, should the barber be summoned at once? Or would the cavaliere first refresh himself with an excellent cup of chocolate, prepared under Cantapresto's own supervision?

Odo turned on him savagely. "Traitor—spy! In whose pay—?"

But the words roused him to a fresh sense of peril. Cantapresto, though he might have guessed Odo's intention, was not privy to his plan of rejoining

Vivaldi and Fulvia; and it flashed across the young man that his self-betrayal must confirm the others' suspicions. His one hope of protecting his friends was to affect indifference to what had happened; and this was made easier, by the reflection that Cantapresto was after all but a tool in more powerful hands. To be spied on was so natural to an Italian of that day that the victim's instinct was rather to circumvent the spy than to denounce him.

Odo dismissed Cantapresto with the reply that he would give orders about the carriage later; desiring that meanwhile the soprano should purchase the handsomest set of filigree ornaments to be found in Vercelli, and carry them with the Cavaliere Valsecca's compliments to the Signorina Malmocco.

Having thus rid himself of observation he dressed as rapidly as possible, trying the while to devise some means of tracing Vivaldi. But the longer he pondered the attempt the more plainly he saw its futility. Vivaldi, doubtless from motives of prudence, had not named the friend with whom he and Fulvia were to take shelter; nor did Odo even know in what quarter of the city to seek them. To question the police was to risk their last chance of safety; and for the same reason he dared not enquire of the posting-master whether any travellers had set out that morning for Lombardy. His natural activity of mind was hampered by a leaden sense of remissness. With what anguish of spirit must Vivaldi and Fulvia have awaited him in that hour of dawn behind the convent! What thoughts must have visited the girl's mind as day broadened, the city woke, and peril pressed on them with every voice and eye! And when at length they saw that he had failed them, which way did their hunted footsteps turn? Perhaps they dared not go back to the friend who had taken them in for the night. Perhaps even now they wandered through the streets, fearing arrest if they revealed themselves by venturing to engage a carriage, at every turn of his thoughts Odo was mocked by some vision of disaster; and an hour of perplexity yielded no happier expedient than that of repairing to the meeting-place behind the Umiliati. It was a deserted lane with few passers; and after vainly questioning the blank wall of the convent and the gates of a sinister-looking alms-house that faced it, he retraced his steps to the inn.

He spent a day of futile research and bitter thoughts, now straying forth in the hope of meeting Vivaldi, now hastening back to the Three Crowns on the chance that some message might await him. He dared not let his mind rest on what might have befallen his friends; yet the alternative of contemplating his own course was scarcely more endurable. Nightfall brought the conviction that the Professor and Fulvia had passed beyond his reach. It was clear that if they were still in Vercelli they did not mean to make their presence known to him, while in the event of their escape he was without means of tracing them farther. He knew indeed that their destination was Milan, but, should they reach there safely, what hope was there of finding them in a city of strangers? By a stroke of folly he had cut himself off from all communication with them, and his misery was enhanced by the discovery of his weakness. He who had fed his fancy on high visions, cherishing in himself the latent patriot and hero, had been driven by a girl's caprice to break the first law of manliness and honour! The event had already justified her; and in a flash of self-contempt he saw himself as she no doubt beheld him— the fribble preying like a summer insect on the slow growths of difficult years...

In bitterness of spirit he set out the next morning for Pianura. A half-melancholy interest drew him back to the scene of his lonely childhood, and he had started early in order to push on that night to Pontesordo. At Valsecca, the regular posting-station between Vercelli and Pianura, he sent Cantapresto forward to the capital, and in a stormy yellow twilight drove alone across the waste land that dipped to the marshes. On his right the woods of the ducal chase hung black against the sky; and presently he saw ahead of him the old square keep, with a flight of swallows circling low about its walls.

In the muddy farm-yard a young man was belabouring a donkey laden with mulberry-shoots. He stared for a moment at Odo's approach and then sullenly returned to his task.

Odo sprang out into the mud. "Why do you beat the brute?" said he indignantly. The other turned a dull face on him and he recognised his old enemy Giannozzo.

"Giannozzo," he cried, "don't you know me? I am the Cavaliere Valsecca, whose ears you used to box when you were a lad. Must you always be pummelling something, that you can't let that poor brute alone at the end of its day's work?"

Giannozzo, dropping his staff, stammered out that he craved his excellency's pardon for not knowing him, but that as for the ass it was a stubborn devil that would not have carried Jesus Christ without gibbing.

"The beast is tired and hungry," cried Odo, his old compassion for the sufferings of the farm-animals suddenly reviving. "How many hours have you worked it without rest or food?"

"No more than I have worked myself," said Giannozzo sulkily; "and as for its being hungry, why should it fare better than its masters?"

Their words had called out of the house a lean bent woman, whose shrivelled skin showed through the rents in her unbleached shift. At sight of Odo she pushed Giannozzo aside and hurried forward to ask how she might serve the gentleman.

"With supper and a bed, my good Filomena," said Odo; and she flung herself at his feet with a cry.

"Saints of heaven, that I should not have known his excellency! But I am half blind with the fever, and who could have dreamed of such an honour?" She clung to his knees in the mud, kissing his hands and calling down blessings on him. "And as for you, Giannozzo, you curd-faced fool, quick, see that his excellency's horses are stabled and go call your father from the cow-house while I prepare his excellency's supper. And fetch me in a faggot to light the fire in the bailiff's parlour."

Odo followed her into the kitchen, where he had so often crouched in a corner to eat his polenta out of reach of her vigorous arm. The roof seemed lower and more smoke-blackened than ever, but the hearth was cold, and he noticed that no supper was laid. Filomena led him into the bailiff's parlour, where a mortal chill seized him. Cobwebs hung from the walls, the window-panes were broken and caked with grime, and the few green twigs which Giannozzo presently threw on the hearth poured a cloud of smoke into the cold heavy air.

There was a long delay while supper was preparing, and when at length Filomena appeared, it was only to produce, with many excuses, a loaf of vetch-bread, a bit of cheese and some dried quinces. There was nothing else in the house, she declared: not so much as a bit of lard to make soup with, a handful of pasti or a flask of wine. In the old days, as his excellency might remember, they had eaten a bit of meat on Sundays, and drunk aquarolle with their supper; but since the new taxes it was as much as the farmers could do to feed their cattle, without having a scrap to spare for themselves. Jacopone, she continued, was bent double with the rheumatism, and had not been able to drive a plough or to work in the mulberries for over two years. He and the farm-lads sat in the cow-stables when their work was over, for the sake of the heat, and she carried their black bread out there to them: a cold supper tasted better in a warm place, and as his excellency knew, all the windows in the house were unglazed save in the bailiff's parlour. Her man would be in presently to pay his duty to his excellency; but he had grown dull-witted since the rheumatism took him, and his excellency must not take it ill if his talk was a little childish.

Thereupon Filomena excused herself, that she might put a clean shirt on Jacopone, and Odo was left to his melancholy musings. His mind had of late run much on economic abuses; but what was any philandering with reform to this close contact with misery? It was as though white hungry faces had suddenly stared in at the windows of his brightly-lit life. What did these people care for education, enlightenment, the religion of humanity? What they wanted was fodder for their cattle, a bit of meat on Sundays and a faggot on the hearth.

Filomena presently returned with her husband; but Jacopone had shrunk into a crippled tremulous old man, who pulled a vague forelock at Odo without sign of recognition. Filomena, it was clear, was master at Pontesordo; for though Giannozzo was a man grown, and did a man's work, he still danced to the tune of his mother's tongue. It was from her that Odo, shivering over the smoky hearth, gathered the details of their wretched state. Pontesordo being a part of the ducal domain, they had led in their old days an easier life than their neighbours; but the new taxes had stripped them as bare as a mulberry-tree in June.

"How is a Christian to live, excellency, with the salt-tax doubled, so that the cows go dry for want of it; with half a zecchin on every pair of oxen, a stajo of wheat and two fowls to the parish, and not so much as a bite of grass allowed on the Duke's lands? In his late Highness's day the poor folk were allowed to graze their cattle on the borders of the chase; but now a man dare not pluck a handful of weeds there, or so much as pick up a fallen twig; though the deer may trample his young wheat, and feed off the patch of beans at his very door. They do say the Duchess has a kind heart, and gives away money to the towns-folk; but we country-people who spend our lives raising fodder for her game never hear of her Highness but when one of her game-keepers comes down on us for poaching or stealing wood.—Yes, by the saints, and it was her Highness who sent a neighbour's lad to the galleys last year for felling a tree in the chase; a good lad as ever dug furrow, but he lacked wood for a new plough-share, and how in God's name was he to plough his field without it?"

So she went on, like a torrent after the spring rains; but when he named Momola she fell silent, and Giannozzo, looking sideways, drummed with his heel on the floor.

Odo glanced from one to the other. "She's dead, then?" he cried.

Filomena opened deprecating palms. "Can one tell, excellency? It may be she is off with the gypsies."

"The gypsies? How long since?"

"Giannozzo," cried his mother, as he stood glowering, "go see that the stable is locked and his excellency's horses bedded down." He slunk out and she began to gather up the remains of Odo's meagre supper.

"But you must remember when this happened."

"Holy Mother! It was the year we had frost in April and lost our hatching for want of leaves. But as for that child of ingratitude, one day she was here, the next she was gone—clean gone, as a nut drops from the tree—and I that had given the blood of my veins to nourish her! Since then, God is my witness, we have had nothing but misfortune. The next year it was the weevils in the wheat; and so it goes."

Odo was silent, seeing it was vain to press her. He fancied that the girl must have died—of neglect perhaps, or ill usage—and that they feared to own it. His heart swelled, but not against them: they seemed to him no more accountable than cowed hunger-driven animals.

He tossed impatiently on the hard bed Filomena had made up for him in the bailiff's parlour, and was afoot again with the first light. Stepping out into the farm-yard he looked abroad over the flat grey face of the land. Around the keep stretched the new-ploughed fields and the pollarded mulberry orchards; but these, with the clustered hovels of the village, formed a mere islet in the surrounding waste of marsh and woodland. The scene symbolised fitly enough of social conditions of the country: the over-crowded peasantry huddled on their scant patches of arable ground, while miles of barren land represented the feudal rights that hemmed them in on every side.

Odo walked across the yard to the chapel. On the threshold he stumbled over a heap of mulberry-shoots and a broken plough-share. Twilight held the place; but as he stood there the frescoes started out in the slant of the sunrise like dead faces floating to the surface of a river. Dead faces, yes: plaintive spectres of his childish fears and longings, lost in the harsh daylight of experience. He had forgotten the very dreams they stood for: Lethe flowed between and only one voice reached across the torrent. It was that of Saint Francis, lover of the poor...

The morning was hot as Odo drove toward Pianura, and limping ahead of him in the midday glare he presently saw the figure of a hump-backed man in a decent black dress and three-cornered hat. There was something familiar in the man's gait, and in the shape of his large head, poised on narrow stooping shoulders, and as the carriage drew abreast of him, Odo, leaning from the window, cried out, "Brutus—this must be Brutus!"

"Your excellency has the advantage of me," said the hunchback, turning on him a thin face lit by the keen eyes that had once searched his childish soul.

Odo met the rebuff with a smile. "Does that," said he, "prevent my suggesting that you might continue your way more comfortably in my carriage? The road is hot and dusty, and, as you see, I am in want of company."

The pedestrian, who seemed unprepared for this affable rejoinder, had the sheepish air of a man whose rudeness has missed the mark.

"Why, sir," said he, recovering himself, "comfort is all a matter of habit, and I daresay the jolting of your carriage might seem to me more unpleasant than the heat and dust of the road, to which necessity has long since accustomed me."

"In that case," returned Odo with increasing amusement, "you will have the additional merit of sacrificing your pleasure to add to mine."

The hunchback stared. "And what have you or yours ever done for me," he retorted, "that I should sacrifice to your pleasure even the wretched privilege of being dusted by the wheels of your coach?"

"Why, that," replied Odo, "is a question I can scarce answer till you give me the opportunity of naming myself.—If you are indeed Carlo Gamba," he continued, "I am your old friend and companion Odo Valsecca."

The hunchback started. "The Cavaliere Valsecca!" he cried. "I had heard that you were expected." He stood gazing at Odo. "Our next Duke!" he muttered.

Odo smiled. "I had rather," he said, "that my past commended me than my future. It is more than doubtful if I am ever able to offer you a seat in the Duke's carriage; but Odo Valsecca's is very much at your service."

Gamba bowed with a kind of awkward dignity. "I am grateful for a friend's kindness," he said, "but I do not ride in a nobleman's carriage."

"There," returned Odo with perfect good-humour, "you have had advantage of ME; for I can no more escape doing so than you can escape spending your life in the company of an ill-tempered man." And courteously lifting his hat he called to the postillion to drive on.

The hunchback at this, flushing red, laid a hand on the carriage door.

"Sir," said he, "I freely own myself in the wrong; but a smooth temper was not one of the blessings my unknown parents bequeathed to me; and I confess I had heard of you as one little concerned with your inferiors except as they might chance to serve your pleasure."

It was Odo's turn to colour. "Look," said he, "at the fallibility of rumour; for I had heard of you as something of a philosopher, and here I find you not only taking a man's character on hearsay but denying him the chance to prove you mistaken!"

"I deny it no longer," said Gamba stepping into the coach; "but as to philosophy, the only claim I can make to it is that of being by birth a peripatetic."

His dignity appeased, the hunchback proved himself a most engaging companion, and as the carriage lumbered slowly toward Pianura he had time not only to recount his own history but to satisfy Odo as to many points of the life awaiting him.

Gamba, it appeared, owed his early schooling to a Jesuit priest who, visiting the foundling asylum, had been struck by the child's quickness, and had taken him home and bred him to be a clerk. The priest's death left his charge adrift, with a smattering of scholarship above his station, and none to whom he could turn for protection. For a while he had lived, as he said, like a street-cat, picking up a meal where he could, and sleeping in church porches and under street-arcades, till one of the Duke's servants took pity on him and he was suffered to hang about the palace and earn his keep by doing the lacquey's errands. The Duke's attention having been called to him as a lad of parts, his Highness had given him to the Marquess of Cerveno, in whose service he remained till shortly before that young nobleman's death. The hunchback passed hastily over this period; but his reticence was lit by the angry flash of his eyes. After the Marquess's death he had lived for a while from hand to mouth, copying music, writing poetry for weddings and funerals, doing pen-and-ink portraits at a scudo apiece, and putting his hand to any honest job that came his way. Count Trescorre, who now and then showed a fitful recognition of the tie that was supposed to connect them, at length heard of the case to which he was come and offered him a trifling pension. This the hunchback refused, asking instead to be given some fixed employment. Trescorre then obtained his appointment as assistant to the Duke's librarian, a good old priest engrossed in compiling the early history of Pianura from the ducal archives; and this post Gamba had now filled for two years.

"It must," said Odo, "be one singularly congenial to you, if, as I have heard, you are of a studious habit. Though I suppose," he tentatively added, "the library is not likely to be rich in works of the new scientific and philosophic schools."

His companion received this observation in silence; and after a moment Odo continued: "I have a motive in asking, since I have been somewhat deeply engaged in the study of these writers, and my dearest wish is to continue while in Pianura my examination of their theories, and if possible to become acquainted with any who share their views."

He was not insensible of the risk of thus opening himself to a stranger; but the sense of peril made him the more eager to proclaim himself on the side of the cause he seemed to have deserted.

Gamba turned as he spoke, and their eyes met in one of those revealing glances that lay the foundations of friendship.

"I fear, Cavaliere," said the hunchback with a smile, "that you will find both branches of investigation somewhat difficult to pursue in Pianura; for the Church takes care that neither the philosophers nor their books shall gain a footing in our most Christian state. Indeed," he added, "not only must the library be free from heretical works, but the librarian clear of heretical leanings; and since you have honoured me with your confidence I will own that, the court having got wind of my supposed tendency to liberalism, I live in daily expectation of dismissal. For the moment they are content to keep their spies on me; but were it not for the protection of the good abate, my superior, I should long since have been turned out."

"And why," asked Odo, "do you speak of the court and the Church as one?"

"Because, sir, in our virtuous duchy the terms are interchangeable. The Duke is in fact so zealous a son of the Church that if the latter showed any leniency to sinners the secular arm would promptly repair her negligence. His Highness, as you may have heard, is ruled by his confessor, an adroit Dominican. The confessor, it is true, has two rivals, the Countess Belverde, a lady distinguished for her piety, and a German astrologer or alchemist, lately come to Pianura, and calling himself a descendant of the Egyptian priesthood and an adept of the higher or secret doctrines of Neoplatonism. These three, however, though ostensibly rivals for the Duke's favour, live on such good terms with one another that they are suspected of having entered into a secret partnership; while some regard them all as the emissaries of the Jesuits, who, since the suppression of the Society, are known to have kept a footing in Pianura, as in most of the Italian states. As to the Duke, the death of the Marquess of Cerveno, the failing health of the little prince, and his own strange physical infirmities, have so preyed on his mind that he is the victim of any who are unscrupulous enough to trade on the fears of a diseased imagination. His counsellors, however divided in doctrine, have at least one end in common; and that is, to keep the light of reason out of the darkened chamber in which they have confined him; and with such a ruler and such principles of government, you may fancy that poor philosophy has not where to lay her head."

"And the people?" Odo pursued. "What of the fiscal administration? In some states where liberty of thought is forbidden the material welfare of the subject is nevertheless considered."

The hunchback shook his head. "It may be so," said he, "though I had thought the principle of moral tyranny must infect every branch of public administration. With us, at all events, where the Church party rules, the privileges and exemptions of the clergy are the chief source of suffering, and the state of passive ignorance in which they have kept the people has bred in the latter a dull resignation that is the surest obstacle to reform. Oh, sir," he cried, his eyes darkening with emotion, "if you could see, as I do, the blind brute misery on which all the magnificence of rank and all the refinements of luxury are built, you would feel, as you drive along this road, that with every turn of the wheels you are passing over the bodies of those who have toiled without ceasing that you might ride in a gilt coach, and have gone hungry that you might feast in Kings' palaces!"

The touch of rhetoric in this adjuration did not discredit it with Odo, to whom the words were as caustic on an open wound. He turned to make some impulsive answer; but as he did so he caught sight of the towers of Pianura rising above the orchards and market-gardens of the suburbs. The sight started a new train of feeling, and Gamba, perceiving it, said quietly: "But this is no time to speak of such things."

A moment later the carriage had passed under the great battlemented gates, with their Etruscan bas-reliefs, and the motto of the house of Valsecca—Humilitas—surmounted by the ducal escutcheon.

Though the hour was close on noon the streets were as animated as at the angelus, and the carriage could hardly proceed for the crowd obstructing its passage. So unusual at that period was such a sight in one of the lesser Italian cities that Odo turned to Gamba for an explanation. At the same moment a roar rose from the crowd; and the coach turning into the Corso which led to the ducal palace and the centre of the town, Odo caught sight of a strange procession advancing from that direction. It was headed by a clerk or usher with a black cap and staff, behind whom marched two bare-foot friars escorting between them a middle-aged man in the dress of an abate, his hands bound behind him and his head surmounted by a paste-board mitre inscribed with the title: A Destroyer of Female Chastity. This man, who was of a simple and decent aspect, was so dazed by the buffeting of the crowd, so spattered by the mud and filth hurled at him from a hundred taunting hands, and his countenance distorted by so piteous a look of animal fear, that he seemed more like a madman being haled to Bedlam than a penitent making public amends for his offence.

"Are such failings always so severely punished in Pianura?" Odo asked, turning ironically to Gamba as the mob and its victim passed out of sight.

The hunchback smiled. "Not," said he, "if the offender be in a position to benefit by the admirable doctrines of probabilism, the direction of intention, or any one of the numerous expedients by which an indulgent Church has smoothed the way of the sinner; but as God does not give the crop unless man sows the seed, so His ministers bestow grace only when the penitent has enriched the treasury. The fellow," he added, "is a man of some learning and of a retired and orderly way of living, and the charge was brought against him by a jeweller and his wife, who owed him a sum of money and are said to have chosen this way of evading payment. The priests are always glad to find a scape-goat of the sort, especially when there are murmurs against the private conduct of those in high places, and the woman, having denounced him, was immediately assured by her confessor that any debt incurred to a seducer was null and void, and that she was entitled to a hundred scudi of damages for having been led into sin."

2.10.

At the Duke's express wish, Odo was to lodge in the palace; and when he entered the courtyard he found Cantapresto waiting to lead him to his apartment.

The rooms assigned to him lay at the end of one of the wings overlooking the gardens; and as he mounted the great stairway and walked down the corridors with their frescoed walls and busts of Roman emperors he recalled the far-off night when he had passed through the same scenes as a frightened awe-struck child. Where he had then beheld a supernatural fabric, peopled with divinities of bronze and marble, and glowing with light and colour, he now saw a many-corridored palace, stately indeed, and full of a faded splendour, but dull and antiquated in comparison with the new-fangled elegance of the Sardinian court. Yet at every turn some object thrilled the fibres of old association or pride of race. Here he traversed a gallery hung with the portraits of his line; there caught a glimpse of the pages' antechamber through which he and his mother had been led when they waited on the Duke; and from the windows of his closet he overlooked the alleys and terraces where he had wandered with the hunchback.

One of the Duke's pages came to say that his Highness would receive the cavaliere when the court rose from dinner; and finding himself with two hours on his hands, Odo determined to await his kinsman's summons in the garden. Thither he presently repaired; and was soon, with a mournful pleasure, retracing the paths he had first explored in such an ecstasy of wonder. The pleached walks and parterres were in all the freshness of June. Roses and jasmine mingled on the terrace-walls, citron-trees ingeniously grafted with red and white carnations stood in Faenza jars before the lemon-house, and marble nymphs and fauns peeped from thickets of flowering camellias. A noise of childish voices presently attracted Odo, and following a tunnel of clipped limes he came out on a theatre cut in the turf and set about with statues of Apollo and the Muses. A handful of boys in military dress were performing a series of evolutions in the centre of this space; and facing them stood a child of about ten years, in a Colonel's uniform covered with orders, his hair curled and powdered, a paste-board sword in his hand, and his frail body supported on one side by a turbaned dwarf, and on the other by an ecclesiastic who was evidently his governor. The child, as Odo approached, was calling out his orders to his regiment in a weak shrill voice, moving now here, now there on his booted tottering legs, as his two supporters guided him, and painfully trying to flourish the paper weapon that was too heavy for his nerveless wrist. Behind this strange group stood another figure, that of a tall heavy man, richly dressed, with a curious Oriental-looking order on his breast and a veiled somnolent eye which he kept fixed on the little prince.

Odo had been about to advance and do homage to his cousin; but a sign from the man in the background arrested him. The manoeuvres were soon over, the heir was lifted into a little gilded chariot drawn by white goats, his regiment formed in line and saluted him, and he disappeared down one of the alleys with his attendants.

This ceremony over, the tall man advanced to Odo with a bow and asked pardon for the liberty he had taken.

"You are doubtless," said he, "his Highness's cousin, the Cavaliere Valsecca; and my excuse for intruding between yourself and the prince is that I am the Duke's physician, Count Heiligenstern, and that the heir is at present undergoing a course of treatment under my care. His health, as you probably know, has long been a cause of anxiety to his illustrious parents, and when I was summoned to Pianura the College of Physicians had given up all hope of saving him. Since my coming, however, I flatter myself that a marked change is perceptible. My method is that of invigorating the blood by exciting the passions most likely to produce a generous vital ardour. Thus, by organising these juvenile manoeuvres, I arouse the prince's martial zeal; by encouraging him to study the history of his ancestors, I evoke his political ambition; by causing him to be led about the gardens on a pony, accompanied by a miniature pack of Maltese dogs in pursuit of a tame doe, I stimulate the passion of the chase; but it is essential to my system that one emotion should not violently counteract another, and I am therefore obliged to protect my noble patient from the sudden intrusion of new impressions."

This explanation, delivered in a sententious tone, and with a strong German accent, seemed to Odo no more than a learned travesty of the familiar and pathetic expedient of distracting a sick child by the pretence of manly diversions. He was struck, however, by the physician's aspect, and would have engaged him in talk had not one of the Duke's gentlemen appeared with the announcement that his Highness would be pleased to receive the Cavaliere Valsecca.

Like most dwellings of its kind in Italy, the palace of Pianura resembled one of those shells which reveal by their outer convolutions the gradual development of the creature housed within. For two or three generations after Bracciaforte, the terrible founder of the line, had made himself master of the republic, his descendants had clung to the old brick fortress or rocca which the great condottiere had held successfully against the burghers' arquebuses and the battering-rams of rival adventurers, and which still glassed its battlements in the slow waters of the Piana beside the city wall. It was Ascanio, the first Duke, the correspondent of Politian and Castiglione, who, finding the ancestral lair too cramped for the court of a humanist prince, had summoned Luciano da Laurana to build a palace better fitted to his state. Duke Ascanio, in bronze by Verocchio, still looked up with pride from the palace-square at the brick and terra-cotta facade with its fruit-wreathed arches crowned by imperial profiles; but a later prince found the small rooms and intricate passages of Laurana's structure inadequate to the pomp of an ally of Leo X., and Vignola added the state apartments, the sculpture gallery and the libraries.

The palace now passed for one of the wonders of Italy. The Duke's guest, the witty and learned Aretino, celebrated it in verse, his friend Cardinal Bembo in prose; Correggio painted the walls of one room, Guilio Romano the ceiling of another. It seemed that magnificence could go no farther, till the seventeenth century brought to the throne a Duke who asked himself how a self-respecting prince could live without a theatre, a riding-school and an additional wing to lodge the ever-growing train of court officials who had by this time replaced the feudal men-at-arms. He answered the question by laying an extra tax on his people and inviting to Pianura the great Roman architect Carlo Borromini, who regretfully admitted that his illustrious patron was on the whole less royally housed than their Highnesses of Mantua and Parma. Within five years the "cavallerizza," the theatre and the gardens flung defiance at these aspiring potentates; and again Pianura took precedence of her rivals. The present Duke's father had expressed the most recent tendency of the race by the erection of a chapel in the florid Jesuit style; and the group of buildings thus chronicled in rich durable lines the varying passions and ambitions of three hundred years of power.

As Odo followed his guide toward the Duke's apartments he remarked a change in the aspect of the palace. Where formerly the corridors had been thronged with pages, lacqueys and gaily-dressed cavaliers and ladies, only a few ecclesiastics now glided by: here a Monsignore in ermine and lace rochet, attended by his chaplain and secretaries, there a cowled Dominican or a sober-looking secular priest. The Duke was lodged in the oldest portion of the palace, and Odo, who had never visited these apartments, looked with interest at the projecting sculptured chimney and vaulted ceiling of the pages' ante-chamber, which had formerly been the guardroom and was still hung with panoplies. Thence he was led into a gallery lined with scriptural tapestries and furnished in the heavy style of the seventeenth century. Here he waited a few moments, hearing the sound of conversation in the room beyond; then the door of this apartment opened, and a handsome Dominican passed out, followed by a page who invited Odo to step into the Duke's cabinet.

This was a very small room, completely panelled in delicate wood-carving touched with gold. Over this panelling, regardless of the beauty of its design, had been hung a mass of reliquaries and small devotional bas-reliefs and paintings, making the room appear more like the chapel of a wonder-working saint than a prince's closet. Here again Odo found himself alone; but the page presently returned to say that his Highness was not well and begged the cavaliere to wait on him in his bed-chamber.

The most conspicuous object in this room was a great bedstead raised on a dais. The plumed posts and sumptuous hangings of the bed gave it an altar-like air, and the Duke himself, who lay between the curtains, his wig replaced by a nightcap, a scapular about his neck, and his shrivelled body wrapped in a brocaded dressing-gown, looked more like a relic than a man. His heavy under-lip trembled slightly as he offered his hand to Odo's salute.

"You find me, cousin," said he after a brief greeting, "much troubled by a question that has of late incessantly disturbed my rest—can the soul, after full intuition of God, be polluted by the sins of the body?" he clutched Odo's hand in his burning grasp. "Is it possible that there are human beings so heedless of their doom that they can go about their earthly pleasures with this awful problem unsolved? Oh, why has not some Pope decided it? Why has God left this hideous uncertainty hanging over us? You know the doctrine of Plotinus—'he who has access to God leaves the virtues behind him as the images of the gods are left in the outer temple.' Many of the fathers believed that the Neoplatonists were permitted to foreshadow in their teachings the revelation of Christ; but on these occult points much doubt remains, and though certain of the great theologians have inclined to this interpretation, there are others who hold that it leans to the heresy of Quietism."

Odo, who had inferred in the Duke's opening words an allusion to the little prince's ill-health, or to some political anxiety, was at a loss how to reply to this strange appeal; but after a moment he said, "I have heard that your Highness's director is a man of great learning and discrimination. Can he not help your Highness to some decision on this point?"

The Duke glanced at him suspiciously. "Father Ignazio," said he, "is in fact well-versed in theology; but there are certain doctrines inaccessible to all but a few who have received the direct illumination of heaven, and on this point I cannot feel that his judgment is final." He wiped the dampness from his sallow forehead and pressed the scapular to his lips. "May you never know," he cried, "the agony of a father whose child is dying, of a sovereign who longs to labour for the welfare of his people, but who is racked by the thought that in giving his mind to temporal duties and domestic affections while such spiritual difficulties are still unsolved, he may be preparing for himself an eternity of torture such as that—" and he pointed to an old and blackened picture of the Last Judgment that hung on the opposite wall.

Odo tried to frame a soothing rejoinder; but the Duke passionately interrupted him. "Alas, cousin, no rest is possible for one who has attained the rapture of the Beatific Vision, yet who trembles lest the mere mechanical indulgence of the senses may still subject him to the common penalty of sin! As a man who has devoted himself to the study of theology is privileged to argue on questions forbidden to the vulgar, so surely fasting, maceration and ecstasy must liberate the body from the bondage of prescribed morality. Shall no distinction be recognised between my conduct and that of the common sot or debauchee whose soul lies in blind subjection to his lower instincts? I, who have laboured early and late to remove temptation from my people— who have punished offences against conduct as unsparingly as spiritual error—I, who have not scrupled to destroy every picture in my galleries that contained a nude figure or a wanton attitude—I, who have been blessed from childhood by tokens of divine favour and miraculous intervention—can I doubt that I have earned the privileges of that higher state in which the soul is no longer responsible for the failings of the body? And yet—and yet— what if I were mistaken?" he moaned. "What if my advisors have deceived me? Si autem et sic impius sum, quare frustra laboravi?" And he sank back on his pillows limp as an empty glove.

Alarmed at his disorder, Odo stood irresolute whether to call for help; but as he hesitated the Duke feebly drew from his bosom a gold key attached to a slender Venetian chain.

"This," said he, "unlocks the small tortoise-shell cabinet yonder. In it you will find a phial of clear liquor, a few drops of which will restore me. 'Tis an essence distilled by the Benedictine nuns of the Perpetual Adoration and peculiarly effective in accesses of spiritual disturbance."

Odo complied, and having poured the liquor into a glass, held it to his cousin's lips. In a moment the Duke's eye revived and he began to speak in a weak but composed voice, with an air of dignity in singular contrast to his previous self-abandonment. "I am," said he, "unhappily subject to such seizures after any prolonged exertion, and a conversation I have just had with my director has left me in no fit state to receive you. The cares of government sit heavy on one who has scarce health enough for the duties of a private station; and were it not for my son I should long since have withdrawn to the shelter of the monastic life." He paused and looked at Odo with a melancholy kindness. "In you," said he, "the native weakness of our complexion appears to have been tempered by the blood of your mother's house, and your countenance gives every promise of health and vivacity."

He broke off with a sigh and continued in a more authoritative tone: "You have learned from Count Trescorre my motive in summoning you to Pianura. My son's health causes me the liveliest concern, my own is subject to such seizures as you have just witnessed. I cannot think that, in this age of infidelity and disorder, God can design to deprive a Christian state of a line of sovereigns uniformly zealous in the defence of truth; but the purposes of Heaven are inscrutable, as the recent suppression of the Society of Jesus has most strangely proved; and should our dynasty be extinguished I am consoled by the thought that the rule will pass to one of our house. Of this I shall have more to say to you in future. Meanwhile your first business is to acquaint yourself with your new surroundings. The Duchess holds a circle this evening, where you will meet the court; but I must advise you that the persons her Highness favours with her intimacy are not those best qualified to guide and instruct a young man in your position. These you will meet at the house of the Countess Belverde, one of the Duchess's ladies, a woman of sound judgment and scrupulous piety, who gathers about her all our most learned and saintly ecclesiastics. Count Trescorre will instruct you in all that becomes your position at court, and my director, Father Ignazio, will aid you in the selection of a confessor. As to the Bishop, a most worthy and conversable prelate, to whom I would have you show all due regard, his zeal in spiritual matters is not as great as I could wish, and in private talk he indulges in a laxity of opinion against which I cannot too emphatically warn you. Happily, however, Pianura offers other opportunities of edification. Father Ignazio is a man of wide learning and inflexible doctrine, and in several of our monasteries, notably that of the Barnabites, you will find examples of sanctity and wisdom such as a young man may well devoutly consider. Our convents also are distinguished for the severity of their rule and the spiritual privileges accorded them. The Carmelites have every reason to hope for the beatification of their aged Prioress, and among the nuns of the Perpetual Adoration is one who has recently received the ineffable grace of the vulnus divinum. In the conversation of these saintly nuns, and of the holy Abbot of the Barnabites, you will find the surest safeguard against those errors and temptations that beset your age." He leaned back with a gesture of dismissal; but added, reddening slightly, as Odo prepared to withdraw: "You will oblige me, cousin, when you meet my physician, Count Heiligenstern, by not touching on the matter of the restorative you have seen me take."

Odo left his cousin's presence with a feeling of deep discouragement. To a spirit aware of the new influences abroad, and fresh from contact with evils rooted in the very foundations of the existing system, there was a peculiar irony in being advised to seek guidance and instruction in the society of ecstatic nuns and cloistered theologians. The Duke, with his sickly soul agrope in a maze of Neoplatonism and probabilism, while his people groaned under unjust taxes, while knowledge and intellectual liberty languished in a kind of moral pest-house, seemed to Odo like a ruler who, in time of famine, should keep the royal granaries locked and spend his days praying for the succour that his own hand might have dispensed.

In the tapestry room one of his Highness's gentlemen waited to reconduct Odo. Their way lay through the portrait gallery of which he had previously caught a glimpse, and here he begged his guide to leave him. He felt a sudden desire to meet his unknown ancestors face to face, and to trace the tendencies which, from the grim Bracciaforte and the stately sceptical humanist of Leo's age, had mysteriously forced the race into its ever-narrowing mould. The dusky canvases, hung high in tarnished escutcheoned frames, presented a continuous chronicle of the line, from Bracciaforte himself, with his predatory profile outlined by some early Tuscan hand against the turrets of his impregnable fortress. Odo lingered long on this image, but it was not till he stood beneath Piero della Francesca's portrait of the first Duke that he felt the thrill of kindred instincts. In this grave face, with its sensuous mouth and melancholy speculative eyes, he recognised the mingled strain of impressionability and unrest that had reached such diverse issues in his cousin and himself. The great Duke of the "Golden Age," in his Titianesque brocade, the statuette of a naked faun at his elbow, and a faun-like smile on his own ruddy lips, represented another aspect of the ancestral spirit: the rounded temperament of an age of Cyrenaicism, in which every moment was a ripe fruit sunned on all sides. A little farther on, the shadow of the Council of Trent began to fall on the ducal faces, as the uniform blackness of the Spanish habit replaced the sumptuous colours of the Renaissance. Here was the persecuting Bishop, Paul IV.'s ally against the Spaniards, painted by Caravaggio in hauberk and mailed gloves, with his motto—Etiam cum gladio—surmounting the episcopal chair; there the Duke who, after a life of hard warfare and stern piety, had resigned his office to his son and died in the "angelica vestis" of the tertiary order; and the "beatified" Duchess who had sold her jewels to buy corn for the poor during the famine of 1670, and had worn a hair-shirt under a corset that seemed stiff enough to serve all the purposes of bodily mortification. So the file descended, the colours fading, the shadows deepening, till it reached a baby porporato of the last century, who had donned the cardinal's habit at four, and stood rigid and a little pale in his red robes and lace, with a crucifix and a skull on the table to which the top of his berretta hardly reached.

It seemed to Odo as he gazed on the long line of faces as though their owners had entered one by one into a narrowing defile, where the sun rose later and set earlier on each successive traveller; and in every countenance, from that of the first Duke to that of his own peruked and cuirassed grandfather, he discerned the same symptom of decadency: that duality of will which, in a delicately-tempered race, is the fatal fruit of an undisturbed pre-eminence. They had ruled too long and enjoyed too much; and the poor creature he had just left to his dismal scruples and forebodings seemed the mere empty husk of long-exhausted passions.

2.11.

The Duchess was lodged in the Borromini wing of the palace, and thither Odo was conducted that evening.

To eyes accustomed to such ceremonial there was no great novelty in the troop of powdered servants, the major-domo in his short cloak and chain, and the florid splendour of the long suite of rooms, decorated in a style that already appeared over-charged to the more fastidious taste of the day. Odo's curiosity centred chiefly in the persons peopling this scene, whose conflicting interests and passions formed, as it were, the framework of the social structure of Pianura, so that there was not a labourer in the mulberry-orchards or a weaver in the silk-looms but depended for his crust of black bread and the leaking roof over his head on the private whim of some member of that brilliant company.

The Duchess, who soon entered, received Odo with the flighty good-nature of a roving mind; but as her deep-blue gaze met his her colour rose, her eyes lingered on his face, and she invited him to a seat at her side. Maria Clementina was of Austrian descent, and something in her free and noble port and the smiling arrogance of her manner recalled the aspect of her distant kinswoman, the young Queen of France. She plied Odo with a hundred questions, interrupting his answers with a playful abruptness, and to all appearances more engaged by his person than his discourse.

"Have you seen my son?" she asked. "I remember you a little boy scarce bigger than Ferrante, whom your mother brought to kiss my hand in the very year of my marriage. Yes—and you pinched my toy spaniel, sir, and I was so angry with you that I got up and turned my back on the company—do you remember? But how should you, being such a child at the time? Ah, cousin how old you make me feel! I would to God my son looked as you did then; but the Duke is killing him with his nostrums. The child was healthy enough when he was born; but what with novenas and touching of relics and animal magnetism and electrical treatment, there's not a bone in his little body but the saints and the surgeons are fighting over its possession. Have you read 'Emile,' cousin, by the new French author—I forget his name? Well, I would have the child brought up like 'Emile,' allowed to run wild in the country and grow up sturdy and hard as a little peasant. But what heresies am I talking! The book is on the Index, I believe, and if my director knew I had it in my library I should be set up in the stocks in the market-place and all my court-gowns burnt at the Church door as a warning against the danger of importing the new fashions from France!—I hope you hunt, cousin?" she cried suddenly. "'Tis my chief diversion and one I would have my friends enjoy with me. His Highness has lately seen fit to cut down my stables, so that I have scarce forty saddle-horses to my name, and the greater part but sorry nags at that; yet I can still find a mount for any friend that will ride with me and I hope to see you among the number if the Duke can spare you now and then from mass and benediction. His Highness complains that I am always surrounded by the same company; but is it my fault if there are not twenty persons at court that can survive a day in the saddle and a night at cards? Have you seen the Belverde, my mistress of the robes? She follows the hunt in a litter, cousin, and tells her beads at the death! I hope you like cards too, cousin, for I would have all my weaknesses shared by my friends, that they may be the less disposed to criticise them."

The impression produced on the Duchess by the cavaliere Valsecca was closely observed by several members of the group surrounding her Highness. One of these was Count Trescorre, who moved among the courtiers with an air of ease that seemed to establish without proclaiming the tie between himself and the Duchess. When Maria Clementina sat down at play, Trescorre joined Odo and with his usual friendliness pointed out the most conspicuous figures in the circle. The Duchess's society, as the Duke had implied, was composed of the livelier members of the court, chief among whom was the same Don Serafino who had figured so vividly in the reminiscences of Mirandolina and Cantapresto. This gentleman, a notorious loose-liver and gamester, with some remains of good looks and a gay boisterous manner, played the leader of revels to her Highness's following; and at his heels came the flock of pretty women and dashing spendthrifts who compose the train of a young and pleasure-loving princess. On such occasions as the present, however, all the members of the court were obliged to pay their duty to her Highness; and conspicuous among these less frequent visitors was the Duke's director, the suave and handsome Dominican whom Odo had seen leaving his Highness's closet that afternoon. This ecclesiastic was engaged in conversation with the Prime Minister, Count Pievepelago, a small feeble mannikin covered with gold lace and orders. The deference with which the latter followed the Dominican's discourse excited Odo's attention; but it was soon diverted by the approach of a lady who joined herself to the group with an air of discreet familiarity. Though no longer young, she was still slender and graceful, and her languid eye and vapourish manner seemed to Odo to veil an uncommon alertness of perception. The rich sobriety of her dress, the jewelled rosary about her wrist, and most of all, perhaps, the murderous sweetness of the smile with which the Duchess addressed her, told him that here was the Countess Belverde; an inference which Trescorre confirmed.

"The Countess," said he, "or I should rather say the Marchioness of Boscofolto, since the Duke has just bestowed on her the fief of that name, is impatient to make your acquaintance; and since you doubtless remember the saying of the Marquis de Montesquieu, that to know a ruler one must know his confessor and his mistress, you will perhaps be glad to seize both opportunities in one."

The Countess greeted Odo with a flattering deference and at once drew him into conversation with Pievepelago and the Dominican.

"We are discussing," said she, "the details of Prince Ferrante's approaching visit to the shrine of our Lady of the Mountain. This shrine lies about half an hour's ride beyond my villa of Boscofolto, where I hope to have the honour of receiving their Highnesses on their return from the pilgrimage. The Madonna del Monte, as you doubtless know, has often preserved the ducal house in seasons of peril, notably during the great plague of 1630 and during the famine in the Duchess Polixena's time, when her Highness, of blessed memory, met our Lady in the streets distributing bread, in the dress of a peasant-woman from the hills, but with a necklace made of blood-drops instead of garnets. Father Ignazio has lately counselled the little prince's visiting in state the protectress of his line, and his Highness's physician, Count Heiligenstern, does not disapprove the plan. In fact," she added, "I understand that he thinks all special acts of piety beneficial, as symbolising the inward act by which the soul incessantly strives to reunite itself to the One."

The Dominican glanced at Odo with a smile. "The Count's dialectics," said he, "might be dangerous were they a little clearer; but we must hope he distinguishes more accurately between his drugs than his dogmas."

"But I am told," the Prime Minister here interposed in a creaking rusty voice, "that her Highness is set against the pilgrimage and will put every obstacle in the way of its being performed."

The Countess sighed and cast down her eyes, the Dominican remained silent, and Trescorre said quietly to Odo, "Her Highness would be pleased to have you join her in a game at basset." As they crossed the room he added in a low tone: "The Duchess, in spite of her remarkable strength of character, is still of an age to be readily open to new influences. I observed she was much taken by your conversation, and you would be doing her a service by engaging her not to oppose this pilgrimage to Boscofolto. We have Heiligenstern's word that it cannot harm the prince, it will produce a good impression on the people, and it is of vital importance to her Highness not to side against the Duke in such matters." And he withdrew with a smile as Odo approached the card-table.

Odo left the Duchess's circle with an increased desire to penetrate more deeply into the organisation of the little world about him, to trace the operation of its various parts, and to put his hand on the mainspring about which they revolved; and he wondered whether Gamba, whose connection with the ducal library must give him some insight into the affairs of the court, might not prove as instructive a guide through this labyrinth as through the mazes of the ducal garden.

The Duke's library filled a series of rooms designed in the classical style of the cinque-cento. On the very threshold Odo was conscious of leaving behind the trivial activities of the palace, with the fantastic architecture which seemed their natural setting. Here all was based on a noble permanence of taste, a convergence of accumulated effort toward a chosen end; and the door was fittingly surmounted by Seneca's definition of the wise man's state: "Omnia illi secula ut deo serviunt."

Odo would gladly have lingered among the books which filled the rooms with an incense-like aroma of old leather. His imagination caressed in passing the yellowish vellum backs, the worn tooling of Aldine folios, the heavy silver clasps of ancient chronicles and psalters; but his first object was to find Gamba and renew the conversation of the previous day. In this he was disappointed. The only occupant of the library was the hunchback's friend and protector, the abate Crescenti, a tall white-haired priest with the roseate gravity and benevolent air of a donator in some Flemish triptych. The abate, courteously welcoming Odo, explained that he had despatched his assistant to the Benedictine monastery to copy certain ancient records of transactions between that order and the Lords of Valsecca, and added that Gamba, on his return, should at once be apprised of the cavaliere's wish to see him.

The abate himself had been engaged, when his visitor entered, in collating manuscripts, but on Odo's begging him to return to his work, he said with a smile: "I do not suffer from an excess of interruptions, for the library is the least visited portion of the palace, and I am glad to welcome any who are disposed to inspect its treasures. I know not, cavaliere," he added, "if the report of my humble labours has ever reached you;" and on Odo's affirmative gesture he went on, with the eagerness of a shy man who gathers assurance from the intelligence of his listener: "Such researches into the rude and uncivilised past seem to me as essential to the comprehension of the present as the mastering of the major premiss to the understanding of a syllogism; and to those who reproach me for wasting my life over the chronicles of barbarian invasions and the records of monkish litigations, instead of contemplating the illustrious deeds of Greek sages and Roman heroes, I confidently reply that it is more useful to a man to know his own father's character than that of a remote ancestor. Even in this quiet retreat," he went on, "I hear much talk of abuses and of the need for reform; and I often think that if they who rail so loudly against existing institutions would take the trouble to trace them to their source, and would, for instance, compare this state as it is today with its condition five hundred or a thousand years ago, instead of measuring it by the standard of some imaginary Platonic republic, they would find, if not less subject for complaint, yet fuller means of understanding and remedying the abuses they discover."

This view of history was one so new in the abate Crescenti's day that it surprised Odo with the revelation of unsuspected possibilities. How was it that among the philosophers whose works he had studied, none had thought of tracing in the social and political tendencies of the race the germ of wrongs so confidently ascribed to the cunning of priests and the rapacity of princes? Odo listened with growing interest while Crescenti, encouraged by his questions, pointed out how the abuses of feudalism had arisen from the small land-owner's need of protection against the northern invader, as the concentration of royal prerogative had been the outcome of the king's intervention between his great vassals and the communes. The discouragement which had obscured Odo's outlook since his visit to Pontesordo was cleared away by the discovery that in a sympathetic study of the past might lie the secret of dealing with present evils. His imagination, taking the intervening obstacles at a bound, arrived at once at the general axiom to which such inductions pointed; and if he afterward learned that human development follows no such direct line of advance, but must painfully stumble across the wastes of error, prejudice and ignorance, while the theoriser traverses the same distance with a stroke of his speculative pinions; yet the influence of these teachings tempered his judgments with charity and dignified his very failures by a tragic sense of their inevitableness.

Crescenti suggested that Gamba should wait on Odo that evening; but the latter, being uncertain how far he might dispose of his time, enquired where the hunchback lodged, with a view of sending for him at a convenient moment. Having dined at the Duchess's table, and soon wearying of the vapid company of her associates, he yielded to the desire for contrast that so often guided his course, and set out toward sunset in search of Gamba's lodging.

It was his first opportunity of inspecting the town at leisure, and for a while he let his curiosity lead him as it would. The streets near the palace were full of noble residences, recording, in their sculptured doorways, in the wrought-iron work of torch-holders and window-grilles, and in every architectural detail, the gradual change of taste that had transformed the machicolations of the mediaeval fighter into the open cortiles and airy balconies of his descendant. Here and there, amid these inveterate records of dominion, rose the monuments of a mightier and more ancient power. Of these churches and monasteries the greater number, dating only from the ascendancy of the Valseccas, showed an ordered and sumptuous architecture; but one or two buildings surviving from the period of the free city stood out among them with the austerity of desert saints in a throng of court ecclesiastics. The columns of the Cathedral porch were still supported on featureless porphyry lions worn smooth by generations of loungers; and above the octagonal baptistery ran a fantastic basrelief wherein the spirals of the vine framed an allegory of men and monsters symbolising, in their mysterious conflicts, the ever-recurring Manicheism of the middle ages. Fresh from his talk with Crescenti, Odo lingered curiously on these sculptures, which but the day before he might have passed by as the efforts of ignorant workmen, but which now seemed full of the significance that belongs to any incomplete expression of human thought or feeling. Of their relation to the growth of art he had as yet no clear notion; but as evidence of sensations that his forefathers had struggled to record, they touched him like the inarticulate stammerings in which childhood strives to convey its meaning.

He found Gamba's lodging on the upper floor of a decayed palace in one of the by-lanes near the Cathedral. The pointed arcades of this ancient building enclosed the remains of floriated mouldings, and the walls of the court showed traces of fresco-painting; but clothes-lines now hung between the arches, and about the well-head in the centre of the court sat a group of tattered women with half-naked children playing in the dirt at their feet. One of these women directed Odo to the staircase which ascended between damp stone walls to Gamba's door. This was opened by the hunchback himself, who, with an astonished exclamation, admitted his visitor to a scantily furnished room littered with books and papers. A child sprawled on the floor, and a young woman, who had been sewing in the fading light of the attic window, snatched him up as Odo entered. Her back being turned to the light, he caught only a slender youthful outline; but something in the turn of the head, the shrinking curve of the shoulders, carried him back to the little barefoot figure cowering in a corner of the kitchen at Pontesordo, while the farm-yard rang with Filomena's call—"Where are you then, child of iniquity?"

"Momola—don't you know me?" he exclaimed.

She hung back trembling, as though the sound of his voice roused an echo of fear; but Gamba, reddening slightly, took her hand and led her forward.

"It is, indeed," said he, "your excellency's old playmate, the Momola of Pontesordo, who consents to share my poverty and who makes me forget it by the tenderness of her devotion."

But Momola, at this, found voice. "Oh, sir," she cried, "it is he who took me in when I was half-dead and starving, who many a time went hungry to feed me, and who cares for the child as if it were his own!"

As she stood there, in her half-wild hollowed-eyed beauty, which seemed a sickly efflorescence of the marshes, pressing to her breast another "child of iniquity" as pale and elfish as her former self, she seemed to Odo the embodiment of ancient wrongs, risen from the wasted soil to haunt the dreams of its oppressors.

Gamba shrugged his shoulders. "Why," said he, "a child of my own is a luxury I am never likely to possess as long as I have wit to remember the fundamental axiom of philosophy: entia non sunt multiplicanda praeter necessitatum; so it is natural enough fate should single me out to repair the negligence of those who have failed to observe that admirable principle. And now," he added, turning gently to Momola, "it is time to put the boy to bed."

When the door had closed on her Odo turned to Gamba. "I could learn nothing at Pontesordo," he said. "They seemed unwilling to speak of her. What is her story and where did you first know her?"

Gamba's face darkened. "You will remember, cavaliere," he said, "that some time after your departure from Pianura I passed into the service of the Marquess of Cerveno, then a youth of about twenty, who combined with graceful manners and a fair exterior a nature so corrupt and cowardly that he seemed like some such noble edifice as this, designed to house great hopes and high ambitions, but fallen to base uses and become the shelter of thieves and prostitutes. Prince Ferrante being sickly from his birth, the Marquess was always looked on as the Duke's successor, and to Trescorre, who even then, as Master of the Horse, cherished the ambitions he has since realised, no prospect could have been more distasteful. My noble brother, to do him justice, has always hated the Jesuits, who, as you doubtless know, were all-powerful here before the recent suppression of the Order. The Marquess of Cerveno was as completely under their control as the Duke is under that of the Dominicans, and Trescorre knew that with the Marquess's accession his own rule must end. He did his best to gain an influence over his future ruler, but failing in this resolved to ruin him.

"Cerveno, like all your house, was passionately addicted to the chase, and spent much time hunting in the forest of Pontesordo. One day the stag was brought to bay in the farm-yard of the old manor, and there Cerveno saw Momola, then a girl of sixteen, of a singular wild beauty which sickness and trouble have since effaced. The young Marquess was instantly taken; and though hitherto indifferent to women, yielded so completely to his infatuation that Trescorre, ever on the alert, saw in it an unexpected means to his end. He instantly married Momola to Giannozzo, whom she feared and hated; he schooled Giannozzo in the part of the jealous and vindictive husband, and by the liberal use of money contrived that Momola, while suffered to encourage the Marquess's addresses, should be kept so close that Cerveno could not see her save by coming to Pontesordo. This was the first step in the plan; the next was to arrange that Momola should lure her lover to the hunting-lodge on the edge of the chase. This lodge, as your excellency may remember, lies level with the marsh, and so open to noxious exhalations that a night's sojourn there may be fatal. The infernal scheme was carried out with the connivance of the scoundrels at the farm, who had no scruples about selling the girl for a few ducats; and as to Momola, can you wonder that her loathing of Giannozzo and of her wretched life at Pontesordo threw her defenceless into Trescorre's toils? All was cunningly planned to exasperate Cerveno's passion and Momola's longing to escape; and at length, pressed by his entreaties and innocently carrying out the designs of his foe, the poor girl promised to meet him after night-fall at the hunting-lodge. The secrecy of the adventure, and the peril to which it exposed him (for Trescorre had taken care to paint Giannozzo and his father in the darkest colours) were fuel to Cerveno's passion, and he went night after night to Pontesordo. The time was August, when the marsh breathes death, and the Duke, apprised of his favourite's imprudence, forbade his returning to the chase.

"Nothing could better have served Trescorre; for opposition spurred the Marquess's languid temper, and he had now the incredible folly to take up his residence in the lodge. Within three weeks the fever held him. He was at once taken to Pianura, and on recovering from his seizure was sent to take the mountain air at the baths of Lucca. But the poison was in his blood. He never regained more than a semblance of health, and his madness having run its course, his passion for Momola turned to hate of the poor girl to whom he ascribed his destruction. Giannozzo, meanwhile, terrified by the report that the Duke had winded the intrigue, and fearing to be charged with connivance, thought to prove his innocence by casting off his wife and disowning her child.

"What part I played in this grim business I leave your excellency to conceive. As the Marquess's creature I was forced to assist at the spectacle without power to stay its consequences; but when the child was born I carried the news to my master and begged him to come to the mother's aid. For answer, he had me beaten by his lacqueys and flung out of his house. I stomached the beating and addressed myself to Trescorre. My noble brother, whose insight is seldom at fault, saw that I knew enough to imperil him. The

Marquess was dying and his enemy could afford to be generous. He gave me a little money and the following year obtained from the Duke my appointment as assistant librarian. In this way I was able to give Momola a home, and to save her child from the Innocenti. She and I, cavaliere, are the misshapen offspring of that cruel foster-parent, who rears more than half the malefactors in the state; but please heaven the boy shall have a better start in life, and perhaps grow up to destroy some of the evils on which that cursed charity thrives."

This narrative, and the sight of Momola and her child, followed so strangely on the spectacle of sordid misery he had witnessed at Pontesordo, that an inarticulate pity held Odo by the throat. Gamba's anger against the people at the farm seemed as senseless as their own cruelty to their animals. What were they all—Momola, her child, and her persecutors—but a sickly growth of the decaying social order? He felt an almost physical longing for fresh air, light, the rush of a purifying wind through the atmosphere of moral darkness that surrounded him.

2.12.

To relieve the tension of his thoughts he set forth to Gamba the purpose of his visit.

"I am," said he, "much like a stranger at a masked ball, where all the masks are acquainted with each other's disguises and concerted to mystify the visitor. Among the persons I have met at court several have shown themselves ready to guide me through this labyrinth; but, till they themselves unmask and declare their true characters, I am doubtful whither they may lead me; nor do I know of any so well fitted as yourself to give me a clue to my surroundings. As for my own disguise," he added with a smile, "I believe I removed it sufficiently on our first meeting to leave you no doubt as to the use to which your information will be put."

Gamba, who seemed touched by this appeal, nevertheless hesitated before replying. At length he said: "I have the fullest trust in your excellency's honour; but I must remind you that during your stay here you will be under the closest observation and that any opinions you express will at once be attributed to the persons you are known to frequent. I would not," he continued hastily, "say this for myself alone, but I have two mouths to feed and my views are already under suspicion."

Reassured by Odo's protestations, or rather, perhaps, by the more convincing warrant of his look and manner, Gamba proceeded to give him a detailed description of the little world in which chance had placed them.

"If you have seen the Duke," said he, "I need not tell you that it is not he who governs the duchy. We are ruled at present by a triumvirate consisting of the Belverde, the Dominican and Trescorre. Pievepelago, the Prime Minister, is a dummy put in place by the Jesuits and kept there by the rivalries of the other three; but he is in his dotage and the courtiers are already laying wagers as to his successor. Many think Father Ignazio will replace him, but I stake my faith on Trescorre. The Duke dislikes him, but he is popular with the middle class, who, since they have shaken off the yoke of the Jesuits, would not willingly see an ecclesiastic at the head of the state. The duchess's influence is also against the Dominican, for her Highness, being, as you know, connected with the Austrian court, is by tradition unfavourable to the Church party. The Duchess's preferences would weigh little with the Duke were it not that she is sole heiress to the old Duke of Monte Alloro, and that any attempt to bring that principality under the control of the Holy See might provoke the interference of Austria.

"In so ticklish a situation I see none but Trescorre to maintain the political balance. He has been adroit enough to make himself necessary to the Duchess without alienating the Duke; he has introduced one or two trifling reforms that have given him a name for liberality in spite of the heavy taxes with which he has loaded the peasantry; and has in short so played his cards as to profit by the foibles of both parties. Her Highness," he continued, in reply to a question of Odo's, "was much taken by him when she first came to Pianura; and before her feeling had cooled he had contrived to make himself indispensable to her. The Duchess is always in debt; and Trescorre, as Comptroller of Finance, holds her by her besetting weakness. Before his appointment her extravagance was the scandal of the town. She borrowed from her ladies, her pages, her very lacqueys; when she went on a visit to her uncle of Monte Alloro she pocketed the money he bestowed on her servants; nay, she was even accused of robbing the Marchioness of Pievepelago, who, having worn one evening a diamond necklace which excited her Highness's admiration, was waylaid on the way home and the jewels torn from her neck by a crowd of masked ruffians among whom she is said to have recognised one of the ducal servants. These are doubtless idle reports; but it is certain that Trescorre's appointment engaged him still more to the Duchess by enabling him to protect her from such calumnies; while by increasing the land taxes he has discharged the worst of her debts and thus made himself popular with the tradesmen she had ruined. Your excellency must excuse my attempting to paint the private character of her Highness. Such facts as I have reported are of public notoriety, but to exceed them would be an unwarranted presumption. I know she has the name of being affable to her dependents, capable of a fitful generosity, and easily moved by distress; and it is certain that her domestic situation has been one to excite pity and disarm criticism.

"With regard to his Highness, it is difficult either to detect his motives or to divine his preferences. His youth was spent in pious practices; and a curious reason is given for the origin of this habit. He was educated, as your excellency is doubtless aware, by a French philosopher of the school of Hobbes; and it is said that in the interval of his tasks the poor Duke, bewildered by his governor's distinctions between conception and cognition, and the object and the sentient, used to spend his time praying the saints to assist him in his atheistical studies; indeed a satire of the day ascribes him as making a novena to the Virgin to obtain a clearer understanding of the universality of matter. Others with more likelihood aver that he frequented the churches to escape from the tyranny of his pedagogue; and it is certain that from one cause or another his education threw him into the opposite extreme of a superstitious and mechanical piety. His marriage, his differences with the Duchess, and the evil influence of Cerveno, exposed him to new temptations, and for a time he led a life which seemed to justify the worst charges of the enemies of materialism. Recent events have flung him back on the exaggerated devotion of his youth, and now, when his health permits, he spends his time serving mass, singing in the choir at benediction and making pilgrimages to the relics of the saints in the different churches of the duchy.

"A few years since, at the instigation of his confessor, he destroyed every picture in the ducal gallery that contained any naked figure or represented any subject offensive to religion. Among them was Titian's famous portrait of Duke Ascanio's mistress, known as the Goldsmith's Daughter, and a Venus by the Venetian painter Giorgione, so highly esteemed in its day that Pope Leo X. is said to have offered in exchange for it the gift of a papal benefice, and a Cardinal's hat for Duke Guidobaldo's younger son. His Highness, moreover, impedes the administration of justice by resisting all attempts to restrict the Church's right of sanctuary, and upholds the decree forbidding his subjects to study at the University of Pavia, where, as you know, the natural sciences are professed by the ablest scholars of Italy. He allows no public duties to interfere with his private devotions, and whatever the urgency of affairs, gives no audience to his ministers on holydays; and a Cardinal a latere recently passing through the duchy on his return to Rome was not received at the Duke's table because he chanced to arrive on a Friday.

"His Highness's fears for Prince Ferrante's health have drawn a swarm of quacks to Pianura, and the influence of the Church is sometimes counteracted by that of the physicians with whom the Duke surrounds himself. The latest of these, the famous Count Heiligenstern, who is said to have performed some remarkable cures by means of the electrical fluid and of animal magnetism, has gained such an ascendancy over the Duke that some suspect him of being an agent of the Austrian court, while others declare that he is a Jesuit en robe courte. But just at present the people scent a Jesuit under every habit, and it is even rumoured that the Belverde is secretly affiliated to a female branch of the Society. With such a sovereign and such ministers, your excellency need not be told how the state is governed. Trescorre, heaven save the mark! represents the liberal party; but his liberalism is like the generosity of the unarmed traveller who throws his purse to a foot-pad; and Father Ignazio is at hand to see that the people are not bettered at the expense of the Church.

"As to the Duke, having no settled policy, and being governed only through his fears, he leans first to one influence and then to another; but since the suppression of the Jesuits nothing can induce him to attack any ecclesiastical privileges. The diocese of Pianura holds a fief known as the Caccia del Vescovo, long noted as the most lawless district of the duchy. Before the death of the late Pope, Trescorre had prevailed on the Duke to annex it to the principality; but the dreadful fate of Ganganelli has checked bolder sovereigns than his Highness in their attempts on the immunities of the Church, and one of the fairest regions of our unhappy state remains a barren waste, the lair of outlaws and assassins, and a menace to the surrounding country. His Highness is not incapable of generous impulses and his occasional acts of humanity might endear him to his people were it not that they despise him for being the creature of his favourites. Thus, the gift of Boscofolto to the Belverde has excited the bitterest discontent; for the Countess is notorious for her cruel exactions, and it is certain that at her death this rich fief will revert to the Church. And now," Gamba ended with a smile, "I have made known to your excellency the chief characters in the masque, as rumour depicts them to the vulgar. As to the court, like the government, it is divided into two parties: the Duke's, headed by the Belverde, and containing the staider and more conservative members of the Church and nobility; and the Duchess's, composed of every fribble and flatterer, every gamester and rake, every intriguing woman and vulgar parvenu that can worm a way into her favour. In such an atmosphere you may fancy how knowledge thrives. The Duke's library consists of a few volumes of theological casuistry, and her Highness never opens a book unless it be to scandalise her husband by reading some prohibited pamphlet from France. The University, since the fall of the Jesuits, has been in charge of the Barnabite order, and, for aught I know, the Ptolemaic system is still taught there, together with the dialectic of Aristotle. As to science, it is anathema; and the press being subject to the restrictions of the Holy Office, and the University closed to modern thought, but few scholars are to be found in the duchy, save those who occupy themselves with belles-lettres, or, like the abate Crescenti, are engaged in historical research. Pianura, even in the late Duke's day, had its circle of lettered noblemen who patronised the arts and founded the local Arcadia; but such pursuits are out of fashion, the

Arcadia languishes, and the Bishop of Pianura is the only dignitary that still plays the Mecaenas. His lordship, whose theological laxity and coolness toward the Holy Office have put him out of favour with the Duke, has, I am told, a fine cabinet of paintings (some of them, it is rumoured, the very pictures that his Highness ordered to be burnt) and the episcopal palace swarms with rhyming abatini, fashionable playwrights and musicians, and the travelling archeologists who hawk their antiques about from one court to another. Here you may assist at interminable disputes as to the relative merits of Tasso and Ariosto, or listen to a learned dissertation on the verse engraved on a carnelian stone; but as to the questions now agitating the world, they are held of less account than a problem in counterpoint or the construction of a doubtful line in Ovid. As long as Truth goes naked she can scarce hope to be received in good company; and her appearance would probably cause as much confusion among the Bishop's literati as in the councils of the Holy Office."

The old analogy likening the human mind to an imperfect mirror, which modifies the images it reflects, occurred more than once to Odo during the hunchback's lively delineation. It was impossible not to remember that the speaker owed his education to the charity of the order he denounced; and this fact suggested to Odo that the other lights and shadows in the picture might be disposed with more art than accuracy. Still, they doubtless embodied a negative truth, and Odo thought it probable that such intellectual diversion as he could hope for must be sought in the Bishop's circle.

It was two days later that he first beheld that prelate, heading the ducal pilgrimage to the shrine of the mountain Virgin. The day had opened with a confused flight of chimes from every bell-tower in Pianura, as though a migratory flock of notes had settled for a moment on the roofs and steeples of the city. The ducal party set forth early from the palace, but the streets were already spanned with arches and garlands of foliage, tapestries and religious paintings decked the facades of the wealthier houses, and at every street-shrine a cluster of candle-flames hovered like yellow butterflies above the freshly-gathered flowers. The windows were packed with spectators, and the crowds who intended to accompany the pilgrimage were already gathering, with their painted and gilt candles, from every corner of the town. Each church and monastery door poured forth its priests or friars to swell the line, and the various lay confraternities, issuing in their distinctive dress from their "lodges" or assembly-rooms, formed a link between the secular and religious divisions of the procession. The market-place was strewn with sand and sweet herbs; and here, on the doorsteps of the Cathedral, between the featureless porphyry lions, the Bishop waited with his red-robed chapter, and the deacons carrying the painted banners of the diocese. Seen thus, with the cloth-of-gold dalmatic above his pontifical tunic, the mitre surmounting his clear-cut impassive face, and the crozier held aloft in his jewelled gloves, he might have stood for a chryselephantine divinity in the porch of some pagan temple.

Odo, riding beside the Duke's litter, had leisure to note not only the diverse features of the procession but their varying effect on the spectators. It was plain that, as Trescorre had said, the pilgrimage was popular with the people. That imaginative sensuousness which has perpetually renewed the Latin Church by giving form and colour to her dogmatic abstractions, by transforming every successive phase of her belief into something to be seen and handled, found an irresistible outlet in a ceremony that seemed to combine with its devotional intent a secret element of expiation. The little prince was dimly felt to be paying for the prodigality of his fathers, to be in some way a link of suffering between the tongue-tied misery of the fields and the insolent splendour of the court; and a vague faith in the vicarious efficacy of his devotion drew the crowd into momentary sympathy with its rulers. Yet this was but an underlying element in the instinctive delight of the people in the outward forms of their religion. Odo's late experiences had wakened him to the influences acting on that obscure substratum of human life that still seemed, to most men of his rank, of no more account than the brick lining of their marble-coated palaces. As he watched the mounting excitement of the throng, and pictured to himself the lives suddenly lit up by this pledge of unseen promises, he wondered that the enemies of the Church should ascribe her predominance to any cause but the natural needs of the heart. The people lived in unlit hovels, for there was a tax on mental as well as on material windows; but here was a light that could pierce the narrowest crevice and scatter the darkness with a single ray.

Odo noted with equal interest the impression produced by the various members of the court and the Church dignitaries. The Duke's litter was coldly received, but a pitying murmur widened about the gilt chair in which Prince Ferrante was seated at his governor's side, and the approach of Trescorre, mounted on a fine horse and dressed with his usual sober elegance, woke a shout that made him for a moment the central figure of the procession. The Bishop was none too warmly welcomed; but when Crescenti appeared, white-haired and erect among the parish priests, the crowd swayed toward him like grasses in the suction of a current; and one of the Duke's gentlemen, seeing Odo's surprise, said with a smile: "No one does more good in Pianura than our learned librarian."

A different and still more striking welcome awaited the Duchess, who presently appeared on her favourite white hackney, surrounded by the members of her household. Her reluctance to take part in the pilgrimage had been overcome by the exhilaration of showing herself to the public, and as she rode along in her gold-embroidered habit and plumed hat she was just such an image of radiant and indulgent sovereignty as turns enforced submission into a romantic allegiance. Her flushing cheek and kindled eye showed the reaction of the effect she produced, and if her subjects forgot her debts, her violences and follies, she was perhaps momentarily transformed into the being their enthusiasm created. She was at any rate keenly alive to the admiration she excited and eager to enhance it by those showy impulses of benevolence that catch the public eye; as when, at the city gates, she stopped her horse to intervene in behalf of a soldier who had been put under arrest for some slight infraction of duty, and then rode on enveloped in the passionate shouting of the crowd.

The shrine at which the young prince was to pay his devotions stood just beyond the city, on the summit of one of the low knolls which pass for hills in the level landscape of Pianura. The white-columned church with its classical dome and portico had been erected as a thank-offering after the plague of 1630, and the nave was lined with life-sized votive figures of Dukes and Duchesses clad in the actual wigs and robes that had dressed their transient grandeur. As the procession wound into the church, to the ringing of bells and the chanting of the choir, Odo was struck by the spectacle of that line of witnesses, watching in glassy-eyed irony the pomp and display to which their moldering robes and tarnished insignia seemed to fix so brief a term. Once or twice already he had felt the shows of human power as no more than vanishing reflections on the tide of being; and now, as he knelt near the shrine, with its central glitter of jewels and its nimbus of wavering lights, and listened to the reiterated ancient wail:

"Mater inviolata, ora pro nobis!
Virgo veneranda, ora pro nobis!
Speculum justitiae, ora pro nobis!"

it seemed to him as though the bounds of life and death were merged, and the sumptuous group of which he formed a part already dusted over with oblivion.

2.13.

Spite of the Mountain Madonna's much-vaunted powers, the first effect of the pilgrimage was to provoke a serious indisposition in the Duke. Exhausted by fasting and emotion, he withdrew to his apartments and for several days denied himself to all but Heiligenstern, who was suspected by some of suffering his patient's disorder to run its course with a view to proving the futility of such remedies. This break in his intercourse with his kinsman left Odo free to take the measure of his new surroundings. The company most naturally engaging him was that which surrounded the Duchess; but he soon wearied of the trivial diversions it offered. It had ever been necessary to him that his pleasures should touch the imagination as well as the senses; and with such refinement of enjoyment the gallants of Pianura were unacquainted. Odo indeed perceived with a touch of amusement that, in a society where Don Serafino set the pace, he must needs lag behind his own lacquey. Cantapresto had, in fact, been hailed by the Bishop's nephew with a cordiality that proclaimed them old associates in folly; and the soprano's manner seemed to declare that, if ever he had held the candle for Don Serafino, he did not grudge the grease that might have dropped on his cassock. He was soon prime favourite and court buffoon in the Duchess's circle, organising pleasure-parties, composing scenarios for her Highness's private theatre, and producing at court any comedian or juggler the report of whose ability reached him from the market-place. Indefatigable in the contriving of such diversions, he soon virtually passed out of Odo's service into that of her Highness: a circumstance which the young man the less regretted as it left him freer to cultivate the acquaintance of Gamba and his friends without exposing them to Cantapresto's espionage.

Odo had felt himself specially drawn toward the abate Crescenti; and the afternoon after their first meeting he had repaired to the librarian's dwelling. Crescenti was the priest of an ancient parish lying near the fortress; and his tiny house was wedged in an angle of the city walls, like a bird's nest in the mouth of a disused canon. A long flight of steps led up to his study, which on the farther side opened level with a vine-shaded patch of herbs and damask roses in the projection of a ruined bastion. This interior, the home of studious peace, was as cheerful and well-ordered as its inmate's mind; and Odo, seated under the vine pergola in the late summer light, and tasting the abate's Val Pulicella while he turned over the warped pages of old codes and chronicles, felt the stealing charm of a sequestered life.

He had learned from Gamba that Crescenti was a faithful parish priest as well as an assiduous scholar, but he saw that the librarian's beneficence took that purely personal form which may coexist with a serene acceptance of the general evils underlying particular hardships. His charities were performed in the old unquestioning spirit of the Roman distribution of corn; and doubtless the good man who carries his loaf of bread and his word of hope into his neighbour's hovel reaps a more tangible return than the lonely thinker who schemes to undermine the strongholds of injustice. Still there was a perplexing contrast between the superficiality of Crescenti's moral judgments and the breadth and penetration of his historic conceptions. Odo was too inexperienced to reflect that a man's sense of the urgency of improvement lies mainly in the line of his talent: as the merchant is persuaded that the roads most in need of mending are those on which his business makes him travel. Odo himself was already conscious of living in a many-windowed house, with outlooks diverse enough to justify more than one view of the universe; but he had no conception of that concentration of purpose that may make the mind's flight to its goal as direct and unvarying as the course of a homing bird. The talk turning on Gamba, Crescenti spoke of the help which the hunchback gave him in his work among the poor.

"His early hardships," said he, "have given him an insight into character that my happier circumstances have denied me; and he has more than once been the means of reclaiming some wretch that I despaired of. Unhappily, his parts and learning are beyond his station, and will not let him rest in the performance of his duties. His mind, I often tell him, is like one of those inn parlours hung with elaborate maps of the three Heretical Cities; whereas the only topography with which the virtuous traveller need be acquainted is that of the Heavenly City to which all our journeyings should tend. The soundness of his heart reassures me as to this distemper of the reason; but others are less familiar with his good qualities and I tremble for the risks to which his rashness may expose him."

The librarian went on to say that Gamba had a pretty poetical gift which he was suspected of employing in the composition of anonymous satires on the court, the government and the Church. At that period every Italian town was as full of lampoons as a marsh of mosquitoes, and it was as difficult in the one case as the other for the sufferer to detect the specific cause of his sting. The moment in Italy was a strange one. The tide of reform had been turned back by the very act devised to hasten it: the suppression of the Society of Jesus. The shout of liberation that rose over the downfall of the order had sunk to a guarded whisper. The dark legend already forming around Ganganelli's death, the hint of that secret liquor distilled for the order's use in a certain convent of Perugia, hung like a menace on the political horizon; and the disbanded Society seemed to have tightened its hold on the public conscience as a dying man's clutch closes on his victorious enemy.

So profoundly had the Jesuits impressed the world with the sense of their mysterious power that they were felt to be like one of those animal organisms which, when torn apart, carry on a separate existence in every fragment. Ganganelli's bull had provided against their exerting any political influence, or controlling opinion as confessors or as public educators; but they were known to be everywhere in Italy, either hidden in other orders, or acting as lay agents of foreign powers, as tutors in private families, or simply as secular priests. Even the confiscation of their wealth did not seem to diminish the popular sense of their strength. Perhaps because that strength had never been completely explained, even by their immense temporal advantages, it was felt to be latent in themselves, and somehow capable of withstanding every kind of external assault. They had moreover benefited by the reaction which always follows on the breaking up of any great organisation. Their detractors were already beginning to forget their faults and remember their merits. The people had been taught to hate the Society as the possessor of wealth and privileges which should have been theirs; but when the Society fell its possessions were absorbed by the other powers, and in many cases the people suffered from abuses and maladministration which they had not known under their Jesuit landlords. The aristocracy had always been in sympathy with the order, and in many states the Jesuits had been banished simply as a measure of political expediency, a sop to the restless masses. In these cases the latent power of the order was concealed rather than diminished by the pretence of a more liberal government, and everywhere, in one form or another, the unseen influence was felt to be on the watch for those who dared to triumph over it too soon.

Such conditions fostered the growth of social satire. Constructive ambition was forced back into its old disguises, and ridicule of individual weaknesses replaced the general attack on beliefs and institutions. Satirical poems in manuscript passed from hand to hand in coffee-houses, casinos and drawing-rooms, and every conspicuous incident in social or political life was borne on a biting quatrain to the confines of the state. The Duke's gift of Boscofolto to the Countess Belverde had stirred up a swarm of epigrams, and the most malignant among them, Crescenti averred, were openly ascribed to Gamba.

"A few more imprudences," he added, "must cost him his post; and if your excellency has any influence with him I would urge its being used to restrain him from such excesses."

Odo, on taking his leave of the librarian, ran across Gamba at the first street-corner; and they had not proceeded a dozen yards together when the eye of the Duke's kinsman fell on a snatch of doggerel scrawled in chalk on an adjacent wall.

"Beware (the quatrain ran) O virtuous wife or maid,
Our ruler's fondness for the shade,
Lest first he woo thee to the leafy glade
And then into the deeper wood persuade."

This crude play on the Belverde's former title and the one she had recently acquired was signed "Carlo Gamba."

Odo glanced curiously at the hunchback, who met the look with a composed smile. "My enemies don't do me justice," said he; "I could do better than that if I tried;" and he effaced the words with a sweep of his shabby sleeve.

Other lampoons of the same quality were continually cropping up on the walls of Pianura, and the ducal police were kept as busy rubbing them out as a band of weeders digging docks out of a garden. The Duchess's debts, the

Duke's devotions, the Belverde's extortions, Heiligenstern's mummery, and the political rivalry between Trescorre and the Dominican, were sauce to the citizen's daily bread; but there was nothing in these popular satires to suggest the hunchback's trenchant irony.

It was in the Bishop's palace that Odo read the first lampoon in which he recognised his friend's touch. In this society of polished dilettanti such documents were valued rather for their literary merits than for their political significance; and the pungent lines in which the Duke's panaceas were hit off (the Belverde figuring among them as a Lenten diet, a dinner of herbs, and a wonder-working bone) caused a flutter of professional envy in the episcopal circle.

The Bishop received company every evening; and Odo soon found that, as Gamba had said, it was the best company in Pianura. His lordship lived in great state in the Gothic palace adjoining the Cathedral. The gloomy vaulted rooms of the original structure had been abandoned to the small fry of the episcopal retinue. In the chambers around the courtyard his lordship drove a thriving trade in wines from his vineyards, while his clients awaited his pleasure in the armoury, where the panoplies of his fighting predecessors still rusted on the walls. Behind this facade a later prelate had built a vast wing overlooking a garden which descended by easy terraces to the Piana. In the high-studded apartments of this wing the Bishop held his court and lived the life of a wealthy secular nobleman. His days were agreeably divided between hunting, inspecting his estates, receiving the visits of antiquarians, artists and literati, and superintending the embellishments of his gardens, then the most famous in North Italy; while his evenings were given to the more private diversions which his age and looks still justified. In religious ceremonies or in formal intercourse with his clergy he was the most imposing and sacerdotal of bishops; but in private life none knew better how to disguise his cloth. He was moreover a man of parts, and from the construction of a Latin hexameter to the growing of a Holland bulb, had a word worth hearing on all subjects likely to engage the dilettante. A liking soon sprang up between Odo and this versatile prelate; and in the retirement of his lordship's cabinet, or pacing with him the garden-alleys set with ancient marbles, the young man gathered many precepts of that philosophy of pleasure which the great churchmen of the eighteenth century practised with such rare completeness.

The Bishop had not, indeed, given much thought to the problems which most deeply engaged his companion. His theory of life took no account of the future and concerned itself little with social conditions outside his own class; but he was acquainted with the classical schools of thought, and, having once acted as the late Duke's envoy to the French court, had frequented the Baron d'Holbach's drawing-room and familiarised himself with the views of the Encyclopaedists; though it was clear that he valued their teachings chiefly as an argument against asceticism.

"Life," said he to Odo, as they sat one afternoon in a garden-pavilion above the river, a marble Mercury confronting them at the end of a vista of clipped myrtle, "life, cavaliere, is a stock on which we may graft what fruit or flower we choose. See the orange-tree in that Capo di Monte jar: in a week or two it will be covered with red roses. Here again is a citron set with carnations; and but yesterday my gardener sent me word that he had at last succeeded in flowering a pomegranate with jasmine. In such cases the gardener chooses as his graft the flower which, by its colour and fragrance, shall most agreeably contrast with the original stock; and he who orders his life on the same principle, grafting it with pleasures that form a refreshing off-set to the obligations of his rank and calling, may regard himself as justified by Nature, who, as you see, smiles on such abnormal unions among her children.—Not long ago," he went on, with a reminiscent smile, "I had here under my roof a young person who practised to perfection this art of engrafting life with the unexpected. Though she was only a player in a strolling company—a sweetheart of my wild nephew's, as you may guess—I have met few of her sex whose conversation was so instructive or who so completely justified the Scriptural adage, "the sweetness of the lips increaseth learning..." He broke off to sip his chocolate. "But why," he continued, "do I talk thus to a young man whose path is lined with such opportunities? The secret of happiness is to say with the great Emperor, 'Everything is fruit to me which thy seasons bring, O Nature.'"

"Such a creed, monsignore," Odo ventured to return, "is as flattering to the intelligence as to the senses; for surely it better becomes a reasoning being to face fate as an equal than to cower before it like a slave; but, since you have opened yourself so freely on the subject, may I carry your argument a point farther and ask how you reconcile your conception of man's destiny with the authorised teachings of the Church?"

The Bishop raised his head with a guarded glance.

"Cavaliere," said he, "the ancients did not admit the rabble to their sacred mysteries; nor dare we permit the unlettered to enter the hollowed precincts of the temple of Reason."

"True," Odo acquiesced; "but if the teachings of Christianity are the best safeguard of the people, should not those teachings at least be stripped of the grotesque excrescences with which the superstitions of the people and— perhaps—the greed and craft of the priesthood have smothered the simple precepts of Jesus?"

The Bishop shrugged his shoulders. "As long," said he, "as the people need the restraint of a dogmatic religion so long must we do our utmost to maintain its outward forms. In our market-place on feast-days there appears the strange figure of a man who carries a banner painted with an image of Saint Paul surrounded by a mass of writhing serpents. This man calls himself a descendant of the apostle and sells to our peasants the miraculous powder with which he killed the great serpent at Malta. If it were not for the banner, the legend, the descent from Saint Paul, how much efficacy do you think those powders would have? And how long do you think the precepts of an invisible divinity would restrain the evil passions of an ignorant peasant? It is because he is afraid of the plaster God in his parish church, and of the priest who represents that God, that he still pays his tithes and forfeitures and keeps his hands from our throats. By Diana," cried the Bishop, taking snuff, "I have no patience with those of my calling who go about whining for apostolic simplicity, and would rob the churches of their ornaments and the faithful of their ceremonies.

"For my part," he added, glancing with a smile about the delicately-stuccoed walls of the pavilion, through the windows of which climbing roses shed their petals on the rich mosaics transferred from a Roman bath, "for my part, when I remember that 'tis to Jesus of Nazareth I owe the good roof over my head and the good nags in my stable; nay, the very venison and pheasants from my preserves, with the gold plate I eat them off, and above all the leisure to enjoy as they deserve these excellent gifts of the Creator—when I consider this, I say, I stand amazed at those who would rob so beneficent a deity of the least of his privileges.—But why," he continued again after a moment, as Odo remained silent, "should we vex ourselves with such questions, when Providence has given us so fair a world to enjoy and such varied faculties with which to apprehend its beauties? I think you have not seen the Venus Callipyge in bronze that I have lately received from Rome?" And he rose and led the way to the house.

This conversation revealed to Odo a third conception of the religious idea. In Piedmont religion imposed itself as a military discipline, the enforced duty of the Christian citizen to the heavenly state; to the Duke it was a means of purchasing spiritual immunity from the consequences of bodily weakness; to the Bishop, it replaced the panem et circenses of ancient Rome. Where, in all this, was the share of those whom Christ had come to save? Where was Saint Francis's devotion to his heavenly bride, the Lady Poverty? Though here and there a good parish priest like Crescenti ministered to the temporal wants of the peasantry, it was only the free-thinker and the atheist who, at the risk of life and fortune, laboured for their moral liberation. Odo listened with a saddened heart, thinking, as he followed his host through the perfumed shade of the gardens, and down the long saloon at the end of which the

Venus stood, of those who for the love of man had denied themselves such delicate emotions and gone forth cheerfully to exile or imprisonment. These were the true lovers of the Lady Poverty, the band in which he longed to be enrolled; yet how restrain a thrill of delight as the slender dusky goddess detached herself against the cool marble of her niche, looking, in the sun-rippled green penumbra of the saloon, with a sound of water falling somewhere out of sight, as though she had just stepped dripping from the wave?

In the Duchess's company life struck another gait. Here was no waiting on subtle pleasures, but a headlong gallop after the cruder sort. Hunting, gaming and masquerading filled her Highness's days; and Odo had felt small inclination to keep pace with the cavalcade, but for the flying huntress at its head. To the Duchess's "view halloo" every drop of blood in him responded; but a vigilant image kept his bosom barred. So they rode, danced, diced together, but like strangers who cross hands at a veglione. Once or twice he fancied the Duchess was for unmasking; but her impulses came and went like fireflies in the dusk, and it suited his humour to remain a looker-on.

So life piped to him during his first days at Pianura: a merry tune in the Bishop's company, a mad one in the Duchess's; but always with the same sad undertone, like the cry of the wind on a warm threshold.

2.14.

Trescorre too kept open house, and here Odo found a warmer welcome than he had expected. Though Trescorre was still the Duchess's accredited lover, it was clear that the tie between them was no longer such as to make him resent her kindness to her young kinsman. He seemed indeed anxious to draw Odo into her Highness's circle, and surprised him by a frankness and affability of which his demeanour at Turin had given no promise. As leader of the anti-clericals he stood for such liberalism as dared show its head in Pianura; and he seemed disposed to invite Odo's confidence in political matters. The latter was, however, too much the child of his race not to hang back from such an invitation. He did not distrust Trescorre more than the other courtiers; but it was a time when every ear was alert for the foot-fall of treachery, and the rashest man did not care to taste first of any cup that was offered him.

These scruples Trescorre made it his business to dispel. He was the only person at court who was willing to discuss politics, and his clear view of affairs excited Odo's admiration if not his concurrence. Odo's was in fact one of those dual visions which instinctively see both sides of a case and take the defence of the less popular. Gamba's principles were dear to him; but he did not therefore believe in the personal baseness of every opponent of the cause. He had refrained from mentioning the hunchback to his supposed brother; but the latter, in one of their talks, brought forward Gamba's name, without reference to the relationship, but with high praise for the young librarian's parts. This, at the moment, put Odo on his guard; but Trescorre having one day begged him to give Gamba warning of some petty danger that threatened him from the clerical side, it became difficult not to believe in an interest so attested; the more so as Trescorre let it be seen that Gamba's political views were not such as to distract from his sympathy.

"The fellow's brains," said he, "would be of infinite use to me; but perhaps he serves us best at a distance. All I ask is that he shall not risk himself too near Father Ignazio's talons, for he would be a pretty morsel to throw to the Holy Office, and the weak point of such a man's position is that, however dangerous in life, he can threaten no one from the grave."

Odo reported this to Gamba, who heard with a two-edged smile. "Yes," was his comment, "he fears me enough to want to see me safe in his fold."

Odo flushed at the implication. "And why not?" said he. "Could you not serve the cause better by attaching yourself openly to the liberals than by lurking in the ditch to throw mud at both parties?"

"The liberals!" sneered Gamba. "Where are they? And what have they done? It was they who drove out the Jesuits; but to whom did the Society's lands go? To the Duke, every acre of them! And the peasantry suffered far less under the fathers, who were good agriculturists, than under the Duke, who is too busy with monks and astrologers to give his mind to irrigation or the reclaiming of waste land. As to the University, who replaced the Jesuits there? Professors from Padua or Pavia? Heaven forbid! But holy Barnabites that have scarce Latin enough to spell out the Lives of the Saints! The Jesuits at least gave a good education to the upper classes; but now the young noblemen are as ignorant as peasants."

Trescorre received at his house, besides the court functionaries, all the liberal faction and the Duchess's personal friends. He kept a lavish state, but lacking the Bishop's social gifts, was less successful in fusing the different elements of his circle. The Duke, for the first few weeks after his kinsman's arrival, received no company; and did not even appear in the Belverde's drawing-rooms; but Odo deemed it none the less politic to show himself there without delay.

The new Marchioness of Boscofolto lived in one of the finest palaces of Pianura, but prodigality was the least of her failings, and the meagreness of her hospitality was an unfailing source of epigram to the drawing-rooms of the opposition. True, she kept open table for half the clergy in the town (omitting, of course, those worldly ecclesiastics who frequented the episcopal palace), but it was whispered that she had persuaded her cook to take half wages in return for the privilege of victualling such holy men, and that the same argument enabled her to obtain her provisions below the market price. In her outer ante-chamber the servants yawned dismally over a cold brazier, without so much as a game of cards to divert them, and the long enfilade of saloons leading to her drawing-room was so scantily lit that her guests could scarce recognise each other in passing. In the room where she sat, a tall crucifix of ebony and gold stood at her elbow and a holy-water cup encrusted with jewels hung on the wall at her side. A dozen or more ecclesiastics were always gathered in stiff seats about the hearth; and the aspect of the apartment, and the Marchioness's semi-monastic costume, justified the nickname of "the sacristy," which the Duchess had bestowed on her rival's drawing-room.

Around the small fire on this cheerless hearth the fortunes of the state were discussed and directed, benefices disposed of, court appointments debated, and reputations made and unmade in tones that suggested the low drone of a group of canons intoning the psalter in an empty cathedral. The Marchioness, who appeared as eager as the others to win Odo to her party, received him with every mark of consideration and pressed him to accompany her on a visit to her brother, the Abbot of the Barnabites; an invitation which he accepted with the more readiness as he had not forgotten the part played by that religious in the adventure of Mirandolina of Chioggia.

He found the Abbot a man with a bland intriguing eye and centuries of pious leisure in his voice. He received his visitors in a room hung with smoky pictures of the Spanish school, showing Saint Jerome in the wilderness, the death of Saint Peter Martyr, and other sanguinary passages in the lives of the saints; and Odo, seated among such surroundings, and hearing the Abbot deplore the loose lives and religious negligence of certain members of the court, could scarce repress a smile as the thought of Mirandolina flitted through his mind.

"She must," he reflected, "have found this a sad change from the Bishop's palace;" and admired with what philosophy she had passed from one protector to the other.

Life in Pianura, after the first few weeks, seemed on the whole a tame business to a youth of his appetite; and he secretly longed for a pretext to resume his travels. None, however, seemed likely to offer; for it was clear that the Duke, in the interval of more pressing concerns, wished to study and observe his kinsman. When sufficiently recovered from the effects of the pilgrimage, he sent for Odo and questioned him closely as to the way in which he had spent his time since coming to Pianura, the acquaintances he had formed and the churches he had frequented. Odo prudently dwelt on the lofty tone of the Belverde's circle, and on the privilege he had enjoyed in attending her on a visit to the holy Abbot of the Barnabites; touching more lightly on his connection with the Bishop, and omitting all mention of Gamba and Crescenti. The Duke assumed a listening air, but it was clear that he could not put off his private thoughts long enough to give an open mind to other matters; and Odo felt that he was nowhere so secure as in his cousin's company. He remembered, however, that the Duke had plenty of eyes to replace his own, and that a secret which was safe in his actual presence might be in mortal danger on his threshold.

His Highness on this occasion was pleased to inform his kinsman that he had ordered Count Trescorre to place at the young man's disposal an income enabling him to keep a carriage and pair, four saddle-horses and five servants. It was scant measure for an heir-presumptive, and Odo wondered if the Belverde had had a hand in the apportionment; but his indifference to such matters (for though personally fastidious he cared little for display) enabled him to show such gratitude that the Duke, fancying he might have been content with less, had nearly withdrawn two of the saddle-horses. This becoming behaviour greatly advanced the young man in the esteem of his Highness, who accorded him on the spot the petites entrees of the ducal apartments. It was a privilege Odo had no mind to abuse; for if life moved slowly in the Belverde's circle it was at a standstill in the Duke's. His Highness never went abroad but to serve mass in some church (his almost daily practice) or to visit one of the numerous monasteries within the city. From Ash Wednesday to Easter Monday it was his custom to transact no public or private business. During this time he received none of his ministers, and saw his son but for a few moments once a day; while in Holy Week he made a retreat with the Barnabites, the Belverde withdrawing for the same period to the convent of the Perpetual Adoration.

Odo, as his new life took shape, found his chief interest in the society of Crescenti and Gamba. In the Duchess's company he might have lost all taste for soberer pleasures, but that his political sympathies wore a girl's reproachful shape. Ever at his side, more vividly than in the body, Fulvia Vivaldi became the symbol of his best aims and deepest failure. Sometimes, indeed, her look drove him forth in the Duchess's train, but more often, drawing him from the crowd of pleasure-seekers, beckoned the way to solitude and study. Under Crescenti's tuition he began the reading of Dante, who just then, after generations of neglect, was once more lifting his voice above the crowd of minor singers. The mighty verse swept Odo out to open seas of thought, and from his vision of that earlier Italy, hapless, bleeding, but alive and breast to breast with the foe, he drew the presage of his country's resurrection.

Passing from this high music to the company of Gamba and his friends was like leaving a church where the penitential psalms are being sung for the market-place where mud and eggs are flying. The change was not agreeable to a fastidious taste; but, as Gamba said, you cannot clean out a stable by waving incense over it. After some hesitation, he had agreed to make Odo acquainted with those who, like himself, were secretly working in the cause of progress. These were mostly of the middle class, physicians, lawyers, and such men of letters as could subsist on the scant wants of an unliterary town. Ablest among them was the bookseller, Andreoni, whose shop was the meeting place of all the literati of Pianura. Andreoni, famous throughout Italy for his editions of the classics, was a man of liberal views and considerable learning, and in his private room were to be found many prohibited volumes, such as Beccaria's Crime and Punishment, Gravina's Hydra Mystica, Concini's History of Probabilism and the Amsterdam editions of the French philosophical works.

The reformers met at various places, and their meetings were conducted with as much secrecy as those of the Honey-Bees. Odo was at first surprised that they should admit him to their conferences; but he soon divined that the gatherings he attended were not those at which the private designs of the party were discussed. It was plain that they belonged to some kind of secret association; and before he had been long in Pianura he learned that the society of the Illuminati, that bugbear of priests and princes, was supposed to have agents at work in the duchy. Odo had heard little of this execrated league, but that it was said to preach atheism, tyrannicide and the complete abolition of territorial rights; but this, being the report of the enemy, was to be received with a measure of doubt. He tried to learn from Gamba whether the Illuminati had a lodge in the city; but on this point he could extract no information. Meanwhile he listened with interest to discussions on taxation, irrigation, and such economic problems as might safely be aired in his presence.

These talks brought vividly before him the political corruption of the state and the misery of the unprivileged classes. All the land in the duchy was farmed on the metayer system, and with such ill results that the peasants were always in debt to their landlords. The weight of the evil lay chiefly on the country-people, who had to pay on every pig they killed, on all the produce they carried to market, on their farm implements, their mulberry-orchards and their silk-worms, to say nothing of the tithes to the parish. So oppressive were these obligations that many of the peasants, forsaking their farms, enrolled themselves in the mendicant orders, thus actually strengthening the hand of their oppressors. Of legislative redress there was no hope, and the Duke was inaccessible to all but his favourites. The previous year, as Odo learned, eight hundred poor labourers, exasperated by want, had petitioned his Highness to relieve them of the corvee; but though they had raised fifteen hundred scudi to bribe the court official who was to present their address, no reply had ever been received. In the city itself, the monopoly of corn and tobacco weighed heavily on the merchants, and the strict censorship of the press made the open ventilation of wrongs impossible, while the Duke's sbirri and the agents of the Holy Office could drag a man's thoughts from his bosom and search his midnight dreams. The Church party, in the interest of their order, fostered the Duke's fears of sedition and branded every innovator as an atheist; the Holy Office having even cast grave doubts on the orthodoxy of a nobleman who had tried to introduce the English system of ploughing on his estates. It was evident to Odo that the secret hopes of the reformers centred in him, and the consciousness of their belief was sweeter than love in his bosom. It diverted him from the follies of his class, fixed his thoughts at an age when they are apt to range, and thus slowly shaped and tempered him for high uses.

In this fashion the weeks passed and summer came. It was the Duchess's habit to escape the August heats by retiring to the dower-house on the Piana, a league beyond the gates; but the little prince being still under the care of the German physician, who would not consent to his removal, her Highness reluctantly lingered in Pianura. With the first leafing of the oaks Odo's old love for the budding earth awoke, and he rode out daily in the forest toward Pontesordo. It was but a flat stretch of shade, lacking the voice of streams and the cold breath of mountain-gorges: a wood without humours or surprises; but the mere spring of the turf was delightful as he cantered down the grass alleys roofed with level boughs, the outer sunlight just gilding the lip of the long green tunnel.

Sometimes he attended the Duchess, but oftener chose to ride alone, setting forth early after a night at cards or a late vigil in Crescenti's study. One of these solitary rides brought him without premeditation to a low building on the fenny edge of the wood. It was a small house, added, it appeared, to an ancient brick front adorned with pilasters, perhaps a fragment of some woodland temple. The door-step was overgrown with a stealthy green moss and tufted with giant fennel; and a shutter swinging loose on its hinge gave a glimpse of inner dimness. Odo guessed at once that this was the hunting lodge where Cerveno had found his death; and as he stood looking out across the oozy secrets of the marsh, the fever seemed to hang on his steps. He turned away with a shiver; but whether it were the sullen aspect of the house, or the close way in which the wood embraced it, the place suddenly laid a detaining hand upon him. It was as though he had reached the heart of solitude. Even the faint woodland noises seemed to recede from that dense circle of shade, and the marsh turned a dead eye to heaven.

Odo tethered his horse to a bough and seated himself on the doorstep; but presently his musings were disturbed by the sound of voices, and the Duchess, attended by her gentlemen, swept by at the end of a long glade. He fancied she waved her hand to him; but being in no humour to join the cavalcade, he remained seated, and the riders soon passed out of sight. As he sat there sombre thoughts came to him, stealing up like exhalations from the fen. He saw his life stretched out before him, full of broken purposes and ineffectual effort. Public affairs were in so perplexed a case that consistent action seemed impossible to either party, and their chief efforts were bent toward directing the choice of a regent. It was this, rather than the possibility of his accession, which fixed the general attention on Odo, and pledged him to circumspection. While not concealing that in economic questions his sympathies were with the liberals, he had carefully abstained from political action, and had hoped, by the strict observance of his religious duties, to avoid the enmity of the Church party. Trescorre's undisguised sympathy seemed the pledge of liberal support, and it could hardly be doubted that the choice of a regent in the Church party would be unpopular enough to imperil the dynasty. With Austria hovering on the horizon the Church herself was not likely to take such risks; and thus all interests seemed to centre in Odo's appointment.

New elements of uncertainty were, however, perpetually disturbing the prospect. Among these was Heiligenstern's growing influence over the Duke. Odo had seen little of the German physician since their first meeting. Hearsay had it that he was close-pressed by the spies of the Holy Office, and perhaps for this reason he remained withdrawn in the Duke's private apartments and rarely showed himself abroad. The little prince, his patient, was as seldom seen, and the accounts of the German's treatment were as conflicting as the other rumours of the court. It was noised on all sides, however, that the Duke was ill-satisfied with the results of the pilgrimage, and resolved upon less hallowed measures to assure his heir's recovery. Hitherto, it was believed, the German had conformed to the ordinary medical treatment; but the clergy now diligently spread among the people the report that supernatural agencies were to be employed. This rumour caused such general agitation that it was said both parties had made secret advances to the Duchess in the hope of inducing her to stay the scandal. Though Maria Clementina felt little real concern for the public welfare, her stirring temper had more than once roused her to active opposition of the government, and her kinship with the old Duke of Monte Alloro made her a strong factor in the political game. Of late, however, she seemed to have wearied of this sport, throwing herself entirely into the private diversions of her station, and alluding with laughing indifference to her husband's necromantic researches.

Such was the conflicting gossip of the hour; but it was in fact idle to forecast the fortunes of a state dependent on a valetudinary's whims; and rumour was driven to feed upon her own conjectures. To Odo the state of affairs seemed a satire on his secret aspirations. In a private station or as a ruling prince he might have served his fellows: as a princeling on the edge of power he was no more than the cardboard sword in a toy armoury.

Suddenly he heard his name pronounced and starting up saw Maria Clementina at his side. She rode alone, and held out her hand as he approached.

"I have had an accident," said she, breathing quickly. "My girth is broke and I have lost the rest of my company."

She was glowing with her quick ride, and as Odo lifted her from the saddle her loosened hair brushed his face like a kiss. For a moment she seemed like life's answer to the dreary riddle of his fate.

"Ah," she sighed, leaning on him, "I am glad I found you, cousin; I hardly knew how weary I was;" and she dropped languidly to the doorstep.

Odo's heart was beating hard. He knew it was only the stir of the spring sap in his veins, but Maria Clementina wore a look of morning brightness that might have made a soberer judgment blink. He turned away to examine her saddle. As he did so, he observed that her girth was not torn, but clean cut, as with sharp scissors. He glanced up in surprise, but she sat with drooping lids, her head thrown back against the lintel; and repressing the question on his lips he busied himself with the adjustment of the saddle. When it was in place he turned to give her a hand; but she only smiled up at him through her lashes.

"What!" said she with an air of lovely lassitude, "are you so impatient to be rid of me? I should have been so glad to linger here a little." She put her hand in his and let him lift her to her feet. "How cool and still it is! Look at that little spring bubbling through the moss. Could you not fetch me a drink from it?"

She tossed aside her riding-hat and pushed back the hair from her warm forehead.

"Your Highness must not drink of the water here," said Odo, releasing her hand.

She gave him a quick derisive glance. "Ah, true," she cried; "this is the house to which that abandoned wretch used to lure poor Cerveno." She drew back to look at the lodge. "Were you ever in it?" she asked curiously. "I should like to see how the place looks."

She laid her hand on the door-latch, and to Odo's surprise it yielded to her touch. "We're in luck, I vow," she declared with a laugh. "Come cousin, let us visit the temple of romance together."

The allusion to Cerveno jarred on Odo, and he followed her in silence. Within doors, the lodge was seen to consist of a single room, gaily painted with hunting-scenes framed in garlands of stucco. In the dusk they could just discern the outlines of carved and gilded furniture, and a Venice mirror gave back their faces like phantoms in a magic crystal.

"This is stifling," said Odo impatiently. "Would your Highness not be better in the open?"

"No, no," she persisted. "Unbar the shutters and we shall have air enough. I love a deserted house: I have always fancied that if one came in noiselessly enough one might catch the ghosts of the people who used to live in it."

He obeyed in silence, and the green-filtered forest noon filled the room with a quiver of light. A chill stole upon Odo as he looked at the dust-shrouded furniture, the painted harpsichord with green mould creeping over its keyboard, the consoles set with empty wine flagons and goblets of Venice glass. The place was like the abandoned corpse of pleasure.

But Maria Clementina laughed and clapped her hands. "This is enchanting," she cried, throwing herself into an arm-chair of threadbare damask, "and I shall rest here while you refresh me with a glass of Lacrima Christi from one of those dusty flagons. They are empty, you say? Never mind, for I have a flask of cordial in my saddle-bag. Fetch it, cousin, and wash these two glasses in the spring, that we may toast all the dead lovers that have drunk out of them."

When Odo returned with the flask and glasses, she had brushed the dust from a slender table of inlaid wood, and drawn a seat near her own. She filled the two goblets with cordial and signed to Odo to seat himself beside her.

"Why do you pull such a glum face?" she cried, leaning over to touch his glass before she emptied hers. "Is it that you are thinking of poor Cerveno? On my soul, I question if he needs your pity! He had his hour of folly, and was too gallant a gentleman not to pay the shot. For my part I would rather drink a poisoned draught than die of thirst."

The wine was rising in waves of colour over her throat and brow, and setting her glass down she suddenly laid her ungloved hand on Odo's.

"Cousin," she said in a low voice, "I could help you if you would let me."

"Help me?" he said, only half-aware of her words in the warm surprise of her touch.

She drew back, but with a look that seemed to leave her hand in his.

"Are you mad," she murmured, "or do you despise your danger?"

"Am I in danger?" he echoed smiling. He was thinking how easily a man might go under in that deep blue gaze of hers. She dropped her lids as though aware of his thought.

"Why do you concern yourself with politics?" she went on with a new note in her voice. "Can you find no diversion more suited to your rank and age? Our court is a dull one, I own—but surely even here a man might find a better use for his time."

Odo's self-possession returned in a flash. "I am not," cried he gaily, "in a position to dispute it at this moment;" and he leaned over to recapture her hand. To his surprise she freed herself with an affronted air.

"Ah," she said, "you think this a device to provoke a gallant conversation." She faced him nobly now. "Look," said she, drawing a folded paper from the breast of her riding-coat. "Have you not frequented these houses?"

Suddenly sobered, he ran his eye over the paper. It contained the dates of the meetings he had attended at the houses of Gamba's friends, with the designation of each house. He turned pale.

"I had no notion," said he, with a smile, "that my movements were of interest in such high places; but why does your Highness speak of danger in this connection?"

"Because it is rumoured that the lodge of the Illuminati, which is known to exist in Pianura, meets secretly at the houses on this list."

Odo hesitated a moment. "Of that," said he, "I have no report. I am acquainted with the houses only as the residences of certain learned and reputable men, who devote their leisure to scientific studies."

"Oh," she interrupted, "call them by what name you please! It is all one to your enemies."

"My enemies?" said he lightly. "And who are they?"

"Who are they?" she repeated impatiently. "Who are they not? Who is there at court that has such cause to love you? The Holy Office? The Duke's party?"

Odo smiled. "I am perhaps not in the best odour with the Church party," said he, "but Count Trescorre has shown himself my friend, and I think my character is safe in his keeping. Nor will it be any news to him that I frequent the company you name."

She threw back her head with a laugh. "Boy," she cried, "you are blinder even than I fancied! Do you know why it was that the Duke summoned you to Pianura? Because he wished his party to mould you to their shape, in case the regency should fall into your hands. And what has Trescorre done? Shown himself your friend, as you say—won your confidence, encouraged you to air your liberal views, allowed you to show yourself continually in the Bishop's company, and to frequent the secret assemblies of free thinkers and conspirators—and all that the Duke may turn against you and perhaps name him regent in your stead! Believe me, cousin," she cried with a mounting urgency, "you never stood in greater need of a friend than now. If you continue on your present course you are undone. The Church party is resolved to hunt down the Illuminati, and both sides would rejoice to see you made the scapegoat of the Holy Office." She sprung up and laid her hand on his arm. "What can I do to convince you?" she said passionately. "Will you believe me if I ask you to go away—to leave Pianura on the instant?"

Odo had risen also, and they faced each other in silence. There was an unmistakable meaning in her tone: a self-revelation so simple and ennobling that she seemed to give herself as hostage for her words.

"Ask me to stay, cousin—not to go," he whispered, her yielding hand in his.

"Ah, madman," she cried, "not to believe me NOW! But it is not too late if you will still be guided."

"I will be guided—but not away from you."

She broke away, but with a glance that drew him after. "It is late now and we must set forward," she said abruptly. "Come to me tomorrow early. I have much more to say to you."

The words seemed to be driven out on her quick breathing, and the blood came and went in her cheek like a hurried messenger. She caught up her riding-hat and turned to put it on before the Venice mirror.

Odo, stepping up behind her, looked over her shoulder to catch the reflection of her blush. Their eyes met for a laughing instant; then he drew back deadly pale, for in the depths of the dim mirror he had seen another face.

The Duchess cried out and glanced behind her. "Who was it? Did you see her?" she said trembling.

Odo mastered himself instantly.

"I saw nothing," he returned quietly. "What can your Highness mean?"

She covered her eyes with her hands. "A girl's face," she shuddered—"there in the mirror—behind mine—a pale face with a black travelling hood over it—"

He gathered up her gloves and riding-whip and threw open the door of the pavilion.

"Your Highness is weary and the air here insalubrious. Shall we not ride?" he said.

Maria Clementina heard him with a blank stare. Suddenly she roused herself and made as though to pass out; but on the threshold she snatched her whip from him and, turning, flung it full at the mirror. Her aim was good and the chiselled handle of the whip shattered the glass to fragments.

She caught up her long skirt and stepped into the open.

"I brook no rivals!" said she with a white-lipped smile. "And now, cousin," she added gaily, "to horse!"

2.15.

Odo, as in duty bound, waited the next morning on the Duchess; but word was brought that her Highness was indisposed, and could not receive him till evening.

He passed a drifting and distracted day. The fear lay much upon him that danger threatened Gamba and his associates; yet to seek them out in the present conjuncture might be to play the stalking-horse to their enemies. Moreover, he fancied the Duchess not incapable of using political rumours to further her private caprice; and scenting no immediate danger he resolved to wait upon events.

On rising from dinner he was surprised by a summons from the Duke. The message, an unusual one at that hour, was brought by a slender pale lad, not in his Highness's service, but in that of the German physician Heiligenstern. The boy, who was said to be a Georgian rescued from the Grand Signior's galleys, and whose small oval face was as smooth as a girl's, accosted Odo in one of the remoter garden alleys with the request to follow him at once to the Duke's apartment. Odo complied, and his guide loitered ahead with an air of unconcern, as though not wishing to have his errand guessed. As they passed through the tapestry gallery preceding the gentlemen's antechamber, footsteps and voices were heard within. Instantly the boy was by Odo's side and had drawn him into the embrasure of a window. A moment later Trescorre left the antechamber and walked rapidly past their hiding-place. As soon as he was out of sight the Georgian led Odo from his concealment and introduced him by a private way to the Duke's closet.

His Highness was in his bed-chamber; and Odo, on being admitted, found him, still in dressing-gown and night-cap, kneeling with a disordered countenance before the ancient picture of the Last Judgment that hung on the wall facing his bed. He seemed to have forgotten that he had asked for his kinsman; for on the latter's entrance he started up with a suspicious glance and hastily closed the panels of the picture, which (as Odo now noticed) appeared to conceal an inner painting. Then, gathering his dressing-gown about him, he led the way to his closet and bade his visitor be seated.

"I have," said he, speaking in a low voice, and glancing apprehensively about him, "summoned you hither privately to speak on a subject which concerns none but ourselves.—You met no one on your way?" he broke off to enquire.

Odo told him that Count Trescorre had passed, but without perceiving him.

The Duke seemed relieved. "My private actions," said he querulously, "are too jealously spied upon by my ministers. Such surveillance is an offence to my authority, and my subjects shall learn that it will not frighten me from my course." He straightened his bent shoulders and tried to put on the majestic look of his official effigy. "It appears," he continued, with one of his sudden changes of manner, "that the Duchess's uncle, the Duke of Monte Alloro, has heard favourable reports of your wit and accomplishments, and is desirous of receiving you at his court." He paused, and Odo concealed his surprise behind a profound bow.

"I own," the Duke went on, "that the invitation comes unseasonably, since I should have preferred to keep you at my side; but his Highness's great age, and his close kinship to my wife, through whom the request is conveyed, make it impossible for me to refuse." The Duke again paused, as though uncertain how to proceed. At length he resumed:—"I will not conceal from you that his Highness is subject to the fantastical humours of his age. He makes it a condition that the length of your stay shall not be limited; but should you fail to suit his mood you may find yourself out of favour in a week. He writes of wishing to send you on a private mission to the court of Naples; but this may be no more than a passing whim. I see no way, however, but to let you go, and to hope for a favourable welcome for you. The Duchess is determined upon giving her uncle this pleasure, and in fact has consented in return to oblige me in an important matter." He flushed and averted his eyes. "I name this," he added with an effort, "only that her Highness may be aware that it depends on herself whether I hold to my side of the bargain. Your papers are already prepared and you have my permission to set out at your convenience. Meanwhile it were well that you should keep your preparations private, at least till you are ready to take leave." And with the air of dignity he could still assume on occasion, he rose and handed Odo his passport.

Odo left the closet with a beating heart. It was clear that his departure from Pianura was as strongly opposed by some one in high authority as it was favoured by the Duchess; and why opposed and by whom he could not so much as hazard a guess. In the web of court intrigues it was difficult for the wariest to grope his way; and Odo was still new to such entanglements. His first sensation was one of release, of a future suddenly enlarged and cleared. The door was open again to opportunity, and he was of an age to greet the unexpected like a bride. Only one thought disturbed him. It was clear that Maria Clementina had paid high for his security; and did not her sacrifice, whatever its nature, constitute a claim upon his future? In sending him to her uncle, whose known favourite she was, she did not let him out of her hand. If he accepted this chance of escape he must hereafter come and go as she bade. At the thought, his bounding fancy slunk back humbled. He saw himself as Trescorre's successor, his sovereign's official lover, taking up again, under more difficult circumstances, and without the zest of inexperience, the dull routine of his former bondage. No, a thousand times no; he would fetter himself to no woman's fancy! Better find a pretext for staying in Pianura, affront the Duchess by refusing her aid, risk his prospects, his life even, than bow his neck twice to the same yoke. All her charm vanished in this vision of unwilling subjection...Disturbed by these considerations, and anxious to compose his spirits, Odo bethought himself of taking refuge in the Bishop's company. Here at least the atmosphere was clear of mystery: the Bishop held aloof from political intrigue and breathed an air untainted by the odium theologicum. Odo found his lordship seated in the cool tessellated saloon which contained his chiefest treasures—marble busts ranged on pedestals between the windows, the bronze Venus Callipyge, and various tables of pietra commessa set out with vases and tazzas of antique pattern. A knot of virtuosi gathered about one of these tables were engaged in examining a collection of engraved gems displayed by a lapidary of Florence; while others inspected a Greek manuscript which the Bishop had lately received from Syria. Beyond the windows, a cedrario or orange-walk stretched its sunlit vista to the terrace above the river; and the black cassocks of one or two priests who were strolling in the clear green shade of a pleached alley made pleasant spots of dimness in the scene.

Even here, however, Odo was aware of a certain disquietude. The Bishop's visitors, instead of engaging in animated disputations over his lordship's treasures, showed a disposition to walk apart, conversing in low tones; and he himself, presently complaining of the heat, invited Odo to accompany him to the grot beneath the terrace. In this shaded retreat, studded with shells and coral and cooled by an artificial wind forced through the conchs of marble Tritons, his lordship at once began to speak of the rumours of public disaffection.

"As you know," said he, "my duties and tastes alike seclude me from political intrigue, and the scandal of the day seldom travels beyond my kitchens. But as creaking signboards announce a storm, the hints and whispers of my household tell me there is mischief abroad. My position protects me from personal risk, and my lack of ambition from political enmity; for it is notorious I would barter the highest honours in the state for a Greek vase or a bronze of Herculanaeum—not to mention the famous Venus of Giorgione, which, if report be true, his Highness has burned at Father Ignazio's instigation. But yours, cavaliere, is a less sheltered walk, and perhaps a friendly warning may be of service. Yet," he added after a pause, "a warning I can scarce call it, since I know not from what quarter the danger impends. Proximus ardet Ucalegon; but there is no telling which way the flames may spread. I can only advise you that the Duke's growing infatuation for his German magician has bred the most violent discontent among his subjects, and that both parties appear resolved to use this disaffection to their advantage. It is said his Highness intends to subject the little prince to some mysterious treatment connected with the rites of the Egyptian priesthood, of whose secret doctrine Heiligenstern pretends to be an adept. Yesterday it was bruited that the Duchess loudly opposed the experiment; this afternoon it is given out that she has yielded. What the result may be, none can foresee; but whichever way the storm blows, the chief danger probably threatens those who have had any connection with the secret societies known to exist in the duchy."

Odo listened attentively, but without betraying any great surprise; and the Bishop, evidently reassured by his composure, suggested that, the heat of the day having declined, they should visit the new Indian pheasants in his volary.

The Bishop's hints had not helped his listener to a decision. Odo indeed gave Cantapresto orders to prepare as privately as possible for their departure; but rather to appear to be carrying out the Duke's instructions than with any fixed intention of so doing. How to find a pretext for remaining he was yet uncertain. To disobey the Duke was impossible; but in the general state of tension it seemed likely enough that both his Highness and the Duchess might change their minds within the next twenty-four hours. He was reluctant to appear that evening in the Duchess's circle; but the command was not to be evaded, and he went thither resolved to excuse himself early.

He found her Highness surrounded by the usual rout that attended her. She was herself in a mood of wild mirth, occasioned by the drolleries of an automatic female figure which a travelling showman introduced by Cantapresto had obtained leave to display at court. This lively puppet performed with surprising skill on the harpsichord, giving the company, among other novelties, selections from the maestro Piccini's latest opera and a concerto of the German composer Gluck.

Maria Clementina seemed at first unaware of her kinsman's presence, and he began to hope he might avoid any private talk with her; but when the automaton had been dismissed and the card-tables were preparing, one of her gentlemen summoned him to her side. As usual, she was highly rouged in the French fashion, and her cold blue eyes had a light which set off the extraordinary fairness of her skin.

"Cousin," said she at once, "have you your papers?" Her tone was haughty and yet eager, as though she scorned to show herself concerned, yet would not have had him believe in her indifference. Odo bowed without speaking.

"And when do you set out?" she continued. "My good uncle is impatient to receive you."

"At the earliest moment, madam," he replied with some hesitation.

The hesitation was not lost on her and he saw her flush through her rouge.

"Ah," said she in a low voice, "the earliest moment is none too early!—Do you go tomorrow?" she persisted; but just then Trescorre advanced toward them, and under a burst of assumed merriment she privately signed to Odo to withdraw.

He was glad to make his escape, for the sense of walking among hidden pitfalls was growing on him. That he had acquitted himself awkwardly with the Duchess he was well aware; but Trescorre's interruption had at least enabled him to gain time. An increasing unwillingness to leave Pianura had replaced his former impatience to be gone. The reluctance to desert his friends was coupled with a boyish desire to stay and see the game out; and behind all his other impulses lurked the instinctive resistance to any feminine influence save one.

The next morning he half-expected another message from the Duchess; but none came, and he judged her to be gravely offended. Cantapresto appeared early with the rumour that some kind of magical ceremony was to be performed that evening in the palace; and toward noon the Georgian boy again came privately to Odo and requested him to wait on the Duke when his Highness rose from supper. This increased Odo's fears for Gamba, Andreoni and the other reformers; yet he dared neither seek them out in person nor entrust a message to Cantapresto. As the day passed, however, he began to throw off his apprehensions. It was not the first time since he had come to Pianura that there had been ominous talk of political disturbances, and he knew that Gamba and his friends were not without means of getting under shelter. As to his own risk, he did not give it a thought. He was not of an age or a temper to weigh personal danger against the excitement of conflict; and as evening drew on he found himself wondering with some impatience if after all nothing unusual would happen.

He supped alone, and at the appointed hour proceeded to the Duke's apartments, taking no farther precaution than to carry his passport about him. The palace seemed deserted. Everywhere an air of apprehension and mystery hung over the long corridors and dimly-lit antechambers. The day had been sultry, with a low sky foreboding great heat, and not a breath of air entered at the windows. There were few persons about, but one or two beggars lurked as usual on the landings of the great staircase, and Odo, in passing, felt his sleeve touched by a woman cowering under the marble ramp in the shadow thrown by a colossal Caesar. Looking down, he heard a voice beg for alms, and as he gave it the woman pressed a paper into his hand and slipped away through the darkness.

Odo hastened on till he could assure himself of being unobserved; then he unfolded the paper and read these words in Gamba's hand: "Have no fear for any one's safety but your own." With a sense of relief he hid the message and entered the Duke's antechamber.

Here he was received by Heiligenstern's Oriental servant, who, with a mute salutation, led him into a large room where the Duke's pages usually waited. The walls of this apartment had been concealed under hangings of black silk worked with cabalistic devices. Oil-lamps set on tripods of antique design shed a faint light over the company seated at one end of the room, among whom Odo recognised the chief dignitaries of the court. The ladies looked pale but curious, the men for the most part indifferent or disapproving. Intense quietness prevailed, broken only by the soft opening and closing of the door through which the guests were admitted. Presently the Duke and Duchess emerged from his Highness's closet. They were followed by Prince Ferrante, supported by his governor and his dwarf, and robed in a silken dressing-gown which hung in voluminous folds about his little shrunken body. Their Highnesses seated themselves in two armchairs in front of the court, and the little prince reclined beside his mother.

No sooner had they taken their places than Heiligenstern stepped forth, wearing a doctor's gown and a quaintly-shaped bonnet or mitre. In his long robes and strange headdress he looked extraordinarily tall and pale, and his features had the glassy-eyed fixity of an ancient mask. He was followed by his two attendants, the Oriental carrying a frame-work of polished metal, not unlike a low narrow bed, which he set down in the middle of the room; while the Georgian lad, who had exchanged his fustanella and embroidered jacket for a flowing white robe, bore in his hands a crystal globe set in a gold stand.

Having reverently placed it on a small table, the boy, at a signal from his master, drew forth a phial and dropped its contents into a bronze vat or brazier which stood at the far end of the room. Instantly clouds of perfumed vapour filled the air, and as these dispersed it was seen that the black hangings of the walls had vanished with them, and the spectators found themselves seated in a kind of open temple through which the eye travelled down colonnaded vistas set with statues and fountains. This magical prospect was bathed in sunlight, and Odo observed that, though the lamps had gone out, the same brightness suffused the room and illuminated the wondering faces of the audience. The little prince uttered a cry of delight, and the magician stepped forward, raising a long white wand in his hand.

"This," said he, in measured accents, "is an evocation of the Temple of Health, into whose blissful precincts the wisdom of the ancients was able to lead the sufferer who put his trust in them. This deceptio visus, or product of rhabdomancy, easily effected by an adept of the Egyptian mysteries, is designed but to prefigure the reality which awaits those who seek health through the ministry of the disciples of Iamblichus. It is no longer denied among men of learning that those who have been instructed in the secret doctrine of the ancients are able, by certain correspondences of nature, revealed only to the initiated, to act on the inanimate world about them, and on the animal economy, by means beyond the common capabilities of man." He paused a moment, and then, turning with a low bow to the Duke, enquired whether his Highness desired the rites to proceed.

The Duke signed his assent, and Heiligenstern, raising his wand, evoked another volume of mist. This time it was shot through with green flames, and as the wild light subsided the room was once more revealed with its black hangings, and the lamps flickered into life again.

After another pause, doubtless intended to increase the tension of the spectators, the magician bade his servant place the crystal before him. He then raised his hands as if in prayer, speaking in a strange chanting jargon, in which Odo detected fragments of Greek and Latin, and the recurring names of the Judaic demons and angels. As this ceased Heiligenstern beckoned to the Georgian boy, who approached him with bowed head and reverently folded hands.

"Your Highness," said Heiligenstern, "and this distinguished company, are doubtless familiar with the magic crystal of the ancients, in which the future may be deciphered by the pure in heart. This lad, whom I rescued from slavery and have bred to my service in the solemn rites of the priesthood of Isis, is as clear in spirit as the crystal which stands before you. The future lies open to him in this translucent sphere and he is prepared to disclose it at your bidding."

There was a moment's silence; but on the magician's repeating his enquiry the Duke said: "Let the boy tell me what he sees."

Heiligenstern at once laid his hands on his acolyte's head and murmured a few words over him; then the boy advanced and bent devoutly above the crystal. Almost immediately the globe was seen to cloud, as though suffused with milk; the cloud gradually faded and the boy began to speak in a low hesitating tone.

"I see," he said, "I see a face...a fair face..." He faltered and glanced up almost apprehensively at Heiligenstern, whose gaze remained impenetrable. The boy began to tremble. "I see nothing," he said in a whisper. "There is one here purer than I...the crystal will not speak for me in that other's presence..."

"Who is that other?" Heiligenstern asked.

The boy fixed his eyes on the little prince. An excited murmur ran through the company and Heiligenstern again advanced to the Duke. "Will your Highness," he asked, "permit the prince to look into the sacred sphere?"

Odo saw the Duchess extend her hand impulsively toward the child; but at a signal from the Duke the little prince's chair was carried to the table on which the crystal stood. Instantly the former phenomenon was repeated, the globe clouding and then clearing itself like a pool after rain.

"Speak, my son," said the Duke. "Tell us what the heavenly powers reveal to you."

The little prince continued to pore over the globe without speaking. Suddenly his thin face reddened and he clung more closely to his companion's arm.

"I see a beautiful place," he began, his small fluting voice rising like a bird's pipe in the stillness, "a place a thousand times more beautiful than this...like a garden...full of golden-haired children...with beautiful strange toys in their hands...they have wings like birds...they ARE birds...ah! they are flying away from me...I see them no more...they vanish through the trees..." He broke off sadly.

Heiligenstern smiled. "That, your Highness, is a vision of the prince's own future, when, restored to health, he is able to disport himself with his playmates in the gardens of the palace."

"But they were not the gardens of the palace!" the little boy exclaimed. "They were much more beautiful than our gardens."

Heiligenstern bowed. "They appeared so to your Highness," he deferentially suggested, "because all the world seems more beautiful to those who have regained their health."

"Enough, my son!" exclaimed the Duchess with a shaken voice. "Why will you weary the child?" she continued, turning to the Duke; and the latter, with evident reluctance, signed to Heiligenstern to cover the crystal. To the general surprise, however, Prince Ferrante pushed back the black velvet covering which the Georgian boy was preparing to throw over it.

"No, no," he exclaimed, in the high obstinate voice of the spoiled child, "let me look again...let me see some more beautiful things...I have never seen anything so beautiful, even in my sleep!" It was the plaintive cry of the child whose happiest hours are those spent in unconsciousness.

"Look again, then," said the Duke, "and ask the heavenly powers what more they have to show you."

The boy gazed in silence; then he broke out: "Ah, now we are in the palace...I see your Highness's cabinet...no, it is the bedchamber...it is night...and I see your Highness lying asleep...very still...very still...your Highness wears the scapular received last Easter from his Holiness...It is very dark...Oh, now a light begins to shine...where does it come from? Through the door? No, there is no door on that side of the room...It shines through the wall at the foot of the bed...ah! I see"—his voice mounted to a cry—"The old picture at the foot of the bed...the picture with the wicked people burning in it...has opened like a door...the light is shining through it...and now a lady steps out from the wall behind the picture...oh, so beautiful...she has yellow hair, as yellow as my mother's...but longer...oh, much longer...she carries a rose in her hand...and there are white doves flying about her shoulders...she is naked, quite naked, poor lady! but she does not seem to mind...she seems to be laughing about it...and your Highness..."

The Duke started up violently. "Enough—enough!" he stammered. "The fever is on the child...this agitation is...most pernicious...Cover the crystal, I say!"

He sank back, his forehead damp with perspiration. In an instant the crystal had been removed, and Prince Ferrante carried back to his mother's side. The boy seemed in nowise affected by his father's commotion. His eyes burned with excitement, and he sat up eagerly, as though not to miss a detail of what was going forward. Maria Clementina leaned over and clasped his hand, but he hardly noticed her. "I want to see some more beautiful things!" he insisted.

The Duke sat speechless, a fallen heap in his chair, and the courtiers looked at each other, their faces shifting spectrally in the faint light, like phantom travellers waiting to be ferried across some mysterious river. At length Heiligenstern advanced and with every mark of deference addressed himself to the Duke.

"Your Highness," said he quietly, "need be under no apprehension as to the effect produced upon the prince. The magic crystal, as your Highness is aware, is under the protection of the blessed spirits, and its revelations cannot harm those who are pure-minded enough to receive them. But the chief purpose of this assemblage was to witness the communication of vital force to the prince, by means of the electrical current. The crystal, by revealing its secrets to the prince, has testified to his perfect purity of mind, and thus declared him to be in a peculiarly fit state to receive what may be designated as the Sacrament of the new faith."

A murmur ran through the room, but Heiligenstern continued without wavering: "I mean thereby to describe that natural religion which, by instructing its adepts in the use of the hidden potencies of earth and air, testifies afresh to the power of the unseen Maker of the Universe."

The murmur subsided, and the Duke, regaining his voice, said with an assumption of authority: "Let the treatment begin."

Heiligenstern immediately spoke a word to the Oriental, who bent over the metal bed which had been set up in the middle of the room. As he did so the air again darkened and the figures of the magician and his assistants were discernible only as flitting shades in the obscurity. Suddenly a soft pure light overflowed the room, the perfume of flowers filled the air, and music seemed to steal out of the very walls. Heiligenstern whispered to the governor and between them they lifted the little prince from his chair and laid him gently on the bed. The magician then leaned over the boy with a slow weaving motion of the hands.

"If your Highness will be pleased to sleep," he said, "I promise your Highness the most beautiful dreams."

The boy smiled back at him and he continued to bend above the bed with flitting hands. Suddenly the little prince began to laugh.

"What does your Highness feel?" the magician asked.

"A prickling...such a soft warm prickling...as if my blood were sunshine with motes dancing in it...or as if that sparkling wine of France were running all over my body."

"It is an agreeable sensation, your Highness?"

The boy nodded.

"It is well with your Highness?"

"Very well."

Heiligenstern began a loud rhythmic chant, and gradually the air darkened, but with the mild dimness of a summer twilight, through which sparks could be seen flickering like fire-flies about the reclining prince. The hush grew deeper; but in the stillness Odo became aware of some unseen influence that seemed to envelope him in waves of exquisite sensation. It was as though the vast silence of the night had poured into the room and, like a dark tepid sea, was lapping about his body and rising to his lips. His thoughts, dissolved into emotion, seemed to waver and float on the stillness like sea-weed on the lift of the tide. He stood spell-bound, lulled, yielding himself to a blissful dissolution.

Suddenly he became aware that the hush was too intense, too complete; and a moment later, as though stretched to the cracking-point, it burst terrifically into sound. A huge uproar shook the room, crashing through it like a tangible mass. The sparks whirled in a menacing dance round the little prince's body, and, abruptly blotted, left a deeper darkness, in which the confused herding movements of startled figures were indistinguishably merged. A flash of silence followed; then the liberated forces of the night broke in rain and thunder on the rocking walls of the room.

"Light—light!" some one stammered; and at the same moment a door was flung open, admitting a burst of candle-light and a group of figures in ecclesiastical dress, against which the white gown and black hood of Father Ignazio detached themselves. The Dominican stepped toward the Duke.

"Your Highness," said he in a tone of quiet resolution, "must pardon this interruption; I act at the bidding of the Holy Office."

Even in that moment of profound disarray the name sent a deeper shudder through his hearers. The Duke, who stood grasping the arms of his chair, raised his head and tried to stare down the intruders; but no one heeded his look. At a signal from the Dominican a servant had brought in a pair of candelabra, and in their commonplace light the cabalistic hangings, the magician's appliances and his fantastically-dressed attendants looked as tawdry as the paraphernalia of a village quack. Heiligenstern alone survived the test. Erect, at bay as it were, his black robe falling in hieratic folds, the white wand raised in his hands, he might have personified the Prince of Darkness drawn up undaunted against the hosts of the Lord. Some one had snatched the little prince from his stretcher, and Maria Clementina, holding him to her breast, sat palely confronting the sorcerer. She alone seemed to measure her strength against his in some mysterious conflict of the will. But meanwhile the Duke had regained his voice.

"My father," said he, "on what information does the Holy Office act?"

The Dominican drew a parchment from his breast. "On that of the Inquisitor General, your Highness," he replied, handing the paper to the Duke, who unfolded it with trembling hands but was plainly unable to master its contents. Father Ignazio beckoned to an ecclesiastic who had entered the room in his train.

"This, your Highness," said he, "is the abate de Crucis of Innsbruck, who was lately commissioned by the Holy Office to enquire into the practises and doctrine of the order of the Illuminati, that corrupt and atheistical sect which has been the cause of so much scandal among the German principalities. In the course of his investigations he became aware that the order had secretly established a lodge in Pianura; and hastening hither from Rome to advise your Highness of the fact, has discovered in the so-called Count Heiligenstern one of the most notorious apostles of the order." He turned to the priest. "Signor abate," he said, "you confirm these facts?"

The abate de Crucis quietly advanced. He was a slight pale man of about thirty, with a thoughtful and indulgent cast of countenance.

"In every particular," said he, bowing profoundly to the Duke, and speaking in a low voice of singular sweetness. "It has been my duty to track this man's career from its ignoble beginning to its infamous culmination, and I have been able to place in the hands of the Holy Office the most complete proofs of his guilt. The so-called Count Heiligenstern is the son of a tailor in a small village of Pomerania. After passing through various vicissitudes with which I need not trouble your Highness, he obtained the confidence of the notorious Dr. Weishaupt, the founder of the German order of the Illuminati, and together this precious couple have indefatigably propagated their obscene and blasphemous doctrines. That they preach atheism and tyrannicide I need not tell your Highness; but it is less generally known that they have made these infamous doctrines the cloak of private vices from which even paganism would have recoiled. The man now before me, among other open offences against society, is known to have seduced a young girl of noble family in Ratisbon and to have murdered her child. His own wife and children he long since abandoned and disowned; and the youth yonder, whom he describes as a Georgian slave rescued from the Grand Signior's galleys, is in fact the wife of a Greek juggler of Ravenna, and has forsaken her husband to live in criminal intercourse with an atheist and assassin."

This indictment, pronounced with an absence of emotion which made each word cut the air like the separate stroke of a lash, was followed by a prolonged silence; then one of the Duchess's ladies cried out suddenly and burst into tears. This was the signal for a general outbreak. The room was filled with a confusion of voices, and among the groups surging about him Odo noticed a number of the Duke's sbirri making their way quietly through the crowd. The notary of the Holy Office advanced toward Heiligenstern, who had placed himself against the wall, with one arm flung about his trembling acolyte. The Duchess, her boy still clasped against her, remained proudly seated; but her eyes met Odo's in a glance of terrified entreaty, and at the same instant he felt a clutch on his sleeve and heard Cantapresto's whisper.

"Cavaliere, a boat waits at the landing below the tanners' lane. The shortest way to it is through the gardens and your excellency will find the gate beyond the Chinese pavilion unlocked."

He had vanished before Odo could look round. The latter still wavered; but as he did so he caught Trescorre's face through the crowd. The minister's eye was fixed on him; and the discovery was enough to make him plunge through the narrow wake left by Cantapresto's retreat.

Odo made his way unhindered to the ante-room, which was also thronged, ecclesiastics, servants and even beggars from the courtyard jostling each other in their struggle to see what was going forward. The confusion favoured his escape, and a moment later he was hastening down the tapestry gallery and through the vacant corridors of the palace. He was familiar with half-a-dozen short-cuts across this network of passages; but in his bewilderment he pressed on down the great stairs and across the echoing guard-room that opened on the terrace. A drowsy sentinel challenged him; and on Odo's explaining that he sought to leave, and not to enter, the palace, replied that he had his Highness's orders to let no one out that night. For a moment Odo was at a loss; then he remembered his passport. It seemed to him an interminable time before the sentinel had scrutinised it by the light of a guttering candle, and to his surprise he found himself in a cold sweat of fear. The rattle of the storm simulated footsteps at his heels and he felt the blind rage of a man within shot of invisible foes.

The passport restored, he plunged out into the night. It was pitch-black in the gardens and the rain drove down with the guttural rush of a midsummer storm. So fierce was its fall that it seemed to suck up the earth in its black eddies, and he felt himself swept along over a heaving hissing surface, with wet boughs lashing out at him as he fled. From one terrace to another he dropped to lower depths of buffeting dripping darkness, till he found his hand on the gate-latch and swung to the black lane below the wall. Thence on a run he wound to the tanners' quarter by the river: a district commonly as foul-tongued as it was ill-favoured, but tonight clean-purged of both evils by the vehement sweep of the storm. Here he groped his way among slippery places and past huddled out-buildings to the piles of the wharf. The rain was now subdued to a noiseless vertical descent, through which he could hear the tap of the river against the piles. Scarce knowing what he fled or whither he was flying, he let himself down the steps and found the flat of a boat's bottom underfoot. A boatman, distinguishable only as a black bulk in the stern, steadied his descent with outstretched hand; then the bow swung round, and after a labouring stroke or two they caught the current and were swept down through the rushing darkness.

BOOK III.
THE CHOICE.

The Vision touched him on the lips and said:
Hereafter thou shalt eat me in thy bread,
Drink me in all thy kisses, feel my hand
Steal 'twixt thy palm and Joy's, and see me stand
Watchful at every crossing of the ways,
The insatiate lover of thy nights and days.

3.1.

It was at Naples, some two years later, that the circumstances of his flight were recalled to Odo Valsecca by the sound of a voice which at once mysteriously connected itself with the incidents of that wild night.

He was seated with a party of gentlemen in the saloon of Sir William Hamilton's famous villa of Posilipo, where they were sipping the ambassador's iced sherbet and examining certain engraved gems and burial-urns recently taken from the excavations. The scene was such as always appealed to Odo's fancy: the spacious room, luxuriously fitted with carpets and curtains in the English style, and opening on a prospect of classical beauty and antique renown; in his hands the rarest specimens of that buried art which, like some belated golden harvest, was now everywhere thrusting itself through the Neapolitan soil; and about him men of taste and understanding, discussing the historic or mythological meaning of the objects before them, and quoting Homer or Horace in corroboration of their guesses.

Several visitors had joined the party since Odo's entrance; and it was from a group of these later arrivals that the voice had reached him. He looked round and saw a man of refined and scholarly appearance, dressed en abbe, as was the general habit in Rome and Naples, and holding in one hand the celebrated blue vase cut in cameo which Sir William had recently purchased from the Barberini family.

"These reliefs," the stranger was saying, "whether cut in the substance itself, or afterward affixed to the glass, certainly belong to the Grecian period of cameo-work, and recall by the purity of their design the finest carvings of Dioskorides." His beautifully-modulated Italian was tinged by a slight foreign accent, which seemed to connect him still more definitely with the episode his voice recalled. Odo turned to a gentleman at his side and asked the speaker's name.

"That," was the reply, "is the abate de Crucis, a scholar and cognoscente, as you perceive, and at present attached to the household of the Papal Nuncio."

Instantly Odo beheld the tumultuous scene in the Duke's apartments, and heard the indictment of Heiligenstern falling in tranquil accents from the very lips which were now, in the same tone, discussing the date of a Greek cameo vase. Even in that moment of disorder he had been struck by the voice and aspect of the agent of the Holy Office, and by a singular distinction that seemed to set the man himself above the coil of passions in which his action was involved. To Odo's spontaneous yet reflective temper there was something peculiarly impressive in the kind of detachment which implies, not obtuseness or indifference, but a higher sensitiveness disciplined by choice. Now he felt a renewed pang of regret that such qualities should be found in the service of the opposition; but the feeling was not incompatible with a wish to be more nearly acquainted with their possessor.

The two years elapsing since Odo's departure from Pianura had widened if they had not lifted his outlook. If he had lost something of his early enthusiasm he had exchanged it for a larger experience of cities and men, and for the self-command born of varied intercourse. He had reached a point where he was able to survey his past dispassionately and to disentangle the threads of the intrigue in which he had so nearly lost his footing. The actual circumstances of his escape were still wrapped in mystery: he could only conjecture that the Duchess, foreseeing the course events would take, had planned with Cantapresto to save him in spite of himself. His nocturnal flight down the river had carried him to Ponte di Po, the point where the Piana flows into the Po, the latter river forming for a few miles the southern frontier of the duchy. Here his passport had taken him safely past the customs-officer, and following the indications of the boatman, he had found, outside the miserable village clustered about the customs, a travelling-chaise which brought him before the next night-fall to Monte Alloro.

Of the real danger from which this timely retreat had removed him, Gamba's subsequent letters had brought ample proof. It was indeed mainly against himself that both parties, perhaps jointly, had directed their attack; designing to take him in the toils ostensibly prepared for the Illuminati. His evasion known, the Holy Office had contented itself with imprisoning Heiligenstern in one of the Papal fortresses near the Adriatic, while his mistress, though bred in the Greek confession, was confined in a convent of the Sepolte Vive and his Oriental servant sent to the Duke's galleys. As to those suspected of affiliations with the forbidden sect, fines and penances were imposed on a few of the least conspicuous, while the chief offenders, either from motives of policy or thanks to their superior adroitness, were suffered to escape without a reprimand. After this, Gamba's letters reported, the duchy had lapsed into its former state of quiescence. Prince Ferrante had been seriously ailing since the night of the electrical treatment, but the Pope having sent his private physician to Pianura, the boy had rallied under the latter's care. The Duke, as was natural, had suffered an acute relapse of piety, spending his time in expiatory pilgrimages to the various votive churches of the duchy, and declining to transact any public business till he should have compiled with his own hand a calendar of the lives of the saints, with the initial letters painted in miniature, which he designed to present to his Holiness at Easter.

Meanwhile Odo, at Monte Alloro, found himself in surroundings so different from those he had left that it seemed incredible they should exist in the same world. The Duke of Monte Alloro was that rare survival of a stronger age, a cynic. In a period of sentimental optimism, of fervid enthusiasms and tearful philanthropy, he represented the pleasure-loving prince of the Renaissance, crushing his people with taxes but dazzling them with festivities; infuriating them by his disregard of the public welfare, but fascinating them by his good looks, his tolerance of old abuses, his ridicule of the monks, and by the careless libertinage which had founded the fortunes of more than one middle-class husband and father—for the Duke always paid well for what he appropriated. He had grown old in his pleasant sins, and these, as such raiment will, had grown old and dingy with him; but if no longer splendid he was still splendour-loving, and drew to his court the most brilliant adventurers of Italy. Spite of his preference for such company, he had a nobler side, the ruins of a fine but uncultivated intelligence, and a taste for all that was young, generous and high in looks and courage. He was at once drawn to Odo, who instinctively addressed himself to these qualities, and whose conversation and manners threw into relief the vulgarity of the old Duke's cronies. The latter was the shrewd enough to enjoy the contrast at the expense of his sycophants' vanity; and the cavaliere Valsecca was for a while the reigning favourite. It would have been hard to say whether his patron was most tickled by his zeal for economic reforms, or by his faith in the perfectibility of man. Both these articles of Odo's creed drew tears of enjoyment from the old Duke's puffy eyes; and he was never tired of declaring that only his hatred for his nephew of Pianura induced him to accord his protection to so dangerous an enemy of society.

Odo at first fancied that it was in response to a mere whim of the Duke's that he had been despatched to Monte Alloro; but he soon perceived that the invitation had been inspired by Maria Clementina's wish. Some three months after Odo's arrival, Cantapresto suddenly appeared with a packet of letters from the Duchess. Among them her Highness had included a few lines to Odo, whom she briefly adjured not to return to Pianura, but to comply in all things with her uncle's desires. Soon after this the old Duke sent for Odo, and asked him how his present mode of life agreed with his tastes. Odo, who had learned that frankness was the surest way to the Duke's favour, replied that, while nothing could be more agreeable than the circumstances of his sojourn at Monte Alloro, he must own to a wish to travel when the occasion offered.

"Why, this is as I fancied," replied the Duke, who held in his hand an open letter on which Odo recognised Maria Clementina's seal. "We have always," he continued, "spoken plainly with each other, and I will not conceal from you that it is for your best interests that you should remain away from Pianura for the present. The Duke, as you doubtless divine, is anxious for your return, and her Highness, for that very reason, is urgent that you should prolong your absence. It is notorious that the Duke soon wearies of those about him, and that your best chance of regaining his favour is to keep out of his reach and let your enemies hang themselves in the noose they have prepared for you. For my part, I am always glad to do an ill-turn to that snivelling friar, my nephew, and the more so when I can seriously oblige a friend; and, as you have perhaps guessed, the Duke dares not ask for your return while I show a fancy for your company. But this," added he with an ironical twinkle, "is a tame place for a young man of your missionary temper, and I have a mind to send you on a visit to that arch-tyrant Ferdinand of Naples, in whose dominions a man may yet burn for heresy or be drawn and quartered for poaching on a nobleman's preserves. I am advised that some rare treasures have lately been taken from the excavations there and I should be glad if you would oblige me by acquiring a few for my gallery. I will give you letters to a cognoscente of my acquaintance, who will put his experience at the disposal of your excellent taste, and the funds at your service will, I hope, enable you to outbid the English brigands who, as the Romans say, would carry off the Colosseum if it were portable."

In all this Odo discerned Maria Clementina's hand, and an instinctive resistance made him hang back upon his patron's proposal. But the only alternative was to return to Pianura; and every letter from Gamba urged on him (for the very reasons the Duke had given) the duty of keeping out of reach as the surest means of saving himself and the cause to which he was pledged. Nothing remained but a graceful acquiescence; and early the next spring he started for Naples.

His first impulse had been to send Cantapresto back to the Duchess. He knew that he owed his escape me grave difficulties to the soprano's prompt action on the night of Heiligenstern's arrest; but he was equally sure that such action might not always be as favourable to his plans. It was plain that Cantapresto was paid to spy on him, and that whenever Odo's intentions clashed with those of his would-be protectors the soprano would side with the latter. But there was something in the air of Monte Alloro which dispelled such considerations, or at least weakened the impulse to act on them. Cantapresto as usual had attracted notice at court. His glibness and versatility amused the Duke, and to Odo he was as difficult to put off as a bad habit. He had become so accomplished a servant that he seemed a sixth sense of his master's; and when the latter prepared to start on his travels Cantapresto took his usual seat in the chaise.

To a traveller of Odo's temper there could be few more agreeable journeys than the one on which he was setting out, and the Duke being in no haste to have his commission executed, his messenger had full leisure to enjoy every stage of the way. He profited by this to visit several of the small principalities north of the Apennines before turning toward Genoa, whence he was to take ship for the South. When he left Monte Alloro the land had worn the bleached face of February, and it was amazing to his northern-bred eyes to find himself, on the sea-coast, in the full exuberance of summer. Seated by this halcyon shore, Genoa, in its carved and frescoed splendour, just then celebrating with the customary gorgeous ritual the accession of a new Doge, seemed to Odo like the richly-inlaid frame of some Renaissance "triumph." But the splendid houses with their marble peristyles, and the painted villas in their orange-groves along the shore, housed a dull and narrow-minded society, content to amass wealth and play biribi under the eyes of their ancestral Vandykes, without any concern as to the questions agitating the world. A kind of fat commercial dulness, a lack of that personal distinction which justifies magnificence, seemed to Odo the prevailing note of the place; nor was he sorry when his packet set sail for Naples.

Here indeed he found all the vivacity that Genoa lacked. Few cities could at first acquaintance be more engaging to the stranger. Dull and brown as it appeared after the rich tints of Genoa, yet so gloriously did sea and land embrace it, so lavishly the sun gild and the moon silver it, that it seemed steeped in the surrounding hues of nature. And what a nature to eyes subdued to the sober tints of the north! Its spectacular quality—that studied sequence of effects ranging from the translucent outline of Capri and the fantastically blue mountains of the coast, to Vesuvius lifting its torch above the plain—this prodigal response to fancy's claims suggested the boundless invention of some great scenic artist, some Olympian Veronese with sea and sky for a palette. And then the city itself, huddled between bay and mountains, and seething and bubbling like a Titan's cauldron! Here was life at its source, not checked, directed, utilised, but gushing forth uncontrollably through every fissure of the brown walls and reeking streets—love and hatred, mirth and folly, impudence and greed, going naked and unashamed as the lazzaroni on the quays. The variegated surface of it all was fascinating to Odo. It set free his powers of purely physical enjoyment, keeping all deeper sensations in abeyance. These, however, presently found satisfaction in that other hidden beauty of which city and plain were but the sumptuous drapery. It is hardly too much to say that to the trained eyes of the day the visible Naples hardly existed, so absorbed were they in the perusal of her buried past. The fever of excavation was on every one. No social or political problem could find a hearing while the subject of the last coin or bas-relief from Pompeii or Herculanaeum remained undecided. Odo, at first an amused spectator, gradually found himself engrossed in the fierce quarrels raging over the date of an intaglio or the myth represented on an amphora. The intrinsic beauty of the objects, and the light they shed on one of the most brilliant phases of human history, were in fact sufficient to justify the prevailing ardour; and the reconstructive habit he had acquired from Crescenti lent a living interest to the driest discussion between rival collectors.

Gradually other influences reasserted themselves. At the house of Sir William Hamilton, then the centre of the most polished society in Naples, he met not only artists and archeologists, but men of letters and of affairs. Among these, he was peculiarly drawn to the two distinguished economists, the abate Galiani and the cavaliere Filangieri, in whose company he enjoyed for the first time sound learning unhampered by pedantry. The lively Galiani proved that social tastes and a broad wit are not incompatible with more serious interests; and Filangieri threw the charm of a graceful personality over any topic he discussed. In the latter, indeed, courtly, young and romantic, a thinker whose intellectual acuteness was steeped in moral emotion, Odo beheld the type of the new chivalry, an ideal leader of the campaign against social injustice. Filangieri represented the extremest optimism of the day. His sense of existing abuses was only equalled by his faith in their speedy amendment. Love was to cure all evils: the love of man for man, the effusive all-embracing sympathy of the school of the Vicaire Savoyard, was to purge the emotions by tenderness and pity. In Gamba, the victim of the conditions he denounced, the sense of present hardship prevailed over the faith in future improvement; while Filangieri's social superiority mitigated his view of the evils and magnified the efficacy of the proposed remedies. Odo's days passed agreeably in such intercourse, or in the excitement of excursions to the ruined cities; and as the court and the higher society of Naples offered little to engage him, he gradually restricted himself to the small circle of chosen spirits gathered at the villa Hamilton. To these he fancied the abate de Crucis might prove an interesting addition; and the desire to learn something of this problematic person induced him to quit the villa at the moment when the abate took leave.

They found themselves together on the threshold; and Odo, recalling to the other the circumstances of their first meeting, proposed that they should dismiss their carriages and regain the city on foot. De Crucis readily consented; and they were soon descending the hill of Posilipo. Here and there a turn in the road brought them to an open space whence they commanded the bay from Procida to Sorrento, with Capri afloat in liquid gold and the long blue shadow of Vesuvius stretching like a menace toward the city. The spectacle was one of which Odo never wearied; but today it barely diverted him from the charms of his companion's talk. The abate de Crucis had that quality of repressed enthusiasm, of an intellectual sensibility tempered by self-possession, which exercises the strongest attraction over a mind not yet master of itself. Though all he said had a personal note he seemed to withhold himself even in the moment of greatest expansion: like some prince who should enrich his favourites from the public treasury but keep his private fortune unimpaired. In the course of their conversation Odo learned that though of Austrian birth his companion was of mingled English and Florentine parentage: a fact perhaps explaining the mixture of urbanity and reserve that lent such charm to his manner. He told Odo that his connection with the Holy Office had been only temporary, and that, having contracted a severe cold the previous winter in Germany, he had accepted a secretaryship in the service of the Papal Nuncio in order to enjoy the benefits of a mild climate. "By profession," he added, "I am a pedagogue, and shall soon travel to Rome, where I have been called by Prince Bracciano to act as governor to his son; and meanwhile I am taking advantage of my residence here to indulge my taste for antiquarian studies."

He went on to praise the company they had just left, declaring that he knew no better way for a young man to form his mind than by frequenting the society of men of conflicting views and equal capacity. "Nothing," said he, "is more injurious to the growth of character than to be secluded from argument and opposition; as nothing is healthier than to be obliged to find good reasons for one's beliefs on pain of surrendering them."

"But," said Odo, struck with this declaration, "to a man of your cloth there is one belief which never surrenders to reason."

The other smiled. "True," he agreed; "but I often marvel to see how little our opponents know of that belief. The wisest of them seem in the case of those children at our country fairs who gape at the incredible things depicted on the curtains of the booths, without asking themselves whether the reality matches its presentment. The weakness of human nature has compelled us to paint the outer curtain of the sanctuary in gaudy colours, and the malicious fancy of our enemies has given a monstrous outline to these pictures; but what are such vanities to one who has passed beyond, and beheld the beauty of the King's daughter, all glorious within?"

As though unwilling to linger on such grave topics, he turned the talk to the scene at their feet, questioning Odo as to the impression Naples had made on him. He listened courteously to the young man's comments on the wretched state of the peasantry, the extravagances of the court and nobility and the judicial corruption which made the lower classes submit to any injustice rather than seek redress through the courts. De Crucis agreed with him in the main, admitting that the monopoly of corn, the maintenance of feudal rights and the King's indifference to the graver duties of his rank placed the kingdom of Naples far below such states as Tuscany or Venetia; "though," he added, "I think our economists, in praising one state at the expense of another, too often overlook those differences of character and climate that must ever make it impossible to govern different races in the same manner. Our peasants have a blunt saying: Cut off the dog's tail and he is still a dog; and so I suspect the most enlightened rule would hardly bring this prompt and choleric people, living on a volcanic soil amid a teeming vegetation, into any resemblance with the clear-headed Tuscan or the gentle and dignified Roman."

As he spoke they emerged upon the Chiaia, where at that hour the quality took the air in their carriages, while the lower classes thronged the footway. A more vivacious scene no city of Europe could present. The gilt coaches drawn by six or eight of the lively Neapolitan horses, decked with plumes and artificial flowers and preceded by running footmen who beat the foot-passengers aside with long staves; the richly-dressed ladies seated in this never-ending file of carriages, bejewelled like miraculous images and languidly bowing to their friends; the throngs of citizens and their wives in holiday dress; the sellers of sherbet, ices and pastry bearing their trays and barrels through the crowd with strange cries and the jingling of bells; the friars of every order in their various habits, the street-musicians, the half-naked lazzaroni, cripples and beggars, who fringed the throng like the line of scum edging a fair lake;—this medley of sound and colour, which in fact resembled some sudden growth of the fiery soil, was an expressive comment on the abate's words.

"Look," he continued, as he and Odo drew aside to escape the mud from an emblazoned chariot, "at the gold-leaf on the panels of that coach and the gold-lace on the liveries of those lacqueys. Is there any other city in the world where gold is so prodigally used? Where the monks gild their relics, the nobility their servants, the apothecaries their pills, the very butchers their mutton? One might fancy their bright sun had set them the example! And how cold and grey all soberer tints must seem to these children of Apollo! Well—so it is with their religion and their daily life. I wager half those naked wretches yonder would rather attend a fine religious service, with abundance of gilt candles, music from gilt organ-pipes, and incense from gilt censers, than eat a good meal or sleep in a decent bed; as they would rather starve under a handsome merry King that has the name of being the best billiard-player in Europe than go full under one of your solemn reforming Austrian Archdukes!"

The words recalled to Odo Crescenti's theory of the influence of character and climate on the course of history; and this subject soon engrossing both speakers, they wandered on, inattentive to their surroundings, till they found themselves in the thickest concourse of the Toledo. Here for a moment the dense crowd hemmed them in; and as they stood observing the humours of the scene, Odo's eye fell on the thick-set figure of a man in doctor's dress, who was being led through the press by two agents of the Inquisition. The sight was too common to have fixed his attention, had he not recognised with a start the irascible red-faced professor who, on his first visit to Vivaldi, had defended the Diluvial theory of creation. The sight raised a host of memories from which Odo would gladly have beaten a retreat; but the crowd held him in check and a moment later he saw that the doctor's eyes were fixed on him with an air of recognition. A movement of pity succeeded his first impulse, and turning to de Crucis he exclaimed:—"I see yonder an old acquaintance who seems in an unlucky plight and with whom I should be glad to speak."

The other, following his glance, beckoned to one of the sbirri, who made his way through the throng with the alacrity of one summoned by a superior. De Crucis exchanged a few words with him, and then signed to him to return to his charge, who presently vanished in some fresh shifting of the crowd.

"Your friend," said de Crucis, "has been summoned before the Holy Office to answer a charge of heresy preferred by the authorities. He has lately been appointed to the chair of physical sciences in the University here, and has doubtless allowed himself to publish openly views that were better expounded in the closet. His offence, however, appears to be a mild one, and I make no doubt he will be set free in a few days."

This, however, did not satisfy Odo; and he asked de Crucis if there were no way of speaking with the doctor at once.

His companion hesitated. "It can easily be arranged," said he; "but—pardon me, cavaliere—are you well-advised in mixing yourself in such matters?"

"I am well-advised in seeking to serve a friend!" Odo somewhat hotly returned; and de Crucis, with a faint smile of approval, replied quietly: "In that case I will obtain permission for you to visit your friend in the morning."

He was true to his word; and the next forenoon Odo, accompanied by an officer of police, was taken to the prison of the Inquisition. Here he found his old acquaintance seated in a clean commodious room and reading Aristotle's "History of Animals," the only volume of his library that he had been permitted to carry with him. He welcomed Odo heartily, and on the latter's enquiring what had brought him to this plight, replied with some dignity that he had been led there in the fulfilment of his duty.

"Some months ago," he continued, "I was summoned hither to profess the natural sciences in the University; a summons I readily accepted, since I hoped, by the study of a volcanic soil, to enlarge my knowledge of the globe's formation. Such in fact was the case, but to my surprise my researches led me to adopt the views I had formerly combated, and I now find myself in the ranks of the Vulcanists, or believers in the secondary origin of the earth: a view you may remember I once opposed with all the zeal of inexperience. Having firmly established every point in my argument according to the Baconian method of investigation, I felt it my duty to enlighten my scholars; and in the course of my last lecture I announced the result of my investigations. I was of course aware of the inevitable result; but the servants of Truth have no choice but to follow where she calls, and many have joyfully traversed stonier places than I am likely to travel."

Nothing could exceed the respect with which Odo heard this simple confession of faith. It was as though the speaker had unconsciously convicted him of remissness, of cowardice even; so vain and windy his theorising seemed, judged by the other's deliberate act! Yet placed as he was, what could he do, how advance their common end, but by passively waiting on events? At least, he reflected, he could perform the trivial service of trying to better his friend's case; and this he eagerly offered to attempt. The doctor thanked him, but without any great appearance of emotion: Odo was struck by the change which had transformed a heady and intemperate speaker into a model of philosophic calm. The doctor, indeed, seemed far more concerned for the safety of his library and his cabinet of minerals than for his own. "Happily," said he, "I am not a man of family, and can therefore sacrifice my liberty with a clear conscience: a fact I am the more thankful for when I recall the moral distress of our poor friend Vivaldi, when compelled to desert his post rather than be separated from his daughter."

The name brought the colour to Odo's brow, and with an embarrassed air he asked what news the doctor had of their friend.

"Alas," said the other, "the last was of his death, which happened two years since in Pavia. The Sardinian government had, as you probably know, confiscated his small property on his leaving the state, and I am told he died in great poverty, and in sore anxiety for his daughter's future." He added that these events had taken place before his own departure from Turin, and that since then he had learned nothing of Fulvia's fate, save that she was said to have made her home with an aunt who lived in a town of the Veneto.

Odo listened in silence. The lapse of time, and the absence of any links of association, had dimmed the girl's image in his breast; but at the mere sound of her name it lived again, and he felt her interwoven with his deepest fibres. The picture of her father's death and of her own need filled him with an ineffectual pity, and for a moment he thought of seeking her out; but the other could recall neither the name of the town she had removed to nor that of the relative who had given her a home.

To aid the good doctor was a simpler business. The intervention of de Crucis and Odo's own influence sufficed to effect his release, and on the payment of a heavy fine (in which Odo privately assisted him) he was reinstated in his chair. The only promise exacted by the Holy Office was that he should in future avoid propounding his own views on questions already decided by Scripture, and to this he readily agreed, since, as he shrewdly remarked to Odo, his opinions were now well-known, and any who wished farther instruction had only to apply to him privately.

The old Duke having invited Odo to return to Monte Alloro with such treasures as he had collected for the ducal galleries, the young man resolved to visit Rome on his way to the North. His acquaintance with de Crucis had grown into something like friendship since their joint effort in behalf of the imprisoned sage, and the abate preparing to set out about the same time, the two agreed to travel together. The road leading from Naples to Rome was at that time one of the worst in Italy, and was besides so ill-provided with inns that there was no inducement to linger on the way. De Crucis, however, succeeded in enlivening even this tedious journey. He was a good linguist and a sound classical scholar, besides having, as he had told Odo, a pronounced taste for antiquarian research. In addition to this, he performed agreeably on the violin, and was well-acquainted with the history of music. His chief distinction, however, lay in the ease with which he wore his accomplishments, and in a breadth of view that made it possible to discuss with him many subjects distasteful to most men of his cloth. The sceptical or licentious ecclesiastic was common enough; but Odo had never before met a priest who united serious piety with this indulgent temper, or who had learning enough to do justice to the arguments of his opponents.

On his venturing one evening to compliment de Crucis on these qualities, the latter replied with a smile: "Whatever has been lately advanced against the Jesuits, it can hardly be denied that they were good school-masters; and it is to them I owe the talents you have been pleased to admire. Indeed," he continued, quietly fingering his violin, "I was myself bred in the order: a fact I do not often make known in the present heated state of public opinion, but which I never conceal when commended for any quality that I owe to the Society rather than to my own merit."

Surprise for the moment silenced Odo; for though it was known that Italy was full of former Jesuits who had been permitted to remain in the country as secular priests, and even to act as tutors or professors in private families, he had never thought of de Crucis in this connection. The latter, seeing his surprise, went on: "Once a Jesuit, always a Jesuit, I suppose. I at least owe the Society too much not to own my debt when the occasion offers. Nor could I ever see the force of the charge so often brought against us: that we sacrifice everything to the glory of the order. For what is the glory of the order? Our own motto has declared it: Ad majorem Dei gloriam—who works for the Society works for its Master. If our zeal has been sometimes misdirected, our blood has a thousand times witnessed to its sincerity. In the Indies, in America, in England during the great persecution, and lately on our own unnatural coasts, the Jesuits have died for Christ as joyfully as His first disciples died for Him. Yet these are but a small number in comparison with the countless servants of the order who, labouring in far countries among savage peoples, or surrounded by the heretical enemies of our faith, have died the far bitterer death of moral isolation: setting themselves to their task with the knowledge that their lives were but so much indistinguishable dust to be added to the sum of human effort. What association founded on human interests has ever commanded such devotion? And what merely human authority could count on such unquestioning obedience, not in a mob of poor illiterate monks, but in men chosen for their capacity and trained to the exercise of their highest faculties? Yet there have never lacked such men to serve the Order; and as one of our enemies has said—our noblest enemy, the great Pascal—'je crois volontiers aux histoires dont les temoins se font egorger.'"

He did not again revert to his connection with the Jesuits; but in the farther course of their acquaintance Odo was often struck by the firmness with which he testified to the faith that was in him, without using the jargon of piety, or seeming, by his own attitude, to cast a reflection on that of others. He was indeed master of that worldly science which the Jesuits excelled in imparting, and which, though it might sink to hypocrisy in smaller natures, became in a finely-tempered spirit, the very flower of Christian courtesy.

Odo had often spoken to de Crucis of the luxurious lives led by many of the monastic orders in Naples. It might be true enough that the monks themselves, and even their abbots, fared on fish and vegetables, and gave their time to charitable and educational work; but it was impossible to visit the famous monastery of San Martino, or that of the Carthusians at Camaldoli, without observing that the anchoret's cell had expanded into a delightful apartment, with bedchamber, library and private chapel, and his cabbage-plot into a princely garden. De Crucis admitted the truth of the charge, explaining it in part by the character of the Neapolitan people, and by the tendency of the northern traveller to forget that such apparent luxuries as spacious rooms, shady groves and the like are regarded as necessities in a hot climate. He urged, moreover, that the monastic life should not be judged by a few isolated instances; and on the way to Rome he proposed that Odo, by way of seeing the other side of the question, should visit the ancient foundation of the Benedictines on Monte Cassino.

The venerable monastery, raised on its height over the busy vale of Garigliano, like some contemplative spirit above the conflicting problems of life, might well be held to represent the nobler side of Christian celibacy. For nearly a thousand years its fortified walls had been the stronghold of the humanities, and generations of students had cherished and added to the treasures of the famous library. But the Benedictine rule was as famous for good works as for learning, and its comparative abstention from dogmatic controversy and from the mechanical devotion of some of the other orders had drawn to it men of superior mind, who sought in the monastic life the free exercise of the noblest activities rather than a sanctified refuge from action. This was especially true of the monastery of Monte Cassino, whither many scholars had been attracted and where the fathers had long had the highest name for learning and beneficence. The monastery, moreover, in addition to its charitable and educational work among the poor, maintained a school of theology to which students came from all parts of Italy; and their presence lent an unwonted life to the great labyrinth of courts and cloisters.

The abbot, with whom de Crucis was well-acquainted, welcomed the travellers warmly, making them free of the library and the archives and pressing them to prolong their visit. Under the spell of these influences they lingered on from day to day; and to Odo they were the pleasantest days he had known. To be waked before dawn by the bell ringing for lauds—to rise from the narrow bed in his white-washed cell, and opening his casement look forth over the haze-enveloped valley, the dark hills of the Abruzzi and the remote gleam of sea touched into being by the sunrise—to hasten through hushed echoing corridors to the church, where in a grey resurrection-light the fathers were intoning the solemn office of renewal—this morning ablution of the spirit, so like the bodily plunge into clear cold water, seemed to attune the mind to the fullest enjoyment of what was to follow: the hours of study, the talks with the monks, the strolls through cloister or garden, all punctuated by the recurring summons to devotion. Yet for all its latent significance it remained to him a purely sensuous impression, the vision of a golden leisure: not a solution of life's perplexities, but at best an honourable escape from them.

3.2.

"To know Rome is to have assisted at the councils of destiny!" This cry of a more famous traveller must have struggled for expression in Odo's breast as the great city, the city of cities, laid her irresistible hold upon him. His first impression, as he drove in the clear evening light from the Porta del Popolo to his lodgings in the Via Sistina, was of a prodigious accumulation of architectural effects, a crowding of century on century, all fused in the crucible of the Roman sun, so that each style seemed linked to the other by some subtle affinity of colour. Nowhere else, surely, is the traveller's first sight so crowded with surprises, with conflicting challenges to eye and brain. Here, as he passed, was a fragment of the ancient Servian wall, there a new stucco shrine embedded in the bricks of a medieval palace; on one hand a lofty terrace crowned by a row of mouldering busts, on the other a tower with machicolated parapet, its flanks encrusted with bits of Roman sculpture and the escutcheons of seventeenth-century Popes. Opposite, perhaps, one of Fuga's golden-brown churches, with windy saints blowing out of their niches, overlooked the nereids of a barocco fountain, or an old house propped itself like a palsied beggar against a row of Corinthian columns; while everywhere flights of steps led up and down to hanging gardens or under archways, and each turn revealed some distant glimpse of convent-walls on the slope of a vineyard or of red-brown ruins profiled against the dim sea-like reaches of the Campagna.

Afterward, as order was born out of chaos, and he began to thread his way among the centuries, this first vision lost something of its intensity; yet it was always, to the last, through the eye that Rome possessed him. Her life, indeed, as though in obedience to such a setting, was an external, a spectacular business, from the wild animation of the cattle-market in the Forum or the hucksters' traffic among the fountains of the Piazza Navona, to the pompous entertainments in the cardinals' palaces and the ever-recurring religious ceremonies and processions. Pius VI., in the reaction from Ganganelli's democratic ways, had restored the pomp and ceremonial of the Vatican with the religious discipline of the Holy Office; and never perhaps had Rome been more splendid on the surface or more silent and empty within. Odo, at times, as he moved through some assemblage of cardinals and nobles, had the sensation of walking through a huge reverberating palace, decked out with all the splendours of art but long since abandoned of men. The superficial animation, the taste for music and antiquities, all the dilettantisms of an idle and irresponsible society, seemed to him to shrivel to dust in the glare of that great past that lit up every corner of the present.

Through his own connections, and the influence of de Crucis, he saw all that was best not only among the nobility, but in that ecclesiastical life now more than ever predominant in Rome. Here at last he was face to face with the mighty Sphinx, and with the bleaching bones of those who had tried to guess her riddle. Wherever he went these "lost adventurers" walked the streets with him, gliding between the Princes of the Church in the ceremonies of Saint Peter's and the Lateran, or mingling in the company that ascended the state staircase at some cardinal's levee.

He met indeed many accomplished and amiable ecclesiastics, but it seemed to him that the more thoughtful among them had either acquired their peace of mind at the cost of a certain sensitiveness, or had taken refuge in a study of the past, as the early hermits fled to the desert from the disorders of Antioch and Alexandria. None seemed disposed to face the actual problems of life, and this attitude of caution or indifference had produced a stagnation of thought that contrasted strongly with the animation of Sir William Hamilton's circle in Naples. The result in Odo's case was a reaction toward the pleasures of his age; and of these Rome had but few to offer. He spent some months in the study of the antique, purchasing a few good examples of sculpture for the Duke, and then, without great reluctance, set out for Monte Alloro.

Here he found a changed atmosphere. The Duke welcomed him handsomely, and bestowed the highest praise on the rarities he had collected; but for the moment the court was ruled by a new favourite, to whom Odo's coming was obviously unwelcome. This adroit adventurer, whose name was soon to become notorious throughout Europe, had taken the old prince by his darling weaknesses, and Odo, having no mind to share in the excesses of the precious couple, seized the first occasion to set out again on his travels.

His course had now become one of aimless wandering; for prudence still forbade his return to Pianura, and his patron's indifference left him free to come and go as he chose. He had brought from Rome—that albergo d'ira— a settled melancholy of spirit, which sought refuge in such distractions as the moment offered. In such a mood change of scene was a necessity, and he resolved to employ the next months in visiting several of the mid-Italian cities. Toward Florence he was specially drawn by the fact that Alfieri now lived there; but, as often happens after such separations, the reunion was a disappointment. Alfieri, indeed, warmly welcomed his friend; but he was engrossed in his dawning passion for the Countess of Albany, and that lady's pitiable situation excluded all other interests from his mind. To Odo, to whom the years had brought an increasing detachment, this self-absorption seemed an arrest in growth; for Alfieri's early worship of liberty had not yet found its destined channel of expression, and for the moment his enthusiasms had shrunk to the compass of a romantic adventure. The friends parted after a few days of unsatisfying intercourse; and it was under the influence of this final disenchantment that Odo set out for Venice.

It was the vintage season, and the travellers descended from the Apennines on a landscape diversified by the picturesque incidents of the grape-gathering. On every slope stood some villa with awnings spread, and merry parties were picnicking among the vines or watching the peasants at their work. Cantapresto, who had shown great reluctance at leaving Monte Alloro, where, as he declared, he found himself as snug as an eel in a pasty, was now all eagerness to press forward; and Odo was in the mood to allow any influence to decide his course. He had an invaluable courier in Cantapresto, whose enormous pretensions generally assured him the best lodging and the fastest conveyance to be obtained, and who was never happier than when outwitting a rival emissary, or bribing a landlord to serve up on Odo's table the repast ordered in advance for some distinguished traveller. His impatience to reach Venice, which he described as the scene of all conceivable delights, had on this occasion tripled his zeal, and they travelled rapidly to Padua, where he had engaged a burchiello for the passage down the Brenta. Here, however, he found he had been outdone at his own game; for the servant of an English Duke had captured the burchiello and embarked his noble party before Cantapresto reached the wharf. This being the season of the villeggiatura, when the Venetian nobility were exchanging visits on the mainland, every conveyance was in motion and no other boat to be had for a week; while as for the "bucentaur" or public bark, which was just then getting under way, it was already packed to the gunwale with Jews, pedlars and such vermin, and the captain swore by the three thousand relics of Saint Justina that he had no room on board for so much as a hungry flea.

Odo, who had accompanied Cantapresto to the water-side, was listening to these assurances and to the soprano's vain invectives, when a well-dressed young man stepped up to the group. This gentleman, whose accent and dress showed him to be a Frenchman of quality, told Odo that he was come from Vicenza, whither he had gone to engage a company of actors for his friend the Procuratore Bra, who was entertaining a distinguished company at his villa on the Brenta; that he was now returning with his players, and that he would be glad to convey Odo so far on his road to Venice. His friend's seat, he added, was near Oriago, but a few miles above Fusina, where a public conveyance might always be found; so that Odo would doubtless be able to proceed the same night to Venice.

This civil offer Odo at once accepted, and the Frenchman thereupon suggested that, as the party was to set out the next day at sunrise, the two should sup together and pass the intervening hours in such diversions as the city offered. They returned to the inn, where the actors were also lodged, and Odo's host having ordered a handsome supper, proposed, with his guest's permission, to invite the leading members of the company to partake of it. He departed on this errand; and great was Odo's wonder, when the door reopened, to discover, among the party it admitted, his old acquaintance of Vercelli, the Count of Castelrovinato. The latter, whose dress and person had been refurbished, and who now wore an air of rakish prosperity, greeted him with evident pleasure, and, while their entertainer was engaged in seating the ladies of the company, gave him a brief account of the situation.

The young French gentleman (whom he named as the Marquis de Coeur-Volant) had come to Italy some months previously on the grand tour, and having fallen a victim to the charms of Venice, had declared that, instead of continuing on his travels, he meant to complete his education in that famous school of pleasure. Being master of his own fortune, he had hired a palace on the Grand Canal, had dispatched his governor (a simple archaeologist) on a mission of exploration to Sicily and Greece, and had devoted himself to an assiduous study of Venetian manners. Among those contributing to his instruction was Mirandolina of Chioggia, who had just completed a successful engagement at the theatre of San Moise in Venice. Wishing to detain her in the neighbourhood, her adorer had prevailed on his friend the Procuratore to give a series of comedies at his villa of Bellocchio and had engaged to provide him with a good company of performers. Miranda was of course selected as prima amorosa; and the Marquess, under Castelrovinato's guidance, had then set out to collect the rest of the company. This he had succeeded in doing, and was now returning to Bellocchio, where Miranda was to meet them. Odo was the more diverted at the hazard which had brought him into such company, as the Procuratore Bra was one of the noblemen to whom the old Duke had specially recommended him. On learning this, the Marquess urged him to present his letter of introduction on arriving at Bellocchio, where the Procuratore, who was noted for hospitality to strangers, would doubtless insist on his joining the assembled party. This Odo declined to do; but his curiosity to see Mirandolina made him hope that chance would soon throw him in the Procuratore's way.

Meanwhile supper was succeeded by music and dancing, and the company broke up only in time to proceed to the landing-place where their barge awaited them. This was a private burchiello of the Procuratore's with a commodious antechamber for the servants, and a cabin cushioned in damask. Into this agreeable retreat the actresses were packed with all their bags and band-boxes; and their travelling-cloaks being rolled into pillows, they were soon asleep in a huddle of tumbled finery.

Odo and his host preferred to take the air on deck. The sun was rising above the willow-clad banks of the Brenta, and it was pleasant to glide in the clear early light past sleeping gardens and villas, and vineyards where the peasants were already at work. The wind setting from the sea, they travelled slowly and had full leisure to view the succession of splendid seats interspersed with gardens, the thriving villages, and the poplar-groves festooned with vines. Coeur-Volant spoke eloquently of the pleasures to be enjoyed in this delightful season of the villeggiatura. "Nowhere," said he, "do people take their pleasures so easily and naturally as in Venice. My countrymen claim a superiority in this art, and it may be they possessed it a generation ago. But what a morose place is France become since philosophy has dethroned enjoyment! If you go on a visit to one of our noblemen's seats, what do you find there, I ask? Cards, comedies, music, the opportunity for an agreeable intrigue in the society of your equals? No—but a hostess engaged in suckling and bathing her brats, or in studying chemistry and optics with some dirty school-master, who is given the seat of honour at table and a pavilion in the park to which he may retire when weary of the homage of the great; while as for the host, he is busy discussing education or political economy with his unfortunate guests, if, indeed, he is not dragging them through leagues of mud and dust to inspect his latest experiments in forestry and agriculture, or to hear a pack of snuffling school-children singing hymns to the God of Nature! And what," he continued, "is the result of it all? The peasants are starving, the taxes are increasing, the virtuous landlords are ruining themselves in farming on scientific principles, the tradespeople are grumbling because the nobility do not spend their money in Paris, the court is dull, the clergy are furious, the Queen mopes, the King is frightened, and the whole French people are yawning themselves to death from Normandy to Provence."

"Yes," said Castelrovinato with his melancholy smile, "the test of success is to have had one's money's worth; but experience, which is dried pleasure, is at best a dusty diet, as we know. Yonder, in a fold of those hills," he added, pointing to the cluster of Euganean mountains just faintly pencilled above the plain, "lies the little fief from which I take my name. Acre by acre, tree by tree, it has gone to pay for my experiments, not in agriculture but in pleasure; and whenever I look over at it from Venice and reflect on what each rood of ground or trunk of tree has purchased, I wonder to see my life as bare as ever for all that I have spent on it."

The young Marquess shrugged his shoulders. "And would your life," he exclaimed, "have been a whit less bare had you passed it in your ancestral keep among those windy hills, in the company of swineherds and charcoal-burners, with a milk-maid for your mistress and the village priest for your partner at picquet?"

"Perhaps not," the other agreed. "There is a tale of a man who spent his life in wishing he had lived differently; and when he died he was surrounded by a throng of spectral shapes, each one exactly like the other, who, on his asking what they were, replied: 'We are all the different lives you might have lived.'"

"If you are going to tell ghost-stories," cried Coeur-Volant, "I will call for a bottle of Canary!"

"And I," rejoined the Count good-humouredly, "will try to coax the ladies forth with a song;" and picking up his lute, which always lay within reach, he began to sing in the Venetian dialect:—

There's a villa on the Brenta
Where the statues, white as snow,
All along the water-terrace
Perch like sea-gulls in a row.

There's a garden on the Brenta
Where the fairest ladies meet,
Picking roses from the trellis
For the gallants at their feet.

There's an arbour on the Brenta
Made of yews that screen the light,
Where I kiss my girl at midday
Close as lovers kiss at night.

The players soon emerged at this call and presently the deck resounded with song and laughter. All the company were familiar with the Venetian bacaroles, and Castelrovinato's lute was passed from hand to hand, as one after another, incited by the Marquess's Canary, tried to recall some favourite measure—"La biondina in gondoleta" or "Guarda, che bella luna."

Meanwhile life was stirring in the villages and gardens, and groups of people appearing on the terraces overhanging the water. Never had Odo beheld a livelier scene. The pillared houses with their rows of statues and vases, the flights of marble steps descending to the gilded river-gates, where boats bobbed against the landings and boatmen gasped in the shade of their awnings; the marble trellises hung with grapes, the gardens where parterres of flowers and parti-coloured gravel alternated with the dusk of tunnelled yew-walks; the company playing at bowls in the long alleys, or drinking chocolate in gazebos above the river; the boats darting hither and thither on the stream itself, the travelling-chaises, market-waggons and pannier-asses crowding the causeway along the bank—all were unrolled before him with as little effect of reality as the episodes woven in some gaily-tinted tapestry. Even the peasants in the vineyards seemed as merry and thoughtless as the quality in their gardens. The vintage-time is the holiday of the rural year and the day's work was interspersed with frequent intervals of relaxation. At the villages where the burchiello touched for refreshments, handsome young women in scarlet bodices came on board with baskets of melons, grapes, figs and peaches; and under the trellises on the landings, lads and girls with flowers in their hair were dancing the monferrina to the rattle of tambourines or the chant of some wandering ballad-singer. These scenes were so engaging to the comedians that they could not be restrained from going ashore and mingling in the village diversions; and the Marquess, though impatient to rejoin his divinity, was too volatile not to be drawn into the adventure. The whole party accordingly disembarked, and were presently giving an exhibition of their talents to the assembled idlers, the Pantaloon, Harlequin and Doctor enacting a comical intermezzo which Cantapresto had that morning composed for them, while Scaramouch and Columbine joined the dancers, and the rest of the company, seizing on a train of donkeys laden with vegetables for the Venetian market, stripped these patient animals of their panniers, and mounting them bareback started a Corso around the village square amid the invectives of the drivers and the applause of the crowd.

Day was declining when the Marquess at last succeeded in driving his flock to their fold, and the moon sent a quiver of brightness across the water as the burchiello touched at the landing of a villa set amid close-massed foliage high above the river. Gardens peopled with statues descended from the portico of the villa to the marble platform on the water's edge, where a throng of boatmen in the Procuratore's livery hurried forward to receive the Marquess and his companions. The comedians, sobered by the magnificence of their surroundings, followed their leader like awe-struck children. Light and music streamed from the long facade overhead, but the lower gardens lay hushed and dark, the air fragrant with unseen flowers, the late moon just burnishing the edges of the laurel-thickets from which, now and again, a nightingale's song gushed in a fountain of sound. Odo, spellbound, followed the others without a thought of his own share in the adventure. Never before had beauty so ministered to every sense. He felt himself lost in his surroundings, absorbed in the scent and murmur of the night.

3.3.

On the upper terrace a dozen lacqueys with wax lights hastened out to receive the travellers. A laughing group followed, headed by a tall vivacious woman covered with jewels, whom Odo guessed to be the Procuratessa Bra. The Marquess, hastening forward, kissed the lady's hand, and turned to summon the actors, who hung back at the farther end of the terrace. The light from the windows and from the lacquey's tapers fell full on the motley band, and Odo, roused to the singularity of his position, was about to seek shelter behind the Pantaloon when he heard a cry of recognition, and Mirandolina, darting out of the Procuratessa's circle, fell at that lady's feet with a whispered word.

The Procuratessa at once advanced with a smile of surprise and bade the Cavaliere Valsecca welcome. Seeing Odo's embarrassment, she added that his Highness of Monte Alloro had already apprised her of the cavaliere's coming, and that she and her husband had the day before despatched a messenger to Venice to enquire if he were already there to invite him to the villa. At the same moment a middle-aged man with an air of careless kindly strength emerged from the house and greeted Odo.

"I am happy," said he bowing, "to receive at Bellocchio a member of the princely house of Pianura; and your excellency will no doubt be as well-pleased as ourselves that accident enables us to make acquaintance without the formalities of an introduction."

This, then, was the famous Procuratore Bra, whose house had given three Doges to Venice, and who was himself regarded as the most powerful if not the most scrupulous noble of his day. Odo had heard many tales of his singularities, for in a generation of elegant triflers his figure stood out with the ruggedness of a granite boulder in a clipped and gravelled garden. To hereditary wealth and influence he added a love of power seconded by great political sagacity and an inflexible will. If his means were not always above suspicion they at least tended to statesmanlike ends, and in his public capacity he was faithful to the highest interests of the state. Reports differed as to his private use of his authority. He was noted for his lavish way of living, and for a hospitality which distinguished him from the majority of his class, who, however showy in their establishments, seldom received strangers, and entertained each other only on the most ceremonious occasions. The Procuratore kept open house both in Venice and on the Brenta, and in his drawing-rooms the foreign traveller was welcomed as freely as in Paris or London. Here, too, were to be met the wits, musicians and literati whom a traditional morgue still excluded from many aristocratic houses. Yet in spite of his hospitality (or perhaps because of it) the Procuratore, as Odo knew, was the butt of the very poets he entertained, and the worst satirised man in Venice. It was his misfortune to be in love with his wife; and this state of mind (in itself sufficiently ridiculous) and the shifts and compromises to which it reduced him, were a source of endless amusement to the humorists. Nor were graver rumours wanting; for it was known that the Procuratore, so proof against other persuasions, was helpless in his wife's hands, and that honest men had been undone and scoundrels exalted at a nod of the beautiful Procuratessa. That lady, as famous in her way as her husband, was noted for quite different qualities; so that, according to one satirist, her hospitality began where his ended, and the Albergo Bra (the nickname their palace went by) was advertised in the lampoons of the day as furnishing both bed and board. In some respects, however, the tastes of the noble couple agreed, both delighting in music, wit, good company, and all the adornments of life; while, with regard to their private conduct, it doubtless suffered by being viewed through the eyes of a narrow and trivial nobility, apt to look with suspicion on any deviation from the customs of their class. Such was the household in which Odo found himself unexpectedly included. He learned that his hosts were in the act of entertaining the English Duke who had captured his burchiello that morning; and having exchanged his travelling-dress for a more suitable toilet he was presently conducted to the private theatre where the company had gathered to witness an improvised performance by Mirandolina and the newly-arrived actors.

The Procuratessa at once beckoned him to the row of gilt armchairs where she sat with the noble Duke and several ladies of distinction. The little theatre sparkled with wax-lights reflected in the facets of glass chandeliers and in the jewels of the richly-habited company, and Odo was struck by the refined brilliancy of the scene. Before he had time to look about him the curtains of the stage were drawn back, and Mirandolina flashed into view, daring and radiant as ever, and dressed with an elegance which spoke well for the liberality of her new protector. She was as much at her ease as before the vulgar audience of Vercelli, and spite of the distinguished eyes fixed upon her, her smiles and sallies were pointedly addressed to Odo. This made him the object of the Procuratessa's banter, but had an opposite effect on the Marquess, who fixed him with an irritated eye and fidgeted restlessly in his seat as the performance went on.

When the curtain fell the Procuratessa led the company to the circular saloon which, as in most villas of the Venetian mainland, formed the central point of the house. If Odo had been charmed by the graceful decorations of the theatre, he was dazzled by the airy splendour of this apartment. Dance-music was pouring from the arched recesses above the doorways, and chandeliers of coloured Murano glass diffused a soft brightness over the pilasters of the stuccoed walls, and the floor of inlaid marbles on which couples were rapidly forming for the contradance. His eye, however, was soon drawn from these to the ceiling which overarched the dancers with what seemed like an Olympian revel reflected in sunset clouds. Over the gilt balustrade surmounting the cornice lolled the figures of fauns, bacchantes, nereids and tritons, hovered over by a cloud of amorini blown like rose-leaves across a rosy sky, while in the centre of the dome Apollo burst in his chariot through the mists of dawn, escorted by a fantastic procession of the human races. These alien subjects of the sun—a fur-clad Laplander, a turbaned figure on a dromedary, a blackamoor and a plumed American Indian—were in turn surrounded by a rout of Maenads and Silenuses, whose flushed advance was checked by the breaking of cool green waves, through which boys wreathed with coral and seaweed disported themselves among shoals of flashing dolphins. It was as though the genius of Pleasure had poured all the riches of his inexhaustible realm on the heads of the revellers below.

The Procuratessa brought Odo to earth by remarking that it was a master-piece of the divine Tiepolo he was admiring. She added that at Bellocchio all formalities were dispensed with, and begged him to observe that, in the rooms opening into the saloon, recreations were provided for every taste. In one of these apartments silver trays were set out with sherbets, cakes, and fruit cooled in snow, while in another stood gaming-tables around which the greater number of the company were already gathering for tresette. A third room was devoted to music; and hither Mirandolina, who was evidently allowed a familiarity of intercourse not accorded to the other comedians, had withdrawn with the pacified Marquess, and perched on the arm of a high gilt chair was pinching the strings of a guitar and humming the first notes of a boatman's song...

After completing the circuit of the rooms Odo stepped out on the terrace, which was now bathed in the whiteness of a soaring moon. The colonnades detached against silver-misted foliage, the gardens spectrally outspread, seemed to enclose him in a magic circle of loveliness which the first ray of daylight must dispel. He wandered on, drawn to the depths of shade on the lower terraces. The hush grew deeper, the murmur of the river more mysterious. A yew-arbour invited him and he seated himself on the bench niched in its inmost dusk. Seen through the black arch of the arbour the moonlight lay like snow on parterres and statues. He thought of Maria Clementina, and of the delight she would have felt in such a scene as he had just left. Then the remembrance of Mirandolina's blandishments stole over him and spite of himself he smiled at the Marquess's discomfiture. Though he was in no humour for an intrigue his fancy was not proof against the romance of his surroundings, and it seemed to him that Miranda's eyes had never been so bright or her smile so full of provocation. No wonder Frattanto followed her like a lost soul and the Marquess abandoned Rome and Baalbec to sit at the feet of such a teacher! Had not that light philosopher after all chosen the true way and guessed the Sphinx's riddle? Why should today always be jilted for tomorrow, sensation sacrificed to thought?

As he sat revolving these questions the yew-branches seemed to stir, and from some deeper recess of shade a figure stole to his side. He started, but a hand was laid on his lips and he was gently forced back into his seat. Dazzled by the outer moonlight he could just guess the outline of the figure pressed against his own. He sat speechless, yielding to the charm of the moment, till suddenly he felt a rapid kiss and the visitor vanished as mysteriously as she had come. He sprang up to follow, but inclination failed with his first step. Let the spell of mystery remain unbroken! He sank down on the seat again lulled by dreamy musings...

When he looked up the moonlight had faded and he felt a chill in the air. He walked out on the terrace. The moon hung low and the tree-tops were beginning to tremble. The villa-front was grey, with oblongs of yellow light marking the windows of the ball-room. As he looked up at it, the dance-music ceased and not a sound was heard but the stir of the foliage and the murmur of the river against its banks. Then, from a loggia above the central portico, a woman's clear contralto notes took flight:

Before the yellow dawn is up,
With pomp of shield and shaft,
Drink we of Night's fast-ebbing cup
One last delicious draught.

The shadowy wine of Night is sweet,
With subtle slumbrous fumes
Crushed by the Hours' melodious feet
From bloodless elder-blooms...

The days at Bellocchio passed in a series of festivities. The mornings were spent in drinking chocolate, strolling in the gardens and visiting the fish-ponds, meanders and other wonders of the villa; thence the greater number of guests were soon drawn to the card-tables, from which they rose only to dine; and after an elaborate dinner prepared by a French cook the whole company set out to explore the country or to exchange visits with the hosts of the adjoining villas. Each evening brought some fresh diversion: a comedy or an operetta in the miniature theatre, an al fresco banquet on the terrace or a ball attended by the principal families of the neighbourhood. Odo soon contrived to reassure the Marquess as to his designs upon Miranda, and when Coeur-Volant was not at cards the two young men spent much of their time together. The Marquess was never tired of extolling the taste and ingenuity with which the Venetians planned and carried out their recreations. "Nature herself," said he, "seems the accomplice of their merry-making, and in no other surroundings could man's natural craving for diversion find so graceful and poetic an expression."

The scene on which they looked out seemed to confirm his words. It was the last evening of their stay at Bellocchio, and the Procuratessa had planned a musical festival on the river. Festoons of coloured lanterns wound from the portico to the water; and opposite the landing lay the Procuratore's Bucentaur, a great barge hung with crimson velvet. In the prow were stationed the comedians, in airy mythological dress, and as the guests stepped on board they were received by Miranda, a rosy Venus who, escorted by Mars and Adonis, recited an ode composed by Cantapresto in the Procuratessa's honour. A banquet was spread in the deck-house, which was hung with silk arras and Venetian mirrors, and, while the guests feasted, dozens of little boats hung with lights and filled with musicians flitted about the Bucentaur like a swarm of musical fireflies...

The next day Odo accompanied the Procuratessa to Venice. Had he been a traveller from beyond the Alps he could hardly have been more unprepared for the spectacle that awaited him. In aspect and customs Venice differed almost as much from other Italian cities as from those of the rest of Europe. From the fanciful stone embroidery of her churches and palaces to a hundred singularities in dress and manners—the full-bottomed wigs and long gowns of the nobles, the black mantles and head-draperies of the ladies, the white masks worn abroad by both sexes, the publicity of social life under the arcades of the Piazza, the extraordinary freedom of intercourse in the casini, gaming-rooms and theatres—the city proclaimed, in every detail of life and architecture, her independence of any tradition but her own. This was the more singular as Saint Mark's square had for centuries been the meeting-place of East and West, and the goal of artists, scholars and pleasure-seekers from all parts of the world. Indeed, as Coeur-Volant pointed out, the Venetian customs almost appeared to have been devised for the convenience of strangers. The privilege of going masked at almost all seasons and the enforced uniformity of dress, which in itself provided a kind of incognito, made the place singularly favourable to every kind of intrigue and amusement; while the mild temper of the people and the watchfulness of the police prevented the public disorders that such license might have occasioned. These seeming anomalies abounded on every side. From the gaming-table where a tinker might set a ducat against a prince it was but a few steps to the Broglio, or arcade under the ducal palace, into which no plebeian might intrude while the nobility walked there. The great ladies, who were subject to strict sumptuary laws, and might not display their jewels or try the new French fashions but on the sly, were yet privileged at all hours to go abroad alone in their gondolas. No society was more haughty and exclusive in its traditions, yet the mask leveled all classes and permitted, during the greater part of the year, an equality of intercourse undreamed of in other cities; while the nobles, though more magnificently housed than in any other capital of Europe, generally sought amusement at the public casini or assembly-rooms instead of receiving company in their own palaces. Such were but a few of the contradictions in a city where the theatres were named after the neighbouring churches, where there were innumerable religious foundations but scarce an ecclesiastic to be met in company, and where the ladies of the laity dressed like nuns, while the nuns in the aristocratic convents went in gala habits and with uncovered heads. No wonder that to the bewildered stranger the Venetians seemed to keep perpetual carnival and Venice herself to be as it were the mere stage of some huge comic interlude.

To Odo the setting was even more astonishing than the performance. Never had he seen pleasure and grace so happily allied, all the arts of life so combined in the single effort after enjoyment. Here was not a mere tendency to linger on the surface, but the essence of superficiality itself; not an ignoring of what lies beneath, but an elimination of it; as though all human experience should be beaten thin and spread out before the eye like some brilliant tenuous plaque of Etruscan gold. And in this science of pleasure—mere jeweller's work though it were—the greatest artists had collaborated, each contributing his page to the philosophy of enjoyment in the form of some radiant allegory flowering from palace wall or ceiling like the enlarged reflection of the life beneath it. Nowhere was the mind arrested by a question or an idea. Thought slunk away like an unmasked guest at the ridotto. Sensation ruled supreme, and each moment was an iridescent bubble fresh-blown from the lips of fancy.

Odo brought to the spectacle the humour best fitted for its enjoyment. His weariness and discouragement sought refuge in the emotional satisfaction of the hour. Here at least the old problem of living had been solved, and from the patrician taking the air in his gondola to the gondolier himself, gambling and singing on the water-steps of his master's palace, all seemed equally satisfied with the solution. Now if ever was the time to cry "halt!" to the present, to forget the travelled road and take no thought for the morrow...

The months passed rapidly and agreeably. The Procuratessa was the most amiable of guides, and in her company Odo enjoyed the best that Venice had to offer, from the matchless music of the churches and hospitals to the petits soupers in the private casini of the nobility; while Coeur-Volant and Castelrovinato introduced him to scenes where even a lady of the Procuratessa's intrepidity might not venture.

Such a life left little time for thoughtful pleasures; nor did Odo find in the society about him any sympathy with his more personal tastes. At first he yielded willingly enough to the pressure of his surroundings, glad to escape from thoughts of the past and speculations about the future; but it was impossible for him to lose his footing in such an element, and at times he felt the lack of such companionship as de Crucis had given him. There was no society in Venice corresponding with the polished circles of Milan or Naples, or with the academic class in such University towns as Padua and Pavia. The few Venetians destined to be remembered among those who had contributed to the intellectual advancement of Italy vegetated in obscurity, suffering not so much from religious persecution—for the Inquisition had little power in Venice—as from the incorrigible indifference of a society which ignored all who did not contribute to its amusement. Odo indeed might have sought out these unhonoured prophets, but that all the influences about him set the other way, and that he was falling more and more into the habit of running with the tide. Now and then, however, a vague ennui drove him to one of the bookshops which, throughout Italy were the chief meeting-places of students and authors. On one of these occasions the dealer invited him into a private room where he kept some rare volumes, and here Odo was surprised to meet Andreoni, the liberal bookseller of Pianura.

Andreoni at first seemed somewhat disconcerted by the meeting; but presently recovering his confidence, he told Odo that he had been recently banished from Pianura, the cause of his banishment being the publication of a book on taxation that was supposed to reflect on the fiscal system of the duchy. Though he did not name the author, Odo at once suspected Gamba; but on his enquiring if the latter had also been banished, Andreoni merely replied that he had been dismissed from his post, and had left Pianura. The bookseller went on to say that he had come to Venice with the idea of setting up his press either there or in Padua, where his wife's family lived. Odo was eager to hear more; but Andreoni courteously declined to wait on him at his lodgings, on the plea that it might harm them both to be seen together. They agreed, however, to meet in San Zaccaria after low mass the next morning, and here Andreoni gave Odo a fuller report of recent events in the duchy.

It appeared that in the incessant see-saw of party influences the Church had once more gained on the liberals. Trescorre was out of favour, the Dominican had begun to show his hand more openly, and the Duke, more than ever apprehensive about his health, was seeking to conciliate heaven by his renewed persecution of the reformers. In the general upheaval even Crescenti had nearly lost his place; and it was rumoured that he kept it only through the intervention of the Pope, who had represented to the Duke that the persecution of a scholar already famous throughout Europe would reflect little credit on the Church.

As for Gamba, Andreoni, though unwilling to admit a knowledge of his exact whereabouts, assured Odo that he was well and had not lost courage. At court matters remained much as usual. The Duchess, surrounded by her familiars, had entered on a new phase of mad expenditure, draining the exchequer to indulge her private whims, filling her apartments with mountebanks and players, and borrowing from courtiers and servants to keep her creditors from the door. Trescorre was no longer able to check her extravagance, and his influence with the Duke being on the wane, the court was once more the scene of unseemly scandals and disorders.

The only new figure to appear there since Odo's departure was that of the little prince's governor, who had come from Rome a few months previously to superintend the heir's education, which was found to have been grievously neglected under his former masters. This was an ecclesiastic, an ex-Jesuit as some said, but without doubt a man of parts, and apparently of more tolerant views than the other churchmen about the court.

"But," Andreoni added, "your excellency may chance to recall him; for he is the same abate de Crucis who was sent to Pianura by the Holy Office to arrest the German astrologer."

Odo heard him with surprise. He had had no news of de Crucis since their parting in Rome, where, as he supposed, the latter was to remain for some years in the service of Prince Bracciano. Odo was at a loss to conceive how or why the Jesuit had come to Pianura; but, whatever his reasons for being there, it was certain that his influence must make itself felt far beyond the range of his immediate duties. Whether this influence would be exerted for good or ill it was impossible to forecast; but much as Odo admired de Crucis, he could not forget that the Jesuit, by his own avowal, was still the servant of the greatest organised opposition to moral and intellectual freedom that the world had ever known. That this opposition was not always actively manifested Odo was well aware. He knew that the Jesuit spirit moved in many directions and that its action was often more beneficial than that of its opponents; but it remained an incalculable element in the composition of human affairs, and one the more to be feared since, in ceasing to have a material existence, it had acquired the dread pervasiveness of an idea.

With the Epiphany the wild carnival-season set in. Nothing could surpass the excesses of this mad time. All classes seemed bitten by the tarantula of mirth, every gondola hid an intrigue, the patrician's tabarro concealed a noble lady, the feminine hood and cloak a young spark bent on mystification, the friar's habit a man of pleasure and the nun's veil a lady of the town. The Piazza swarmed with merry-makers of all degrees. The square itself was taken up by the booths of hucksters, rope-dancers and astrologers, while promenaders in travesty thronged the arcades, and the ladies of the nobility, in their white masks and black zendaletti, surveyed the scene from the windows of the assembly-rooms in the Procuratie, or, threading the crowd on the arms of their gallants, visited the various peep-shows and flocked about the rhinoceros exhibited in a great canvas tent in the Piazzetta. The characteristic contrasts of Venetian life seemed to be emphasised by the vagaries of the carnival, and Odo never ceased to be diverted by the sight of a long line of masqueraders in every kind of comic disguise kneeling devoutly before the brilliantly-lit shrine of the Virgin under the arches of the Procuratie, while the friar who led their devotions interrupted his litany whenever the quack on an adjoining platform began to bawl through a tin trumpet the praise of his miraculous pills.

The mounting madness culminated on Giovedi Grasso, the last Thursday before Lent, when the Piazzetta became the scene of ceremonies in which the Doge himself took part. These opened with the decapitation of three bulls: a rite said to commemorate some long-forgotten dispute between the inveterate enemies, Venice and Aquileia. The bulls, preceded by halberdiers and trumpeters, and surrounded by armed attendants, were led in state before the ducal palace, and the executioner, practised in his bloody work, struck off each head with a single stroke of his huge sword. This slaughter was succeeded by pleasanter sights, such as the famous Vola, or flight of a boy from the bell-tower of Saint Mark's to a window of the palace, where he presented a nosegay to his Serenity and was caught up again to his airy vaulting-ground. After this ingenious feat came another called the "Force of Hercules," given by a band of youths who, building themselves into a kind of pyramid, shifted their postures with inexhaustible agility, while bursts of fireworks wove yellow arches through the midday light. Meanwhile the crowds in the streets fled this way and that as a throng of uproarious young fellows drove before them the bulls that were to be baited in the open squares; and wherever a recessed doorway or the angle of a building afforded shelter from the rout, some posture-maker or ballad-singer had gathered a crowd about his carpet.

Ash Wednesday brought about a dramatic transformation. Every travesty laid aside, every tent and stall swept away, the people again gathered in the Piazza to receive the ashes of penitence on their heads, the churches now became the chief centres of interest. Venice was noted for her sacred music and for the lavish illumination of her favourite shrines and chapels; and few religious spectacles were more impressive than the Forty Hours' devotion in the wealthier churches of the city. All the magic of music, painting and sculpture were combined in the service of religion, and Odo's sense of the dramatic quality of the Catholic rites found gratification in the moving scenes where, amid the imperishable splendours of his own creation, man owned himself but dust. Never before had he been so alive to the symbolism of the penitential season, so awed by the beauty and symmetry of that great structure of the Liturgical Year that leads the soul up, step by step, to the awful heights of Calvary. The very carelessness of those about him seemed to deepen the solemnity of the scenes enacted—as though the Church, after all her centuries of dominion, were still, as in those early days, but a voice crying in the wilderness.

The Easter bells ushered in the reign of another spirit. If the carnival folly was spent, the joy of returning life replaced it. After the winter diversions of cards, concerts and theatres, came the excursions to the island-gardens of the lagoon and the evening promenade of the fresca on the Grand Canal. Now the palace-windows were hung with awnings, the oleanders in the balconies grew rosy against the sea-worn marble, and yellow snap-dragons blossomed from the crumbling walls. The market-boats brought early fruits and vegetables from the Brenta and roses and gilly-flowers from the Paduan gardens; and when the wind set from shore it carried with it the scent of lime-blossoms and flowering fields. Now also was the season when the great civic and religious processions took place, dyeing the water with sunset hues as they swept from the steps of the Piazzetta to San Giorgio, the Redentore or the Salute. In the fashionable convents the nuns celebrated the festivals of their patron saints with musical and dramatic entertainments to which secular visitors were invited. These entertainments were a noted feature of Venetian life, and the subject of much scandalous comment among visitors from beyond the Alps. The nuns of the stricter orders were as closely cloistered as elsewhere; but in the convents of Santa Croce, Santa Chiara, and a few others, mostly filled by the daughters of the nobility, an unusual liberty prevailed. It was known that the inmates had taken the veil for family reasons, and to the indulgent Venetian temper it seemed natural that their seclusion should be made as little irksome as possible. As a rule the privileges accorded to the nuns consisted merely in their being allowed to receive visits in the presence of a lay-sister, and to perform in concerts on the feast-days of the order; but some few convents had a name for far greater license, and it was a common thing for the noble libertine returned from Italy to boast of his intrigue with a Venetian nun.

Odo, in the Procuratessa's train, had of course visited many of the principal convents. Whether it were owing to the malicious pleasure of contrasting their own state with that of their cloistered sisters, or to the discreet shelter which the parlour afforded to their private intrigues, the Venetian ladies were exceedingly partial to these visits. The Procuratessa was no exception to the rule, and as was natural to one of her complexion, she preferred the convents where the greatest freedom prevailed. Odo, however, had hitherto found little to tempt him in these glimpses of forbidden fruit. The nuns, though often young and pretty, had the insipidity of women secluded from the passions and sorrows of life without being raised above them; and he preferred the frank coarseness of the Procuratessa's circle to the simpering graces of the cloister.

Even Coeur-Volant's mysterious boast of a conquest he had made among the sisters failed to excite his friend's curiosity. The Marquess, though still devoted to Miranda, was too much the child of his race not to seek variety in his emotions; indeed he often declared that the one fault of the Italian character was its unimaginative fidelity in love-affairs.

"Does a man," he asked, "dine off one dish at a gourmet's banquet? And why should I restrict myself to one course at the most richly-spread table in Europe? One must love at least two women to appreciate either; and, did the silly creatures but know it, a rival becomes them like a patch."

Sister Mary of the Crucifix, he went on to explain, possessed the very qualities that Miranda lacked. The daughter of a rich nobleman of Treviso, she was skilled in music, drawing and all the operations of the needle, and was early promised in marriage to a young man whose estates adjoined her father's. The jealousy of a younger sister, who was secretly in love with the suitor, caused her to accuse Coeur-Volant's mistress of misconduct and thus broke off the marriage; and the unhappy girl, repudiated by her bridegroom, was at once despatched to a convent in Venice. Enraged at her fate, she had repeatedly appealed to the authorities to release her; but her father's wealth and influence prevailed against all her efforts. The abbess, however, felt such pity for her that she was allowed more freedom than the other nuns, with whom her wit and beauty made her a favourite in spite of her exceptional privileges. These, as Coeur-Volant hinted, included the liberty of leaving the convent after night-fall to visit her friends; and he professed to be one of those whom she had thus honoured. Always eager to have his good taste ratified by the envy of his friends, he was urgent with Odo to make the lady's acquaintance, and it was agreed that, on the first favourable occasion, a meeting should take place at Coeur-Volant's casino. The weeks elapsed, however, without Odo's hearing further of the matter, and it had nearly passed from his mind when one August day he received word that the Marquess hoped for his company that evening.

He was in that mood of careless acquiescence when any novelty invites, and the heavy warmth of the summer night seemed the accomplice of his humour. Cloaked and masked, he stepped into his gondola and was swept rapidly along the Grand Canal and through winding channels to the Giudecca. It was close on midnight and all Venice was abroad. Gondolas laden with musicians and hung with coloured lamps lay beneath the palace windows or drifted out on the oily reaches of the lagoon. There was no moon, and the side-canals were dark and noiseless but for the hundreds of caged nightingales that made every byway musical. As his prow slipped past garden walls and under the blackness of low-ached bridges Odo felt the fathomless mystery of the Venetian night: not the open night of the lagoons, but the secret dusk of nameless waterways between blind windows and complaisant gates.

At one of these his gondola presently touched. The gate was cautiously unbarred and Odo found himself in a strip of garden preceding a low pavilion in which not a light was visible. A woman-servant led him indoors and the Marquess greeted him on the threshold.

"You are late!" he exclaimed. "I began to fear you would not be here to receive our guests with me."

"Your guests?" Odo repeated. "I had fancied there was but one."

The Marquess smiled. "My dear Mary of the Crucifix," he said, "is too well-born to venture out alone at this late hour, and has prevailed on her bosom friend to accompany her.—Besides," he added with his deprecating shrug, "I own I have had too recent an experience of your success to trust you alone with my enchantress; and she has promised to bring the most fascinating nun in the convent to protect her from your wiles."

As he spoke he led Odo into a room furnished in the luxurious style of a French boudoir. A Savonnerie carpet covered the floor, the lounges and easy-chairs were heaped with cushions, and the panels hung with pastel drawings of a lively or sentimental character. The windows toward the garden were close-shuttered, but those on the farther side of the room stood open on a starlit terrace whence the eye looked out over the lagoon to the outer line of islands.

"Confess," cried Coeur-Volant, pointing to a table set with delicacies and flanked by silver wine-coolers, "that I have spared no pains to do my goddess honour and that this interior must present an agreeable contrast to the whitewashed cells and dismal refectory of her convent! No passion," he continued, with his quaint didactic air, "is so susceptible as love to the influence of its surroundings; and principles which might have held out against a horse-hair sofa and soupe a l'oignon have before now been known to succumb to silk cushions and champagne."

He received with perfect good-humour the retort that if he failed in his designs his cook and his upholsterer would not be to blame; and the young men were still engaged in such banter when the servant returned to say that a gondola was at the water-gate. The Marquess hastened out and presently reappeared with two masked and hooded figures. The first of these, whom he led by the hand, entered with the air of one not unaccustomed to her surroundings; but the other hung back, and on the Marquess's inviting them to unmask, hurriedly signed to her friend to refuse.

"Very well, fair strangers," said Coeur-Volant with a laugh; "if you insist on prolonging our suspense we shall avenge ourselves by prolonging yours, and neither my friend nor I will unmask till you are pleased to set us the example."

The first lady echoed his laugh. "Shall I own," she cried, "that I suspect in this unflattering compliance a pretext to conceal your friend's features from me as long as possible? For my part," she continued, throwing back her hood, "the mask of hypocrisy I am compelled to wear in the convent makes me hate every form of disguise, and with all my defects I prefer to be known as I am." And with that she detached her mask and dropped the cloak from her shoulders.

The gesture revealed a beauty of the laughing sensuous type best suited to such surroundings. Sister Mary of the Crucifix, in her sumptuous gown of shot-silk, with pearls wound through her reddish hair and hanging on her bare shoulders, might have stepped from some festal canvas of Bonifazio's. She had laid aside even the light gauze veil worn by the nuns in gala habit, and no vestige of her calling showed itself in dress or bearing.

"Do you accept my challenge, cavaliere?" she exclaimed, turning on Odo a glance confident of victory.

The Marquess meanwhile had approached the other nun with the intention of inducing her to unmask; but as Sister Mary of the Crucifix advanced to perform the same service for his friend, his irrepressible jealousy made him step hastily between them.

"Come cavaliere," he cried, drawing Odo gaily toward the unknown nun, "since you have induced one of our fair guests to unmask perhaps you may be equally successful with the other, who appears provokingly indifferent to my advances."

The masked nun had in fact retreated to a corner of the room and stood there, drawing her cloak about her, rather in the attitude of a frightened child than in that of a lady bent on a gallant adventure.

Sister Mary of the Crucifix approached her playfully. "My dear Sister Veronica," said she, throwing her arm about the other's neck, "hesitates to reveal charms which she knows must cast mine in the shade; but I am not to be outdone in generosity, and if the Marquess will unmask his friend I will do the same by mine."

As she spoke she deftly pinioned the nun's hands and snatched off her mask with a malicious laugh. The Marquess, entering into her humour, removed Odo's at the same instant, and the latter, turning with a laugh, found himself face to face with Fulvia Vivaldi. He grew white, and Mary of the Crucifix sprang forward to catch her friend.

"Good God! What is this?" gasped the Marquess, staring from one to the other.

A glance of entreaty from Fulvia checked the answer on Odo's lips, and for a moment there was silence in the room; then Fulvia, breaking away from her companion, fled out on the terrace. The other was about to follow; but Odo, controlling himself, stepped between them.

"Madam," said he in a low voice, "I recognise in your companion a friend of whom I have long had no word. Will you pardon me if I speak with her alone?"

Sister Mary drew back with a meaning sparkle in her handsome eyes. "Why, this," she cried, not without a touch of resentment, "is the prettiest ending imaginable; but what a sly creature, to be sure, to make me think it was her first assignation!"

Odo, without answering, hastened out on the terrace. It was so dark after the brightly lit room that for a moment he did not distinguish the figure which had sprung to the low parapet above the water; and he stumbled forward just in time to snatch Fulvia back to safety.

"This is madness!" he cried, as she hung upon him trembling.

"The boat," she stammered in a strange sobbing voice—"the boat should be somewhere below—"

"The boat lies at the water-gate on the other side," he answered.

She drew away from him with a gesture of despair. The struggle with Sister Mary had disordered her hair and it fell on her white neck in loosened strands. "My cloak—my mask—" she faltered vaguely, clasping her hands across her bosom; then suddenly dropped to a seat and burst into tears. Once before—but in how different a case!—he had seen her thus thrilled with weeping. Then fate had thrown him humbled at her feet, now it was she who cried him mercy in every line of her bowed head and shaken breast; and the thought of that other meeting flooded his heart with pity.

He knelt before her, seeking her hands. "Fulvia, why do you shrink from me?" he whispered. But she shook her head and wept on.

At last her sobs subsided and she rose to her feet. "I must go back," said she in a low tone, and would have passed him.

"Back? To the convent?"

"To the convent," she said after him; but she made no farther effort to move.

The question that tortured him sprang forth. "You have taken the vows?"

"A month since," she answered.

He hid his face in his hands and for a moment both were silent. "And you have no other word for me—none?" he faltered at last.

She fixed him with a hard bright stare. "Yes—one," she cried; "keep a place for me among your gallant recollections."

"Fulvia!" he said with sudden strength, and caught her by the arm.

"Let me pass!" she cried.

"No, by heaven!" he retorted; "not till you listen to me—not till you tell me how it is that I come upon you here!—Ah, child," he broke out, "do you fancy I don't see how little you belong in such scenes? That I don't know you are here through some dreadful error? Fulvia," he pleaded, "will you never trust me?" And at the word he burned with blushes in the darkness.

His voice, perhaps, rather than what he said, seemed to have struck a yielding fibre. He felt her arm tremble in his hold; but after a moment she said with cruel distinctness: "There was no error. I came knowingly. It was the company and not the place I was deceived in."

Odo drew back with a start; then, as if in spite of himself, he broke into a laugh. "By the saints," said he, almost joyously, "I am sorry to be where I am not wanted; but since no better company offers, will you not make the best of mine and suffer me to hand you in to supper with our friends?" And with a low bow he offered her his arm.

The effect was instantaneous. He saw her catch at the balustrade for support.

"Sancta simplicitas!" he exulted, "and did you think to play the part at such short notice?" He fell at her feet and covered her hands with kisses. "My Fulvia! My poor child! come with me, come away from here," he entreated. "I know not what mad hazard has brought us thus together, but I thank God on my knees for the encounter. You shall tell me all or nothing, as you please—you shall presently dismiss me at your convent-gate, and never see me again if you so will it—but till then, I swear, you are in my charge, and no human power shall come between us!"

As he ended the Marquess's voice called gaily through the open window: "Friends, the burgundy is uncorked! Will you not join us in a glass of good French wine?"

Fulvia flung herself upon Odo. "Yes—yes; away—take me away from here!" she cried, clinging to him. She had gathered her cloak about her and drawn the hood over her disordered hair. "Away! Away!" she repeated. "I cannot see them again. Good God, is there no other way out?"

With a gesture he warned her to be silent and drew her along the terrace in the shadow of the house. The gravel creaked beneath their feet, and she shook at the least sound; but her hand lay in his like a child's and he felt himself her master. At the farther end of the terrace a flight of steps led to a narrow strip of shore. He helped her down and after listening a moment gave a whistle. Presently they heard a low plash of oars and saw the prow of a gondola cautiously rounding the angle of the terrace. The water was shallow and the boatmen proceeded slowly and at length paused a few yards from the land.

"We can come no nearer," one of them called; "what is it?"

"Your mistress is unwell and wishes to return," Odo answered; and catching Fulvia in his arms he waded out with her to the gondola and lifted her over the side. "To Santa Chiara!" he ordered, as he laid her on the cushions beneath the felze; and the boatmen, recognising her as one of their late fares, without more ado began to row rapidly toward the city.

3.4.

In the pitying darkness of the gondola she lay beyond speech, her hand in his, her breath coming fitfully. Odo waited in suspense, not daring to question her, yet sure that if she did not speak then she would never do so. All doubt and perplexity of spirit had vanished in the simple sense of her nearness. The throb of her hand in his was like the heart-beat of hope. He felt himself no longer a drifting spectator of life but a sharer in its gifts and renunciations. Which this meeting would bring he dared not yet surmise: it was enough that he was with Fulvia and that love had freed his spirit.

At length she began to speak. Her agitation was so great that he had difficulty in piecing together the fragments of her story; but for the moment he was more concerned in regaining her confidence than in seeking to obtain a clear picture of the past. Before she could end, the gondola rounded the corner of the narrow canal skirting the garden-wall of Santa Chiara. Alarmed lest he should lose her again he passionately urged her to receive him on the morrow; and after some hesitation she consented. A moment later their prow touched the postern and the boatman gave a low call which proved him no novice at the business. Fulvia signed to Odo not to speak or move; and they sat listening intently for the opening of the gate. As soon as it was unbarred she sprang ashore and vanished in the darkness of the garden; and with a cold sense of failure Odo heard the bolt slipping back and the stealthy fall of the oars as the gondola slid away under the shadow of the convent-wall. Whither was he being carried and would that bolt ever be drawn for him again? In the sultry dawn the convent loomed forbiddingly as a prison, and he could hardly believe that a few hours earlier the very doors now closed against him had stood open to all the world. They would open again; but whether to him, who could conjecture? He was resolved to see Fulvia again, but he shrank from the thought of forcing himself upon her. She had promised to receive him; but what revulsion of feeling might not the morrow bring?

Unable to sleep, he bade the boatmen carry him to the Lido. The sun was just rising above the Friulian Alps and the lagoon lay dull and smooth as a breathed-on mirror. As he paced the lonely sands he tried to reconstruct Fulvia's broken story, supplementing it with such details as his experience of Venetian life suggested. It appeared that after her father's death she had found herself possessed of a small sum of money which he had painfully accumulated for her during the two years they had spent in Pavia. Her only thought was to employ this inheritance in publishing the great work on the origin of civilisation which Vivaldi had completed a few days before his last seizure. Through one of the professors of the University, who had been her father's friend, she negotiated with a printer of Amsterdam for the production of the book, and the terms being agreed on, despatched the money and the manuscript thither by a sure hand. Both were duly delivered and the publisher had advanced so far in his work as to send Fulvia the proof-sheets of the first chapters, when he took alarm at the renewed activity of the Holy Office in France and Italy, declared there would be no market for the book in the present state of affairs, and refused either to continue printing it, or to restore the money, which he said had barely covered the setting-up of the type. Fulvia then attempted to recover the manuscript; but the publisher refusing to surrender it, she found herself doubly beggared at a stroke.

In this extremity she turned to a sister of her father's, who lived near Treviso; and this excellent woman, though persuaded that her brother's heretical views had doomed him to everlasting torment, did not scruple to offer his child a home. Here Fulvia had lived for two years when her aunt's sudden death left her destitute; for the good lady, to atone for having given shelter to a niece of doubtful orthodoxy, had left the whole of her small property to the Church.

Fulvia's only other relations were certain distant cousins of her mother's, members of the Venetian nobility, but of the indigent class called Barnabotti, who lived on the bounty of the state. While in Treviso she had made the acquaintance of one of these cousins, a stirring noisy fellow involved in all the political agitations of the state. It was among the Barnabotti, the class most indebted to the government, that these seditious movements generally arose; and Fulvia's cousin was one of the most notorious malcontents of his order. She had mistaken his revolutionary bluster for philosophic enlightenment; and, persuaded that he shared in her views, she rashly appealed to him for help. With the most eloquent expressions of sympathy he offered her a home under his own roof; but on reaching Venice she was but ill-received by his wife and family, who made no scruple of declaring that, being but pensioners themselves, they were in no state to nourish their pauper relatives. Fulvia could not but own that they were right; for they lived in the garret of a half-ruined house, pawning their very beds to pay for ices in the Piazza and sitting at home all the week in dirty shifts and night-caps that they might go to mass in silk and powder on a Sunday. After two months of wretchedness with these unfriendly hosts, whom she vainly tried to conciliate by a hundred little services and attentions the poor girl resolved to return to Milan, where she hoped to obtain some menial position in the household of one of her father's friends. Her cousins, at this, made a great outcry, protesting that none of their blood should so demean herself, and that they would spare no efforts to find some better way of providing for her. Their noble connections gave Fulvia the hope that they might obtain a small pension for her, and she unsuspiciously yielded to their wishes; but to her dismay she learned a few weeks later, that, thanks to their exertions, she was to be admitted as a novice to the convent of Santa Chiara. Though it was the common way of disposing of portionless girls, the liberal views of her cousins had reassured Fulvia, and she woke to her fate too late to escape it. She was to enter on her novitiate on the morrow; but even had delay been possible she knew that both the civil and religious authorities would sustain her family in their course.

Her cousins, knowing her independent spirit, and perhaps fearing an outcry if they sequestered her too closely, had thought to soften her resistance by placing her in a convent noted for its leniencies; but to Fulvia such surroundings were more repugnant than the strictest monastic discipline. The corruption of the religious orders was a favourite topic with her father's friends, and the Venetian nuns were noted throughout Italy for their frivolous and dissipated lives; but nothing that Fulvia had heard or imagined approached the realities that awaited her. At first the mere sense of imprisonment, of being cut off forever from the world of free thought and action which had been her native element, overwhelmed every other feeling, and she lay numb in the clutch of fate. But she was too young for this merciful torpor to last, and with the returning consciousness of her situation came the instinctive effort to amend it. How she longed then to have been buried in some strict order, where she might have spent her days in solitary work and meditation! How she loathed the petty gossip of the nuns, their furtive reaching after forbidden pleasures! The blindest bigotry would have been less insufferable than this clandestine commerce with the world, the strictest sequestration than this open parody of the monastic calling. She sought in vain among her companions for an answering mind. Many, like herself, were in open rebellion against their lot; but for reasons so different that the feeling was an added estrangement. At last the longing to escape over-mastered every other sensation. It became a fixed idea, a devouring passion. She did not trust herself to think of what must follow, but centred every faculty on the effort of evasion.

At this point in her story her growing distress had made it hard for Odo to gather more than a general hint of her meaning. It was clear, however, that she had found her sole hope of escape lay in gaining the friendship of one of the more favoured nuns. Her own position in the community was of the humblest, for she had neither rank nor wealth to commend her; but her skill on the harpsichord had attracted the notice of the music-mistress and she had been enrolled in the convent orchestra before her novitiate was over. This had brought her into contact with a few of the more favoured sisters, and among them she had recognised in Sister Mary of the Crucifix the daughter of the nobleman who had been her aunt's landlord at Treviso. Fulvia's name was not unknown to the handsome nun, and the coincidence was enough to draw them together in a community where such trivial affinities must replace the ties of nature. Fulvia soon learned that Mary of the

Crucifix was the spoiled darling of the convent. Her beauty and spirit, as much perhaps as her family connections, had given her this predominance; and no scruples interfered with her use of it. Finding herself, as she declared, on the wrong side of the grate, she determined to gather in all the pleasures she could reach through it; and her reach was certainly prodigious. Here Odo had been obliged to fall back on his knowledge of Venetian customs to conjecture the incidents leading up to the scene of the previous night. He divined that Fulvia, maddened by having had to pronounce the irrevocable vows, had resolved to fly at all hazards; that Sister Mary, unconscious of her designs, had proposed to take her on a party of pleasure, and that the rash girl, blind to every risk but that of delay, had seized on this desperate means of escape. What must have followed had she not chanced on Odo, she had clearly neither the courage nor the experience to picture; but she seemed to have had some confused idea of throwing herself on the mercy of the foreign nobleman she believed she was to meet.

So much Odo had gathered; and her voice, her gesture, the disorder of her spirit, supplied what her words omitted. Not for a moment, either in listening to her or in the soberer period of revision, did he question the exact truth of her narrative. It was the second time that they had met under strange circumstances; yet now as before the sense of her candour was his ruling thought. He concluded that, whatever plight she found herself in, she would be its immediate justification; and felt sure he must have reached this conclusion though love had not had a stake in the verdict. This perhaps but proved him the more deeply taken; for it is when passion tightens the net that reason flaps her wings most loudly.

Day was high when he returned to his lodgings, impatient for a word from Fulvia. None had come; and as the hours passed he yielded to the most disheartening fancies. His wretchedness was increased by the thought that he had once inflicted on her such suspense he was now enduring; and he went so far as to wonder if this were her revenge for Vercelli. But if the past was intolerable to consider the future was all baffling fears. His immediate study was how to see her; and this her continued silence seemed to refuse him. The extremity of her plight was his best ally; yet here again anxiety suggested that his having been the witness of her humiliation must insensibly turn her against him. Never perhaps does a man show less knowledge of human nature than in speculating on the conduct of his beloved; and every step in the labyrinth of his conjectures carried Odo farther from the truth. This rose on him at nightfall, in the shape of a letter slipped in his hand by a lay-sister as he crossed the square before his lodgings. He stepped to the light of the nearest shrine and read the few words in a tumult. "This being Friday, no visitors are admitted to the convent; but I entreat you to come to me tomorrow an hour before benediction." A postcript added: "It is the hour when visitors are most frequent."

He saw her meaning in a flash: his best chance of speaking with her was in a crowd, and his heart bounded at the significance of her admission. Now indeed he felt himself lord of the future. Nothing counted but that he was to see her. His horizon was narrowed to the bars through which her hand would greet him; yet never had the world appeared so vast.

Long before the hour appointed he was at the gate of Santa Chiara. He asked to speak with Sister Veronica and the portress led him to the parlour. Several nuns were already behind the grate, chatting with a group of fashionable ladies and their gallants; but Fulvia was not among them. In a few moments the portress returned and informed Odo that Sister Veronica was indisposed and unable to leave her cell. His heart sank, and he asked if she had sent no message. The portress answered in the negative, but added that the abbess begged him to come to her parlour; and at this his hopes took wing again.

The abbess's parlour was preceded by a handsome antechamber, where Odo was bidden to wait. It was doubtless the Reverend Mother's hour for receiving company, for through the door beyond he heard laughter and music and the sound of lively talk. Presently this door opened and Mary of the Crucifix entered. In her monastic habit she looked coarse and overblown: the severe lines and sober tints of the dress did not become her. Odo felt an insurmountable repugnance at seeing her. He could not conceive why Fulvia had chosen such an intermediary, and for the first time a stealing doubt tainted his thoughts of her.

Sister Mary seemed to read his mind. "You bear me a grudge," said she gaily; "but I think you will live to own that I do not return it. Come with me if you wish to speak with Sister Veronica."

Odo flushed with surprise. "She is not too unwell to receive me?"

Sister Mary raised her eyebrows in astonishment. "To receive her cousin? Her nearest male relative, come from Treviso purposely to visit her? The saints forbid!" she cried. "The poor child is indeed dying—but only to see her cousin!" And with that she seized his hand and hurried him down the corridor to a door on which she tapped three times. It opened at once, and catching Odo by the shoulder she pushed him laughingly over the threshold and cried out as she vanished: "Be careful not to agitate the sufferer!"

Odo found himself in a neat plain cell; but he had no eyes for his surroundings. All that he saw was Fulvia, dressed in her nun's habit and seated near the window, through which the afternoon light fell softly on her white coif and the austere folds of her dress. She rose and greeted him with a smile.

"You are not ill, then?" he cried, stupidly, and the colour rose to her pale face.

"No," she said, "I am not ill, and at first I was reluctant to make use of such a subterfuge; but to feign an indisposition was the only way of speaking with you privately, and, alas, in this school one soon becomes a proficient in deceit." She paused a moment and then added with an effort: "Even this favour I could not have obtained save through Sister Mary of the Crucifix; but she now understands that you are an old friend of my father's, and that my motive for wishing to see you is not what she at first supposed."

This was said with such noble simplicity and so direct a glance, that Odo, confused by the sense of his own doubts, could only murmur as he bent over her hand: "Fuoco di quest' incendio non v' assale."

She drew back gently and signed him to a seat. "I trust not," she said, answering his citation; "but I think the flame through which Beatrice walked must have been less contaminating than this morass in which I flounder."

She was silent a moment and he had leisure to steal a closer look at her. It was the first time since their meeting that he had really seen her face; and he was struck by the touch of awe that had come upon her beauty. Perhaps her recent suffering had spiritualised a countenance already pure and lofty; for as he looked at her it seemed to him that she was transformed into a being beyond earthly contact, and his heart sank with the sense of her remoteness. Presently she began to speak and his consciousness of the distance between them was increased by the composure of her manner. All signs of confusion and distress had vanished. She faced him with the same innocent freedom as under her father's roof, and all that had since passed between them seemed to have slipped from her without a trace.

She began by thanking him for coming, and then at once reverted to her desperate situation and to her determination to escape.

"I am alone and friendless," she said, "and though the length of our past acquaintance" (and here indeed she blushed) "scarce warrants such a presumption, yet I believe that in my father's name I may appeal to you. It may be that with the best will to help me you can discover no way of doing so, but at least I shall have the benefit of your advice. I now see," she added, again deeply blushing, but keeping her eyes on his, "the madness of my late attempt, and the depth of the abyss from which you rescued me. Death were indeed preferable to such chances; but I do not mean to die while life holds out a hope of liberation."

As she spoke there flashed on Odo the reason of her remoteness and composure. He had come to her as a lover: she received him as a friend. His longing to aid her was inspired by passion: she saw in it only the natural impulse of benevolence. So mortifying was the discovery that he hardly followed her words. All his thoughts were engaged in reviewing the past; and he now saw that if, as she said, their acquaintance scarce warranted her appealing to him as a friend, it still less justified his addressing her as a lover. Only once before had he spoken to her of love, and that under circumstances which almost forbade a return to the subject, or at least compelled an added prudence in approaching it. Once again he found himself the prisoner of his folly, and stood aghast at the ingenuity of the punishment. To play the part she ascribed to him was his only portion; and he resolved at least to play it like a man.

With what composure he might, he assured Fulvia of his desire to serve her, and asked if she had no hope of obtaining her release from the Holy See. She answered: none, since enquiry must reveal that she was the daughter of a man who had been prosecuted for heresy, and that after his death she had devoted the small sum he had left her to the publication of his writings. She added that his Holiness, resolved to counteract the effects of the late Pope's leniency, had greatly enlarged the powers of the Inquisition, and had taken special measures to prevent those who entered the religious life from renouncing their calling.

"Since I have been here," she said, "three nuns have tried to obtain their release, and one has conclusively proved that she was forced to take the vows by fraud; but their pleas have been rejected, and mine would meet the same fate. Indeed, the only result would be to deprive me of what little liberty I am allowed; for the three nuns I speak of are now the most closely watched in the convent."

She went on to explain that, thanks to the connivance of Sister Mary of the Crucifix, her actual escape might be effected without much difficulty; but that she was now awake to the madness of taking so desperate a step without knowing whither it would lead her.

"To be safe," she said, "I must cross the borders of Switzerland. If I could reach Geneva I should be beyond the arm of the Holy Office, and at the University there I should find friends of my father who would surely take pity on my situation and help me to a living. But the journey is long and difficult, and not to be safely attempted without some assurance of shelter on the way."

It was on Odo's lips to declare that he would provide her with shelter and escort; but at this moment three warning taps announced the return of Sister Mary of the Crucifix.

She entered merrily and at once laid one hand on Fulvia's brow and caught her wrist in the other. "The patient's pulse has risen," she declared, "and rest and a lowering treatment are essential. I must ask the cavaliere to withdraw."

Fulvia, with an air of constraint, held out her hand to Odo.

"I shall see you soon again?" he whispered; and Sister Mary, as though she had guessed his words, cried out, "I think your excellency may count on a recurrence of the seizure two days hence at the same hour!"

3.5.

With this Odo was forced to be content; and he passed the intervening time in devising the means of Fulvia's rescue. He was resolved to let no rashness or negligence hinder the attempt, and to prove, by the discretion of his course, that he was no longer the light fool who had once hazarded her safety. He went about his preparations as one that had no private stake in the venture; but he was therefore the more punctilious to show himself worthy of her trust and sensible of the charge it laid upon him.

At their next meeting he found her in the same open and friendly mood, and she listened gratefully as he set forth his plan. This was that she should first write to a doctor of the University in Geneva, who had been her father's friend, stating her plight and asking if he could help her to a living should she contrive to reach Geneva. Pending the reply, Odo was to plan the stages of the journey in such fashion that she might count on concealment in case of pursuit; and she was not to attempt her escape till these details were decided. Fulvia was the more ready to acquiesce in this postponement as she did not wish to involve Sister Mary in her adventure, but hoped to escape unassisted during an entertainment which was to take place in the convent on the feast of Saint Michael, some six weeks later.

To Odo the delay was still more welcome; for it gave him what he must needs regard as his last opportunity of being in the girl's company. She had accepted his companionship on the journey with a readiness in which he saw only the magnanimity of pardon; but in Geneva they must part, and what hope had he of seeing her again? The first smart of vanity allayed, he was glad she chose to treat him as a friend. It was in this character that he could best prove his disinterestedness, his resolve to make amends for the past; and in this character only—as he now felt—would it be possible for him to part from her.

On his second visit he ventured to discharge his mind of its heaviest burden by enquiring what had befallen her and her father after he had lost trace of them at Vercelli. She told him quite simply that, failing to meet him at the appointed place, they at once guessed that his plan had been winded by the abate who travelled with him; and that after a few hours' delay her father had succeeded in securing a chaise which had taken them safely across the border. She went on to speak of the hardships they had suffered after reaching Milan. Even under a comparatively liberal government it was small advantage to be marked by the Holy Office; and though he received much kindness, and even material aid, from those of his way of thinking, Vivaldi was unable to obtain the professorship he had hoped for.

From Milan they went to Pavia; but in this University, the most liberal in Italy, the chairs were so sought after that there was no hope of his receiving a charge worthy of his talents. Here, however, his spirit breathed its natural air, and reluctant to lose the privileges of such intercourse he decided to accept the post of librarian to an eccentric nobleman of the town. If his pay was modest his duties left him leisure for the work which was his chief concern; for his patron, who had houses in Milan and Brescia, came seldom to Pavia, and Fulvia and her father had the vast palace to themselves. They lodged in a corner adjoining the library, spending their days in studious seclusion, their evenings in conversation with some of the first scholars of Europe: the learned botanist Scopoli, Spallanzani, Volta, and Father Fontana, the famous mathematician. In such surroundings Vivaldi might have pursued his task contentedly enough, but for the thought of Fulvia's future. This, his daughter said, continually preyed on him, driving him to labours beyond his strength; for he hoped by the publication of his book to make good, at least in part, the loss of the small property which the Sardinian government had confiscated. All her entreaties could not dissuade him from over-exertion; and in addition to his regular duties he took on himself (as she afterward learned) the tedious work of revising proofs and copying manuscripts for the professors. This drudgery, combined with severe intellectual effort, exceeded his flagging powers; and the book was hardly completed when his patron, apprised of its contents, abruptly removed him from his post. From that day Vivaldi sank in health; but he ended as became a sage, content to have discharged the task for which he had given up home and substance, and dying with the great Stoic's words upon his lips:—

Lex non poena mors.

Vivaldi's friends in Milan came generously to Fulvia's aid, and she would gladly have remained among them; but after the loss of her small inheritance and of her father's manuscript she was without means of repaying their kindness, and nothing remained but to turn to her own kin.

As Odo sat in the quiet cell, listening to her story, and hearing again the great names his youth had reverenced, he felt himself an exile returning to his own, mounting the familiar heights and breathing the air that was his birthright.

Looking back from this recovered standpoint he saw how far behind his early hopes had been left. Since his departure from Naples there had been nothing to remind him of that vast noiseless labour of the spirit going on everywhere beneath the social surface: that baffled but undiscouraged endeavour in which he had once so impatiently claimed his share. Now every word of Fulvia's smote the bones of some dead purpose, till his bosom seemed a very valley of Ezekiel. Her own trials had fanned her love of freedom, and the near hope of release lent an exaltation to her words. Of bitterness, of resentment she gave no sign; and he was awed by the same serenity of spirit which had struck him in the imprisoned doctor. But perhaps the strongest impression she produced was that of increasing his points of contact with life. His other sentimental ties had been a barrier between himself and the outer world; but the feeling which drew him to Fulvia had the effect of levelling the bounds of egoism, of letting into the circle of his nearest emotions that great tide of human longing and effort that had always faintly sounded on the shores of self. Perhaps it was her power of evoking this wider life that gave a sense of permanence, of security almost, to the stolen moments of their intercourse, lulling the lover's impatience of actual conditions with the sense of something that must survive the accidents of fortune. Only in some such way could he explain, in looking back, the completeness of each moment spent with her. He was conscious even at the time of a suspension of the emotional laws, a charmed surrender to the limitations of his fate. When he was away his impatience reasserted itself; but her presence was like a soothing hand on his spirit, and he knew that his quiet hours with her would count among those intervals between the crises of life that flower in memory when the crises themselves have faded.

It was natural that in the course of these visits she in turn should question him; and as his past rearranged itself beneath her scrutiny he seemed once more to trace the thread of purpose on which its fragments hung. He told her of his connection with the liberals of Pianura, of the situation at court, and of the reason for his prolonged travels. As he talked her eyes conveyed the exquisite sense of her complete comprehension. She saw, before he could justify himself, how the uncertainty of his future, and his inability to act, had cast him adrift upon a life of superficial enjoyment; and how his latent dissatisfaction with this life had inevitably resulted in self-distrust and vacillation. "You wait your hour," she said of him; and he seized on the phrase as a justification of his inactivity and, when chance should offer, a spur to fresh endeavour. Her interest in the liberal cause had been intensified and exalted by her father's death—his martyrdom, as she described it. Like most women possessed of an abstract idea she had unconsciously personified the idea and made a religion of it; but it was a religion of charity and not of vindictiveness. "I should like my father's death avenged by love and not by hate," she said; "I would have it bring peace, not a sword."

On one point only she remained, if not hostile yet unresponsive. This was when he spoke of de Crucis. Her manner hardened instantly, and he perceived that, though he dwelt on the Jesuit's tolerant view and cultivated tastes, she beheld only the priest and not the man. She had been eager to hear of Crescenti, whom she knew by name as a student of European repute, and to the praise of whose parochial charities she listened with outspoken sympathy; but the Jesuits stood for the Holy Office, and she had suffered too deeply at the hands of the Holy Office to regard with an open mind any who might be supposed to represent its principles. It was impossible for Odo to make her understand how distinctly, in de Crucis's case, the man predominated over the order; and conscious of the painfulness of the subject, he gave up the attempt to interest her in his friend.

Three or four times he was permitted to visit her in her cell: after that they met almost daily in the parlour, where, about the hour of benediction, they could talk almost as privately under cover of the general chatter. In due time Fulvia received an answer from the Calvinist professor, who assured her of a welcome in Geneva and shelter under his roof. Odo, meanwhile, had perfected the plan of their journey; but as Michaelmas approached he began to fear Cantapresto's observation. He now bitterly regretted that he had not held to his purpose of sending the soprano back to Pianura; but to do so at this point would be to challenge observation and he resolved instead on despatching him to Monte Alloro with a letter to the old Duke. As the way to Geneva lay in the opposite direction this would at least give the fugitives a three days' lead; and they had little cause to fear pursuit from any other quarter. The convent indeed might raise a hue and cry; but the nuns of Santa Chiara had lately given the devout so much cause for scandal that the abbess would probably be disposed to hush up any fresh delinquency. The time too was well-chosen; for the sisters had prevailed on the Reverend Mother to celebrate the saint's day by a masked ball, and the whole convent was engrossed in the invention of whimsical disguises. The nuns indeed were not to take part in the ball; but a number of them were to appear in an allegorical entertainment with which the evening was to open. The new Papal Nuncio, who was lately arrived in Venice, had promised to be present; and as he was known to be a man of pleasure there was scarce a sister in the convent but had an eye to his conquest. These circumstances gave to Fulvia's plans the shelter of indifference; for in the delightful effort of surpassing the other nuns even Mary of the Crucifix lost interest in her friend's affairs.

Odo, to preserve the secrecy of his designs, had been obliged to keep up a pretence of his former habits, showing himself abroad with Coeur-Volant and Castelrovinato and frequenting the Procuratessa's routs and card-parties. This lady, though lately returned to the Brenta, had announced her intention of coming to Venice for the ball at Santa Chiara; and Coeur-Volant was mightily preoccupied with the entertainment, at which he purposed his mistress should outshine all her companions.

The evening came at last, and Odo found himself entering the gates of Santa Chiara with a throng of merry-makers. The convent was noted for its splendid hospitality, and unwonted preparations had been made to honour the saint. The brightly-illuminated bridge leading to the square of Santa Chiara was decked with a colonnade of pasteboard and stiffened linen cunningly painted, and a classical portico masked the entrance gate. A flourish of trumpets and hautboys, and the firing of miniature cannon, greeted the arrival of the guests, who were escorted to the parlour, which was hung with tapestries and glowing with lights like a Lady Chapel. Here they were received by the abbess, who, on the arrival of the Nuncio, led the way to the garden, where a stage had been erected.

The nuns who were not to take part in the play had been seated directly under the stage, divided from the rest of the company by a low screen of foliage. Ranged beneath the footlights, which shone on their bare shoulders and white gowns, and on the gauze veils replacing their monastic coifs, they seemed a choir of pagan virgins grouped in the proscenium of an antique theatre. Everything indeed combined to produce the impression of some classic festival: the setting of motionless foliage, the mild autumnal sky in which the stars hung near and vivid, and the foreground thronged with a motley company lit by the shifting brightness of torches.

As Odo, in mask and travesty, stood observing the fantastically-dressed audience, the pasteboard theatre adorned with statuary, and the nuns flitting across the stage, his imagination, strung to the highest pitch by his own impending venture, was thrilled by the contrast between the outward appearance of the scene and its underlying reality. From where he stood he looked directly at the abbess, who was seated with the Nuncio and his suite under the tall crucifix in the centre of the garden. As if to emphasise the irony of the situation, the torch fixed behind this noble group cast an enlarged shadow of the cross over the abbess's white gown and the splendid robes of her companions, who, though they wore the mask, had not laid aside their clerical dress. To Odo the juxtaposition had the effect of some supernatural warning, the shadow of the divine wrath projected on its heedless ministers; an impression heightened by the fact that, just opposite the cross, a lively figure of Pan, surmounting the pediment of the theatre, seemed to fling defiance at the Galilean intruder.

The nuns, like the rest of the company, were masked; and it had been agreed between Odo and Fulvia that the latter should wear a wreath of myrtle above her veil. As almost all her companions had chosen brightly-coloured flowers this dark green chaplet was easily distinguished among the clustered heads beneath the stage, and Odo had no doubt of being able to rejoin Fulvia in the moment of dispersal that should follow the conclusion of the play. He knew that the sisters were to precede their guests and be locked behind the grate before the ball began; but as they passed through the garden and cloisters the barrier between nuns and visitors would probably not be too strictly maintained. As he had foreseen, the company, attracted by the graceful procession, pressed forward regardless of the assistant mistresses' protests, and the shadowy arcades were full of laughter and whispered snatches of talk as the white flock was driven back to its fold.

Odo had withdrawn to the darkest angle of the cloister, close to a door leading to the pharmacy. It was here that Fulvia had told him to wait; and though he had lost sight of her when the audience rose, he stood confidently watching for the reappearance of the myrtle-wreath. Presently he saw it close at hand; and just then the line of sisters flowed toward him, driven forward by a group of lively masqueraders, among whom he seemed to recognise Coeur-Volant's voice and figure. Nothing could have been more opportune, for the pressure swept the wearer of the myrtle-wreath almost into his arms; and as the intruders were dispersed and the nuns laughingly reformed their lines, her hand lingered in his and he felt himself drawn toward the door.

It yielded to her touch and Odo followed her down a dark passageway to the empty room where rows of old Faenza jars and quaintly-shaped flagons glimmered in the dusk. Beyond the pharmacy was another door, the key of which hung on the wall with the portress's hood and cloak. Without a word the girl wrapped herself in the cloak and, fitting the key to the lock, softly opened the door. All this was done with a rapidity and assurance for which Odo was unprepared; but, reflecting that Fulvia's whole future hung on the promptness with which each detail of her plan was executed, he concluded that her natural force of character enabled her to assume an ease she could hardly feel.

The door opened on the kitchen-garden, and brushing the lavender-hedges with her flying skirts she sped on ahead of Odo to the postern which the nuns were accustomed to use for their nocturnal escapades. Only the thickness of an oaken gate stood between Fulvia and the outer world. To her the opening of the gate meant the first step toward freedom, but to Odo the passing from their enchanted weeks of fellowship to the inner loneliness of his former life. He hung back silent while she drew the bolt.

A moment later they had crossed the threshold and his gondola was slipping toward them out of the shadow of the wall. Fulvia sprang on board and he followed her under the felze. The warm darkness enclosing them stirred impulses which their daily intercourse had subdued, and in the sense of her nearness he lost sight of the conditions which had brought them together.

The feeling seemed to communicate itself; for as the gondola rounded the angle of the convent-wall and swung out on the open, she drooped toward him with the turn of the boat and their lips met under the loosened masks.

At the same instant the light of the Virgin's shrine in the corner of the convent-wall fell through the window of the felze on the face lifted to Odo's; and he found himself suddenly confronted by the tender eyes and malicious smile of Sister Mary of the Crucifix.

"By Diana," she cried as he started back, "I did but claim my pay in advance; nor do I think that, when she knows all, Sister Veronica will grudge me my reward!"

He continued to stare at her in speechless bewilderment, and she went on with a kind of tender impatience: "You simpleton, can you not guess that you were watched, and that but for me your Veronica would at this moment be lying under lock and key in her cell? Instead of which," she continued, speaking more slowly, and leaning back as though to enjoy the full savour of his suspense, "instead of which she now awaits you in a safe nook of my choosing, where, within half an hour's time, you may atone to her with interest for the infidelity into which I have betrayed you."

"She knows, then?" Odo faltered, not daring to say more in his ignorance of Sister Mary's share in the secret.

Sister Mary shook her head with a tantalising laugh. "That you are coming? Alas, no, poor angel! She fancies that she has been sent from the convent to avoid you—as indeed she was, and by the Reverend Mother's own order, who, it seems, had wind of the intrigue this morning. But, the saints be praised, the excellent sister who was ordered to attend her is in my pay and instead of conducting her to her relatives of San Barnado, who were to keep her locked up over night, has, if I mistake not, taken her to a good woman of my acquaintance—an old servant, in fact—who will guard her as jealously as the family plate till you and I come to her release."

As she spoke she put out her head and gave a whispered order to the gondolier; and at the word the boat swung round and headed for the city.

In the violent reaction which this strange encounter produced, Odo was for the moment incapable of taking any clear note of his surroundings. Uncertain if he were not once more the victim of some such mischance as seemed to attend all his efforts to succour Fulvia, he sat in silent apprehension as the gondola shot across the Grand Canal and entered the labyrinth of water-ways behind San Moise. Sister Mary took his silence philosophically.

"You dare not speak to me, for fear of betraying yourself," she said, "and I scarce wonder at your distrust; for your plans were so well laid that I had no notion of what was on foot, and must have remained in ignorance if Veronica had not been put in Sister Martha's charge. But you will both live to thank me, and I hope," she added, laughing, "to own that you would have done better to take me into your confidence from the first."

As she spoke the gondola touched at the head of a narrow passage which lost itself in the blackness of the overhanging houses. Sister Mary sprang out and drew Odo after her. A few yards down the alley she entered a plain low-storied house somewhat withdrawn behind its neighbours. Followed by Odo she groped her way up a dark flight of stairs and knocked at a door on the upper landing. A vague flutter within, indicative of whispers and uncertain movements, was followed by the slipping of the bolt, and a middle-aged woman looked out. She drew back with an exclamation of welcome, and Sister Mary, seizing Odo by the shoulders, pushed him across the threshold of a small dimly-lit kitchen.

Fulvia, in her nun's habit, cowered in the darkest corner; but at sight of Odo she sprang up, and ran toward him with a happy cry.

3.6.

An hour later the two were well on their way toward Mestre, where a travelling-chaise awaited them. Odo, having learned that Andreoni was settled in Padua, had asked him to receive Fulvia in his house till the next night-fall; and the bookseller, whom he had taken into his confidence, was eager to welcome the daughter of the revered Vivaldi.

The extremes of hope and apprehension had left Fulvia too exhausted for many words, and Odo, after she had confirmed every particular of Sister Mary's story, refrained from questioning her farther. Thanks to her friend's resources she had been able to exchange her nun's dress for the plain gown and travelling-cloak of a young woman of the middle class; and this dress painfully recalled to Odo the day when he had found her standing beside the broken-down chaise on the road to Vercelli.

The recollection was not calculated to put him at his ease; and indeed it was only now that he began to feel the peculiar constraint of his position. To Andreoni his explanation of Fulvia's flight had seemed natural enough; but on the subsequent stages of their journey she must pass for his mistress or his wife, and he hardly knew in what spirit she would take the misapprehensions that must inevitably arise.

At Mestre their carriage waited, and they drove rapidly toward Padua through the waning night. Andreoni, in his concern for Fulvia's safety, had prepared for her reception a little farm-house of his wife's, in a vineyard beyond the town; and here at daybreak it was almost a relief to Odo to commit his charge to the Signora Andreoni's care.

The day was spent indoors, and Andreoni having thought it more prudent to bring no servant from Padua, his wife prepared the meals for their guests and the bookseller drew a jar of his own wine from the cellar. Fulvia kept to herself during the day; but at dusk she surprised Odo by entering the room with a trayful of plates and glasses, and helping their hostess to set out the supper-table. The few hours of rest had restored to her not only the serenity of the convent, but a lightness of step and glance that Odo had not seen in her since the early days of their friendship. He marvelled to see how the first breath of freedom had set her blood in motion and fanned her languid eye; but he could not suppress the accompanying thought that his own presence had failed to work such miracles.

They had planned to ride that night to a little village in the hills beyond Vicenza, where Fulvia's foster-mother, a peasant of the Vicentine, lived with her son, who was a vine-dresser; and supper was hardly over when they were told that their horses waited. Their kind hosts dared not urge them to linger; and after a hurried farewell they rode forth into the fresh darkness of the September night.

The new moon was down and they had to thread their way slowly through the stony lanes between the vineyards. At length they gained the open country, and growing more accustomed to the darkness put their horses to a trot. The change of pace, and the exhilaration of traversing an unknown country in the hush and mystery of night, combined to free their spirits, and Odo began to be aware that the barrier between them was lifted. To the charm of their intercourse at Santa Chiara was added that closer sympathy produced by the sense of isolation. They were enclosed in their common risk as in some secret meeting-place where no consciousness of the outer world intruded; and though their talk kept the safe level of their immediate concerns he felt the change in every inflection of Fulvia's voice and in the subtler emphasis of her silences.

The way was long, and he had feared that she would be taxed beyond her strength; but the miles seemed to fly beneath their horses' feet, and they could scarcely believe that the dark hills which rose ahead of them against a whitening sky marked the limit of their journey.

With some difficulty they found their way to the vine-dresser's house, a mere hut in a remote fold of the hills. From motives of prudence they had not warned the nurse of their coming; but they found the old woman already at work in her melon-patch and learned from her that her son had gone down to his day's labour in the valley. She received Fulvia with a tender wonder, as at some supernatural presence descending into her life, too much awed, till the first embraces were over, to risk any conjecture as to Odo's presence. But with the returning sense of familiarity—the fancied recovery of the nurseling's features in the girl's definite outline—came the inevitable reaction of curiosity, and the fugitives felt themselves coupled in the old woman's meaning smiles. To Odo's surprise Fulvia received these innuendoes with baffling composure, parrying the questions she seemed to answer, and finally taking refuge in a plea for rest. But the accord of the previous night was broken; and when the travellers set out again, starting a little before sunset to avoid the vine-dresser's return, the constraint of the day began to weigh upon them. In Fulvia's case physical weariness perhaps had a share in the change; but whatever the cause, its effect was to make this stage of the journey strangely tedious to both.

Their way lay through the country north of Vicenza, whence they hoped by dawn to gain Peschiera on the lake of Garda, and hire a chaise which should take them across the border. For the first hour or two they had the new moon to light them; but as it set the sky clouded and drops of rain began to fall. Fulvia had hitherto shown a gay indifference to the discomforts of the journey; but she presently began to complain of the cold and to question Odo anxiously as to the length of the way. The hilliness of the country forced them to travel slowly, and it seemed to Odo that hours had elapsed before they saw lights in the valley below them. Their plan had been to avoid the towns on their way, and Fulvia, the night before, had contented herself with a half-hour's rest by the roadside; but a heavy rain was now falling, and she at once assented to Odo's tentative proposal that they should take shelter till the storm was over.

They dismounted at an inn on the outskirts of the village. The sleepy landlord stared as he unbarred the door and led them into the kitchen; but he offered no comment beyond remarking that it was a good night to be under cover.

Fulvia sank down on the wooden settle near the chimney, where a fire had been hastily kindled. She took no notice of Odo when he removed the dripping cloak from her shoulders, but sat gazing before her in a kind of apathy.

"I cannot eat," she said, as Odo pressed her to take her place at the table.

The innkeeper turned to him with a confidential nod. "Your lady looks fairly beaten," he said. "I've a notion that one of my good beds would be more to her taste than the best supper in the land. Shall I have a room made ready for your excellencies?"

"No, no," said Fulvia, starting up. "We must set out again as soon as we have supped."

She approached the table and hastily emptied the glass of country wine that Odo had poured out for her.

The innkeeper seemed a simple unsuspicious fellow, but at this he put down the plate of cheese he was carrying and looked at her curiously.

"Start out again at this hour of the night?" he exclaimed. "By the saints, your excellencies must be running a race with the sun! Or do you doubt my being able to provide you with decent lodgings, that you prefer mud and rain to my good sheets and pillows?"

"Indeed, no," Odo amicably interposed; "but we are hurrying to meet a friend who is to rejoin us tomorrow at Peschiera."

"Ah—at Peschiera," said the other, as though the name had struck him. He took a dish of eggs from the fire and set it before Fulvia. "Well," he went on with a shrug, "it is written that none of my beds shall be slept in tonight. Not two hours since I had a gentleman here that gave the very same excuse for hurrying forward; though his horses were so spent that I had to provide him with another pair before he could continue his journey." He laughed and uncorked a second bottle.

"That reminds me," he went on, pausing suddenly before Fulvia, "that the other gentleman was travelling to meet a friend too; a lady, he said—a young lady. He fancied she might have passed this way and questioned me closely; but as it happened there had been no petticoat under my roof for three days.—I wonder, now, if he could have been looking for your excellencies?"

Fulvia flushed high at this, but a sign from Odo checked the denial on her lips.

"Why," said he, "it is not unlikely, though I had fancied our friend would come from another direction. What was this gentleman like?"

The landlord hesitated, evidently not so much from any reluctance to impart what he knew as from the inability to express it. "Well," said he, trying to supplement his words by a vaguely descriptive gesture, "he was a handsome personable-looking man—smallish built, but with a fine manner, and dressed not unlike your excellency."

"Ah," said Odo carelessly, "our friend is an ecclesiastic.—And which way did this gentleman travel?" he went on, pouring himself another glass.

The landlord assumed an air of country cunning. "There's the fishy part of it," said he. "He gave orders to go toward Verona; but my boy, who chased the carriage down the road, as lads will, says that at the cross-ways below the old mill the driver took the turn for Peschiera."

Fulvia at this seemed no longer able to control herself. She came close to Odo and said in a low urgent tone: "For heaven's sake, let us set forward!"

Odo again signed to her to keep silent, and with an effort she resumed her seat and made a pretence of eating. A moment later he despatched the landlord to the stable, to see that the horses had been rubbed down; and as soon as the door closed she broke out passionately.

"It is my fault," she cried, "it is all my fault for coming here. If I had had the courage to keep on this would never have happened!"

"No," said Odo quietly, "and we should have gone straight to Peschiera and landed in the arms of our pursuer—if this mysterious traveller is in pursuit of us."

His tone seemed to steady her. "Oh," she said, and the colour flickered out of her face.

"As it happens," he went on, "nothing could have been more fortunate than our coming here."

"I see—I see—; but now we must go on at once," she persisted.

He looked at her gravely. "This is your wish?"

She seemed seized with a panic fear. "I cannot stay here!" she repeated.

"Which way shall we go, then? If we continue to Peschiera, and this man is after us, we are lost."

"But if he does not find us he may return here—he will surely return here!"

"He cannot return before morning. It is close on midnight already. Meanwhile you can take a few hours' rest while I devise means of reaching the lake by some mule-track across the mountain."

It cost him an effort to take this tone with her; but he saw that in her high-strung mood any other would have been less effective. She rose slowly, keeping her eyes on him with the look of a frightened child. "I will do as you wish," she said.

"Let the landlord prepare a bed for you, then. I will keep watch down here and the horses shall be saddled at daylight."

She stood silent while he went to the door to call the innkeeper; but when the order was given, and the door closed again, she disconcerted him by a sudden sob.

"What a burden I am!" she cried. "I had no right to accept this of you." And she turned and fled up the dark stairs.

The night passed and toward dawn the rain ceased. Odo rose from his dreary vigil in the kitchen, and called to the innkeeper to carry up bread and wine to Fulvia's room. Then he went out to see that the horses were fed and watered. He had not dared to question the landlord as to the roads, lest his doing so should excite suspicion; but he hoped to find an ostler who would give him the information he needed.

The stable was empty, however; and he prepared to bait the horses himself. As he stooped to place his lantern on the floor he caught the gleam of a small polished object at his feet. He picked it up and found that it was a silver coat-of-arms, such as are attached to the blinders and saddles of a carriage-harness. His curiosity was aroused, and holding the light closer he recognised the ducal crown of Pianura surmounting the "Humilitas" of the Valseccas.

The discovery was so startling that for some moments he stood gazing at the small object in his hand without being able to steady his confused ideas. Gradually they took shape, and he saw that, if the ornament had fallen from the harness of the traveller who had just preceded them, it was not Fulvia but he himself who was being pursued. But who was it who sought him and to what purpose? One fact alone was clear: the traveller, whoever he was, rode in one of the Duke's carriages, and therefore presumably upon his sovereign's business.

Odo was still trying to thread a way through these conjectures when a yawning ostler pushed open the stable-door.

"Your excellency is in a hurry to be gone," he said, with a surprised glance.

Odo handed him the coat-of-arms. "Can you tell me what this is?" he asked carelessly. "I picked it up here a moment ago."

The other turned it over and stared. "Why," said he, "that's off the harness of the gentleman that supped here last night—the same that went on later to Peschiera."

Odo proceeded to question him about the mule-tracks over Monte Baldo, and having bidden him saddle the horses in half an hour, crossed the courtyard and re-entered the inn. A grey light was already falling through the windows, and he mounted the stairs and knocked on the door which he thought must be Fulvia's. Her voice bade him enter and he found her seated fully dressed beside the window. She rose with a smile and he saw that she had regained her usual self-possession.

"Do we set out at once?" she asked.

"There is no great haste," he answered. "You must eat first, and by that time the horses will be saddled."

"As you please," she returned, with a readiness in which he divined the wish to make amends for her wilfulness the previous night. Her eyes and cheeks glowed with an excitement which counterfeited the effects of a night's rest, and he thought he had never seen her more radiant. She approached the table on which the wine and bread had been placed, and drew another chair beside her own.

"Will you not share with me?" she asked, filling a glass for him.

He took it from her with a smile. "I have good news for you," he said, holding out the bit of silver which he had brought from the stable.

She examined it wonderingly. "What does this mean?" she asked, looking up at him.

"That it is I who am being followed—and not you."

She started and the ornament slipped from her hand.

"You?" she faltered with a quick change of colour.

"This coat-of-arms," he explained, "dropped from the harness of the traveller who left the inn just before our arrival last night."

"Well—" she said, still without understanding; "and do you know the coat?"

Odo smiled. "It is mine," he answered; "and the crown is my cousin's. The traveller must have been a messenger of the Duke's."

She stood leaning against the seat from which she had risen, one hand still grasping it while the other hung inert. Her lips parted but she did not speak. Her pallor troubled Odo and he went up to her and took her hand.

"Do you not understand," he said gently, "that there is no farther cause for alarm? I have no reason to think that the Duke's messenger is in pursuit of me; but should he be so, and should he overtake us, he has no authority over you and no reason for betraying you to your enemies."

The blood poured back to her face. "Me! My enemies!" she stammered. "It is not of them I think." She raised her head and faced him in a glow.

For a moment he stood stupidly gazing at her; then the mist lifted and through it he saw a great light.

The landlord's knock warned them that their horses waited, and they rode out in the grey morning. The world about them still lay in shade, and as they climbed the wooded defile above the valley Odo was reminded of the days at Donnaz when he had ridden up the mountain in the same early light. Never since then had he felt, as he did now, the boy's easy kinship with the unexpected, the sense that no encounter could be too wonderful to fit in with the mere wonder of living.

To avoid the road to Peschiera they had resolved to cross the Monte Baldo by a mule-track which should bring them out at one of the villages on the eastern shore of Garda; and the search for this path led them up through steep rain-scented woods where they had to part the wet boughs as they passed. From time to time they regained the highway and rode abreast, almost silent at first with the weight of their new nearness, and then breaking into talk that was the mere overflow of what they were thinking. There was in truth more to be felt between them than to be said; since, as each was aware, the new light that suffused the present left the future as obscure as before. But what mattered, when the hour was theirs? The narrow kingdom of today is better worth ruling over than the widest past or future; but not more than once does a man hold its fugitive sceptre. The past, however, was theirs also: a past so transformed that he must revisit it with her, joyously confronting her new self with the image of her that met them at each turn. Then he had himself to trace in her memories, his transfigured likeness to linger over in the Narcissus-mirror of her faith in him. This interchange of recollections served them as well as any outspoken expression of feeling, and the most commonplace allusion was charged with happy meanings.

Arabia Petraea had been an Eden to such travellers; how much more the happy slopes they were now descending! All the afternoon their path wound down the western incline of Monte Baldo, first under huge olives, then through thickets of laurel and acacia, to emerge on a lower level of lemon and orange groves, with the blue lake showing through a diaper of golden-fruited boughs. Fulvia, to whom this clear-cut southern foliage was as new as the pure intensity of light that bathed it, seemed to herself to be moving through the landscape of a dream. It was as though nature had been remodelled, transformed almost, under the touch of their love: as though they had found their way to the Hesperian glades in which poets and painters placed the legendary lovers of antiquity.

Such feelings were intensified by the strangeness of the situation. In Italy the young girls of the middle class, though seemingly allowed a greater freedom of intercourse than the daughters of noblemen, were in reality as strictly guarded. Though, like Fulvia, they might converse with the elderly merchants or scholars frequenting the family table, they were never alone in the company of men, and the high standard of conduct prevailing in the bourgeoisie forbade all thought of clandestine intercourse. This was especially true of the families of men of letters, where the liberal education of the young girls, and their habit of associating as equals with men of serious and cultivated minds, gave them a self-possession disconcerting to the young blood accustomed to conquer with a glance. These girls as a rule, were married early to men of their own standing, and though the cicisbeo was not unknown after marriage he was not an authorised member of the household. Fulvia, indeed, belonged to the class most inaccessible to men of Odo's rank: the only class in Italy in which the wife's fidelity was as much esteemed as the innocence of the girl. Such principles had long been ridiculed by persons of quality and satirised by poets and playwrights. From Aristophanes to Beaumarchais the cheated husband and the outwitted guardian had been the figures on which the dramatist relied for his comic effects. Even the miser tricked out of his savings was a shade less ridiculous, less grotesquely deserving of his fate, than the husband defrauded of his wife's affection. The plausible adulteress and the adroit seducer had a recognised claim on the sympathy of the public. But the inevitable reaction was at hand; and the new teachers to whom Odo's contemporaries were beginning to listen had thrown a strangely poetic light over the dull figures of the domestic virtues. Faithfulness to the family sanctities, reverence for the marriage tie, courage to sacrifice the loftiest passion to the most plodding duty: these were qualities to touch the fancy of a generation sated with derision. If love as a sentiment was the discovery of the medieval poets, love as a moral emotion might be called that of the eighteenth-century philosophers, who, for all their celebration of free unions and fatal passions, were really on the side of the angels, were fighting the battle of the spiritual against the sensual, of conscience against appetite.

The imperceptible action of these new influences formed the real barrier between Odo and Fulvia. The girl stood for the embodiment of the purifying emotions that were to renew the world. Her candour, her unapproachableness, her simple trust in him, were a part of the magic light which the new idealism had shed over the old social structure. His was, in short, a love large enough to include other emotions: a widening rather than a contraction of the emotional range. Youth and propinquity have before now broken down stronger defences; but Fulvia's situation was an unspoken appeal to her lover's forbearance. The sense that her safety depended on him kept his sentimental impulses in check and made the happiness of the moment seem, in its exquisite unreality, a mere dreamlike interlude between the facts of life.

Toward sunset they rested in an olive-orchard, tethering their horses to the low boughs. Overhead, through the thin foliage of tarnished silver, the sky, as the moon suffused it, melted from steel blue to a clearer silver. A peasant-woman whose hut stood close by brought them a goat's cheese on a vine-leaf and a jug of spring-water; and as they supped, a little goat-herd, driving his flock down the hill, paused to watch them with furtive woodland eyes.

Odo, questioning him, learned that at the village on the shore below they could obtain a boat to carry them across the lake. Fulvia, for lack of a passport, dared not set foot on Austrian soil; but the Swiss authorities were less exacting and Odo had hopes of crossing the border without difficulty. They set out again presently, descending through the grey dusk of the olives till the path became too steep for riding; then Odo lifted Fulvia from the saddle and led the two horses after her. Here and there, between the trees, they caught a momentary glimpse of lights on the shore and the pale gleam of the lake enclosed in black foliage. From the village below came snatches of song and the shrill wail of a pipe; and as the night deepened they saw, far out on the water, the wild flare of the fish-spearers' torches, like comets in an inverted sky.

With nightfall the spirits of both had sunk. Fulvia walked ahead in silence and Odo read a mute apprehension in her drooping outline. Every step brought them nearer to the point they both feared to face, and though each knew what lay in the other's thoughts neither dared break the silence. Odo's mind turned anxiously to the incidents of the morning, to the finding of the ducal coat-of-arms, and to all the possibilities it suggested. What errand save one could have carried an envoy from Pianura to that remote hamlet among the hills? He could scarcely doubt that it was in pursuit of himself that the ducal messenger travelled; but with what object was the journey undertaken? Was he to be recalled in obedience to some new whim of the Duke's? Or had some unforeseen change—he dared not let his thoughts define it—suddenly made his presence needful in Pianura? It was more probable that the possibility of his flight with Fulvia had been suggested to the Duke by the ecclesiastical authorities, and that the same hand which had parted them before was again secretly at work. In any case, it was Odo's first business to see his companion safely across the border; and in that endeavour he had now little fear of being thwarted. If the Duke's messenger awaited them at Peschiera he waited in vain; and though their flight across the lake might be known before dawn it would then be no easy matter to overtake them.

In an hour's time, as Odo had hoped, they were putting off from the shore in a blunt-nosed fishing-boat which was the lightest craft the village could provide. The lake was stark calm, and the two boatmen, silhouetted against the moonlight, drove the boat forward with even vigorous strokes. Fulvia, shivering in the autumnal chill, had drawn her hood close about her and sat silent, her face in shade. Measured by their secret apprehensions the boat's progress seemed at first indescribably slow; but gradually the sounds from the shore grew fainter, and the fugitives felt themselves alone in a world enclosed by the moonlit circle of the waters.

As they advanced this sense of isolation and security grew deeper and more impressive. The motionless surface of the lake was enclosed in a wall of mountains which the moonlight seemed to vein with marble. A sky in which the stars were dissolved in white radiance curved high above their heads; and not a sail flecked the lake or a cloud the sky. The boat seemed suspended alone in some ethereal medium.

Presently one of the boatmen spoke to the other and glanced toward the north. Then the second silently shipped his oar and hoisted the sail. Hardly had he made it fast when a fresh of wind came down the lake and they began to stretch across the bay with spreading canvas. The wind was contrary, but Odo welcomed it, for he saw at once that it would be quicker work to tack to the other shore than to depend on the oars. The scene underwent a sudden change. The silver mirror over which they had appeared to glide was shivered into sparkling fragments, and in the enveloping rush and murmur of the night the boat woke to a creaking straining activity.

The man at the rudder suddenly pointed to a huddle of lights to the south. "Peschiera."

Odo laughed. "We shall soon show it our heels," said he.

The other boatman shrugged his shoulders. "Even an enemy's roof may serve to keep out the storm," he observed philosophically.

"The storm? What storm?"

The man pointed to the north. Against the sky hung a little black cloud, the merest flaw in the perfect curve of the night.

"The lake is shrewish at this season," the boatman continued. "Did your excellencies burn a candle before starting?"

Odo sat silent, his eyes fixed on the cloud. It was growing visibly now. With every moment its outline seemed to shift and spread, till its black menace dilated to the zenith. The bright water still broke about them in diamond spray; but as the shadow travelled the lake beneath it turned to lead. Then the storm dropped on them. It fell suddenly out of mid-heaven. Sky and water grew black and a long shudder ran through the boat. For a moment she hung back, staggering under a white fury of blows; then the gale seemed to lift and swing her about and she shot forward through a long tunnel of glistening blackness, bows on for Peschiera.

"The enemy's roof!" thought Odo. He reached for Fulvia's hand and found it in the darkness. The rain was driving against them now and he drew her close and wrapped his cloak about her. She lay still, without a tremor, as though in that shelter no fears could reach her. The night roared about them and the waters seemed to divide beneath their keel. Through the tumult Odo shouted to the boatmen to try to make some harbour north of Peschiera. They shouted back that they must go where the wind willed and bless the saints if they made any harbour at all; and Odo saw that Peschiera was their destiny.

It was past midnight when they set foot on shore. The rain still fell in torrents and they could hardly grope their way up the steps of the landing-stage. Odo's first concern was to avoid the inn; but the boatmen, exhausted by their efforts and impatient to be under shelter, could not be bribed to seek out at that hour another lodging for the travellers. Odo dared not expose Fulvia longer to the storm, and reluctantly they turned toward the inn, trusting that at that hour their coming would attract little notice.

A travelling-carriage stood in the courtyard, and somewhat to Odo's surprise the landlord was still afoot. He led them into the public parlour, which was alight, with a good fire on the hearth. A gentleman in travelling-dress sat near this fire, his back to the door, reading by a shaded candle. He rose as the travellers entered, and Odo recognised the abate de Crucis.

The latter advanced with a smile in which pleasure was more visible than surprise. He bowed slightly to Fulvia, who had shrunk back into the shadow of the doorway; then he turned to Odo and said: "Cavaliere, I have travelled six days to overtake you. The Duke of Pianura is dying and has named you regent."

3.7.

Odo heard a slight movement behind him. He turned and saw that Fulvia had vanished. He understood her wish for concealment, but its futility was written in the glance with which de Crucis followed her flight.

The abate continued to speak in urgent tones. "I implore you," he said, "to lose no time in accompanying me to Pianura. The situation there is critical and before now his Highness's death may have placed the reins in your hands." He glanced at his watch. "If your excellency is not too tired to set out at once, my horses can be harnessed within the half hour."

Odo's heart sank. To have let his thoughts dwell on such a possibility seemed to have done little to prepare him for its realisation. He hardly understood what de Crucis was saying: he knew only that an hour before he had fancied himself master of his fate and that now he was again in bonds. His first clear thought was that nothing should part him from Fulvia.

De Crucis seemed to read the thought.

"Cavaliere," he said, "at a moment when time is so valuable you will pardon my directness. You are accompanying to Switzerland a lady who has placed herself in your charge—"

Odo made no reply, and the other went on in the same firm but courteous tone: "Foreseeing that it would be difficult for you to leave her so abruptly I provided myself, in Venice, with a passport which will take her safely across the border." He drew a paper from his coat. "This," said he, handing it to Odo, "is the Papal Nuncio's authorisation to the Signorina Fulvia Vivaldi, known in religion as Sister Veronica, to absent herself from Italy for an indefinite period. With this passport and a good escort your companion will have no difficulty in joining her friends."

Excess of astonishment kept Odo silent for a moment; and in that moment he had as it were a fugitive glimpse into the workings of the great power which still strove for predominance in Italy. A safe-conduct from the Papal Nuncio to Fulvia Vivaldi was equivalent to her release from her vows; and this in turn implied that, for the moment, religious discipline had been frankly sacrificed to the pressure of political necessities. How the invisible hands made and unmade the destinies of those who came in their way! How boldly the Church swept aside her own defences when they obstructed her course! He was conscious, even at the moment, of all that men like de Crucis had to say in defence of this higher expediency, this avowed discrimination between the factors in each fresh combination of circumstances. He had himself felt the complex wonder of thoughtful minds before the Church's perpetual miracle of change disguised in immutability; but now he saw only the meaner side of the game, its elements of cruelty and falseness; and he felt himself no more than a frail bark on the dark and tossing seas of ecclesiastical intrigue. For a moment his heart shuddered back from its fate.

"No passport, no safe-conduct," he said at length, "can release me from my duty to the lady who has placed herself in my care. I shall not leave her till she has joined her friends."

De Crucis bowed. "This is the answer I expected," he said, not without sadness.

Odo glanced at him in surprise. The two men, hitherto, had addressed each other as strangers; but now something in the abate's tone recalled to Odo the familiarity of their former intercourse, their deep community of thought, the significance of the days they had spent together in the monastery of Monte Cassino. The association of ideas brought before him the profound sense of responsibility with which, at that time, he had looked forward to such an hour as this.

The abate was watching him gravely.

"Cavaliere," he said, "every instant counts, all you had once hoped to do for Pianura is now yours to accomplish. But in your absence your enemies are not idle. His Highness may revoke your appointment at any hour. Of late I have had his ear, but I have now been near a week absent, and you know the Duke is not long constant to one purpose.—Cavaliere," he exclaimed, "I appeal to you not in the name of the God whom you have come to doubt, but in that of your fellow-men, whom you have wished to serve."

Odo looked at him, not without a confused sense of the irony of such an appeal on such lips, yet with the distinct consciousness that it was uttered in all sincerity, and that, whatever their superficial diversity of view, he and de Crucis were at one on those deeper questions that gave the moment its real significance.

"It is impossible," he repeated, "that I should go with you."

De Crucis was again silent, and Odo was aware of the renewed intentness of his scrutiny. "If the lady—" broke from him once; but he checked himself and took a turn in the room.

Meanwhile a resolve was slowly forming itself in Odo. He would not be false to the call which, since his boyhood, had so often made itself heard before the voice of pleasure and self-interest; but he would at least reserve the right to obey it in his own fashion and under conditions which left his private inclination free.

"There may be more than one way of serving one's fellows," he said quietly. "Go back without me, abate. Tell my cousin that I resign my rights to the succession. I shall live my own life elsewhere, not unworthily, I hope, but as a private person."

De Crucis had turned pale. For a moment his habitual self-command seemed about to fail him; and Odo could not but see that a sincere personal regret was mingled with the political agent's consciousness of failure.

He himself was chiefly aware of a sense of relief, of self-recovery, as though he had at last solved a baffling enigma and found himself once more at one with his fate.

Suddenly he heard a step behind him. Fulvia had re-entered the room. She had put off her drenched cloak, but the hair lay in damp strands on her forehead, deepening her pallor and the lines of weariness under her eyes. She moved across the room, carrying her head high and advancing tranquilly to Odo's side. Even in that moment of confused emotions he was struck by the nobility of her gait and gesture.

She turned to de Crucis, and Odo had the immediate intuition that she had recognised him.

"Will you let me speak a word privately to the cavaliere Valsecca?" she said.

The other bowed silently and turned away. The door closed on him, and Odo and Fulvia remained alone. For a moment neither spoke; then she said: "That was the abate de Crucis?"

He assented.

She looked at him sadly. "You still believe him to be your friend?"

"Yes," he answered frankly, "I still believe him to be my friend, and, spite of his cloth, the friend of justice and humanity. But he is here simply as the Duke's agent. He has been for some time the governor of Prince Ferrante."

"I knew," she murmured, "I knew—"

He went up to her and caught her hands. "Why do we waste our time upon him?" he exclaimed impatiently. "Nothing matters but that I am free at last."

She drew back, gently releasing herself. "Free—?"

"My choice is made. I have resigned my right to the succession. I shall not return to Pianura."

She continued to stare at him, leaning against the chair from which de Crucis had risen.

"Your choice is made! Your choice is made!" she repeated. "And you have chosen—"

"You," he said simply. "Will you go to France with me, Fulvia? Will you be my wife and work with me at a distance for the cause that, in Italy, we may not serve together? I have never abandoned the aims your father taught me to strive for; they are dearer, more sacred to me than ever; but I cannot strive for them alone. I must feel your hand in mine, I must know that your heart beats with mine, I must hear the voice of liberty speak to me in your voice—" He broke off suddenly and went up to her. "All this is nothing," he said. "I love you. I cannot give you up. That is all."

For a moment, as he spoke, her face shone with an extraordinary light. She looked at him intently, as one who seemed to gaze beyond and through him, at some mystic vision that his words evoked. Then the brightness faded.

"The picture you draw is a beautiful one," she said, speaking slowly, in sweet deliberate tones, "but it is not for me to look on. What you said last is not true. If you love me it is because we have thought the same thoughts, dreamed the same dream, heard the same voice—in each other's voices, perhaps, as you say, but none the less a real voice, apart from us and above us, and one which would speak to us as loudly if we were apart—one which both of us must follow to the end."

He gazed at her eagerly as she spoke; and while he gazed there came to him, perversely enough, a vision of the life he was renouncing, not as it concerned the public welfare but in its merely personal aspect: a vision of the power, the luxury, the sumptuous background of traditional state and prerogative in which his artistic and intellectual tastes, as well as his easy impulses of benevolence, would find unchecked and immediate gratification. It was the first time that he had been aware of such lurking influences under his most generous aspirations; but even as Fulvia ceased to speak the vision faded, leaving only an intenser longing to bend her will to his.

"You are right," he rejoined; "we must follow that voice to the end; but why not together? Your father himself often questioned whether the patriot could not serve his people better at a distance than in their midst. In France, where the new ideas are not only tolerated but put in practice, we shall be able to study their effects and to learn how they may best be applied to the relief of our own unhappy people; and as a private person, independent of party and patronage, could I not do more than as the nominal head of a narrow priest-ridden government, where every act and word would be used by my enemies to injure me and the cause I represent?"

The vigour and rapidity of the attack, and the promptness with which he converted her argument to his own use, were not without visible effect. Odo saw his words reflected in the wavering glow of Fulvia's cheek; but almost at once she regained control of her pulses and faced him with that serenity which seemed to come to her at such moments.

"What you say might be true," she answered, "were your opportunities indeed restricted to the regency. But the little prince's life is known to hang on a thread: at any moment you may be Duke. And you will not deny that as Duke of Pianura you can serve your people better than as an obscure pamphleteer in Paris."

Odo made an impatient gesture. "Are you so sure?" he said. "Even as Duke I must be the puppet of powers greater than myself—of Austria, of Rome, nay, of the wealthy nobles who will always league themselves with their sovereign's enemies rather than suffer a hand upon their privileges. And even if I were fortunate enough to outwit my masters and rule indeed, over what a toy kingdom should I reign! How small a number would be benefited! How little the cause would be helped by my example! As an obscure pamphleteer I might reach the hearts of thousands and speak to great kings on their thrones; as Duke of Pianura, fighting single-handed to reform the laws of my little state, I should rank at best with the other petty sovereigns who are amusing themselves all over Italy with agricultural experiments and improved methods of cheese-making."

Again the brightness shone in Fulvia's face. "How you love me!" she said as he paused; and went on, restraining him with a gesture of the gentlest dignity: "For it is love that speaks thus in you and not reason; and you know as I do that the duty to which a man is born comes before any of his own choosing. You are called to serve liberty on a throne, I in some obscure corner of the

- 230 -

private life. We can no more exchange our duties than our stations; but if our lives divide, our purpose remains one, and as pious persons recall each other in the mystery of the Sacrament, so we shall meet in spirit in the new religion we profess."

Her voice gained strength and measure as she spoke, and Odo felt that all that passion could urge must spend itself in vain against such high security of spirit.

"Go, cavaliere," she continued, "I implore you to lose no time in reaching Pianura. Occasion is short-lived, and an hour's lingering may cost you the regency, and with it the chance of gaining a hold on your people. I will not expatiate, as some might, on the power and dignities that await you. You are no adventurer plotting to steal a throne, but a soldier pledged to his post." She moved close to him and suddenly caught his hand and raised it to her lips. "Your excellency," said she, "has deigned to look for a moment on a poor girl that crossed your path. Now your eyes must be on your people, who will yet have cause to love and bless you as she does."

She shone on him with a weeping brightness that dissolved his very soul.

"Ah," he cried, "you have indeed learned your lesson well! I admire with what stoic calmness you pronounce my doom, with what readiness you dispose of my future!"

"It is not mine to dispose of," she caught him up, "nor yours; but belongs, as much as any slave's to his master, to the people you are called to rule. Think for how many generations their unheeded sufferings, their unrewarded toil, have paid for the pomp and pleasure of your house! That is the debt you are called on to acquit, the wrong you are pledged to set right."

Odo was silent. She had found the unanswerable word. Yes, he was called on to acquit the accumulated debt of that long unrighteous rule: it was he who must pay, if need be with the last drop of his blood, for the savage victories of Bracciaforte, the rapacity of Guidobaldo, the magnificence of Ascanio, the religious terrors and secret vices of the poor Duke now nearing his end. All these passions had preyed on the people, on the tillers and weavers and vine-dressers, obscure servants of a wasteful greatness: theirs had been the blood that renewed the exhausted veins of their rulers, through generation after generation of dumb labour and privation. And the noblest passions, as well as the basest, had been nourished at the same cost. Every flower in the ducal gardens, every picture on the palace walls, every honour in the ancient annals of the house, had been planted, paid for, fought for by the people. With mute inconscient irony the two powers had faced each other for generations: the subjects never guessing that their sovereigns were puppets of their own making, the Dukes that all their pomp and circumstance were but a borrowed motley. Now the evil wrought in ignorance remained to be undone in the light of the world's new knowledge: the discovery of that universal brotherhood which Christ had long ago proclaimed, and which, after so many centuries, those who denied Christ were the first to put in practice. Hour by hour, day by day, at the cost of every personal inclination, of all that endears life and ennobles failure, Odo must set himself to redeem the credit of his house. He saw his way straight before him; but in that hour of insight his heart's instinct of self-preservation made one last effort against fate.

He turned to Fulvia.

"You are right," he said; "I have no choice. You have shown me the way; but must I travel it alone? You ask me to give up at a stroke all that makes life desirable: to set forth, without a backward glance, on the very road that leads me farthest from you! Yesterday I might have obeyed; but how can I turn today from this near view of my happiness?"

He paused a moment and she seemed about to answer; but he hurried on without giving her time. "Fulvia, if you ask this sacrifice of me, is there none you will make in return? If you bid me go forth and work for my people, will you not come with me and work for them too?" He stretched out his hands, in a gesture that seemed to sum up his infinite need of her, and for a moment they faced each other, silenced by the nearness of great issues.

She knew well enough what he offered. According to the code of the day there was no dishonour in the offer and it did not occur to her to resent it. But she looked at him sadly and he read her refusal in the look.

"The Regent's mistress?" she said slowly. "The key to the treasury, the back-door to preferment, the secret trafficker in titles and appointments? That is what I should stand for—and it is not to such services that you must even appear to owe your power. I will not say that I have my own work to do; for the dearest service I could perform would be to help you in yours. But to do this I must stand aside. To be near you I must go from you. To love you I must give you up."

She looked him full in the eyes as she spoke; then she went up to him and kissed him. It was the first kiss she had given him since she had thrown herself in his arms in her father's garden; but now he felt her whole being on her lips.

He would have held her fast, forgetting everything in the sweetness of her surrender; but she drew back quickly and, before he could guess her intention, throw open the door of the room to which de Crucis had withdrawn.

"Signor abate!" she said.

The Jesuit came forward. Odo was dimly aware that, for an instant, the two measured each other; then Fulvia said quietly:

"His excellency goes with you to Pianura."

What more she said, or what de Crucis answered, he could never afterward recall. He had a confused sense of having cried out a last unavailing protest, faintly, inarticulately, like a man struggling to make himself heard in a dream; then the room grew dark about him, and in its stead he saw the old chapel at Donnaz, with its dimly-gleaming shrine, and heard the voice of the chaplain, harsh and yet strangely shaken:—"My chief prayer for you is that, should you be raised to this eminence, it may be at a moment when such advancement seems to thrust you in the dust."

Odo lifted his head and saw de Crucis standing alone before him.

"I am ready," he said.

BOOK IV.
THE REWARD.

Where are the portraits of those who have perished in spite of their vows?

4.1.

One bright March day in the year 1783 the bells of Pianura began to ring at sunrise, and with their first peal the townsfolk were abroad.

The city was already dressed for a festival. A canopy of crimson velvet, surmounted by the ducal crown and by the "Humilitas" of the Valseccas, concealed the columns of the Cathedral porch and fell in royal folds about the featureless porphyry lions who had seen so many successive rulers ascend the steps between their outstretched paws. The frieze of ramping and running animals around the ancient baptistery was concealed by heavy green garlands alternating with religious banners; and every church and chapel had draped its doorway with crimson and placed above the image of its patron saint the ducal crown of Pianura.

No less sumptuous was the adornment of the private dwellings. The great families—the Trescorri, the Belverdi, the Pievepelaghi—had outdone each other in the display of golden-threaded tapestries and Genoese velvets emblazoned with armorial bearings; and even the sombre facade of the Boscofolto palace showed a rich drapery surmounted by the quarterings of the new Marchioness.

But it was not only the palace-fronts that had put on a holiday dress. The contagion had spread to the poorer quarters, and in many a narrow street and crooked lane, where surely no part of the coming pageant might be expected to pass, the crazy balconies and unglazed windows were decked out with scraps of finery: a yard or two of velvet filched from the state hangings of some noble house, a torn and discoloured church banner, even a cast-off sacque of brocade or a peasant's holiday kerchief, skilfully draped about the rusty iron and held in place by pots of clove-pink and sweet basil. The half-ruined palace which had once housed Gamba and Momola showed a few shreds of colour on its sullen front, and the abate Crescenti's modest house, wedged in a corner of the city walls, was dressed like the altar of a Lady Chapel; while even the tanners' quarter by the river displayed its festoons of coloured paper and tinsel, ingeniously twisted into the semblance of a crown.

For the new Duke, who was about to enter his capital in state, was extraordinarily popular with all classes. His popularity, as yet, was mainly due to a general detestation of the rule he had replaced; but such a sentiment gives to a new sovereign an impetus which, if he knows how to use it, will carry him a long way toward success; and among those in the Duke's confidence it was rumoured that he was qualified not only to profit by the expectations he had raised but to fulfil them. The last months of the late Duke's life had plunged the duchy into such political and financial disorder that all parties were agreed in welcoming a change. Even those that had most to lose by the accession of the new sovereign, or most to fear from the policy he was known to favour, preferred the possibility of new evils to a continuance of present conditions. The expertest angler in troubled waters may find waters too troubled for his sport; and under a government where power is passed from hand to hand like the handkerchief in a children's game, the most adroit time-server may find himself grasping the empty air.

It would indeed have been difficult to say who had ruled during the year preceding the Duke's death. Prime ministers had succeeded each other like the clowns in a harlequinade. Just as the Church seemed to have gained the upper hand some mysterious revulsion of feeling would fling the Duke toward Trescorre and the liberals; and when these had attempted, by some trifling concession to popular feeling, to restore the credit of the government, their sovereign, seized by religious scruples, would hastily recall the clerical party. So the administration staggered on, reeling from one policy to another, clutching now at this support and now at that, while Austria and the Holy See hung on its steps, awaiting the inevitable fall.

A cruel winter and a fresh outbreak of the silkworm disease had aggravated the misery of the people, while the mounting extravagance of the Duchess had put a last strain on the exhausted treasury. The consequent increase of the salt-tax roused such popular fury that Father Ignazio, who was responsible for the measure, was dismissed by the panic-stricken Duke, and Trescorre, as usual, called in to repair his rival's mistake. But it would have taken a greater statesman than Trescorre to reach the root of such evils; and the new minister succeeded neither in pacifying the people nor in reassuring his sovereign.

Meanwhile the Duke was sinking under the mysterious disease which had hung upon him since his birth. It was hinted that his last hours were darkened by hallucinations, and the pious pictured him as haunted by profligate visions, while the free-thinkers maintained that he was the dupe of priestly jugglery. Toward the end there was the inevitable rumour of acqua tofana, and the populace cried out that the Jesuits were at work again. It seems more probable, however, that his Highness, who had assisted at the annual festival of the Madonna del Monte, and had mingled on foot with the swarm of devotees thronging thither from all parts, had contracted a pestilent disorder from one of the pilgrims. Certain it is that death came in a dreadful form. The Duchess, alarmed for the health of Prince Ferrante, fled with him to the dower-house by the Piana; and the strange nature of his Highness's distemper caused many to follow her example. Even the Duke's servants, and the quacks that lived on his bounty, were said to have abandoned the death-chamber; and an English traveller passing through Pianura boasted that, by the payment of a small fee to the palace porter, he had obtained leave to enter his Highness's closet and peer through the doorway at the dying man. However this may be, it would appear that the Duke's confessor—a monk of the Barnabite order—was not to be found when his Highness called for him; and the servant sent forth in haste to fetch a priest returned, strangely enough, with the abate Crescenti, whose suspected orthodoxy had so long made him the object of the Duke's detestation. He it was who alone witnessed the end of that tormented life, and knew upon what hopes or fears it closed.

Meanwhile it appeared that the Duchess's precautions were not unfounded; for Prince Ferrante presently sickened of the same malady which had cut off his father, and when the Regent, travelling post-haste, arrived in Pianura, he had barely time to pass from the Duke's obsequies to the death-bed of the heir.

Etiquette required that a year of mourning should elapse between the accession of the new sovereign and his state entry into his capital; so that if Duke Odo's character and intentions were still matter of conjecture to his subjects, his appearance was already familiar to them. His youth, his good looks, his open mien, his known affability of manner, were so many arguments in his favour with an impressionable and impulsive people; and it was perhaps natural that he should interpret as a tribute to his principles the sympathy which his person aroused.

It is certain that he fancied himself, at that time, as well-acquainted with his subjects as they believed themselves to be with him; and the understanding supposed to exist was productive of equal satisfaction to both sides. The new Duke had thrown himself with extraordinary zeal into the task of loving and understanding his people. It had been his refuge from a hundred doubts and uncertainties, the one clearly-defined object in an obscure and troubled fate. And their response had, almost immediately, turned his task into a pleasure. It was so easy to rule if one's subjects loved one! And so easy to be loved if only one loved enough in return! If he did not, like the Pope, describe himself to his people as the servant of the servants of God, he at least longed to make them feel that this new gospel of service was the base on which all sovereignty must henceforth repose.

It was not that his first year of power had been without moments of disillusionment. He had had more than one embittering experience of intrigue and perfidy, more than one glimpse of the pitfalls besetting his course; but his confidence in his own powers and his faith in his people remained unshaken, and with two such beliefs to sustain him it seemed as though no difficulties would prove insurmountable.

Such at least was the mood in which, on the morning of his entry into Pianura, he prepared to face his subjects. Strangely enough, the state entry began at Ponte di Po, the very spot where, on a stormy midnight some seven years earlier, the new Duke had landed, a fugitive from his future realm. Here, according to an ancient custom, the sovereign awaited the arrival of his ministers and court; and then, taking seat in his state barge, proceeded by water to Pianura, followed by an escort of galleys.

A great tent hung with tapestries had been set up on the river-bank; and here Odo awaited the approach of the barge. As it touched at the landing-stage he stepped out, and his prime minister, Count Trescorre, advanced toward him, accompanied by the dignitaries of the court. Trescorre had aged in the intervening years. His delicate features had withered like a woman's, and the fine irony of his smile had taken an edge of cruelty. His face suggested a worn engraving, the lines of which have been deepened by a too-incisive instrument.

The functionaries attending him were, with few exceptions, the same who had figured in a like capacity at the late sovereign's court. With the passing of the years they had grown heavier or thinner, more ponderous or stiffer in their movements, and as they advanced, in their splendid but unwieldy court dress, they seemed to Odo like superannuated marionettes whose springs and wires have rusted from disuse.

The barge was a magnificent gilded Bucentaur, presented to the late Duke's father by the Doge of Venice, and carved by his Serenity's most famous sculptors in wood. Tritons and sea-goddesses encircled the prow and throned above the stern, and the interior of the deck-house was adorned with delicate rilievi and painted by Tiepolo with scenes from the myth of Amphitrite. Here the new Duke seated himself, surrounded by his household, and presently the heavy craft, rowed by sixty galley-slaves, was moving slowly up the river toward Pianura.

In the clear spring light the old walled city, with its domes and towers, rose pleasantly among budding orchards and fields. Close at hand were the crenellations of Bracciaforte's keep, and just beyond, the ornate cupola of the royal chapel, symbolising in their proximity the successive ambitions of the ducal race; while the round-arched campanile of the Cathedral and the square tower of the mediaeval town-hall sprang up side by side, marking the centre of the free city which the Valseccas had subjugated. It seemed to the new Duke, who was given to such reflections, that he could read his race's history in that broken skyline; but he was soon snatched from its perusal by the cheers of the crowd who thronged the river-bank to greet his approach.

As the Bucentaur touched at the landing-stage and Odo stepped out on the red carpet strewn with flowers, while cannon thundered from the walls and the bells burst into renewed jubilation, he felt himself for the first time face to face with his people. The very ceremonial which in other cases kept them apart was now a means of closer communication; for it was to show himself to them that he was making a public entry into his capital, and it was to see him that the city had poured forth her shouting throngs. The shouts rose and widened as he advanced, enveloping him in a mounting tide of welcome, in which cannon, bells and voices—the decreed and the spontaneous acclamations—were indistinguishably merged. In like manner, approbation of his person was mingled with a simple enjoyment of the show of which he formed a part; and it must have taken a more experienced head than Odo's to distinguish between the two currents of enthusiasm on which he felt himself swept forward.

The pageant was indeed brilliant enough to justify the popular transport; and the fact that the new Duke formed a worthy centre to so much magnificence was not lost on his splendour-loving subjects. The late sovereign had so long held himself aloof that the city was unaccustomed to such shows, and as the procession wound into the square before the Cathedral, where the thickest of the crowd was massed, the very pealing of the church-bells was lost in the roar of human voices.

Don Serafino, the Bishop's nephew, and now Master of the Horse, rode first, on a splendid charger, preceded by four trumpets and followed by his esquires; then came the court dignitaries, attended by their pages and staffieri in gala liveries, the marshals with their staves, the masters of ceremony, and the clergy mounted on mules trapped with velvet, each led by two running footmen. The Duke rode next, alone and somewhat pale. Two pages of arms, helmeted and carrying lances, walked at his horse's bridle; and behind him came his household and ministers, with their gentlemen and a long train of servants, followed by the regiment of light horse which closed the procession.

The houses surrounding the square afforded the best point of view to those unwilling to mix with the crowd in the streets; and among the spectators thronging the windows and balconies, and leaning over the edge of the leads, were many who, from one motive or another, felt a personal interest in the new Duke. The Marchioness of Boscofolto had accepted a seat in the windows of the Pievepelaghi palace, which formed an angle of the square, and she and her hostess—the same lady who had been relieved of her diamond necklace by footpads suspected of wearing the Duchess's livery—

sat observing the scene behind the garlanded balconies of the piano nobile. In the mezzanin windows of a neighbouring wine-shop the bookseller Andreoni, with half a dozen members of the philosophical society to which Odo had belonged, peered above the heads of the crowd thronging the arcade, and through a dormer of the leads Carlo Gamba, the assistant in the ducal library, looked out on the triumph of his former patron. Among the Church dignities grouped about his Highness was Father Ignazio, the late Duke's confessor, now Prior of the Dominicans, and said to be withdrawn from political life. Seated on his richly-trapped mule he observed the scene with impassive face; while from his place in the long line of minor clergy, the abate Crescenti, with eyes of infinite tenderness and concern, watched the young Duke solemnly ascending the Cathedral steps.

In the porch the Bishop waited, impressive as ever in his white and gold dalmatic, against the red robes of the chapter. Preceded by two chamberlains Odo mounted the steps amid the sudden silence of the people. The great bronze portals of the Cathedral, which were never opened save on occasions of state, swung slowly inward, pouring a wave of music and incense out upon the hushed sunlit square; then they closed again, engulphing the brilliant procession—the Duke, the Bishop, the clergy and the court—and leaving the populace to scatter in search of the diversions prepared for them at every street-corner.

It was not till late that night that the new Duke found himself alone. He had withdrawn at last from the torch-lit balcony overlooking the square, whither the shouts of his subjects had persistently recalled him. Silence was falling on the illuminated streets, and the dimness of midnight upon the sky through which rocket after rocket had torn its brilliant furrows. In the palace a profounder stillness reigned. Since his accession Odo, out of respect for the late Duke, had lodged in one of the wings of the great building; but tradition demanded that he should henceforth inhabit the ducal apartments, and thither, at the close of the day's ceremonies, his gentlemen had conducted him.

Trescorre had asked permission to wait on him before he slept; and he knew that the prime minister would be kept late by his conference with the secret police, whose nightly report could not be handed in till the festivities were over. Meanwhile Odo was in no mood for sleep. He sat alone in the closet, still hung with saints' images and jewelled reliquaries, where his cousin had so often given him audience, and whence, through the open door, he could see the embroidered curtains and plumed baldachin of the state bed which was presently to receive him. All day his heart had beat with high ambitions; but now a weight sank upon his spirit. The reaction from the tumultuous welcome of the streets to the closely-guarded silence of the palace made him feel how unreal was the fancied union between himself and his people, how insuperable the distance that tradition and habit had placed between them. In the narrow closet where his predecessor had taken refuge from the detested task of reigning, the new Duke felt the same moral lassitude steal over him. How was such a puny will as his to contend against the great forces of greed and prejudice? All the influences arrayed against him—tradition, superstition, the lust of power, the arrogance of race—seemed concentrated in the atmosphere of that silent room, with its guarded threshold, its pious relics, and lying on the desk in the embrasure of the window, the manuscript litany which the late Duke had not lived to complete.

Oppressed by his surroundings, Odo rose and entered the bed-chamber. A lamp burned before the image of the Madonna at the head of the bed, and two lighted flambeaux flanked the picture of the Last Judgment on the opposite wall. Odo remembered the look of terror which the Duke had fixed on the picture during their first strange conversation. A praying-stool stood beneath it, and it was said that here, rather than before the Virgin's image, the melancholy prince performed his private devotions. The horrors of the scene were depicted with a childish minuteness of detail, as though the painter had sought to produce an impression of moral anguish by the accumulation of physical sufferings; and just such puerile images of the wrath to come may have haunted the mysterious recesses of the Duke's imagination. Crescenti had told Odo how the dying man's thoughts had seemed to centre upon this dreadful subject, and how again and again, amid his ravings, he had cried out that the picture must be burned, as though the sight of it was become intolerable to him.

Odo's own mind, across which the events and emotions of the day still threw the fantastic shadows of an expiring illumination, was wrought to the highest state of impressionability. He saw in a flash all that the picture must have symbolised to his cousin's fancy; and in his desire to reconstruct that dying vision of fleshly retribution, he stepped close to the diptych, resting a knee on the stool beneath it. As he did so, the picture suddenly opened, disclosing the inner panel. Odo caught up one of the flambeaux, and in its light, as on a sunlit wave, there stepped forth to him the lost Venus of Giorgione.

He knew the picture in an instant. There was no mistaking the glow of the limbs, the midsummer languor of the smile, the magical atmosphere in which the gold of sunlight, of autumn leaves, of amber grapes, seemed fused by some lost alchemy of the brush. As he gazed, the scene changed, and he saw himself in a darkened room with cabalistic hangings. He saw Heiligenstern's tall figure, towering in supernatural light, the Duke leaning eagerly forward, the Duchess with set lips and troubled eyes, the little prince bent wonderingly above the magic crystal...

A step in the antechamber announced Trescorre's approach. Odo returned to the cabinet and the minister advanced with a low bow. The two men had had time to grow accustomed to the new relation in which they stood to one another, yet there were moments when, to Odo, the past seemed to lie like fallen leaves beneath Trescorre's steps—Donna Laura, fond and foolish in her weeds, Gamba, Momola, and the pure featherhead Cerveno, dying at nineteen of a distemper because he had stood in the other's way. The impression was strong on him now—but it was only momentary. Habit reasserted itself, and the minister effaced the man. Odo signed to Trescorre to seat himself and the latter silently presented his report.

He was a diligent and capable administrator, and however mixed might be the motives which attached him to his sovereign, they did not interfere with the exact performance of his duties. Odo knew this and was grateful for it. He knew that Trescorre, ambitious of the regency, had intrigued against him to the last. He knew that an intemperate love of power was the mainspring of that seemingly dispassionate nature. But death had crossed Trescorre's schemes; and he was too adroit an opportunist not to see that his best chance now lay in making himself indispensable to his new sovereign. Of all this Odo was aware; but his own motives in appointing Trescorre did not justify his looking for great disinterestedness in his minister. The irony of circumstances had forced them upon each other, and each knew that the other understood the situation and was prepared to make the best of it.

The Duke presently rose, and handed back to Trescorre the reports of the secret police. They were the documents he most disliked to handle.

"You have acquitted yourself admirably of your disagreeable duties," he said with a smile. "I hope I have done as well. At any rate the day is over."

Trescorre returned the smile, with his usual tinge of irony. "Another has already begun," said he.

"Ah," said Odo, with a touch of impatience, "are we not to sleep on our laurels?"

Trescorre bowed. "Austria, your Highness, never sleeps."

Odo looked at him with surprise. "What do you mean?"

"That I have to remind your Highness—"

"Of what—?"

Trescorre had one of his characteristic pauses.

"That the Duke of Monte Alloro is in failing health—and that her Highness's year of widowhood ended yesterday."

There was a silence. Odo, who had reseated himself, rose and walked to the window. The shutters stood open and he looked out over the formless obscurity of the gardens. Above the intervening masses of foliage the Borromini wing raised its vague grey bulk. He saw lights in Maria Clementina's apartments and wondered if she still waked. An hour or two earlier she had given him her hand in the contra-dance at the state ball. It was her first public appearance since the late Duke's death, and with the laying off of her weeds she had regained something of her former brilliancy. At the moment he had hardly observed her: she had seemed a mere inanimate part of the pageant of which he formed the throbbing centre. But now the sense of her nearness pressed upon him. She seemed close to him, ingrown with his fate; and with the curious duality of vision that belongs to such moments he beheld her again as she had first shone on him—the imperious child whom he had angered by stroking her spaniel, the radiant girl who had welcomed him on his return to Pianura. Trescorre's voice aroused him.

"At any moment," the minister was saying, "her Highness may fall heir to Monte Alloro. It is the moment for which Austria waits. There is always an Archduke ready—and her Highness is still a young woman."

Odo turned slowly from the window. "I have told you that this is impossible," he murmured.

Trescorre looked down and thoughtfully fingered the documents in his hands.

"Your Highness," said he, "is as well-acquainted as your ministers with the difficulties that beset us. Monte Alloro is one of the richest states in Italy. It is a pity to alienate such revenues from Pianura."

The new Duke was silent. His minister's words were merely the audible expression of his own thoughts. He knew that the future welfare of Pianura depended on the annexation of Monte Alloro. He owed it to his people to unite the two sovereignties.

At length he said: "You are building on an unwarrantable assumption."

Trescorre raised an interrogative glance.

"You assume her Highness's consent."

The minister again paused; and his pause seemed to flash an ironical light on the poverty of the other's defences.

"I come straight from her Highness," said he quietly, "and I assume nothing that I am not in a position to affirm."

Odo turned on him with a start. "Do I understand that you have presumed—?"

His minister raised a deprecating hand. "Sir," said he, "the Archduke's envoy is in Pianura."

4.2.

Odo, on his return to Pianura, had taken it for granted that de Crucis would remain in his service.

There had been little talk between the two on the way. The one was deep in his own wretchedness, and the other had too fine a tact to intrude on it; but Odo felt the nearness of that penetrating sympathy which was almost a gift of divination. He was glad to have de Crucis at his side at a moment when any other companionship had been intolerable; and in the egotism of his misery he imagined that he could dispose as he pleased of his friend's future.

After the little Prince's death, however, de Crucis had at once asked permission to leave Pianura. He was perhaps not displeased by Odo's expressions of surprise and disappointment; but they did not alter his decision. He reminded the new Duke that he had been called to Pianura as governor to the late heir, and that, death having cut short his task, he had now no farther pretext for remaining.

Odo listened with a strange sense of loneliness. The responsibilities of his new state weighed heavily on the musing speculative side of his nature. Face to face with the sudden summons to action, with the necessity for prompt and not too-curious choice of means and method, he felt a stealing apathy of the will, an inclination toward the subtle duality of judgment that had so often weakened and diffused his energies. At such a crisis it seemed to him that, de Crucis gone, he remained without a friend. He urged the abate to reconsider his decision, begging him to choose a post about his person.

De Crucis shook his head.

"The offer," said he, "is more tempting to me than your Highness can guess; but my business here is at an end, and must be taken up elsewhere. My calling is that of a pedagogue. When I was summoned to take charge of Prince Ferrante's education I gave up my position in the household of Prince Bracciano not only because I believed that I could make myself more useful in training a future sovereign than the son of a private nobleman, but also," he added with a smile, "because I was curious to visit a state of which your Highness had so often spoken, and because I believed that my residence here might enable me to be of service to your Highness. In this I was not mistaken; and I will gladly remain in Pianura long enough to give your Highness such counsels as my experience suggests; but that business discharged, I must ask leave to go."

From this position no entreaties could move him; and so fixed was his resolve that it confirmed the idea that he was still a secret agent of the Jesuits. Strangely enough, this did not prejudice Odo, who was more than ever under the spell of de Crucis's personal influence. Though Odo had been acquainted with many professed philosophers he had never met among them a character so nearly resembling the old stoical ideal of temperance and serenity, and he could never be long with de Crucis without reflecting that the training which could form and nourish so noble a nature must be other than the world conceived it.

De Crucis, however, frankly pointed out that his former connection with the Jesuits was too well known in Pianura not to be an obstacle in the way of his usefulness.

"I own," said he, "that before the late Duke's death I exerted such influence as I possessed to bring about your Highness's appointment as regent; but the very connections that favoured me with your predecessor must stand in the way of my serving your Highness. Nothing could be more fatal to your prospects than to have it said that you had chosen a former Jesuit as your advisor. In the present juncture of affairs it is needful that you should appear to be in sympathy with the liberals, and that whatever reforms you attempt should seem the result of popular pressure rather than of your own free choice. Such an attitude may not flatter the sovereign's pride, and is in fact merely a higher form of expediency; but it is one which the proudest monarchs of Europe are finding themselves constrained to take if they would preserve their power and use it effectually."

Soon afterward de Crucis left Pianura; but before leaving he imparted to Odo the result of his observations while in the late Duke's service. De Crucis's view was that of the more thoughtful men of his day who had not broken with the Church, yet were conscious that the whole social system of Europe was in need of renovation. The movement of ideas in France, and their rapid transformation into legislative measures of unforeseen importance, had as yet made little impression in Italy; and the clergy in particular lived in serene unconsciousness of any impending change. De Crucis, however, had been much in France, and had frequented the French churchmen, who (save in the highest ranks of the hierarchy) were keenly alive to the need of reform, and ready, in many instances, to sacrifice their own privileges in the public cause. These men, living in their provincial cures or abbeys, were necessarily in closer contact with the people, better acquainted with their needs and more competent to relieve them, than the city demagogues theorising in Parisian coffee-houses on the Rights of Man and the Code of Nature. But the voice of the demagogues carried farther than that of the clergy; and such revolutionary notions as crossed the Alps had more to do with the founding of future Utopias than with the remedy of present evils.

Even in France the temperate counsels of the clergy were being overruled by the sentimental imprudences of the nobles and by the bluster of the politicians. It was to put Odo on his guard against these two influences that de Crucis was chiefly anxious; but the intelligent cooperation of the clergy was sadly lacking in his administrative scheme. He knew that Odo could not count on the support of the Church party, and that he must make what use he could of the liberals in his attempts at reform. The clergy of Pianura had been in power too long to believe in the necessity of conceding anything to the new spirit; and since the banishment of the Society of Jesus the presumption of the other orders had increased instead of diminishing. The priests, whatever their failings, had attached the needy by a lavish bounty; and they had a powerful auxiliary in the Madonna of the Mountain, who drew pilgrims from all parts of Italy and thus contributed to the material welfare of the state as well as to its spiritual privileges. To the common people their Virgin was not only a protection against disease and famine, but a kind of oracle, who by divers signs and tokens gave evidence of divine approval or displeasure; and it was naturally to the priests that the faithful looked for a reading of these phenomena. This gave the clergy a powerful hold on the religious sensibilities of the people; and more than once the manifest disapproval of the Mountain Madonna had turned the scales against some economic measure which threatened the rights of her augurs.

De Crucis understood the force of these traditional influences; but Odo, in common with the more cultivated men of his day, had lived too long in an atmosphere of polite scepticism to measure the profound hold of religion on the consciousness of the people. Christ had been so long banished from the drawing-room that it was has hard to believe that He still ruled in field and vineyard. To men of Odo's stamp the piety of the masses was a mere superficial growth, a kind of mental mould to be dried off by the first beams of knowledge. He did not conceive it as a habit of thought so old that it had become instinctive, so closely intertwined with every sense that to hope to eradicate it was like trying to drain all the blood from a man's body without killing him. He knew nothing of the unwearied workings of that power, patient as a natural force, which, to reach spirits darkened by ignorance and eyes dulled by toil, had stooped to a thousand disguises, humble, tender and grotesque—peopling the earth with a new race of avenging or protecting deities, guarding the babe in the cradle and the cattle in the stalls, blessing the good man's vineyard or blighting the crops of the blasphemer, guiding the lonely traveller over torrents and precipices, smoothing the sea and hushing the whirlwind, praying with the mother over her sick child, and watching beside the dead in plague-house and lazaret and galley—entering into every joy and grief of the obscurest consciousness, penetrating to depths of misery which no human compassion ever reached, and redressing by a prompt and summary justice wrongs of which no human legislation took account.

Odo's first act after his accession had been to recall the political offenders banished by his predecessor; and so general was the custom of marking the opening of a new reign by an amnesty to political exiles, that Trescorre offered no opposition to the measure. Andreoni and his friends at once returned to Pianura, and Gamba at the same time emerged from his mysterious hiding-place. He was the only one of the group who struck Odo as having any administrative capacity; yet he was more likely to be of use as a pamphleteer than as an office-holder. As to the other philosophers, they were what their name implied: thoughtful and high-minded men, with a generous conception of their civic duties, and a noble readiness to fulfil them at any cost, but untrained to action, and totally ignorant of the complex science of government.

Odo found the hunchback changed. He had withered like Trescorre, but under the harsher blight of physical privations; and his tongue had an added bitterness. He replied evasively to all enquiries as to what had become of him during his absence from Pianura; but on Odo's asking for news of Momola and the child he said coldly: "They are both dead."

"Dead?" Odo exclaimed. "Together?"

"There was scarce an hour between them," Gamba answered. "She said she must keep alive as long as the boy needed her—after that she turned on her side and died."

"But of what disorder? How came they to sicken at the same time?"

The hunchback stood silent, his eyes on the ground. Suddenly he raised them and looked full at the Duke.

"Those that saw them called it the plague."

"The plague? Good God!" Odo slowly returned his stare. "Is it possible—" he paused—"that she too was at the feast of the Madonna?"

"She was there, but it was not there that she contracted the distemper."

"Not there—?"

"No; for she dragged herself from her bed to go."

There was another silence. The hunchback had lowered his eyes. The Duke sat motionless, resting his head on his hand. Suddenly he made a gesture of dismissal...

Two months after his state entry into Pianura Odo married his cousin's widow.

It surprised him, in looking back, to see how completely the thought of Maria Clementina had passed out of his life, how wholly he had ceased to reckon with her as one of the factors in his destiny. At her child's death-bed he had seen in her only the stricken mother, centred in her loss, and recalling, in an agony of tears, the little prince's prophetic vision of the winged playmates who came to him carrying toys from Paradise. After Prince Ferrante's death she had gone on a long visit to her uncle of Monte Alloro; and since her return to Pianura she had lived in the dower-house, refusing Odo's offer of a palace in the town. She had first shown herself to the public on the day of the state entry; and now, her year of widowhood over, she was again the consort of a reigning Duke of Pianura.

No one was more ignorant than her husband of the motives determining her act. As Duchess of Monte Alloro she might have enjoyed the wealth and independence which her uncle's death had bestowed on her, but in marrying again she resigned the right to her new possessions, which became vested in the crown of Pianura. Was it love that had prompted the sacrifice? As she stood beside him on the altar steps of the Cathedral, as she rode home beside him between their shouting subjects, Odo asked himself the question again and again. The years had dealt lightly with her, and she had crossed the threshold of the thirties with the assured step of a woman who has no cause to fear what awaits her. But her blood no longer spoke her thoughts, and the transparence of youth had changed to a brilliant density. He could not penetrate beneath the surface of her smile: she seemed to him like a beautiful toy which might conceal a lacerating weapon.

Meanwhile between himself and any better understanding of her stood the remembrance of their talk in the hunting-lodge of Pontesordo. What she had offered then he had refused to take: was she the woman to forget such a refusal? Was it not rather to keep its memory alive that she had married him? Or was she but the flighty girl he had once imagined her, driven hither and thither by spasmodic impulses, and incapable of consistent action, whether for good or ill? The barrier of their past—of all that lay unsaid and undone between them—so completely cut her off from him that he had, in her presence, the strange sensation of a man who believes himself to be alone yet feels that he is watched...The first months of their marriage were oppressed by this sense of constraint; but gradually habit bridged the distance between them and he found himself at once nearer to her and less acutely aware of her. In the second year an heir was born and died; and the hopes and grief thus shared drew them insensibly into the relation of the ordinary husband and wife, knitted together at the roots in spite of superficial divergencies.

In his passionate need of sympathy and counsel Odo longed to make the most of this enforced community of interests. Already his first zeal was flagging, his belief in his mission wavering: he needed the encouragement of a kindred faith. He had no hope of finding in Maria Clementina that pure passion for justice which seemed to him the noblest ardour of the soul. He had read it in one woman's eyes, but these had long been turned from him. Unconsciously perhaps he counted rather on his wife's less generous qualities: the passion for dominion, the blind arrogance of temper that, for the mere pleasure of making her power felt, had so often drawn her into public affairs. Might not this waste force—which implied, after all, a certain prodigality of courage—be used for good as well as evil? Might not his influence make of the undisciplined creature at his side an unconscious instrument in the great work of order and reconstruction?

His first appeal to her brought the answer. At his request his ministers had drawn up a plan of financial reorganisation, which should include the two duchies; for Monte Alloro, though wealthier than Pianura, was in even greater need of fiscal reform. As a first step towards replenishing the treasury the Duke had declared himself ready to limit his private expenditure to a fixed sum; and he now asked the Duchess to pledge herself in the same manner. Maria Clementina, since her uncle's death, had been in receipt of a third of the annual revenues of Monte Alloro. This should have enabled her to pay her debts and put some dignity and order into her establishment; but the first year's income had gone in the building of a villa on the Piana, in imitation of the country-seats along the Brenta; the second was spent in establishing a menagerie of wild animals like that of the French Queen at Versailles; and rumour had it that the Duchess carried her imitation of her royal cousin so far as to be involved in an ugly quarrel with her jewellers about a necklace for which she owed a thousand ducats.

All these reports had of course reached Odo; but he still hoped that an appeal to her love of dominion might prove stronger than the habit of self-indulgence. He said to himself that nothing had ever been done to rouse her ambition, that hitherto, if she had meddled in politics, it had been merely from thwarted vanity or the desire to gratify some personal spite. Now he hoped to take her by higher passions, and by associating her with his own schemes to utilise her dormant energies.

For the first moments she listened with the strained fixity of a child; then her attention flickered and died out. The life-long habit of referring every question to a personal standpoint made it difficult for her to follow a general argument, and she leaned back with the resigned eyelids of piety under the pulpit. Odo, resolved to be patient, and seeing that the subject was too large for her, tried to take it apart, putting it before her bit by bit, and at such an angle that she should catch her own reflection in it. He thought to take her by the Austrian side, touching on the well-known antagonism between Vienna and Rome, on the reforms of the Tuscan Grand-Duke, on the

Emperor Joseph's open defiance of the Church's feudal claims. But she scented a personal application.

"My cousin the Emperor should be a priest himself," she shrugged, "for he belongs to the preaching order. He never goes to France but he gives the poor Queen such a scolding that her eyes are red for a week. Has Joseph been trying to set our house in order?"

Discouraged, but more than ever bent on patience, he tried the chord of vanity, of her love of popularity. The people called her the beautiful Duchess—why not let history name her the great? But the mention of history was unfortunate. It reminded her of her lesson-books, and of the stupid Greeks and Romans, whose dates she could never recall. She hoped she should never be anything so dull as an historical personage! And besides, greatness was for the men—it was enough for a princess to be virtuous. And she looked as edifying as her own epitaph.

He caught this up and tried to make her distinguish between the public and the private virtues. But the word "responsibility" slipped from him and he felt her stiffen. This was preaching, and she hated preaching even more than history. Her attention strayed again and he rallied his forces in a last appeal. But he knew it was a lost battle: every argument broke against the close front of her indifference. He was talking a language she had never learned—it was all as remote from her as Church Latin. A princess did not need to know Latin. She let her eye linger suggestively on the clock. It was a fine hunting morning, and she had meant to kill a stag in the Caccia del Vescovo.

When he began to sum up, and the question narrowed to a direct appeal, her eyes left the clock and returned to him. Now she was listening. He pressed on to the matter of retrenchment. Would she join him, would she help to make the great work possible? At first she seemed hardly to understand; but as his meaning grew clear to her—"Is the money no longer ours?" she exclaimed.

He hesitated. "I suppose it is as much ours as ever," he said.

"And how much is that?" she asked impatiently.

"It is ours as a trust for our people."

She stared in honest wonder. These were new signs in her heaven.

"A trust? A trust? I am not sure that I know what that means. Is the money ours or theirs?"

He hesitated. "In strict honour, it is ours only as long as we spend it for their benefit."

She turned aside to examine an enamelled patch-box by Van Blarenberghe which the court jeweller had newly received from Paris. When she raised her eyes she said: "And if we do not spend it for their benefit—?"

Odo glanced about the room. He looked at the delicate adornment of the walls, the curtains of Lyons damask, the crystal girandoles, the toys in porcelain of Saxony and Sevres, in bronze and ivory and Chinese lacquer, crowding the tables and cabinets of inlaid wood. Overhead floated a rosy allegory by Luca Giordano; underfoot lay a carpet of the royal manufactory of France; and through the open windows he heard the plash of the garden fountains and saw the alignment of the long green alleys set with the statues of Roman patriots.

"Then," said he—and the words sounded strangely in his own ears—"then they may take it from us some day—and all this with it, to the very toy you are playing with."

She rose, and from her fullest height dropped a brilliant smile on him; then her eyes turned to the portrait of the great fighting Duke set in the monumental stucchi of the chimney-piece.

"If you take after your ancestors you will know how to defend it," she said.

4.3.

The new Duke sat in his closet. The walls had been stripped of their pious relics and lined with books, and above the fireplace hung the Venus of Giorgione, liberated at last from her long imprisonment. The windows stood open, admitting the soft September air. Twilight had fallen on the gardens, and through it a young moon floated above the cypresses.

On just such an evening three years earlier he had ridden down the slope of the Monte Baldo with Fulvia Vivaldi at his side. How often, since, he had relived the incidents of that night! With singular precision they succeeded each other in his thoughts. He felt the wild sweep of the storm across the lake, the warmth of her nearness, the sense of her complete trust in him; then their arrival at the inn, the dazzle of light as they crossed the threshold, and de Crucis confronting them within. He heard her voice pleading with him in every accent that pride and tenderness and a noble loyalty could command; he felt her will slowly dominating his, like a supernatural power forcing him into his destined path; he felt—and with how profound an irony of spirit!— the passion of self-dedication in which he had taken up his task.

He had known moments of happiness since; moments when he believed in himself and in his calling, and felt himself indeed the man she thought him. That was in the exaltation of the first months, when his opportunities had seemed as boundless as his dreams, and he had not yet learned that the sovereign's power may be a kind of spiritual prison to the man. Since then, indeed, he had known another kind of happiness, had been aware of a secret voice whispering within him that she was right and had chosen wisely for him; but this was when he had realised that he lived in a prison, and had begun to admire the sumptuous adornment of its walls. For a while the mere external show of power amused him, and his imagination was charmed by the historic dignity of his surroundings. In such a setting, against the background of such a past, it seemed easy to play the benefactor and friend of the people. His sensibility was touched by the contrast, and he saw himself as a picturesque figure linking the new dreams of liberty and equality to the feudal traditions of a thousand years. But this masquerading soon ceased to divert him. The round of court ceremonial wearied him, and books and art lost their fascination. The more he varied his amusements the more monotonous they became, the more he crowded his life with petty duties the more empty of achievement it seemed.

At first he had hoped to bury his personal disappointments in the task of reconstructing his little state; but on every side he felt a mute resistance to his efforts. The philosophical faction had indeed poured forth pamphlets celebrating his reforms, and comparing his reign to the return of the Golden Age. But it was not for the philosophers that he laboured; and the benefits of free speech, a free press, a secular education did not, after all, reach those over whom his heart yearned. It was the people he longed to serve; and the people were hungry, were fever-stricken, were crushed with tithes and taxes. It was hopeless to try to reach them by the diffusion of popular knowledge. They must first be fed and clothed; and before they could be fed and clothed the chains of feudalism must be broken.

Men like Gamba and Andreoni saw this clearly enough; but it was not from them that help could come. The nobility and clergy must be coaxed or coerced into sympathy with the new movement; and to accomplish this exceeded Odo's powers. In France, the revolt from feudalism had found some of its boldest leaders in the very class that had most to lose by the change; but in Italy fewer causes were at work to set such disinterested passions in motion. South of the Alps liberalism was merely one of the new fashions from France: the men ran after the pamphlets from Paris as the women ran after the cosmetics; and the politics went no deeper than the powder. Even among the freest intellects liberalism resulted in a new way of thinking rather in a new way of living. Nowhere among the better classes was there any desire to attack existing institutions. The Church had never troubled the Latin consciousness. The Renaissance had taught cultivated Italians how to live at peace with a creed in which they no longer believed; and their easy-going scepticism was combined with a traditional conviction that the priest knew better than any one how to deal with the poor, and that the clergy were of distinct use in relieving the individual conscience of its obligation to its fellows.

It was against such deep-seated habits of thought that Odo had to struggle. Centuries of fierce individualism, or of sullen apathy under a foreign rule, had left the Italians incapable of any concerted political action; but suspicion, avarice and vanity, combined with a lurking fear of the Church, united all parties in a kind of passive opposition to reform. Thus the Duke's resolve to put the University under lay direction had excited the enmity of the Barnabites, who had been at its head since the suppression of the Society of Jesus; his efforts to partition among the peasantry the Caccia del Vescovo, that great waste domain of the see of Pianura, had roused a storm of fear among all who laid claim to feudal rights; and his own personal attempts at retrenchment, which necessitated the suppression of numerous court offices, had done more than anything else to increase his unpopularity. Even the people, in whose behalf these sacrifices were made, looked askance at his diminished state, and showed a perverse sympathy with the dispossessed officials who had taken so picturesque a part in the public ceremonials of the court. All Odo's philosophy could not fortify him against such disillusionments. He felt the lack of Fulvia's unquestioning faith not only in the abstract beauty of the new ideals but in their immediate adaptability to the complex conditions of life. Only a woman's convictions, nourished on sentiment and self-sacrifice, could burn with that clear unwavering flame: his own beliefs were at the mercy of every wind of doubt or ingratitude that blew across his unsheltered sensibilities.

It was more than a year since he had had news of Fulvia. For a while they had exchanged letters, and it had been a consolation to tell her of his struggles and experiments, of his many failures and few results. She had encouraged him to continue the struggle, had analysed his various plans of reform, and had given her enthusiastic support to the partitioning of the Bishop's fief and the secularisation of the University. Her own life, she said, was too uneventful to write of; but she spoke of the kindness of her hosts, the Professor and his wife, of the simple unceremonious way of living in the old Calvinist city, and of the number of distinguished persons drawn thither by its atmosphere of intellectual and social freedom.

Odo suspected a certain colourlessness in the life she depicted. The tone of her letters was too uniformly cheerful not to suggest a lack of emotional variety; and he knew that Fulvia's nature, however much she fancied it under the rule of reason, was in reality fed by profound currents of feeling. Something of her old ardour reappeared when she wrote of the possibility of publishing her father's book. Her friends in Geneva, having heard of her difficulty with the Dutch publisher, had undertaken to vindicate her claims;

and they had every hope that the matter would be successfully concluded. The joy of renewed activity with which this letter glowed would have communicated itself to Odo had he received it at a different time; but it came on the day of his marriage, and since then he had never written to her.

Now he felt a sudden longing to break the silence between them, and seating himself at his desk he began to write. A moment later there was a knock on the door and one of his gentlemen entered. The Count Vittorio Alfieri, with a dozen horses and as many servants, was newly arrived at the Golden Cross, and desired to know when he might have the honour of waiting on his Highness.

Odo felt the sudden glow of pleasure that the news of Alfieri's coming always brought. Here was a friend at last! He forgot the constraint of their last meeting in Florence, and remembered only the happy interchange of ideas and emotions that had been one of the quickening influences of his youth.

Alfieri, in the intervening years, was grown to be one of the foremost figures in Italy. His love for the Countess of Albany, persisting through the vicissitudes of her tragic marriage, had rallied the scattered forces of his nature. Ambitious to excel for her sake, to show himself worthy of such a love, he had at last shaken off the strange torpor of his youth, and revealed himself as the poet for whom Italy waited. In ten months of feverish effort he had poured forth fourteen tragedies—among them the Antigone, the Virginia, and the Conjuration of the Pazzi. Italy started up at the sound of a new voice vibrating with passions she had long since unlearned. Since Filicaja's thrilling appeal to his enslaved country no poet had challenged the old Roman spirit which Petrarch had striven to rouse. While the literati were busy discussing Alfieri's blank verse, while the grammarians wrangled over his syntax and ridiculed his solecisms, the public, heedless of such niceties, was glowing with the new wine which he had poured into the old vessels of classic story. "Liberty" was the cry that rang on the lips of all his heroes, in accents so new and stirring that his audience never wearied of its repetition. It was no secret that his stories of ancient Greece and Rome were but allegories meant to teach the love of freedom; yet the Antigone had been performed in the private theatre of the Spanish Ambassador at Rome, the Virginia had been received with applause on the public boards at Turin, and after the usual difficulties with the censorship the happy author had actually succeeded in publishing his plays at Siena. These volumes were already in Odo's hands, and a manuscript copy of the Odes to Free America was being circulated among the liberals in Pianura, and had been brought to his notice by Andreoni.

To those hopeful spirits who looked for the near approach of a happier era, Alfieri was the inspired spokesman of reform, the heaven-sent prophet who was to lead his country out of bondage. The eyes of the Italian reformers were fixed with passionate eagerness on the course of events in England and France. The conclusion of peace between England and America, recently celebrated in Alfieri's fifth Ode, seemed to the most sceptical convincing proof that the rights of man were destined to a speedy triumph throughout the civilised world. It was not of a united Italy that these enthusiasts dreamed. They were not so much patriots as philanthropists; for the teachings of Rousseau and his school, while intensifying the love of man for man, had proportionately weakened the sense of patriotism, of the interets du clocher. The new man prided himself on being a citizen of the world, on sympathising as warmly with the poetic savage of Peru as with his own prosaic and narrow-minded neighbours. Indeed, the prevalent belief that the savage's mode of life was much nearer the truth than that of civilised Europeans, made it appear superfluous to enter into the grievances and difficulties of what was but a passing phase of human development. To cast off clothes and codes, and live in a peaceful socialism "under the amiable reign of Truth and Nature," seemed on the whole much easier than to undertake the systematic reform of existing abuses.

To such dreamers—whose ideas were those of the majority of intelligent men in France and Italy—Alfieri's high-sounding tirades embodied the noblest of political creeds; and even the soberer judgment of statesmen and men of affairs was captivated by the grandeur of his verse and the heroic audacity of his theme. For the first time in centuries the Italian Muse spoke with the voice of a man; and every man's heart in Italy sprang up at the call.

In the midst of these triumphs, fate in the shape of Cardinal York had momentarily separated Alfieri from his mistress, despatching the too-tender Countess to a discreet retreat in Alsace, and signifying to her turbulent adorer that he was not to follow her. Distracted by this prohibition, Alfieri had resumed the nomadic habits of his youth, now wandering from one Italian city to another, now pushing as far as Paris, which he hated but was always revisiting, now dashing across the Channel to buy thoroughbreds in England—for his passion for horses was unabated. He was lately returned from such an expedition, having led his cavalcade across the Alps in person, with a boyish delight in the astonishment which this fantastic exploit excited.

The meeting between the two friends was all that Odo could have wished. Though affecting to scorn the courts of princes, Alfieri was not averse to showing himself there as the poet of the democracy, and to hearing his heroes mouth their tyrannicidal speeches on the boards of royal and ducal stages. He had lately made some stay in Milan, where he had arrived in time to see his Antigone performed before the vice-regal court, and to be enthusiastically acclaimed as the high-priest of liberty by a community living placidly under the Austrian yoke. Alfieri was not the man to be struck by such incongruities. It was his fate to formulate creeds in which he had no faith: to recreate the political ideals of Italy while bitterly opposed to any actual effort at reform, and to be regarded as the mouthpiece of the Revolution while he execrated the Revolution with the whole force of his traditional instincts. As usual he was too deeply engrossed in his own affairs to feel much interest in any others; but it was enough for Odo to clasp the hand of the man who had given a voice to the highest aspirations of his countrymen. The poet gave more than he could expect from the friend; and he was satisfied to listen to Alfieri's account of his triumphs, interspersed with bitter diatribes against the public whose applause he courted, and the Pope to whom, on bended knee, he had offered a copy of his plays.

Odo eagerly pressed Alfieri to remain in Pianura, offering to put one of the ducal villas at his disposal, and suggesting that the Virginia should be performed before the court on the Duchess's birthday.

"It is true," he said, "that we can offer you but an indifferent company of actors; but it might be possible to obtain one or two of the leading tragedians from Turin or Milan, so that the principal parts should at least be worthily filled."

Alfieri replied with a contemptuous gesture. "Your Highness, our leading tragedians are monkeys trained to dance to the tune of Goldoni and Metastasio. The best are no better than the worst. We have no tragedians in Italy because—hitherto—we have had no tragic dramatist." He drew himself up and thrust a hand in his bosom. "Ah!" he exclaimed, "if I could see the part of Virginia acted by the lady who recently recited, before a small company in Milan, my Odes to Free America! There indeed were fire, sublimity and passion! And the countenance had not lost its freshness, the eye its lustre. But," he suddenly added, "your Highness knows of whom I speak. The lady is Fulvia Vivaldi, the daughter of the philosopher at whose feet we sat in our youth."

Fulvia Vivaldi! Odo raised his head with a start. She had left Geneva then, had returned to Italy. The Alps no longer divided them—a scant day's journey would bring him to her side! It was strange how the mere thought seemed to fill the room with her presence. He felt her in the quickened beat of his pulses, in the sudden lightness of the air, in a lifting and widening of the very bounds of thought.

From Alfieri he learned that she had lived for some months in the household of the distinguished naturalist, Count Castiglione, with whose daughter's education she was charged. In such surroundings her wit and learning could not fail to attract the best company of Milan, and she was become one of the most noted figures of the capital. There had been some talk of offering her the chair of poetry at the Brera; but the report of her liberal views had deterred the faculty. Meanwhile the very fact that she represented the new school of thought gave an added zest to her conversation in a society which made up for its mild servitude under the Austrian by much talk of liberalism and independence. The Signorina Vivaldi became the fashion. The literati celebrated her scholarship, the sonneteers her eloquence and beauty; and no foreigner on the grand tour was content to leave Milan without having beheld the fair prodigy and heard her recite Petrarch's Ode to Italy, or the latest elegy of Pindamonte.

Odo scarce knew with what feelings he listened. He could not but acknowledge that such a life was better suited to one of Fulvia's gifts and ambitions than the humdrum existence of a Swiss town; yet his first sensation was one of obscure jealousy, of reluctance to think of her as having definitely broken with the past. He had pictured her as adrift, like himself, on a dark sea of uncertainties; and to learn that she had found a safe anchorage was almost to feel himself deserted.

The court was soon busy with preparations for the coming performance. A celebrated actress from Venice was engaged to play the part of Virginia, and the rehearsals went rapidly forward under the noble author's supervision. At last the great day arrived, and for the first time in the history of the little theatre, operetta and pastoral were replaced by the buskined Muse of tragedy. The court and all the nobility were present, and though it was no longer thought becoming for ecclesiastics to visit the theatre, the easy-going Bishop appeared in a side-box in company with his chaplains and the Vicar-general.

The performance was brilliantly successful. Frantic applause greeted the tirades of the young Icilius. Every outburst against the abuse of privileges and the insolence of the patricians was acclaimed by ministers and courtiers, and the loudest in approval were the Marquess Pievepelago, the recognised representative of the clericals, the Marchioness of Boscofolto, whose harsh enforcement of her feudal rights was among the bitterest grievances of the peasantry, and the good Bishop, who had lately roused himself from his habitual indolence to oppose the threatened annexation of the Caccia del Vescovo. One and all proclaimed their ardent sympathy with the proletariat, their scorn of tyranny and extortion in high places; and if the Marchioness, on her return home, ordered one of her linkmen to be flogged for having trod on her gown; if Pievepelago the next morning refused to give audience to a poor devil of a pamphleteer that was come to ask his intercession with the Holy Office; if the Bishop at the same moment concluded the purchase of six able-bodied Turks from the galleys of his Serenity the Doge of Genoa—it is probable that, like the illustrious author of the drama, all were unconscious of any incongruity between their sentiments and actions.

As to Odo, seated in the state box, with Maria Clementina at his side, and the court dignitaries grouped in the background, he had not listened to a dozen lines before all sense of his surroundings vanished and he became the passive instrument on which the poet played his mighty harmonies. All the incidental difficulties of life, all the vacillations of an unsatisfied spirit, were consumed in that energising emotion which seemed to leave every faculty stripped for action. Profounder meaning and more subtle music he had found in the great poets of the past; but here was an appeal to the immediate needs of the hour, uttered in notes as thrilling as a trumpet-call, and brought home to every sense by the vivid imagery of the stage. Once more he felt the old ardour of belief that Fulvia's nearness had fanned in him. His convictions had flagged rather than his courage: now they started up as at her summons, and he heard the ring of her voice in every line.

He left the theatre still vibrating with this new inrush of life, and jealous of any interruption that should check it. The Duchess's birthday was being celebrated by illuminations and fireworks, and throngs of merry-makers filled the moonlit streets; but Odo, after appearing for a moment at his wife's side on the balcony above the public square, withdrew quietly to his own apartments. The casement of his closet stood wide, and he leaned against the window-frame, looking out on the silent radiance of the gardens. As he stood there he saw two figures flit across the farther end of one of the long alleys. The moonlight surrendered them for a moment, the shade almost instantly reclaiming them—strayed revellers, doubtless, escaping from the lights and music of the Duchess's circle.

A knock roused the Duke and he remembered that he had bidden Gamba wait on him after the performance. He had been curious to hear what impression Alfieri's drama had produced upon the hunchback; but now any interruption seemed unwelcome, and he turned to Gamba with a gesture of dismissal.

The latter however remained on the threshold.

"Your Highness," he said, "the bookseller Andreoni craves the privilege of an audience."

"Andreoni? At this hour?"

"For reasons so urgent that he makes no doubt of your Highness's consent; and to prove his good faith, and the need of presenting himself at so undue an hour, and in this private manner, he charged me to give this to your Highness."

He laid in the Duke's hand a small object in blackened silver, which on nearer inspection proved to be the ducal coat-of-arms.

Odo stood gazing fixedly at this mysterious token, which seemed to come as an answer to his inmost thoughts. His heart beat high with confused hopes and fears, and he could hardly control the voice in which he answered: "Bid Andreoni come to me."

4.4.

The bookseller began by excusing himself for the liberty he had taken. He explained that the Signorina Fulvia Vivaldi, in whose behalf he came, was in urgent need of aid, and had begged him to wait on the Duke as soon as the court had risen from the play.

"She is in Pianura, then?" Odo exclaimed.

"Since yesterday, your Highness. Three days since she was ordered by the police to leave Milan within twenty-four hours, and she came at once to Pianura, knowing that my wife and I would gladly receive her. But today we learned that the Holy Office was advised of her presence here, and of the reason of her banishment from Lombardy; and this fresh danger has forced her to implore your Highness's protection."

Andreoni went on to explain that the publication of her father's book was the immediate cause of Fulvia's persecution. The Origin of Civilisation, which had been printed some months previously in Amsterdam, had stirred Italy more profoundly than any book since Beccaria's great work on Crime and Punishment. The author's historical investigations were but a pretext for the development of his political theories, which were set forth with singular daring and audacity, and supported by all the arguments that his long study of the past commanded. The temperate and judicial tone which he had succeeded in preserving enhanced the effect of his arraignment of Church and state, and while his immense erudition commended his work to the learned, its directness of style gave it an immediate popularity with the general reader. It was an age when every book or pamphlet bearing on the great question of personal liberty was eagerly devoured by an insatiable public; and a few weeks after Vivaldi's volume had been smuggled into Italy it was the talk of every club and coffee-house from Calabria to Piedmont. The inevitable result soon followed. The Holy Office got wind of the business, and the book was at once put on the Index. In Naples and Bologna it was publicly burned, and in Modena a professor of the University who was found to have a copy in his possession was fined and removed from his chair.

In Milan, where the strong liberal faction among the nobility, and the comparative leniency of the Austrian rule, permitted a more unrestrained discussion of political questions, the Origin of Civilisation was received with open enthusiasm, and the story of the difficulties that Fulvia had encountered in its publication made her the heroine of the moment. She had never concealed her devotion to her father's doctrines, and in the first glow of filial pride she may have yielded too openly to the desire to propagate them. Certain it is that she began to be looked on as having shared in the writing of the book, or as being at least an active exponent of its principles. Even in Lombardy it was not well to be too openly associated with the authorship of a condemned book; and Fulvia was suddenly advised by the police that her presence in Milan was no longer acceptable to the government.

The news excited great indignation among her friends, and Count Castiglione and several other gentlemen of rank hastened to intervene in her behalf; but the governor declared himself unwilling to take issue with the Holy Office on a doctrinal point, and privately added that it would be well for the Signorina Vivaldi to withdraw from Lombardy before the clergy brought any direct charge against her. To ignore this hint would have been to risk not only her own safety but that of the gentlemen who had befriended her; and Fulvia at once set out for Pianura, the only place in Italy where she could count on friendship and protection.

Andreoni and his wife would gladly have given her a home; but on learning that the Holy Office was on her track, she had refused to compromise them by remaining under their roof, and had insisted that Andreoni should wait on the Duke and obtain a safe-conduct for her that very night.

Odo listened to this story with an agitation compounded of strangely contradictory sensations. To learn that Fulvia, at the very moment when he had pictured her as separated from him by the happiness and security of her life, was in reality a proscribed wanderer with none but himself to turn to, filled him with a confused sense of happiness; but the discovery that, in his own dominions, the political refugee was not safe from the threats of the Holy Office, excited a different emotion. All these considerations, however, were subordinate to the thought that he must see Fulvia at once. It was impossible to summon her to the palace at that hour, or even to secure her safety till morning, without compromising Andreoni by calling attention to the fact that a suspected person was under his roof; and for a moment Odo was at a loss how to detain her in Pianura without seeming to go counter to her wishes.

Suddenly he remembered that Gamba was fertile in expedients, and calling in the hunchback, asked what plan he could devise. Gamba, after a moment's reflection, drew a key from his pocket.

"May it please your Highness," he said, "this unlocks the door of the hunting-lodge at Pontesordo. The place has been deserted these many years, because of its bad name, and I have more than once found it a convenient shelter when I had reasons for wishing to be private. At this season there is no fear of poison from the marshes, and if your Highness desires I will see that the lady finds her way there before sunrise."

The sun had hardly risen the next morning when the Duke himself set forth. He rode alone, dressed like one of his own esquires, and gave the word unremarked to the sleepy sentinel at the gate. As it closed behind him and he set out down the long road that led to the chase, it seemed to him that the morning solitude was thronged with spectral memories. Melancholy and fanciful they flitted before him, now in the guise of Cerveno and Momola, now of Maria Clementina and himself. Every detail of the scene was interwoven with the fibres of early association, from the far off years when, as a lonely child on the farm at Pontesordo, he had gazed across the marsh at the mysterious woodlands of the chase, to the later day when, in the deserted hunting-lodge, the Duchess had flung her whip at the face in the Venice mirror.

He pressed forward impatiently, and presently the lodge rose before him in its grassy solitude. The level sunbeams had not yet penetrated the surrounding palisade of boughs, and the house lay in a chill twilight that seemed an emanation from its mouldering walls. As Odo approached, Gamba appeared from the shadow and took his horse; and the next moment he had pushed open the door, and stood in Fulvia's presence.

She was seated at the farther end of the room, and as she rose to meet him it chanced that her head, enveloped in its black travelling-hood, was relieved for a moment against the tarnished background of the broken mirror. The impression struck a chill to his heart; but it was replaced by a glow of boyish happiness as their eyes met and he felt her hands in his.

For a moment all his thoughts were lost in the mere sense of her nearness. She seemed simply an enveloping atmosphere in which he drew fresh breath; but gradually her outline emerged from this haze of feeling, and he found himself looking at her with the wondering gaze of a stranger. She had been a girl of sixteen when they first met. Twelve years had passed since then, and she was now a woman of twenty-eight, belonging to a race in which beauty ripens early and as soon declines. But some happy property of nature— whether the rare mould of her features or the gift of the spirit that informed them—had held her loveliness intact, preserving the clear lines of youth after its bloom was gone, and making her seem like a lover's memory of herself. So she appeared at first, a bright imponderable presence gliding toward him out of the past; but as her hands lay in his the warm current of life was renewed between them, and the woman dispossessed the shade.

4.5.

Unpublished fragment from Mr. Arthur Young's diary of his travels in Italy in the year 1789.

October 1st.

Having agreed with a vetturino to carry me to Pianura, set out this morning from Mantua. The country mostly arable, with rows of elm and maple pollard. Dined at Casal Maggiore, in an infamous filthy inn. At dinner was joined by a gentleman who had taken the other seat in the vettura as far as Pianura. We engaged in conversation and I found him a man of lively intelligence and the most polished address. Though dressed in the foreign style, en abbe, he spoke English with as much fluency as myself, and but for the philosophical tone of his remarks I had taken him for an ecclesiastic. Altogether a striking and somewhat perplexing character: able, keen, intelligent, evidently used to the best company, yet acquainted with the condition of the people, the methods of farming, and other economical subjects such as are seldom thought worthy of attention among Italians of quality.

It appeared he was newly from France, where he had been as much struck as myself by the general state of ferment. Though owning that there was much reason for discontent, and that the conduct of the court and ministers was blind and infatuated beyond belief, he yet declared himself gravely apprehensive of the future, saying that the people knew not what they wanted, and were unwilling to listen to those that might have proved their best advisors. Whether by this he meant the clergy I know not; though I observed he spoke favourably of that body in France, pointing out that, long before the recent agitations, they had defended the civil rights of the Third Estate, and citing many cases in which the country curates had shown themselves the truest friends of the people: a fact my own observation hath confirmed.

I remarked to him that I was surprised to find how little talk there was in Italy of the distracted conditions in France; and this though the country is overrun with French refugees, or emigres, as they call themselves, who bring with them reports that might well excite the alarm of neighbouring governments. He said he had remarked the same indifference, but that this was consonant with the Italian character, which never looked to the morrow; and he added that the mild disposition of the people, and their profound respect for religion, were sufficient assurance against any political excess.

To this I could not forbear replying that I could not regard as excesses the just protests of the poor against the unlawful tyranny of the privileged classes, nor forbear to hail with joy the dawn of that light of freedom which hath already shed so sublime an effulgence on the wilds of the New World. The abate took this in good part, though I could see he was not wholly of my way of thinking; but he declared that in his opinion different races needed different laws, and that the sturdy and temperate American colonists were fitted to enjoy a greater measure of political freedom than the more volatile French and Italians—as though liberty were not destined by the Creator to be equally shared by all mankind! (Footnote: I let this passage stand, though the late unhappy events in France have, alas! proved that my friend the abate was nearer right than myself. June, 1794.)

In the afternoon through a poor country to Ponte di Po, a miserable village on the borders of the duchy, where we lay, not slept, in our clothes, at the worst inn I have yet encountered. Here our luggage was plumbed for Pianura. The impertinence of the petty sovereigns to travellers in Italy is often intolerable, and the customs officers show the utmost insolence in the search for seditious pamphlets and other contraband articles; but here I was agreeably surprised by the courtesy of the officials and the despatch with which our luggage was examined. On my remarking this, my companion replied that the Duke of Pianura was a man of liberal views, anxious to encourage foreigners to visit his state, and the last to put petty obstacles in the way of travel. I answered, this was the report I had heard of him; and it was in the hope of learning something more of the reforms he was said to have effected, that I had turned aside to visit the duchy. My companion replied that his Highness had in fact introduced some innovations in the government; but that changes which seemed the most beneficial in one direction often worked mischief in another, so that the wisest ruler was perhaps not he that did the greatest amount of good, but he that was cause of the fewest evils.

The 2nd.

From Ponte di Po to Pianura the most convenient way is by water; but the river Piana being greatly swollen by the late rains, my friend, who seems well-acquainted with the country, proposed driving thither: a suggestion I readily accepted, as it gave me a good opportunity to study the roads and farms of the duchy.

Crossing the Piana, drove near four hours over horrible roads across waste land, thinly wooded, without houses or cultivation. On my expressing surprise that the territory of so enlightened a prince would lie thus neglected, the abate said this land was a fief of the see of Pianura, and that the Duke was desirous of annexing it to the duchy. I asked if it were true that his Highness had given his people a constitution modelled on that of the Duke of Tuscany. He said he had heard the report; but that for his part he must deplore any measure tending to debar the clergy from the possession of land.

Seeing my surprise, he explained that, in Italy at least, the religious orders were far better landlords than the great nobles or the petty sovereigns, who, being for the most part absent from their estates, left their peasantry to be pillaged by rapacious middlemen and stewards: an argument I have heard advanced by other travellers, and have myself had frequent occasion to corroborate.

On leaving the Bishop's domain, remarked an improvement in the roads. Flat land, well irrigated, and divided as usual into small holdings. The pernicious metayer system exists everywhere, but I am told the Duke is opposed to it, though it is upheld not only by the landed class, but by the numerous economists that write on agriculture from their closets, but would doubtless be sorely puzzled to distinguish a beet-root from a turnip.

The 3rd.

Set out early to visit Pianura. The city clean and well-kept. The Duke has introduced street-lamps, such as are used in Turin, and the pavement is remarkably fair and even. Few beggars are to be seen and the people have a thriving look. Visited the Cathedral and Baptistery, in the Gothic style, more curious than beautiful; also the Duke's picture gallery.

Learning that the Duchess was to ride out in the afternoon, had the curiosity to walk abroad to see her. A good view of her as she left the palace. Though no longer in her first youth she is one of the handsomest women I have seen. Remarked a decided likeness to the Queen of France, though the eye and smile are less engaging. The people in the streets received her sullenly, and I am told her debts and disorders are the scandal of the town. She has, of course, her cicisbeo, and the Duke is the devoted slave of a learned lady, who is said to exert an unlimited influence over him, and to have done much to better the condition of the people. A new part for a prince's mistress to play!

In the evening to the theatre, a handsome building, well-lit with wax, where Cimarosa's Due Baroni was agreeably sung.

The 4th.

My lord Hervey, in Florence, having favoured me with a letter to Count Trescorre, the Duke's prime minister, I waited on that gentleman yesterday. His excellency received me politely and assured me that he knew me by reputation and would do all he could to put me in the way of investigating the agricultural conditions of the duchy. Contrary to the Italian custom, he invited me to dine with him the next day. As a rule these great nobles do not open their doors to foreigners, however well recommended.

Visited, by appointment, the press of the celebrated Andreoni, who was banished during the late Duke's reign for suspected liberal tendencies, but is now restored to favour and placed at the head of the Royal Typography. Signor Andreoni received me with every mark of esteem, and after having shown me some of the finest examples of his work—such as the Pindar, the Lucretius and the Dante—accompanied me to a neighbouring coffee-house, where I was introduced to several lovers of agriculture. Here I learned some particulars of the Duke's attempted reforms. He has undertaken the work of draining the vast marsh of Pontesordo, to the west of the city, notorious for its mal'aria; has renounced the monopoly of corn and tobacco; has taken the University out of the hands of the Barnabites, and introduced the teaching of the physical sciences, formerly prohibited by the Church; has spent since his accession near 200,000 liv. on improving the roads throughout the duchy, and is now engaged in framing a constitution which shall deprive the clergy of the greatest part of their privileges and confirm the sovereign's right to annex ecclesiastical territory for the benefit of the people.

In spite of these radical measures, his Highness is not popular with the masses. He is accused of irreligion by the monks that he has removed from the University, and his mistress, the daughter of a noted free-thinker who was driven from Piedmont by the Inquisition, is said to have an unholy influence over him. I am told these rumours are diligently fomented by the late Duke's minister, now Prior of the Dominican monastery, a man of bigoted views but great astuteness. The truth is, the people are so completely under the influence of the friars that a word is enough to turn them against their truest benefactors.

In the afternoon I was setting out to visit the Bishop's gallery when Count Trescorre's secretary waited on me with an invitation to inspect the estates of the Marchioness of Boscofolto: an offer I readily accepted—for what are the masterpieces of Raphael or Cleomenes to the sight of a good turnip field or of a well-kept dairy?

I had heard of Boscofolto, which was given by the late Duke to his mistress, as one of the most productive estates of the duchy; but great was my disappointment on beholding it. Fine gardens there are, to be sure, clipt walks, leaden statues, and water-works; but as for the farms, all is dirt, neglect, disorder. Spite of the lady's wealth, all are let out alla meta, and farmed on principles that would disgrace a savage. The spade used instead of the plough, the hedges neglected, mole-casts in the pastures, good land run to waste, the peasants starving and indebted—where, with a little thrift and humanity, all had been smiling plenty! Learned that on the owner's death this great property reverts to the Barnabites.

From Boscofolto to the church of the Madonna del Monte, where is one of their wonder-working images, said to be annually visited by close on thirty thousand pilgrims; but there is always some exaggeration in such figures. A fine building, richly adorned, and hung with an extraordinary number of votive offerings: silver arms, legs, hearts, wax images, and paintings. Some of these latter are clearly the work of village artists, and depict the miraculous escape of the peasantry from various calamities, and the preservation of their crops from floods, drought, lightning and so forth. These poor wretches had done more to better their crops by spending their savings in good ploughshares and harrows than by hanging gew-gaws on a wooden idol.

The Rector received us civilly and showed us the treasury, full of jewels and costly plate, and the buildings where the pilgrims are lodged. Learned that the Giubileo or centenary festival of the Madonna is shortly to be celebrated with great pomp. The poorer classes delight in these ceremonies, and I am told this is to surpass all previous ones, the clergy intending to work on the superstitions of the people and thus turn them against the new charter. It is said the Duke hopes to counteract these designs by offering a jewelled diadem to the Virgin; but this will no doubt do him a bad turn with the esprits libres. These little states are as full of intrigues as a foul fruit of maggots.

The 5th.

To dinner at Count Trescorre's where, as usual, I was the plainest-dressed man in the company. Have long since ceased to be concerned by this: why should a mere English farmer compete in elegance with these Monsignori and Illustrissimi? Surprised to find among the company my travelling-companion of the other day. Learned that he is the abate de Crucis, a personal friend of the Duke's. He greeted me cordially, and on hearing my name, said that he was acquainted with my works in the translation of Mons. Freville, and now understood how it was that I had got the better of him in our farming disputations on the way hither.

Was surprised to be told by Count Trescorre that the Duke desired me to wait on him that evening. Though in general not ambitious of such honours, yet in this case nothing could be more gratifying.

The 6th.

Yesterday evening to the palace, where his Highness received me with great affability. He was in his private apartments, with the abate de Crucis and several other learned men; among them the famous abate Crescenti, librarian to his Highness and author of the celebrated Chronicles of the Italian States. Happy indeed is the prince who surrounds himself with scholars instead of courtiers! Yet I cannot say that the impression his Highness produced on me was one of HAPPINESS. His countenance is sad, almost careworn, though with a smile of engaging sweetness; his manner affable without condescension, and open without familiarity. I am told he is oppressed by the cares of his station; and from a certain irresolution of voice and eye, that bespeaks not so much weakness as a speculative cast of mind, I can believe him less fitted for active government than for the meditations of the closet. He appears, however, zealous to perform his duties; questioned me eagerly about my impressions of Italy, and showed a flattering familiarity with my works, and a desire to profit by what he was pleased to call my exceptional knowledge of agriculture. I thought I perceived in him a sincere wish to study the welfare of his people; but was disappointed to find among his chosen associates not one practical farmer or economist, but only the usual closet-theorists that are too busy planning Utopias to think of planting turnips.

The 7th.

Visited his Highness's estate at Valsecca. Here he has converted a handsome seat into a school of agriculture, tearing down an immense orangery to plant mulberries, and replacing costly gardens and statuary by well-tilled fields: a good example to his wealthy subjects. Unfortunately his bailiff is not what we should call a practical farmer; and many acres of valuable ground are given up to a botanic garden, where exotic plants are grown at great expense, and rather for curiosity than use: a common error of noble agriculturists.

In the afternoon with the abate de Crucis to the Benedictine monastery, a league beyond the city. Here I saw the best farming in the duchy. The Prior received us politely and conversed with intelligence on drainage, crops and irrigation. I urged on him the cultivation of turnips and he appeared struck by my arguments. The tenants on this great estate appeared better housed and fed than any I have seen in Pianura. The monks have a school of agriculture, less pretentious but better-managed than the Duke's. Some of them study physics and chemistry, and there are good chirurgeons among them, who care for the poor without pay. The aged and infirm peasants are housed in a neat almshouse, and the sick nursed in a clean well-built lazaret. Altogether an agreeable picture of rural prosperity, though I had rather it had been the result of FREE LABOUR than of MONASTIC BOUNTY.

The 8th.

By appointment, to the Duke's Egeria. This lady, the Signorina F.V., having heard that I was in Pianura, had desired the Signor Andreoni to bring me to her.

I had expected a female of the loud declamatory type: something of the Corilla Olimpica order; but in this was agreeably disappointed. The Signorina V. is modestly lodged, lives in the frugal style of the middle class, and refuses to accept a title, though she is thus debarred from going to court. Were it not indiscreet to speculate on a lady's age, I should put hers at somewhat above thirty. Though without the Duchess's commanding elegance she has, I believe, more beauty of a quiet sort: a countenance at once soft and animated, agreeably tinged with melancholy, yet lit up by the incessant play of thought and emotion that succeed each other in her talk. Better conversation I never heard; and can heartily confirm the assurances of those who had told me that the lady was as agreeable in discourse as learned in the closet. (Footnote: It has before now been observed that the FREE and VOLATILE manners of foreign ladies tend to blind the English traveller to the inferiority of their PHYSICAL charms. Note by a Female Friend of the Author.)

On entering, found a numerous company assembled to compliment my hostess on her recent appointment as doctor of the University. This is an honour not uncommonly conferred in Italy, where female learning, perhaps from its rarity, is highly esteemed; but I am told the ladies thus distinguished seldom speak in public, though their degree entitles them to a chair in the University. In the Signorina V.'s society I found the most advanced reformers of the duchy: among others Signor Gamba, the famous pamphleteer, author of a remarkable treatise on taxation, which had nearly cost him his liberty under the late Duke's reign. He is a man of extreme views and sarcastic tongue, with an irritability of manner that is perhaps the result of bodily infirmities. His ideas, I am told, have much weight with the fair doctoress; and in the lampoons of the day the new constitution is said to be the offspring of their amours, and to have inherited its father's deformity.

The company presently withdrawing, my hostess pressed me to remain. She was eager for news from France, spoke admiringly of the new constitution, and recited in a moving manner an Ode of her own composition on the Fall of the Bastille. Though living so retired she makes no secret of her connection with the Duke; said he had told her of his conversation with me, and asked what I thought of his plan for draining the marsh of Pontesordo. On my attempting to reply to this in detail, I saw that, like some of the most accomplished of her sex, she was impatient of minutiae, and preferred general ideas to particular instances; but when the talk turned on the rights of the people I was struck by the energy and justice of her remarks, and by a tone of resolution and courage that made me to say to myself: "Here is the hand that rules the state."

She questioned me earnestly about the state of affairs in France, begged me to lend her what pamphlets I could procure, and while making no secret of her republican sympathies, expressed herself with a moderation not always found in her sex. Of the clergy alone she appeared intolerant: a fact hardly to be wondered at, considering the persecution to which she and her father have been subjected. She detained me near two hours in such discourse, and on my taking leave asked with some show of feeling what I, as a practical economist, would advise the Duke to do for the benefit of his people; to which I replied, "Plant turnips, madam!" and she laughed heartily, and said no doubt I was right. But I fear all the heads here are too full of fine theories to condescend to such simple improvements...

4.6.

Fulvia, in the twilight, sat awaiting the Duke.

The room in which she sat looked out on a stone-flagged cloister enclosing a plot of ground planted with yews; and at the farther end of this cloister a door communicated by a covered way with the ducal gardens. The house had formed a part of the convent of the Perpetual Adoration, which had been sold by the nuns when they moved to the new buildings the late Duke had given them. A portion had been torn down to make way for the Marquess of Cerveno's palace, and in the remaining fragment, a low building wedged between high walls, Fulvia had found a lodging. Her whole dwelling consisted of the Abbess's parlour, in which she now sat, and the two or three adjoining cells. The tall presses in the parlour had been filled with her father's books, and surmounted by his globes and other scientific instruments. But for this the apartment remained as unadorned as in her predecessor's day; and Fulvia, in her austere black gown, with a lawn kerchief folded over her breast, and the unpowdered hair drawn back from her pale face, might herself have passed for the head of a religious community.

She cultivated with almost morbid care this severity of dress and surroundings. There were moments when she could hardly tolerate the pale autumnal beauty which her glass reflected, when even this phantom of youth and radiance became a stumbling-block to her spiritual pride. She was not ashamed of being the Duke of Pianura's mistress; but she had a horror of being thought like the mistresses of other princes. She loathed all that the position represented in men's minds; she had refused all that, according to the conventions of the day, it entitled her to claim: wealth, patronage, and the rank and estates which it was customary for the sovereign to confer. She had taken nothing from Odo but his love, and the little house in which he had lodged her.

Three years had passed since Fulvia's flight to Pianura. From the moment when she and Odo had stood face to face again, it had been clear to him that he could never give her up, to her that she could never leave him. Fate seemed to have thrown them together in derision of their long struggle, and both felt that lassitude of the will which is the reaction from vain endeavour. The discovery that he needed her, that the task for which he had given her up could after all not be accomplished without her, served to overcome her last resistance. If the end for which both strove could best be attained together—if he needed the aid of her unfaltering faith as much as she needed that of his wealth and power—why should any personal scruple stand between them? Why should she who had given all else to the cause—ease, fortune, safety, and even the happiness that lay in her hand—hesitate to make the final sacrifice of a private ideal? According to the standards of her day there was no dishonour to a woman in being the mistress of a man whose rank forbade his marrying her: the dishonour lay in the conduct which had come to be associated with such relations. Under the old dispensation the influence of the prince's mistress had stood for the last excesses of moral and political corruption; why might it not, under the new law, come to represent as unlimited a power for good?

So love, the casuist, argued; and during those first months, when happiness seemed at last its own justification, Fulvia lived in every fibre. But always, even then, she was on the defensive against that higher tribunal which her own conception of life had created. In spite of herself she was a child of the new era, of the universal reaction against the falseness and egotism of the old social code. A standard of conduct regulated by the needs of the race rather than by individual passion, a conception of each existence as a link in the great chain of human endeavour, had slowly shaped itself out of the wild theories and vague "codes" of the eighteenth-century moralists; and with this sense of the sacramental nature of human ties, came a renewed reverence for moral and physical purity.

Fulvia was of those who require that their lives shall be an affirmation of themselves; and the lack of inner harmony drove her to seek some outward expression of her ideals. She threw herself with renewed passion into the political struggle. The best, the only justification of her power, was to use it boldly, openly, for the good of the people. All the repressed forces of her nature were poured into this single channel. She had no desire to conceal her situation, to disguise her influence over Odo. She wished it rather to be so visible a factor in his relations with his people that she should come to be regarded as the ultimate pledge of his good faith. But, like all the casuistical virtues, this position had the rigidity of something created to fit a special case; and the result was a fixity of attitude, which spread benumbingly over her whole nature. She was conscious of the change, yet dared not struggle against it, since to do so was to confess the weakness of her case. She had chosen to be regarded as a symbol rather than a woman, and there were moments when she felt as isolated from life as some marble allegory in its niche above the market-place.

It was the desire to associate herself with the Duke's public life that had induced her, after much hesitation, to accept the degree which the University had conferred on her. She had shared eagerly in the work of reconstructing the University, and had been the means of drawing to Pianura several teachers of distinction from Padua and Pavia. It was her dream to build up a seat of learning which should attract students from all parts of Italy; and though many young men of good family had withdrawn from the classes when the Barnabites were dispossessed, she was confident that they would soon be replaced by scholars from other states. She was resolved to identify herself openly with the educational reform which seemed to her one of the most important steps toward civic emancipation; and she had therefore acceded to the request of the faculty that, on receiving her degree, she should sustain a thesis before the University. This ceremony was to take place a few days hence, on the Duke's birthday; and, as the new charter was to be proclaimed on the same day, Fulvia had chosen as the subject of her discourse the Constitution recently promulgated in France.

She pushed aside the bundle of political pamphlets which she had been studying, and sat looking out at the strip of garden beyond the arches of the cloister. The narrow horizon bounded by convent walls symbolised fitly enough the life she had chosen to lead: a life of artificial restraints and renunciations, passive, conventual almost, in which even the central point of her love burned, now, with a calm devotional glow.

The door in the cloister opened and the Duke crossed the garden. He walked slowly, with the listless step she had observed in him of late; and as he entered she saw that he looked pale and weary.

"You have been at work again," she said. "A cabinet-meeting?"

"Yes," he answered, sinking into the Abbess's high carved chair.

He glanced musingly about the dim room, in which the shadow of the cloister made an early dusk. Its atmosphere of monastic calm, of which the significance did not escape him, fell soothingly on his spirit. It simplified his relation to Fulvia by tacitly restricting it within the bounds of a tranquil tenderness. Any other setting would have seemed less in harmony with their fate.

Better, perhaps, than Fulvia, he knew what ailed them both. Happiness had come to them, but it had come too late; it had come tinged with disloyalty to their early ideals; it had come when delay and disillusionment had imperceptibly weakened the springs of passion. For it is the saddest thing about sorrow that it deadens the capacity for happiness; and to Fulvia and Odo the joy they had renounced had returned with an exile's alien face.

Seeing that he remained silent, she rose and lit the shaded lamp on the table. He watched her as she moved across the room. Her step had lost none of its flowing grace, of that harmonious impetus which years ago had drawn his boyish fancy in its wake. As she bent above the lamp, the circle of light threw her face into relief against the deepening shadows of the room. She had changed, indeed, but as those change in whom the springs of life are clear and abundant: it was a development rather than a diminution. The old purity of outline remained; and deep below the surface, but still visible sometimes to his lessening insight, the old girlish spirit, radiant, tender and impetuous, stirred for a moment in her eyes.

The lamplight fell on the pamphlets she had pushed aside. Odo picked one up. "What are these?" he asked.

"They were sent to me by the English traveller whom Andreoni brought here."

He turned a few pages. "The old story," he said. "Do you never weary of it?"

"An old story?" she exclaimed. "I thought it had been the newest in the world. Is it not being written, chapter by chapter, before our very eyes?"

Odo laid the treatise aside. "Are you never afraid to turn the next page?" he asked.

"Afraid? Afraid of what?"

"That it may be written in blood."

She uttered a quick exclamation; then her face hardened, and she said in a low tone: "De Crucis has been with you."

He made the half-resigned, half-impatient gesture of the man who feels himself drawn into a familiar argument from which there is no issue.

"He left yesterday for Germany."

"He was here too long!" she said, with an uncontrollable escape of bitterness.

Odo sighed. "If you would but let me bring him to you, you would see that his influence over me is not what you think it."

She was silent a moment; then she said: "You are tired tonight. Let us not talk of these things."

"As you please," he answered, with an air of relief; and she rose and went to the harpsichord.

She played softly, with a veiled touch, gliding from one crepuscular melody to another, till the room was filled with drifts of sound that seemed like the voice of its own shadows. There had been times when he could have yielded himself to this languid tide of music, letting it loosen the ties of thought till he floated out into the soothing dimness of sensation; but now the present held him. To Fulvia, too, he knew the music was but a forced interlude, a mechanical refuge from thought. She had deliberately narrowed their intercourse to one central idea; and it was her punishment that silence had come to be merely an intensified expression of this idea.

When she turned to Odo she saw the same consciousness in his face. It was useless for them to talk of other things. With a pang of unreasoning regret she felt that she had become to him the embodiment of a single thought—a formula, rather than a woman.

"Tell me what you have been doing," she said.

The question was a relief. At once he began to separation of his work. All his thoughts, all his time, were given to the constitution which was to define the powers of Church and state. The difficulties increased as the work advanced; but the gravest difficulty was one of which he dared not tell her: his own growing distrust of the ideas for which he laboured. He was too keenly aware of the difference in their mental operations. With Fulvia, ideas were either rejected or at once converted into principles; with himself, they remained stored in the mind, serving rather as commentaries on life than as incentives to action. This perpetual accessibility to new impressions was a quality she could not understand, or could conceive of only as a weakness. Her own mind was like a garden in which nothing is ever transplanted. She allowed for no intermediate stages between error and dogma, for no shifting of the bounds of conviction; and this security gave her the singleness of purpose in which he found himself more and more deficient.

Odo remembered that he had once thought her nearness would dispel his hesitations. At first it had been so; but gradually the contact with her fixed enthusiasms had set up within him an opposing sense of the claims ignored. The element of dogmatism in her faith showed the discouraging sameness of the human mind. He perceived that to a spirit like Fulvia's it might become possible to shed blood in the cause of tolerance.

The rapid march of events in France had necessarily produced an opposite effect on minds so differently constituted. To Fulvia the year had been a year of victory, a glorious affirmation of her political creed. Step by step she had seen, as in some old allegorical painting, error fly before the shafts of truth. Where Odo beheld a conflagration she saw a sunrise; and all that was bare and cold in her own life was warmed and transfigured by that ineffable brightness.

She listened patiently while he enlarged on the difficulties of the case. The constitution was framed in all its details, but with its completion he felt more than ever doubtful of the wisdom of granting it. He would have welcomed any postponement that did not seem an admission of fear. He dreaded the inevitable break with the clergy, not so much because of the consequent danger to his own authority, as because he was increasingly conscious of the newness and clumsiness of the instrument with which he proposed to replace their tried and complex system. He mentioned to Fulvia the rumours of popular disaffection; but she swept them aside with a smile.

"The people mistrust you," she said. "And what does that mean? That you have given your enemies time to work on their credulity. The longer you delay the more opposition you will encounter. Father Ignazio would rather destroy the state than let it be saved by any hand but his."

Odo reflected. "Of all my enemies," he said, "Father Ignazio is the one I most respect, because he is the most sincere."

"He is the most dangerous, then," she returned. "A fanatic is always more powerful than a knave."

He was struck with her undiminished faith in the sufficiency of such generalisations. Did she really think that to solve such a problem it was only necessary to define it? The contact with her unfaltering assurance would once have given him a momentary glow; but now it left him cold.

She was speaking more urgently. "Surely," she said, "the noblest use a man can make of his own freedom is to set others free. My father said it was the only justification of kingship."

He glanced at her half-sadly. "Do you still fancy that kings are free? I am bound hand and foot."

"So was my father," she flashed back at him; "but he had the Promethean spirit."

She coloured at her own quickness, but Odo took the thrust tranquilly.

"Yes," he said, "your father had the Promethean spirit: I have not. The flesh that is daily torn from me does not grow again."

"Your courage is as great as his," she exclaimed, her tenderness in arms.

"No," he answered, "for his was hopeful." There was a pause, and then he began to speak of the day's work.

All the afternoon he had been in consultation with Crescenti, whose vast historical knowledge was of service in determining many disputed points in the tenure of land. The librarian was in sympathy with any measures tending to relieve the condition of the peasantry; yet he was almost as strongly opposed as Trescorre to any reproduction of the Tuscan constitution.

"He is afraid!" broke from Fulvia. She admired and respected Crescenti, yet she had never fully trusted him. The taint of ecclesiasticism was on him.

Odo smiled. "He has never been afraid of facing the charge of Jansenism," he replied. "All his life he has stood in open opposition to the Church party."

"It is one thing to criticise their dogmas, another to attack their privileges. At such a time he is bound to remember that he is a priest—that he is one of them."

"Yet, as you have often pointed out, it is to the clergy that France in great measure owes her release from feudalism."

She smiled coldly. "France would have won her cause without the clergy!"

"This is not France, then," he said with a sigh. After a moment he began again: "Can you not see that any reform which aims at reducing the power of the clergy must be more easily and successfully carried out if they can be induced to take part in it? That, in short, we need them at this moment as we have never needed them before? The example of France ought at least to show you that."

"The example of France shows me that, to gain a point in such a struggle, any means must be used! In France, as you say, the clergy were with the people—here they are against them. Where persuasion fails coercion must be used!"

Odo smiled faintly. "You might have borrowed that from their own armoury," he said.

She coloured at the sarcasm. "Why not?" she retorted. "Let them have a taste of their own methods! They know the kind of pressure that makes men yield—when they feel it they will know what to do."

He looked at her with astonishment. "This is Gamba's tone," he said. "I have never heard you speak in this way before."

She coloured again; and now with a profound emotion. "Yes," she said, "it is Gamba's tone. He and I speak for the same cause and with the same voice. We are of the people and we speak for the people. Who are your other counsellors? Priests and noblemen! It is natural enough that they should wish to make their side of the question heard. Listen to them, if you will—conciliate them, if you can! We need all the allies we can win. Only do not fancy they are really speaking for the people. Do not think it is the people's voice you hear. The people do not ask you to weigh this claim against that, to look too curiously into the defects and merits of every clause in their charter. All they ask is that the charter should be given them!"

She spoke with the low-voiced passion that possessed her at such moments. All acrimony had vanished from her tone. The expression of a great conviction had swept aside every personal animosity, and cleared the sources of her deepest feeling. Odo felt the pressure of her emotion. He leaned to her and their hands met.

"It shall be given them," he said.

She lifted her face to his. It shone with a great light. Once before he had seen it so illumined, but with how different a brightness! The remembrance stirred in him some old habit of the senses. He bent over and kissed her.

4.7.

Never before had Odo so keenly felt the difference between theoretical visions of liberty and their practical application. His deepest heart-searchings showed him as sincerely devoted as ever to the cause which had enlisted his youth. He still longed above all things to serve his fellows; but the conditions of such service were not what he had dreamed. How different a calling it had been in Saint Francis's day, when hearts inflamed with the new sense of brotherhood had but to set forth on their simple mission of almsgiving and admonition! To love one's neighbour had become a much more complex business, one that taxed the intelligence as much as the heart, and in the course of which feeling must be held in firm subjection to reason. He was discouraged by Fulvia's inability to understand the change. Hers was the missionary spirit; and he could not but reflect how much happier she would have been as a nun in a charitable order, a unit in some organised system of beneficence.

He too would have been happier to serve than to command! But it is not given to the lovers of the Lady Poverty to choose their special rank in her household. Don Gervaso's words came back to him with deepening significance, and he thought how truly the old chaplain's prayer had been fulfilled. Honour and power had come to him, and they had abased him to the dust. The "Humilitas" of his fathers, woven, carved and painted on every side, pursued him with an ironical reminder of his impotence.

Fulvia had not been mistaken in attributing his depression of spirit to de Crucis's visit. It was the first time that de Crucis had returned to Pianura since the new Duke's accession. Odo had welcomed him eagerly, had again pressed him to remain; but de Crucis was on his way to Germany, bound on some business which could not be deferred. Odo, aware of the renewed activity of the Jesuits, supposed that this business was connected with the flight of the French refugees, many of whom were gone to Coblentz; but on this point the abate was silent. Of the state of affairs in France he spoke openly and despondently. The immoderate haste with which the reforms had been granted filled him with fears for the future. Odo knew that Crescenti shared these fears, and the judgment of these two men, with whom he differed on fundamental principles, weighed with him far more than the opinions of the party he was supposed to represent. But he was in the case of many greater sovereigns of his day. He had set free the waters of reform, and the frail bark of his authority had been torn from its moorings and swept headlong into the central current.

The next morning, to his surprise, the Duchess sent one of her gentlemen to ask an audience. Odo at once replied that he would wait on her Highness; and a few moments later he was ushered into his wife's closet.

She had just left her toilet, and was still in the morning negligee worn during that prolonged and public ceremonial. Freshly perfumed and powdered, her eyes bright, her lips set in a nervous smile, she curiously recalled the arrogant child who had snatched her spaniel away from him years ago in that same room. And was she not that child, after all? Had she ever grown beyond the imperious instincts of her youth? It seemed to him now that he had judged her harshly in the first months of their marriage. He had felt a momentary impatience when he had tried to force her roving impulses into the line of his own endeavour: it was easier to view her leniently now that she had almost passed out of his life.

He wondered why she had sent for him. Some dispute with her household, doubtless; a quarrel with a servant, even—or perhaps some sordid difficulty with her creditors. But she began in a new key.

"Your Highness," she said, "is not given to taking my advice."

Odo looked at her in surprise. "The opportunity is not often accorded me," he replied with a smile.

Maria Clementina made an impatient gesture; then her face softened. Contradictory emotions flitted over it like the reflections cast by a hurrying sky. She came close to him and then drew away and seated herself in the high-backed chair where she had throned when he first saw her. Suddenly she blushed and began to speak.

"Once," she said in a low, almost inaudible voice, "I was able to give your Highness warning of an impending danger—" She paused and her eyes rested full on Odo.

He felt his colour rise as he returned her gaze. It was her first allusion to the past. He had supposed she had forgotten. For a moment he remained awkwardly silent.

"Do you remember?" she asked.

"I remember."

"The danger was a grave one. Your Highness may recall that but for my warning you would not have been advised of it."

"I remember," he said again.

She paused a moment. "The danger," she repeated, "was a grave one; but it threatened only your Highness's person. Your Highness listened to me then; will you listen again if I advise you of a greater—a peril threatening not only your person but your throne?"

Odo smiled. He could guess now what was coming. She had been drilled to act as the mouthpiece of the opposition. He composed his features and said quietly: "These are grave words, madam. I know of no such peril—but I am always ready to listen to your Highness."

His smile had betrayed him, and a quick flame of anger passed over her face.

"Why should you listen to me, since you never heed what I say?"

"Your Highness has just reminded me that I did so once—"

"Once!" she repeated bitterly. "You were younger then—and so was I!" She glanced at herself in the mirror with a dissatisfied laugh. Something in her look and movement touched the springs of compassion.

"Try me again," he said gently. "If I am older, perhaps I am also wiser, and therefore even more willing to be guided—we all knew that." She broke off, as though she felt her mistake and wished to make a fresh beginning. Again her face was full of fluctuating meaning; and he saw, beneath its shallow surface, the eddy of incoherent impulses. When she spoke, it was with a noble gravity.

"Your Highness," she said, "does not take me into your counsels; but it is no secret at court and in the town that you have in contemplation a grave political measure."

"I have made no secret of it," he replied.

"No—or I should be the last to know it!" she exclaimed, with one of her sudden lapses into petulance.

Odo made no reply. Her futility was beginning to weary him. She saw it and again attempted an impersonal dignity of manner.

"It has been your Highness's choice," she said, "to exclude me from public affairs. Perhaps I was not fitted by education or intelligence to share in the cares of government. Your Highness will at least bear witness that I have scrupulously respected your decision, and have never attempted to intrude upon your counsels."

Odo bowed. It would have been useless to remind her that he had sought her help and failed to obtain it.

"I have accepted my position," she continued. "I have led the life to which it has pleased your Highness to restrict me. But I have not been able to detach my heart as well as my thoughts from your Highness's interests. I have not learned to be indifferent to your danger."

Odo looked up quickly. She ceased to interest him when she spoke by the book, and he was impatient to make an end.

"You spoke of danger before," he said. "What danger?"

"That of forcing on your subjects liberties which they do not desire!"

"Ah," said he thoughtfully. That was all, then. What a poor tool she made! He marvelled that, in all these years, Trescorre's skilful hands should not have fashioned her to better purpose.

"Your Highness," he said, "has reminded me that since our marriage you had lived withdrawn from public affairs. I will not pause to dispute by whose choice this has been; I will in turn merely remind your Highness that such a life does not afford much opportunity of gauging public opinion."

In spite of himself a note of sarcasm had again crept into his voice; but to his surprise she did not seem to resent it.

"Ah," she exclaimed, with more feeling than she had hitherto shown, "you fancy that, because I am kept in ignorance of what you think, I am ignorant also of what others think of you! Believe me," she said, with a flash of insight that startled him, "I know more of you than if we stood closer. But you mistake my purpose. I have not sent for you to force my counsels on you. I have no desire to appear ridiculous. I do not ask you to hear what *I* think of your course, but what others think of it."

"What others?"

The question did not disconcert her. "Your subjects," she said quickly.

"My subjects are of many classes."

"All are of one class in resenting this charter. I am told you intend to proclaim it within a few days. I entreat you at least to delay, to reconsider your course. Oh, believe me when I say you are in danger! Of what use to offer a crown to our Lady, when you have it in your heart to slight her servants? But I will not speak of the clergy, since you despise them—nor of the nobles, since you ignore their claims. I will speak only of the people—the people, in whose interest you profess to act. Believe me, in striking at the Church you wound the poor. It is not their bodily welfare I mean—though Heaven knows how many sources of bounty must now run dry! It is their faith you insult. First you turn them against their masters, then against their God. They may acclaim you for it now—but I tell you they will hate you for it in the end!"

She paused, flushed with the vehemence of her argument, and eager to press it farther. But her last words had touched an unexpected fibre in Odo. He looked at her with his unseeing visionary gaze.

"The end?" he murmured. "Who knows what the end will be?"

"Do you still need to be told?" she exclaimed. "Must you always come to me to learn that you are in danger?"

"If the state is in danger the danger must be faced. The state exists for the people; if they do not need it, it has ceased to serve its purpose."

She clasped her hands in an ecstasy of wonder. "Oh, fool, madman—but it is not of the state I speak! It is you who are in danger—you—you—you—"

He raised his head with an impatient gesture.

"I?" he said. "I had thought you meant a graver peril."

She looked at him in silence. Her pride met his and thrilled with it; and for a moment the two were one.

"Odo!" she cried. She sank into a chair, and he went to her and took her hand.

"Such fears are worthy neither of us," he said gravely.

"I am not ashamed of them," she said. Her hand clung to him and she lifted her eyes to his face. "You will listen to me?" she whispered in a glow.

He drew back chilled. If only she had kept the feminine in abeyance! But sex was her only weapon.

"I have listened," he said quietly. "And I thank you."

"But you will not be counselled?"

"In the last issue one must be one's own counsellor."

Her face flamed. "If you were but that!" she tossed back at him.

The taunt struck him full. He knew that he should have let it lie; but he caught it up in spite of himself.

"Madam!" he said.

"I should have appealed to our sovereign, not to her servant!" she cried, dashing into the breach she had made.

He stood motionless, stunned almost. For what she had said was true. He was no longer the sovereign: the rule had passed out of his hands.

His silence frightened her. With an instinctive jealousy she saw that her words had started a train of thought in which she had no part. She felt herself ignored, abandoned; and all her passions rushed to the defence of her wounded vanity.

"Oh, believe me," she cried, "I speak as your Duchess, not as your wife. That is a name in which I should never dream of appealing to you. I have ever stood apart from your private pleasures, as became a woman of my house." She faced him with a flash of the Austrian insolence. "But when I see the state drifting to ruin as the result of your caprice, when I see your own life endangered, your people turned against you, religion openly insulted, law and authority made the plaything of this—this—false atheistical creature, that has robbed me—robbed me of all—" She broke off helplessly and hid her face with a sob.

Odo stood speechless, spell-bound. He could not mistake what had happened. The woman had surged to the surface at last—the real woman, passionate, self-centred, undisciplined, but so piteous, after all, in this sudden subjection to the one tenderness that survived in her. She loved him and was jealous of her rival. That was the instinct which had swept all others aside. At that moment she cared nothing for her safety or his. The state might perish if they but fell together. It was the distance between them that maddened her.

The tragic simplicity of the revelation left Odo silent. For a fantastic moment he yielded to the vision of what that waste power might have accomplished. Life seemed to him a confusion of roving force that met only to crash in ruins.

His silence drew her to her feet. She repossessed herself, throbbing but valiant.

"My fears for your Highness's safety have led my speech astray. I have given your Highness the warning it was my duty to give. Beyond that I had no thought of trespassing."

And still Odo was silent. A dozen answers struggled to his lips; but they were checked by the stealing sense of duality that so often paralysed his action. He had recovered his lucidity of vision, and his impulses faded before it like mist. He saw life again as it was, an incomplete and shabby business, a patchwork of torn and ravelled effort. Everywhere the shears of Atropos were busy, and never could the cut threads be joined again.

He took his wife's hand and bent over it ceremoniously. It lay in his like a stone.

4.8.

The jubilee of the Mountain Madonna fell on the feast of the Purification. It was mid-November, but with a sky of June. The autumn rains had ceased for the moment, and fields and orchards glistened with a late verdure.

Never had the faithful gathered in such numbers to do honour to the wonder-working Virgin. A widespread resistance to the influences of free thought and Jansenism was pouring fresh life into the old formulas of devotion. Though many motives combined to strengthen this movement, it was still mainly a simple expression of loyalty to old ideals, an instinctive rallying around a threatened cause. It is the honest conviction underlying all great popular impulses that gives them their real strength; and in this case the thousands of pilgrims flocking on foot to the mountain shrine embodied a greater moral force than the powerful ecclesiastics at whose call they had gathered.

The clergy themselves were come from all sides; while those that were unable to attend had sent costly gifts to the miraculous Virgin. The Bishops of Mantua, Modena, Vercelli and Cremona had travelled to Pianura in state, the people flocking out beyond the gates to welcome them. Four mitred Abbots, several Monsignori, and Priors, Rectors, Vicars-general and canons innumerable rode in the procession, followed on foot by the humble army of parish priests and by interminable confraternities of all orders.

The approach of the great dignitaries was hailed with enthusiasm by the crowds lining the roads. Even the Bishop of Pianura, never popular with the people, received an unwonted measure of applause, and the white-cowled Prior of the Dominicans, riding by stern and close-lipped as a monk of Zurbaran's, was greeted with frenzied acclamations. The report that the Bishop and the heads of the religious houses in Pianura were to set free suppers for the pilgrims had doubtless quickened this outburst of piety; yet it was perhaps chiefly due to the sense of coming peril that had gradually permeated the dim consciousness of the crowd.

In the church, the glow of lights, the thrilling beauty of the music and the glitter of the priestly vestments were blent in a melting harmony of sound and colour. The shrine of the Madonna shone with unearthly radiance. Hundreds of candles formed an elongated nimbus about her hieratic figure, which was surmounted by the canopy of cloth-of-gold presented by the Duke of Modena. The Bishops of Vercelli and Cremona had offered a robe of silver brocade studded with coral and turquoises, the devout Princess Clotilda of Savoy an emerald necklace, the Bishop of Pianura a marvellous veil of rose-point made in a Flemish convent; while on the statue's brow rested the Duke's jewelled diadem.

The Duke himself, seated in his tribune above the choir, observed the scene with a renewed appreciation of the Church's unfailing dramatic instinct. At first he saw in the spectacle only this outer and symbolic side, of which the mere sensuous beauty had always deeply moved him; but as he watched the effect produced on the great throng filling the aisles, he began to see that this external splendour was but the veil before the sanctuary, and to realise what de Crucis meant when he spoke of the deep hold of the Church upon the people. Every colour, every gesture, every word and note of music that made up the texture of the gorgeous ceremonial might indeed seem part of a long-studied and astutely-planned effect. Yet each had its root in some instinct of the heart, some natural development of the inner life, so that they were in fact not the cunningly-adjusted fragments of an arbitrary pattern but the inseparable fibres of a living organism. It was Odo's misfortune to see too far ahead on the road along which his destiny was urging him. As he sat there, face to face with the people he was trying to lead, he heard above the music of the mass and the chant of the kneeling throng an echo of the question that Don Gervaso had once put to him:—"If you take Christ from the people, what have you to give them instead?"

He was roused by a burst of silver clarions. The mass was over, and the Duke and Duchess were to descend from their tribune and venerate the holy image before it was carried through the church.

Odo rose and gave his hand to his wife. They had not seen each other, save in public, since their last conversation in her closet. The Duchess walked with set lips and head erect, keeping her profile turned to him as they descended the steps and advanced to the choir. None knew better how to take her part in such a pageant. She had the gift of drawing upon herself the undivided attention of any assemblage in which she moved; and the consciousness of this power lent a kind of Olympian buoyancy to her gait. The richness of her dress and her extravagant display of jewels seemed almost a challenge to the sacred image blazing like a rainbow beneath its golden canopy; and Odo smiled to think that his childish fancy had once compared the brilliant being at his side to the humble tinsel-decked Virgin of the church at Pontesordo.

As the couple advanced, stillness fell on the church. The air was full of the lingering haze of incense, through which the sunlight from the clerestory poured in prismatic splendours on the statue of the Virgin. Rigid, superhuman, a molten flamboyancy of gold and gems, the wonder-working Madonna shone out above her worshippers. The Duke and Duchess paused, bowing deeply, below the choir. Then they mounted the steps and knelt before the shrine. As they did so a crash broke the silence, and the startled devotees saw that the ducal diadem had fallen from the Madonna's head.

The hush prolonged itself a moment; then a canon sprang forward to pick up the crown, and with the movement a murmur rose and spread through the church. The Duke's offering had fallen to the ground as he approached to venerate the blessed image. That this was an omen no man could doubt. It needed no augur to interpret it. The murmur, gathering force as it swept through the packed aisles, passed from surprise to fear, from fear to a deep hum of anger;—for the people understood, as plainly as though she had spoken, that the Virgin of the Valseccas had cast from her the gift of an unbeliever...

The ceremonies over, the long procession was formed again and set out toward the city. The crowd had surged ahead, and when the Duke rode through the gates the streets were already thronged. Moving slowly between the compact mass of people he felt himself as closely observed as on the day of his state entry; but with far different effect. Enthusiasm had given way to a cold curiosity. The excitement of the spectators had spent itself in the morning, and the sight of their sovereign failed to rouse their flagging ardour. Now and then a cheer broke out, but it died again without kindling another in the uninflammable mass. Odo could not tell how much of this indifference was due to a natural reaction from the emotions of the morning, how much to his personal unpopularity, how much to the ominous impression produced by the falling of the Virgin's crown. He rode between his people oppressed by a sense of estrangement such as he had never known. He felt himself shut off from them by an impassable barrier of superstition and ignorance; and every effort to reach them was like the wrong turn in a labyrinth, drawing him farther away from the issue to which it seemed to lead.

As he advanced under this indifferent or hostile scrutiny, he thought how much easier it would be to face a rain of bullets than this withering glare of criticism. A sudden longing to escape, to be done with it all, came over him with sickening force. His nerves ached with the physical strain of holding himself upright on his horse, of preserving the statuesque erectness proper to the occasion. He felt like one of his own ancestral effigies, of which the wooden framework had rotted under the splendid robes. A congestion at the head of a narrow street had checked the procession, and he was obliged to rein in his horse. He looked about and found himself in the centre of the square near the Baptistery. A few feet off, directly in a line with him, was the weather-worn front of the Royal Printing-Press. He raised his head and saw a group of people on the balcony. Though they were close at hand, he saw them in a blur, against which Fulvia's figure suddenly detached itself. She had told him that she was to view the procession with the Andreonis; but through the mental haze which enveloped him her apparition struck a vague surprise.

He looked at her intently, and their eyes met. A faint happiness stole over her face, but no recognition was possible, and she continued to gaze out steadily upon the throng below the balcony. Involuntarily his glance followed hers, and he saw that she was herself the centre of the crowd's attention. Her plain, almost Quakerish habit, and the tranquil dignity of her carriage, made her a conspicuous figure among the animated groups in the adjoining windows, and Odo, with the acuteness of perception which a public life develops, was instantly aware that her name was on every lip. At the same moment he saw a woman close to his horse's feet snatch up her child and make the sign against the evil eye. A boy who stood staring open-mouthed at Fulvia caught the gesture and repeated it; a barefoot friar imitated the boy, and it seemed to Odo that the familiar sign was spreading with malignant rapidity to the furthest limits of the crowd. The impression was only momentary; for the cavalcade was again in motion, and without raising his eyes he rode on, sick at heart...

At nightfall a man opened the gate of the ducal gardens below the Chinese pavilion and stepped out into the deserted lane. He locked the gate and slipped the key into his pocket; then he turned and walked toward the centre of the town. As he reached the more populous quarters his walk slackened to a stroll; and now and then he paused to observe a knot of merry-makers or look through the curtains of the tents set up in the squares.

The man was plainly but decently dressed, like a petty tradesman or a lawyer's clerk, and the night being chill he wore a cloak, and had drawn his hat-brim over his forehead. He sauntered on, letting the crowd carry him, with the air of one who has an hour to kill, and whose holiday-making takes the form of an amused spectatorship. To such an observer the streets offered ample entertainment. The shrewd air discouraged lounging and kept the crowd in motion; but the open platforms built for dancing were thronged with couples, and every peep-show, wine-shop and astrologer's booth was packed to the doors. The shrines and street-lamps being all alight, and booths and platforms hung with countless lanterns, the scene was as bright as day; but in the ever-shifting medley of peasant-dresses, liveries, monkish cowls and carnival disguises, a soberly-clad man might easily go unremarked.

Reaching the square before the Cathedral, the solitary observer pushed his way through the idlers gathered about a dais with a curtain at the back. Before the curtain stood a Milanese quack, dressed like a noble gentleman, with sword and plumed hat, and rehearsing his cures in stentorian tones, while his zany, in the short mask and green-and-white habit of Brighella, cracked jokes and turned hand-springs for the diversion of the vulgar.

"Behold," the charlatan was shouting, "the marvellous Egyptian love-philter distilled from the pearl that the great Emperor Antony dropped into Queen Cleopatra's cup. This infallible fluid, handed down for generations in the family of my ancestor, the High Priest of Isis—" The bray of a neighbouring show-man's trumpet cut him short, and yielding to circumstances he drew back the curtain, and a tumbling-girl sprang out and began her antics on the front of the stage.

"What did he say was the price of that drink, Giannina?" asked a young maid-servant pulling her neighbour's sleeve.

"Are you thinking of buying it for Pietrino, my beauty?" the other returned with a laugh. "Believe me, it is a sound proverb that says: When the fruit is ripe it falls of itself."

The girl drew away angrily, and the quack took up his harangue:—"The same philter, ladies and gentlemen—though in confessing it I betray a professional secret—the same philter, I declare to you on the honour of a nobleman, whereby, in your own city, a lady no longer young and no way remarkable in looks or station, has captured and subjugated the affections of one so high, so exalted, so above all others in beauty, rank, wealth, power and dignities—"

"Oh, oh, that's the Duke!" sniggered a voice in the crowd.

"Ladies and gentlemen, I name no names!" cried the quack impressively.

"No need to," retorted the voice.

"They do say, though, she gave him something to drink," said a young woman to a youth in a clerk's dress. "The saying is she studied medicine with the Turks."

"The Moors, you mean," said the clerk with an air of superiority.

"Well, they say her mother was a Turkey slave and her father a murderer from the Sultan's galleys."

"No, no, she's plain Piedmontese, I tell you. Her father was a physician in Turin, and was driven out of the country for poisoning his patients in order to watch their death-agonies."

"They say she's good to the poor, though," said another voice doubtfully.

"Good to the poor? Ay, that's what they said of her father. All I know is that she heard Stefano the weaver's lad had the falling sickness, and she carried him a potion with her own hands, and the next day the child was dead, and a Carmelite friar, who saw the phial he drank from, said it was the same shape and size as one that was found in a witch's grave when they were digging the foundations for the new monastery."

"Ladies and gentlemen," shrieked the quack, "what am I offered for a drop of this priceless liquor?"

The listener turned aside and pushed his way toward the farther end of the square. As he did so he ran against a merry-andrew who thrust a long printed sheet in his hand.

"Buy my satirical ballads, ladies and gentlemen!" the fellow shouted. "Two for a farthing, invented and written by an own cousin of the great Pasquino of Rome! What will you have, sir? Here's the secret history of a famous Prince's amours with an atheist—here's the true scandal of an illustrious lady's necklace—two for a farthing...and my humblest thanks to your excellency." He pocketed the coin, and the other, thrusting the broadsheets beneath his cloak, pushed on to the nearest coffee-house.

Here every table was thronged, and the babble of talk so loud that the stranger, hopeless of obtaining refreshment, pressed his way into the remotest corner of the room and seated himself on an empty cask. At first he sat motionless, silently observing the crowd; then he drew forth the ballads and ran his eye over them. He was still engaged in this study when his notice was attracted by a loud discussion going forward between a party of men at the nearest table. The disputants, petty tradesman or artisans by their dress, had evidently been warmed by a good flagon of wine, and their tones were so lively that every word reached the listener on the cask.

"Reform, reform!" cried one, who appeared by his dress and manner to be the weightiest of the company—"it's all very well to cry reform; but what I say is that most of those that are howling for it no more know what they're asking than a parrot that's been taught the litany. Now the first question is: who benefits by your reform? And what's the answer to that, eh? Is it the tradesmen? The merchants? The clerks, artisans, household servants, I ask you? I hear some of my fellow-tradesmen complaining that the nobility don't pay their bills. Will they be better paid, think you, when the Duke has halved their revenues? Will the quality keep up as large households, employ as many lacqueys, set as lavish tables, wear as fine clothes, collect as many rarities, buy as many horses, give us, in short, as many opportunities of making our profit out of their pleasure? What I say is, if we're to have new taxes, don't let them fall on the very class we live by!"

"That's true enough," said another speaker, a lean bilious man with a pen behind his ear. "The peasantry are the only class that are going to profit by this constitution."

"And what do the peasantry do for us, I should like to know?" the first speaker went on triumphantly. "As far as the fat friars go, I'm not sorry to see them squeezed a trifle, for they've wrung enough money out of our women-folk to lie between feathers from now till doomsday; but I say, if you care for your pockets, don't lay hands on the nobility!"

"Gently, gently, my friend," exclaimed a cautious flaccid-looking man setting down his glass. "Father and son, for four generations, my family have served Pianura with Church candles, and I can tell you that since these new atheistical notions came in, the nobility are not the good patrons they used to be. But as for the friars, I should be sorry to see them meddled with. It's true they may get the best morsel in the pot and the warmest seat on the hearth—and one of them, now and then, may take too long to teach a pretty girl her Pater Noster—but I'm not sure we shall be better off when they're gone. Formerly, if a child too many came to poor folk they could always comfort themselves with the thought that, if there was no room for him at home, the Church was there to provide for him. But if we drive out the good friars, a man will have to count mouths before he dares look at his wife too lovingly."

"Well," said the scribe with a dry smile, "I've a notion the good friars have always taken more than they gave; and if it were not for the gaping mouths under the cowl even a poor man might have victuals enough for his own."

The first speaker turned on him contentiously.

"Do I understand you are for this new charter, then?" he asked.

"No, no," said the other. "Better hot polenta than a cold ortolan. Things are none too good as they are, but I never care to taste first of a new dish. And in this case I don't fancy the cook."

"Ah, that's it," said the soft man. "It's too much like the apothecary's wife mixing his drugs for him. Men of Roman lineage want no women to govern them!" He puffed himself out and thrust a hand in his bosom. "Besides, gentlemen," he added, dropping his voice and glancing cautiously about the room, "the saints are my witness I'm not superstitious—but frankly, now, I don't much fancy this business of the Virgin's crown."

"What do you mean?" asked a lean visionary-looking youth who had been drinking and listening.

"Why, sir, I needn't say I'm the last man in Pianura to listen to women's tattle; but my wife had it straight from Cino the barber, whose sister is portress of the Benedictines, that, two days since, one of the nuns foretold the whole business, precisely as it happened—and what's more, many that were in the

Church this morning will tell you that they distinctly saw the blessed image raise both arms and tear the crown from her head."

"H'm," said the young man flippantly, "what became of the Bambino meanwhile, I wonder?"

The scribe shrugged his shoulders. "We all know," said he, "that Cino the barber lies like a christened Jew; but I'm not surprised the thing was known in advance, for I make no doubt the priests pulled the wires that brought down the crown."

The fat man looked scandalised, and the first speaker waved the subject aside as unworthy of attention.

"Such tales are for women and monks," he said impatiently. "But the business has its serious side. I tell you we are being hurried to our ruin. Here's this matter of draining the marshes at Pontesordo. Who's to pay for that? The class that profits by it? Not by a long way. It's we who drain the land, and the peasants are to live on it."

The visionary youth tossed back his hair. "But isn't that an inspiration to you, sir?" he exclaimed. "Does not your heart dilate at the thought of uplifting the condition of your down-trodden fellows?"

"My fellows? The peasantry my fellows?" cried the other. "I'd have you know, my young master, that I come of a long and honourable line of cloth-merchants, that have had their names on the Guild for two hundred years and over. I've nothing to do with the peasantry, thank God!"

The youth had emptied another glass. "What?" he screamed. "You deny the universal kinship of man? You disown your starving brothers? Proud tyrant, remember the Bastille!" He burst into tears and began to quote Alfieri.

"Well," said the fat man, turning a disgusted shoulder on this display of emotion, "to my mind this business of draining Pontesordo is too much like telling the Almighty what to do. If God made the land wet, what right have we to dry it? Those that begin by meddling with the Creator's works may end by laying hands on the Creator."

"You're right," said another. "There's no knowing where these new-fangled notions may land us. For my part, I was rather taken by them at first; but since I find that his Highness, to pay for all his good works, is cutting down his household and throwing decent people out of a job—like my own son, for instance, that was one of the under-steward's boys at the palace—why, since then, I begin to see a little farther into the game."

A shabby shrewd-looking fellow in a dirty coat and snuff-stained stock had sauntered up to the table and stood listening with an amused smile.

"Ah," said the scribe, glancing up, "here's a thoroughgoing reformer, who'll be asking us all to throw up our hats for the new charter."

The new-comer laughed contemptuously. "I?" he said. "God forbid! The new charter's none of my making. It's only another dodge for getting round the populace—for appearing to give them what they would rise up and take if it were denied them any longer."

"Why, I thought you were hot for these reforms?" exclaimed the fat man with surprise.

The other shrugged. "You might as well say I was in favour of having the sun rise tomorrow. It would probably rise at the same hour if I voted against it. Reform is bound to come, whether your Dukes and Princes are for it or against it; and those that grant constitutions instead of refusing them are like men who tie a string to their hats before going out in a gale. The string may hold for a while—but if it blows hard enough the hats will all come off in the end."

"Ay, ay; and meanwhile we furnish the string from our own pockets," said the scribe with a chuckle.

The shabby man grinned. "It won't be the last thing to come out of your pockets," said he, turning to push his way toward another table.

The others rose and called for their reckoning; and the listener on the cask slipped out of his corner, elbowed a passage to the door and stepped forth into the square.

It was after midnight, a thin drizzle was falling, and the crowd had scattered. The rain was beginning to extinguish the paper lanterns and the torches, and the canvas sides of the tents flapped dismally, like wet sheets on a clothes-line. The man drew his cloak closer, and avoiding the stragglers who crossed his path, turned into the first street that led to the palace. He walked fast over the slippery cobble-stones, buffeted by a rising wind and threading his way between dark walls and sleeping house-fronts till he reached the lane below the ducal gardens. He unlocked the door by which he had come forth, entered the gardens, and paused a moment on the terrace above the lane.

Behind him rose the palace, a dark irregular bulk, with a lighted window showing here and there. Before him lay the city, an indistinguishable huddle of roofs and towers under the rainy night. He stood awhile gazing out over it; then he turned and walked toward the palace. The garden alleys were deserted, the pleached walks dark as subterranean passages, with the wet gleam of statues starting spectrally out of the blackness. The man walked rapidly, leaving the Borromini wing on his left, and skirting the outstanding mass of the older buildings. Behind the marble buttresses of the chapel, he crossed the dense obscurity of a court between high walls, found a door under an archway, turned a key in the lock, and gained a spiral stairway as dark as the court. He groped his way up the stairs and paused a moment on the landing to listen. Then he opened another door, lifted a heavy hanging of tapestry, and stepped into the Duke's closet. It stood empty, with a lamp burning low on the desk.

The man threw off his cloak and hat, dropped into a chair beside the desk, and hid his face in his hands.

4.9.

It was the eve of the Duke's birthday. A cabinet council had been called in the morning, and his Highness's ministers had submitted to him the revised draft of the constitution which was to be proclaimed on the morrow.

Throughout the conference, which was brief and formal, Odo had been conscious of a subtle change in the ministerial atmosphere. Instead of the current of resistance against which he had grown used to forcing his way, he became aware of a tacit yielding to his will. Trescorre had apparently withdrawn his opposition to the charter, and the other ministers had followed suit. To Odo's overwrought imagination there was something ominous in the change. He had counted on the goad of opposition to fight off the fatal languor which he had learned to expect at such crises. Now that he found there was to be no struggle he understood how largely his zeal had of late depended on such factitious incentives. He felt an irrational longing to throw himself on the other side of the conflict, to tear in bits the paper awaiting his signature, and disown the policy which had dictated it. But the tide of acquiescence on which he was afloat was no stagnant back-water of indifference, but the glassy reach just above the fall of a river. The current was as swift as it was smooth, and he felt himself hurried forward to an end he could no longer escape. He took the pen which Trescorre handed him, and signed the constitution.

The meeting over, he summoned Gamba. He felt the need of such encouragement as the hunchback alone could give. Fulvia's enthusiasms were too unreal, too abstract. She lived in a region of ideals, whence ugly facts were swept out by some process of mental housewifery which kept her world perpetually smiling and immaculate. Gamba at least fed his convictions on facts. If his outlook was narrow it was direct: no roseate medium of fancy was interposed between his vision and the truth.

He stood listening thoughtfully while Odo poured forth his doubts.

"Your Highness may well hesitate," he said at last. "There are always more good reasons against a new state of things than for it. I am not surprised that Count Trescorre appears to have withdrawn his opposition. I believe he now honestly wishes your Highness to proclaim the constitution."

Odo looked up in surprise. "You do not mean that he has come to believe in it?"

Gamba smiled. "Probably not in your Highness's sense; but he may have found a use of his own for it."

"What do you mean?" Odo asked.

"If he does not believe it will benefit the state he may think it will injure your Highness."

"Ah—" said the Duke slowly.

There was a pause, during which he was possessed by the same shuddering reluctance to fix his mind on the facts before him as when he had questioned the hunchback about Momola's death. He longed to cast the whole business aside, to be up and away from it, drawing breath in a new world where every air was not tainted with corruption. He raised his head with an effort.

"You think, then, that the liberals are secretly acting against me in this matter?"

"I am persuaded of it, your Highness."

Odo hesitated. "You have always told me," he began again, "that the love of dominion was your brother's ruling passion. If he really believes this movement will be popular with the people, why should he secretly oppose it, instead of making the most of his own share in it as the minister of a popular sovereign?"

"For several reasons," Gamba answered promptly. "In the first place, the reforms your Highness has introduced are not of his own choosing, and Trescorre has little sympathy with any policy he has not dictated. In the second place, the powers and opportunities of a constitutional minister are too restricted to satisfy his appetite for rule; and thirdly—" he paused a moment, as though doubtful how his words would be received—"I suspect Trescorre of having a private score against your Highness, which he would be glad to pay off publicly."

Odo fell silent, yielding himself to a fresh current of thought.

"I know not what score he may have against me," he said at length; "but what injures me must injure the state, and if Trescorre has any such motive for withdrawing his opposition, it must be because he believes the constitution will defeat its own ends."

"He does believe that, assuredly; but he is not the only one of your Highness's ministers that would ruin the state on the chance of finding an opportunity among the ruins."

"That is as it may be," said Odo with a touch of weariness. "I have seen enough of human ambition to learn how limited and unimaginative a passion it is. If it saw farther I should fear it more. But if it is short-sighted it sees clearly at close range; and the motive you ascribe to Trescorre would imply that he believes the constitution will be a failure."

"Without doubt, your Highness. I am convinced that your ministers have done all they could to prevent the proclamation of the charter, and failing that, to thwart its workings if it be proclaimed. In this they have gone hand in hand with the clergy, and their measures have been well taken. But I do not believe that any state of mind produced by external influences can long withstand the natural drift of opinion; and your Highness may be sure that, though the talkers and writers are mostly against you in this matter, the mass of the people are with you."

Odo answered with a despairing gesture. "How can I be sure, when the people have no means of expressing their needs? It is like trying to guess the wants of a deaf and dumb man!"

The hunchback flushed suddenly. "The people will not always be deaf and dumb," he said. "Some day they will speak."

"Not in my day," said Odo wearily. "And meanwhile we blunder on, without ever really knowing what incalculable instincts and prejudices are pitted against us. You and your party tell me the people are sick of the burdens the clergy lay on them—yet their blind devotion to the Church is manifest at every turn, and it did not need the business of the Virgin's crown to show me how little reason and justice can avail against such influences."

Gamba replied by an impatient gesture. "As to the Virgin's crown," he said, "your Highness must have guessed it was one of the friars' tricks: a last expedient to turn the people against you. I was not bred up by a priest for nothing; I know what past masters those gentry are in raising ghosts and reading portents. They know the minds of the poor folk as the herdsman knows the habits of his cattle; and for generations they have used that knowledge to bring the people more completely under their control."

"And what have we to oppose to such a power?" Odo exclaimed. "We are fighting the battle of ideas against passions, of reflection against instinct; and you have but to look in the human heart to guess which side will win in such a struggle. We have science and truth and common-sense with us, you say—yes, but the Church has love and fear and tradition, and the solidarity of nigh two thousand years of dominion."

Gamba listened in respectful silence; then he replied with a faint smile: "All that your Highness says is true; but I beg leave to relate to your Highness a tale which I read lately in an old book of your library. According to this story it appears that when the early Christians of Alexandria set out to destroy the pagan idols in the temples they were seized with great dread at sight of the god Serapis; for even those that did not believe in the old gods feared them, and none dared raise a hand against the sacred image. But suddenly a soldier who was bolder than the rest flung his battle-axe at the figure—and when it broke in pieces, there rushed out nothing worse than a great company of rats."...

The Duke had promised to visit Fulvia that evening. For several days his state of indecision had made him find pretexts for avoiding her; but now that the charter was signed and he had ordered its proclamation, he craved the contact of her unwavering faith.

He found her alone in the dusk of the convent parlour; but he had hardly crossed the threshold before he was aware of an indefinable change in his surroundings. She advanced with an impulsiveness out of harmony with the usual tranquillity of their meetings, and he felt her hand tremble and burn in his. In the twilight it seemed to him that her very dress had a warmer rustle and glimmer, that there emanated from her glance and movements some heady fragrance of a long-past summer. He smiled to think that this phantom coquetry should have risen at the summons of an academic degree; but some deeper sense in him was stirred as by a vision of waste riches adrift on the dim seas of chance.

For a moment she sat silent, as in the days when they had been too near each other for many words; and there was something indescribably soothing in this dreamlike return to the past. It was he who roused himself first.

"How young you look!" he said, giving involuntary utterance to his thought.

"Do I?" she answered gaily. "I am glad of that, for I feel extraordinarily young tonight. Perhaps it is because I have been thinking a great deal of the old days—of Venice and Turin—and of the high-road to Vercelli, for instance." She glanced at him with a smile.

"Do you know," she went on, moving to a seat at his side, and laying a hand on the arm of his chair, "that there is one secret of mine you have never guessed in all these years?"

Odo returned her smile. "What is it, I wonder?" he said.

She fixed him with bright bantering eyes. "I knew why you deserted us at Vercelli." He uttered an exclamation, but she lifted a hand to his lips. "Ah, how angry I was then—but why be angry now? It all happened so long ago; and if it had not happened—who knows?—perhaps you would never have pitied me enough to love me as you did." She laughed softly, reminiscently, leaning back as if to let the tide of memories ripple over her. Then she raised her head suddenly, and said in a changed voice: "Are your plans fixed for tomorrow?"

Odo glanced at her in surprise. Her mind seemed to move as capriciously as Maria Clementina's.

"The constitution is signed," he answered, "and my ministers proclaim it tomorrow morning." He looked at her a moment, and lifted her hand to his lips. "Everything has been done according to your wishes," he said.

She drew away with a start, and he saw that she had turned pale. "No, no—not as I wish," she murmured. "It must not be because *I* wish—" she broke off and her hand slipped from his.

"You have taught me to wish as you wish," he answered gently. "Surely you would not disown your pupil now?"

Her agitation increased. "Do not call yourself that!" she exclaimed. "Not even in jest. What you have done has been done of your own choice—because you thought it best for your people. My nearness or absence could have made no difference."

He looked at her with growing wonder. "Why this sudden modesty?" he said with a smile. "I thought you prided yourself on your share in the great work."

She tried to force an answering smile, but the curve broke into a quiver of distress, and she came close to him, with a gesture that seemed to take flight from herself.

"Don't say it, don't say it!" she broke out. "What right have they to call it my doing? I but stood aside and watched you and gloried in you—is there any guilt to a woman in THAT?" She clung to him a moment, hiding her face in his breast.

He loosened her arms gently, that he might draw back and look at her. "Fulvia," he asked, "what ails you? You are not yourself tonight. Has anything happened to distress you? Have you been annoyed or alarmed in any way?— It is not possible," he broke off, "that Trescorre has been here—?"

She drew away, flushed and protesting. "No, no," she exclaimed. "Why should Trescorre come here? Why should you fancy that any one has been here? I am excited, I know; I talk idly; but it is because I have been thinking too long of these things—"

"Of what things?"

"Of what people say—how can one help hearing that? I sometimes fancy that the more withdrawn one lives the more distinctly one hears the outer noises."

"But why should you heed the outer noises? You have never done so before."

"Perhaps I was wrong not to do so before. Perhaps I should have listened sooner. Perhaps others have seen—understood—sooner than I—oh, the thought is intolerable!"

She moved a pace or two away, and then, regaining the mastery of her lips and eyes, turned to him with a show of calmness.

"Your heart was never in this charter—" she began.

"Fulvia!" he cried protestingly; but she lifted a silencing hand. "Ah, I have seen it—I have felt it—but I was never willing to own that you were right. My pride in you blinded me, I suppose. I could not bear to dream any fate for you but the greatest. I saw you always leading events, rather than waiting on them. But true greatness lies in the man, not in his actions. Compromise, delay, renunciation—these may be as heroic as conflict. A woman's vision is so narrow that I did not see this at first. You have always told me that I looked only at one side of the question; but I see the other side now—I see that you were right."

Odo stood silent. He had followed her with growing wonder. A volte-face so little in keeping with her mental habits immediately struck him as a feint; yet so strangely did it accord with his own secret reluctances that these inclined him to let it pass unquestioned.

Some instinctive loyalty to his past checked the temptation. "I am not sure that I understand you," he said slowly. "Have you lost faith in the ideas we have worked for?"

She hesitated, and he saw the struggle beneath her surface calmness. "No, no," she exclaimed quickly, "I have not lost faith in them—"

"In me, then?"

She smiled with a disarming sadness. "That would be so much simpler!" she murmured.

"What do you mean, then?" he urged. "We must understand each other." He paused, and measured his words out slowly. "Do you think it a mistake to proclaim the constitution tomorrow?"

Again her face was full of shadowy contradictions. "I entreat you not to proclaim it tomorrow," she said in a low voice.

Odo felt the blood drum in his ears. Was not this the word for which he had waited? But still some deeper instinct held him back, warning him, as it seemed, that to fall below his purpose at such a juncture was the only measurable failure. He must know more before he yielded, see deeper into her heart and his; and each moment brought the clearer conviction that there was more to know and see.

"This is unlike you, Fulvia," he said. "You cannot make such a request on impulse. You must have a reason."

She smiled. "You told me once that a woman's reasons are only impulses in men's clothes."

But he was not to be diverted by this thrust. "I shall think so now," he said, "unless you can give me some better account of yours!"

She was silent, and he pressed on with a persistency for which he himself could hardly account: "You must have a reason for this request."

"I have one," she said, dropping her attempts at evasion.

"And it is—?"

She paused again, with a look of appeal against which he had to stiffen himself.

"I do not believe the time has come," she said at length.

"You think the people are not ready for the constitution?"

She answered with an effort: "I think the people are not ready for it."

He fell silent, and they sat facing each other, but with eyes apart.

"You have received this impression from Gamba, from Andreoni—from the members of our party?" he asked.

She made no reply.

"Remember, Fulvia," he went on almost sternly, "that this is the end for which we have worked together all these years—the end for which we renounced each other and went forth in our youth, you to exile and I to an unwilling sovereignty. It was because we loved this cause better than ourselves that we had strength to give up for it our personal hopes of happiness. If we betray the cause from any merely personal motive we shall have fallen below our earlier selves." He waited again, but she was still silent. "Can you swear to me," he went on, "that no such motive influences you now? That you honestly believe we have been deceived and mistaken? That our years of faith and labour have been wasted, and that, if mankind is to be helped, it is to be in other ways and by other efforts than ours?"

He stood before her accusingly, almost, the passion of the long fight surging up in him as he felt the weapon drop from his hand.

Fulvia had sat motionless under his appeal; but as he paused she rose with an impulsive gesture. "Oh, why do you torment me with questions?" she cried, half-sobbing. "I venture to counsel a delay, and you arraign me as though I stood at the day of judgment!"

"It IS our day of judgment," he retorted. "It is the day on which life confronts us with our own actions, and we must justify them or own ourselves deluded." He went up to her and caught her hands entreatingly. "Fulvia," he said, "I too have doubted, wavered—and if you will give me one honest reason that is worthy of us both—"

She broke from him to hide her weeping. "Reasons! reasons!" she stammered. "What does the heart know of reasons? I ask a favour—the first I ever asked of you—and you answer it by haggling with me for reasons!"

Something in her voice and gesture was like a lightning-flash over a dark landscape. In an instant he saw the pit at his feet.

"Some one has been with you. Those words were not yours," he cried.

She rallied instantly. "That is a pretext for not heeding them!" she returned.

The lightning glared again. He stepped close and faced her.

"The Duchess has been here," he said.

She dropped into a chair and hid her face from him. A wave of anger mounted from his heart, choking back his words and filling his brain with its fumes. But as it subsided he felt himself suddenly cool, firm, attempered. There could be no wavering, no self-questioning now.

"When did this happen?" he asked.

She shook her head despairingly.

"Fulvia," he said, "if you will not speak I will speak for you. I can guess what arguments were used—what threats, even. Were there threats?" burst from him in a fresh leap of anger.

She raised her head slowly. "Threats would not have mattered," she said.

"But your fears were played on—your fears for my safety?—Fulvia, answer me!" he insisted.

She rose suddenly and laid her arms about his shoulders, with a gesture half-tender, half-maternal.

"Oh," she said, "why will you torture me? I have borne much for our love's sake, and would have borne this too—in silence, like the rest—but to speak of it is to relieve it; and my strength fails me!"

He held her hands fast, keeping his eyes on hers. "No," he said, "for your strength never failed you when there was any call on it; and our whole past calls on it now. Rouse yourself, Fulvia: look life in the face! You were told there might be troubles tomorrow—that I was in danger, perhaps?"

"There was worse—there was worse," she shuddered.

"Worse?"

"The blame was laid on me—the responsibility. Your love for me, my power over you, were accused. The people hate me—they hate you for loving me! Oh, I have destroyed you!" she cried.

Odo felt a slow cold strength pouring into all his veins. It was as though his enemies, in thinking to mix a mortal poison, had rendered him invulnerable. He bent over her with great gentleness.

"Fulvia, this is madness," he said. "A moment's thought must show you what passions are here at work. Can you not rise above such fears? No one can judge between us but ourselves."

"Ah, but you do not know—you will not understand. Your life may be in danger!" she cried.

"I have been told that before," he said contemptuously. "It is a common trick of the political game."

"This is no trick," she exclaimed. "I was made to see—to understand—and I swear to you that the danger is real."

"And what if it were? Is the Church to have all the martyrs?" said he gaily. "Come, Fulvia, shake off such fancies. My life is as safe as yours. At worst there may be a little hissing to be faced. That is easy enough compared to facing one's own doubts. And I have no doubts now—that is all past, thank heaven! I see the road straight before me—as straight as when you showed it to me once before, years ago, in the inn-parlour at Peschiera. You pointed the way to it then; surely you would not hold me back from it now?"

He took her in his arms and kissed her lips to silence.

"When we meet tomorrow," he said, releasing her, "It will be as teacher and pupil, you in your doctor's gown and I a learner at your feet. Put your old faith in me into your argument, and we shall have all Pianura converted."

He hastened away through the dim gardens, carrying a boy's heart in his breast.

4.10.

The University of Pianura was lodged in the ancient Signoria or Town Hall of the free city; and here, on the afternoon of the Duke's birthday, the civic dignitaries and the leading men of the learned professions had assembled to see the doctorate conferred on the Signorina Fulvia Vivaldi and on several less conspicuous candidates of the other sex.

The city was again in gala dress. Early that morning the new constitution had been proclaimed, with much firing of cannon and display of official fireworks; but even these great news, and their attendant manifestations, had failed to enliven the populace, who, instead of filling the streets with their usual stir, hung massed at certain points, as though curiously waiting on events. There are few sights more ominous than that of a crowd thus observing itself, watching in inconscient suspense for the unknown crisis which its own passions have engendered.

It was known that his Highness, after the public banquet at the palace, was to proceed in state to the University; and the throng was thick about the palace gates and in the streets betwixt it and the Signoria. Here the square was close-packed, and every window choked with gazers, as the Duke's coach came in sight, escorted meagrely by his equerries and the half-dozen light-horse that preceded him. The small escort, and the marked absence of military display, perhaps disappointed the splendour-loving crowd; and from this cause or another, scarce a cheer was heard as his Highness descended from his coach, and walked up the steps to the porch of ancient carved stone where the faculty awaited him.

The hall was already filled with students and graduates, and with the guests of the University. Through this grave assemblage the Duke passed up to the row of armchairs beneath the dais at the farther end of the room. Trescorre, who was to have attended his Highness, had excused himself on the plea of indisposition, and only a few gentlemen-in-waiting accompanied the Duke; but in the brown half-light of the old Gothic hall their glittering uniforms contrasted brilliantly with the black gowns of the students, and the sober broadcloth of the learned professions. A discreet murmur of enthusiasm rose at their approach, mounting almost to a cheer as the Duke bowed before taking his seat; for the audience represented the class most in sympathy with his policy and most confident of its success.

The meetings of the faculty were held in the great council-chamber where the Rectors of the old free city had assembled; and such a setting was regarded as peculiarly appropriate to the present occasion. The fact was alluded to, with much wealth of historical and mythological analogy, by the President, who opened the ceremonies with a polysyllabic Latin oration, in which the Duke was compared to Apollo, Hercules and Jason, as well as to the flower of sublunary heroes.

This feat of rhetoric over, the candidates were called on to advance and receive their degrees. The men came first, profiting by the momentary advantage of sex, but clearly aware of its inability to confer even momentary importance in the eyes of the impatient audience. A pause followed, and then Fulvia appeared. Against the red-robed faculty at the back of the dais, she stood tall and slender in her black cap and gown. The high windows of painted glass shed a paleness on her face, but her carriage was light and assured as she advanced to the President and knelt to receive her degree. The parchment was placed in her hand, the furred hood laid on her shoulders; then, after another flourish of rhetoric, she was led to the lectern from which her discourse was to be delivered. Odo sat just below her, and as she took her place their eyes met for an instant. He was caught up in the serene exaltation of her look, as though she soared with him above wind and cloud to a region of unshadowed calm; then her eyes fell and she began to speak.

She had a pretty mastery of Latin, and though she had never before spoken in public, her poetical recitations, and the early habit of intercourse with her father's friends, had given her a fair measure of fluency and self-possession. These qualities were raised to eloquence by the sweetness of her voice, and by the grave beauty which made the academic gown seem her natural wear, rather than a travesty of learning. Odo at first had some difficulty in fixing his attention on what she said; and when he controlled his thoughts she was in the height of her panegyric of constitutional liberty. She had begun slowly, almost coldly; but now her theme possessed her. One by one she evoked the familiar formulas with which his mind had once reverberated. They woke no echo in him now; but he saw that she could still set them ringing through the sensibilities of her hearers. As she stood there, a slight impassioned figure, warming to her high argument, his sense of irony was touched by the incongruity of her background. The wall behind her was covered by an ancient fresco, fast fading under its touches of renewed gilding, and representing the patron scholars of the mediaeval world: the theologians, law-givers and logicians under whose protection the free city had placed its budding liberties. There they sat, rigid and sumptuous on their Gothic thrones: Origen, Zeno, David, Lycurgus, Aristotle; listening in a kind of cataleptic helplessness to a confession of faith that scattered their doctrines to the winds. As he looked and listened, a weary sense of the reiterance of things came over him. For what were these ancient manipulators of ideas, prestidigitators of a vanished world of thought, but the forbears of the long line of theorists of whom Fulvia was the last inconscient mouthpiece? The new game was still played with the old counters, the new jugglers repeated the old tricks; and the very words now poured out in defence of the new cause were but mercenaries scarred in the service of its enemies. For generations, for centuries, man had fought on; crying for liberty, dreaming it was won, waking to find himself the slave of the new forces he had generated, burning and being burnt for the same beliefs under different guises, calling his instinct ideas and his ideas revelations; destroying, rebuilding, falling, rising, mending broken weapons, championing extinct illusions, mistaking his failures for achievements and planting his flag on the ramparts as they fell. And as the vision of this inveterate conflict rose before him, Odo saw that the beauty, the power, the immortality, dwelt not in the idea but in the struggle for it.

His resistance yielded as this sense stole over him, and with an almost physical relief he felt himself drawn once more into the familiar current of emotion. Yes, it was better after all to be one of that great unconquerable army, though, like the Trojans fighting for a phantom Helen, they might be doing battle for the shadow of a shade; better to march in their ranks, endure with them, fight with them, fall with them, than to miss the great enveloping sense of brotherhood that turned defeat to victory.

As the conviction grew in him, Fulvia's words regained their lost significance. Through the set mask of language the living thoughts looked forth, old indeed as the world, but renewed with the new life of every heart that bore them. She had left the abstract and dropped to concrete issues: to the gift of the constitution, the benefits and obligations it implied, the new relations it established between ruler and subject and between man and man. Odo saw that she approached the question without flinching. No trace remained of the trembling woman who had clung to him the night before. Her old convictions repossessed her and she soared above human fears.

So engrossed was he that he had been unaware of a growing murmur of sound which seemed to be forcing its way from without through the walls of the ancient building. As Fulvia's oration neared its end the murmur rose to a roar. Startled faces were turned toward the doors of the council-chamber, and one of the Duke's gentlemen left his seat and made his way through the audience. Odo sat motionless, his eyes on Fulvia. He noticed that her face paled as the sound reached her, but there was no break in the voice with which she uttered the closing words of her peroration. As she ended, the noise was momentarily drowned under a loud burst of clapping; but this died in a hush of apprehension through which the outer tumult became more ominously audible. The equerry reentered the hall with a disordered countenance. He hastened to the Duke and addressed him urgently.

"Your Highness," he said, "the crowd has thickened and wears an ugly look. There are many friars abroad, and images of the Mountain Virgin being carried in procession. Will your Highness be pleased to remain here while I summon an escort from the barracks?"

Odo was still watching Fulvia. She had received the applause of the audience with a deep reverence, and was now in the act of withdrawing to the inner room at the back of the dais. Her eyes met Odo's; she smiled and the door closed on her. He turned to the equerry.

"There is no need of an escort," he said. "I trust my people if they do not trust me."

"But, your Highness, the streets are full of demagogues who have been haranguing the people since morning. The crowd is shouting against the constitution and against the Signorina Vivaldi."

A flame of anger passed over the Duke's face; but he subdued it instantly.

"Go to the Signorina Vivaldi," he said, pointing to the door by which Fulvia had left the hall. "Assure her that there is no danger, but ask her to remain where she is till the crowd disperses, and request the faculty in my name to remain with her."

The equerry bowed, and hurried up the steps of the dais, while the Duke signed to his other companions to precede him to the door of the hall. As they walked down the long room, between the close-packed ranks of the audience, the outer tumult surged threateningly toward them. Near the doorway, another of the gentlemen-in-waiting was seen to speak with the Duke.

"Your Highness," he said, "there is a private way at the back by which you may yet leave the building unobserved."

"You appear to forget that I entered it publicly," said Odo.

"But, your Highness, we cannot answer for the consequences—"

The Duke signed to the ushers to throw open the doors. They obeyed, and he stepped out into the stone vestibule preceding the porch. The iron-barred outer doors of this vestibule were securely bolted, and the porter hung back in affright at the order to unlock them.

"Your Highness, the people are raving mad," he said, flinging himself on his knees.

Odo turned impatiently to his escort. "Unbar the doors, gentlemen," he said. The blood was drumming in his ears, but his eye was clear and steady, and he noted with curious detachment the comic agony of the fat porter's face, and the strain and swell of the equerry's muscles as he dragged back the ponderous bolts.

The doors swung open, and the Duke emerged. Below him, still with that unimpaired distinctness of vision which seemed a part of his heightened vitality, he saw a great gesticulating mass of people. They packed the square so closely that their own numbers held them immovable, save for their swaying arms and heads; and those whom the square could not contain had climbed to porticoes, balconies and cornices, and massed themselves in the neck of the adjoining streets. The handful of light-horse who had escorted the Duke's carriage formed a single line at the foot of the steps, so that the approach to the porch was still clear; but it was plain that the crowd, with its next movement, would break through this slender barrier and hem in the Duke.

At Odo's appearance the shouting had ceased and every eye was turned on him. He stood there, a brilliant target, in his laced coat of peach-coloured velvet, his breast covered with orders, a hand on his jewelled sword-hilt. For a moment sovereign and subjects measured each other; and in that moment Odo drank his deepest draught of life. He was not thinking now of the constitution or its opponents. His present business was to get down the steps and into the carriage, returning to the palace as openly as he had come. He was conscious of neither pity nor hatred for the throng in his path. For the moment he regarded them merely as a natural force, to be fought against like storm or flood. His clearest sensation was one of relief at having at last some material obstacle to spend his strength against, instead of the impalpable powers which had so long beset him. He felt, too, a boyish satisfaction at his own steadiness of pulse and eye, at the absence of that fatal inertia which he had come to dread. So clear was his mental horizon that it embraced not only the present crisis, but a dozen incidents leading up to it. He remembered that Trescorre had urged him to take a larger escort, and that he had refused on the ground that any military display might imply a doubt of his people. He was glad now that he had done so. He would have hated to slink to his carriage behind a barrier of drawn swords. He wanted no help to see him through this business. The blood sang in his veins at the thought of facing it alone.

The silence lasted but a moment; then an image of the Mountain Virgin was suddenly thrust in air, and a voice cried out: "Down with our Lady's enemies! We want no laws against the friars!"

A howl caught up the words and tossed them to and fro above the seething heads. Images of the Virgin, religious banners, the blue-and-white of the Madonna's colours, suddenly canopied the crowd.

"We want the Barnabites back!" sang out another voice.

"Down with the free-thinkers!" yelled a hundred angry throats.

A stone or two sped through the air and struck the sculptures of the porch.

"Your Highness!" cried the equerry who stood nearest, and would have snatched the Duke back within doors.

For all answer, Odo stepped clear of the porch and advanced to the edge of the steps. As he did so, a shower of missiles hummed about him, and a stone struck him on the lip. The blood rushed to his head, and he swayed in the sudden grip of anger; but he mastered himself and raised his lace handkerchief to the cut.

His gentlemen had drawn their swords; but he signed to them to sheathe again. His first thought was that he must somehow make the people hear him. He lifted his hand and advanced a step; but as he did so a shot rang out, followed by a loud cry. The lieutenant of the light-horse, infuriated by the insult to his master, had drawn the pistol from his holster and fired blindly into the crowd. His bullet had found a mark, and the throng hissed and seethed about the spot where a man had fallen. At the same instant Odo was aware of a commotion in the group behind him, and with a great plunge of the heart he saw Fulvia at his side. She still wore the academic dress, and her black gown detached itself sharply against the bright colours of the ducal uniforms.

Groans and hisses received her, but the mob hung back, as though her look had checked them. Then a voice shrieked out: "Down with the atheist! We want no foreign witches!" and another caught it up with the yell: "She poisoned the weaver's boy! Her father was hanged for murdering Christian children!"

The cry set the crowd in motion again, and it rolled toward the line of mounted soldiers at the foot of the steps. The men had their hands on their holsters; but the Duke's call rang out: "No firing!" and drawing their blades, they sat motionless to receive the shock.

It came, dashed against them and dispersed them. Only a few yards lay now between the people and their sovereign. But at that moment another shot was fired. This time it came from the thick of the crowd. The equerries' swords leapt forth again, and they closed around the Duke and Fulvia.

"Save yourself, sir! Back into the building!" one of the gentlemen shouted; but Odo had no eyes for what was coming. For as the shot was heard he had seen a change in Fulvia. A moment they had stood together, smiling, undaunted, hands locked and wedded eyes, then he felt her dissolve against him and drop between his arms.

A cry had gone out that the Duke was wounded, and a leaden silence fell on the crowd. In that silence Odo knelt, lifting Fulvia's head to his breast. No wound showed through her black gown. She lay as though smitten by some invisible hand. So deep was the hush that her least whisper must have reached him; but though he bent close no whisper came. The invisible hand had struck the very source of life; and to these two, in their moment of final reunion, with so much unsaid between them that now at last they longed to say, there was left only the dumb communion of fast-clouding eyes...

A clatter of cavalry was heard down the streets that led to the square. The equerry sent to warn Fulvia had escaped from the back of the building and hastened to the barracks to summon a regiment. But the soldiery were no longer needed. The blind fury of the mob had died of its own excess. The rumour that the Duke was hurt brought a chill reaction of dismay, and the rioters were already scattering when the cavalry came in sight. Their approach turned the slow dispersal to a stampede. A few arrests were made, the remaining groups were charged by the soldiers, and presently the square lay bare as a storm-swept plain, though the people still hung on its outskirts, ready to disband at the first threat of the troops.

It was on this solitude that the Duke looked out as he regained a sense of his surroundings. Fulvia had been carried into the audience-chamber and laid on the dais, her head resting on the velvet cushions of the ducal chair. She had died instantly, shot through the heart, and the surgeons summoned in haste had soon ceased from their ineffectual efforts. For a long time Odo knelt beside her, unconscious of all but that one wild moment when life at its highest had been dashed into the gulf of death. Thought had ceased, and neither rage nor grief moved as yet across the chaos of his being. All his life was in his eyes, as they drew up, drop by drop, the precious essence of her loveliness. For she had grown, beneath the simplifying hand of death, strangely yet most humanly beautiful. Life had fallen from her like the husk from the flower, and she wore the face of her first hopes. The transition had been too swift for any backward look, any anguished rending of the fibres, and he felt himself, not detached by the stroke, but caught up with her into some great calm within the heart of change.

He knew not how he found himself once more on the steps above the square. Below him his state carriage stood in the same place, flanked by the regiment of cavalry. Down the narrow streets he saw the brooding cloud of people, and the sight roused his blood. They were his enemies now—he felt the warm hate in his veins. They were his enemies, and he would face them openly. No closed chariot guarded by troops—he would not have so much as a pane of glass between himself and his subjects. He descended the steps, bade the colonel of the regiment dismount, and sprang into his saddle. Then, at the head of his soldiers, at a foot-pace, he rode back through the packed streets to the palace.

In the palace, courtyard and vestibule were thronged with courtiers and lacqueys. He walked through them with his head high, the cut on his lip like the mark of a hot iron in the dead whiteness of his face. At the head of the great staircase Maria Clementina waited. She sprang forward, distraught and trembling, her face as blanched as his.

"You are safe—you are safe—you are not hurt—" she stammered, catching at his hands.

A shudder seized him as he put her aside.

"Odo! Odo!" she cried passionately, and made as though to bar his way.

He gave her a blind look and passed on down the long gallery to his closet.

4.11.

The joy of reprisals lasted no longer than a summer storm. To hurt, to silence, to destroy, was too easy to be satisfying. The passions of his ancestors burned low in Odo's breast: though he felt Bracciaforte's fury in his veins he could taste no answering gratification of revenge. And the spirit on which he would have spent his hatred was not here or there, as an embodied faction, but everywhere as an intangible influence. The acqua tofana of his enemies had pervaded every fibre of the state.

The mist of anguish lifted, he saw himself alone among ruins. For a moment Fulvia's glowing faith had hung between him and a final vision of the truth; and as his convictions weakened he had replaced them with an immense pity, an all-sufficing hope. Sentimental verbiage: he saw it clearly now. He had been the dupe of the old word-jugglery which was forever confounding fact and fancy in men's minds. For it was essentially an age of words: the world was drunk with them, as it had once been drunk with action; and the former was the deadlier drug of the two. He looked about him languidly, letting the facts of life filter slowly through his faculties. The sources of energy were so benumbed in him that he felt like a man whom long disease had reduced to helplessness and who must laboriously begin his bodily education again. Hate was the only passion which survived, and that was but a deaf intransitive emotion coiled in his nature's depths.

Sickness at last brought its obliteration. He sank into gulfs of weakness and oblivion, and when the rise of the tide floated him back to life, it was to a life as faint and colourless as infancy. Colourless too were the boundaries on which he looked out: the narrow enclosure of white walls, opening on a slit of pale spring landscape. His hands lay before him, white and helpless on the white coverlet of his bed. He raised his eyes and saw de Crucis at his side. Then he began to remember. There had been preceding intervals of consciousness, and in one of them, in answer perhaps to some vaguely-uttered wish for light and air, he had been carried out of the palace and the city to the Benedictine monastery on its wooded knoll beyond the Piana. Then the veil had dropped again, and his spirit had wandered in a dim place of shades. There was a faint sweetness in coming back at last to familiar sights and sounds. They no longer hurt like pressure on an aching nerve: they seemed rather, now, the touch of a reassuring hand.

As the contact with life became closer and more sustained he began to watch himself curiously, wondering what instincts and habits of thought would survive his long mental death. It was with a bitter, almost pitiable disappointment that he found the old man growing again in him. Life, with a mocking hand, brought him the cast-off vesture of his past, and he felt himself gradually compressed again into the old passions and prejudices. Yet he wore them with a difference—they were a cramping garment rather than a living sheath. He had brought back from his lonely voyagings a sense of estrangement deeper than any surface-affinity with things.

As his physical strength returned, and he was able to leave his room and walk through the long corridors to the outer air, he felt the old spell which the life of Monte Cassino had cast on him. The quiet garden, with its clumps of box and lavender between paths converging to the statue of Saint Benedict; the cloisters paved with the monks' nameless graves; the traces of devotional painting left here and there on the weather-beaten walls, like fragments of prayer in a world-worn mind: these formed a circle of tranquillising influences in which he could gradually reacquire the habit of living.

He had never deceived himself as to the cause of the riots. He knew from Gamba and Andreoni that the liberals and the court, for once working in unison, had provoked the blind outburst of fanaticism which a rasher judgment might have ascribed to the clergy. The Dominicans, bigoted and eager for power, had been ready enough to serve such an end, and some of the begging orders had furnished the necessary points of contact with the people; but the movement was at bottom purely political, and represented the resistance of the privileged classes to any attack on their inherited rights.

As such, he could no longer regard it as completely unreasonable. He was beginning to feel the social and political significance of those old restrictions and barriers against which his early zeal had tilted. Certainly in the ideal state the rights and obligations of the different classes would be more evenly adjusted. But the ideal state was a figment of the brain. The real one, as Crescenti had long ago pointed out, was the gradual and heterogeneous product of remote social conditions, wherein every seeming inconsistency had its roots in some bygone need, and the character of each class, with its special passions, ignorances and prejudices, was the sum total of influences so ingrown and inveterate that they had become a law of thought. All this, however, seemed rather matter for philosophic musing than for definite action. His predominant feeling was still that of remoteness from the immediate issues of life: the soeva indignatio had been succeeded by a great calm.

The soothing influences of the monastic life had doubtless helped to tide him over the stormy passage of returning consciousness. His sensitiveness to these influences inclined him for the first time to consider them analytically. Hitherto he had regarded the Church as a skilfully-adjusted engine, the product of human passions scientifically combined to obtain the greatest sum of tangible results. Now he saw that he had never penetrated beneath the surface. For the Church which grasped, contrived, calculated, struggled for temporal possessions and used material weapons against spiritual foes—this outer Church was nothing more than the body, which, like any other animal body, had to care for its own gross needs, nourish, clothe, defend itself, fight for a footing among the material resistances of life—while the soul, the inner animating principle, might dwell aloof from all these things, in a clear medium of its own.

To this soul of the Church his daily life now brought him close. He felt it in the ordered beneficence of the great community, in the simplicity of its external life and the richness and suavity of its inner relations. No alliance based on material interests, no love of power working toward a common end, could have created that harmony of thought and act which was reflected in every face about him. Each of these men seemed to have FOUND OUT SOMETHING of which he was still ignorant.

What it was, de Crucis tried to tell him as they paced the cloisters together or sat in the warm stillness of the budding garden. At the first news of the Duke's illness the Jesuit had hastened to Pianura. No companionship could have been so satisfying to Odo. De Crucis's mental attitude toward mankind might have been defined as an illuminated charity. To love men, or to understand them, is not as unusual as to do both together; and it was the intellectual acuteness of his friend's judgments that made their Christian amenity so seductive to Odo.

"The highest claim of Christianity," the Jesuit said one morning, as they sat on a worn stone bench at the end of the sunny vine-walk, "is that it has come nearer to solving the problem of men's relations to each other than any system invented by themselves. This, after all, is the secret principle of the Church's vitality. She gave a spiritual charter of equality to mankind long before the philosophers thought of giving them a material one. If, all the while, she has been fighting for dominion, arrogating to herself special privileges, struggling to preserve the old lines of social and legal demarcation, it has been because for nigh two thousand years she has cherished in her breast the one free city of the spirit, because to guard its liberties she has had to defend and strengthen her own position. I do not ask you to consider whence comes this insight into the needs of man, this mysterious power over him; I ask you simply to confess them in their results. I am not of those who believe that God permits good to come to mankind through one channel only, and I doubt not that now and in times past the thinkers whom your Highness follows have done much to raise the condition of their fellows; but I would have you observe that, where they have done so, it has been because, at bottom, their aims coincided with the Church's. The deeper you probe into her secret sources of power, the more you find there, in the germ if you will, but still potentially active, all those humanising energies which work together for the lifting of the race. In her wisdom and her patience she may have seen fit to withhold their expression, to let them seek another outlet; but they are there, stored in her consciousness like the archetypes of the Platonists in the Universal Mind. It is the knowledge of this, the sure knowledge of it, which creates the atmosphere of serenity that you feel about you. From the tilling of the vineyards, or the dressing of a beggar's sores, to the loftiest and most complicated intellectual labour imposed on him, each brother knows that his daily task is part of a great scheme of action, working ever from imperfection to perfection, from human incompleteness to the divine completion. This sense of being, not straws on a blind wind of chance, but units in an ordered force, gives to the humblest Christian an individual security and dignity which kings on their thrones might envy.

"But not only does the Church anticipate every tendency of mankind; alone of all powers she knows how to control and direct the passions she excites. This it is which makes her an auxiliary that no temporal prince can well despise. It is in this aspect that I would have your Highness consider her. Do not underrate her power because it seems based on the commoner instincts rather than on the higher faculties of man. That is one of the sources of her strength. She can support her claims by reason and argument, but it is because her work, like that of her divine Founder, lies chiefly among those who can neither reason nor argue, that she chooses to rest her appeal on the simplest and most universal emotions. As, in our towns, the streets are lit mainly by the tapers before the shrines of the saints, so the way of life would be dark to the great multitude of men but for the light of faith burning within them..."

Meanwhile the shufflings of destiny had brought to Trescorre the prize for which he waited. During the Duke's illness he had been appointed regent of

Pianura, and his sovereign's reluctance to take up the cares of government had now left him for six months in authority. The day after the proclaiming of the constitution Odo had withdrawn his signature from it, on the ground that the concessions it contained were inopportune. The functions of government went on again in the old way. The old abuses persisted, the old offences were condoned: it was as though the apathy of the sovereign had been communicated to his people. Centuries of submission were in their blood, and for two generations there had been no warfare south of the Alps.

For the moment men's minds were turned to the great events going forward in France. It had not yet occurred to the Italians that the recoil of these events might be felt among themselves. They were simply amused spectators, roused at last to the significance of the show, but never dreaming that they might soon be called from the wings to the footlights. To de Crucis, however, the possibility of such a call was already present, and it was he who pressed the Duke to return to his post. A deep reluctance held Odo back. He would have liked to linger on in the monastery, leading the tranquil yet busy life of the monks, and trying to read the baffling riddle of its completeness. At that moment it seemed to him of vastly more importance to discover the exact nature of the soul—whether it was in fact a metaphysical entity, as these men believed, or a mere secretion of the brain, as he had been taught to think— than to go back and govern his people. For what mattered the rest, if he had been mistaken about the soul?

With a start he realised that he was going as his cousin had gone—that this was but another form of the fatal lethargy that hung upon his race. An effort of the will drew him back to Pianura, and made him resume the semblance of authority; but it carried him no farther. Trescorre ostensibly became prime minister, and in reality remained the head of the state. The Duke was present at the cabinet meetings but took no part in the direction of affairs. His mind was lost in a maze of metaphysical speculations; and even these served him merely as some cunningly-contrived toy with which to trick his leisure.

His revocation of the charter had necessarily separated him from Gamba and the advanced liberals. He knew that the hunchback, ever scornful of expediency, charged him with disloyalty to the people; but such charges could no longer wound. The events following the Duke's birthday had served to crystallise the schemes of the little liberal group, and they now formed a campaign of active opposition to the government, attacking it by means of pamphlets and lampoons, and by such public speaking as the police allowed. The new professors of the University, ardently in sympathy with the constitutional movement, used their lectures as means of political teaching, and the old stronghold of dogma became the centre of destructive criticism. But as yet these ideas formed but a single live point in the general numbness.

Two years passed in this way. North of the Alps, all Europe was convulsed, while Italy was still but a sleeper who tosses in his sleep. In the two Sicilies, the arrogance and perfidy of the government gave a few martyrs to the cause, and in Bologna there was a brief revolutionary outbreak; but for the most part the Italian states were sinking into inanition. Venice, by recalling her fleet from Greece, let fall the dominion of the sea. Twenty years earlier Genoa had basely yielded Corsica to France. The Pope condemned the French for their outrages on religion, and his subjects murdered Basseville, the agent of the new republic. The sympathies and impulses of the various states were as contradictory as they were ineffectual.

Meanwhile, in France, Europe was trying to solve at a stroke the problems of a thousand years. All the repressed passions which civilisation had sought, however imperfectly, to curb, stalked abroad destructive as flood and fire. The great generation of the Encyclopaedists had passed away, and the teachings of Rousseau had prevailed over those of Montesquieu and Voltaire. The sober sense of the economists was swept aside by the sound and fury of the demagogues, and France was become a very Babel of tongues. The old malady of words had swept over the world like a pestilence.

To the little Italian courts, still dozing in fancied security under the wing of Bourbon and Hapsburg suzerains, these rumours were borne by the wild flight of emigres—dead leaves loosened by the first blast of the storm. Month by month they poured across the Alps in ever-increasing numbers, bringing confused contradictory tales of anarchy and outrage. Among those whom chance thus carried to Pianura were certain familiars of the Duke's earlier life—the Count Alfieri and his royal mistress, flying from Paris, and arriving breathless with the tale of their private injuries. To the poet of revolt this sudden realisation of his doctrines seemed in fact a purely personal outrage. It was as though a man writing an epic poem on an earthquake should suddenly find himself engulphed. To Alfieri the downfall of the French monarchy and the triumph of democratic ideas meant simply that his French investments had shrunk to nothing, and that he, the greatest poet of the age, had been obliged, at an immense sacrifice of personal dignity, to plead with a drunken mob for leave to escape from Paris. To the wider aspect of the "tragic farce," as he called it, his eyes remained obstinately closed. He viewed the whole revolutionary movement as a conspiracy against his comfort, and boasted that during his enforced residence in France he had not so much as exchanged a word with one of the "French slaves, instigators of false liberty," who, by trying to put into action the principles taught in his previous works, had so grievously interfered with the composition of fresh masterpieces.

The royal pretensions of the Countess of Albany—pretensions affirmed rather than abated as the tide of revolution rose—made it impossible that she should be received at the court of Pianura; but the Duke found a mild entertainment in Alfieri's company. The poet's revulsion of feeling seemed to Odo like the ironic laughter of the fates. His thoughts returned to the midnight meetings of the Honey Bees, and to the first vision of that face which men had lain down their lives to see. Men had looked on that face since then, and its horror was reflected in their own.

Other fugitives to Pianura brought another impression of events—that comic note which life, the supreme dramatic artist, never omits from her tragedies. These were the Duke's old friend the Marquis de Coeur-Volant, fleeing from his chateau as the peasants put the torch to it, and arriving in Pianura destitute, gouty and middle-aged, but imperturbable and epigrammatic as ever. With him came his Marquise, a dark-eyed lady, stout to unwieldiness and much given to devotion, in whom it was whispered (though he introduced her as the daughter of a Venetian Senator) that a reminiscent eye might still detect the outline of the gracefullest Columbine who had ever flitted across the Italian stage. These visitors were lodged by the Duke's kindness in the Palazzo Cerveno, near the ducal residence; and though the ladies of Pianura were inclined to look askance on the Marquise's genealogy, yet his Highness's condescension, and her own edifying piety, had soon allayed these scruples, and the salon of Madame de Coeur-Volant became the rival of Madame d'Albany's.

It was, in fact, the more entertaining of the two; for, in spite of his lady's austere views, the Marquis retained that gift of social flexibility that was already becoming the tradition of a happier day. To the Marquis, indeed, the revolution was execrable not so much because of the hardships it inflicted, as because it was the forerunner of social dissolution—the breaking-up of the regime which had made manners the highest morality, and conversation the chief end of man. He could have lived gaily on a crust in good company and amid smiling faces; but the social deficiencies of Pianura were more difficult to endure than any material privation. In Italy, as the Marquis had more than once remarked, people loved, gambled, wrote poetry, and patronised the arts; but, alas, they did not converse. Coeur-Volant could not conceal from his Highness that there was no conversation in Pianura; but he did his best to fill the void by the constant exercise of his own gift in that direction, and to Odo at least his talk seemed as good as it was copious. Misfortune had given a finer savour to the Marquis's philosophy, and there was a kind of heroic grace in his undisturbed cultivation of the amenities.

While the Marquis was struggling to preserve the conversational art, and Alfieri planning the savage revenge of the Misogallo, the course of affairs in France had gained a wilder impetus. The abolition of the nobility, the flight and capture of the King, his enforced declaration of war against Austria, the massacres of Avignon, the sack of the Tuileries—such events seemed incredible enough till the next had crowded them out of mind. The new year rose in blood and mounted to a bloodier noon. All the old defences were falling. Religion, monarchy, law, were sucked down into the whirlpool of liberated passions. Across that sanguinary scene passed, like a mocking ghost, the philosophers' vision of the perfectibility of man. Man was free at last—freer than his would-be liberators had ever dreamed of making him—and he used his freedom like a beast. For the multitude had risen—that multitude which no man could number, which even the demagogues who ranted in its name had never seriously reckoned with—that dim, grovelling indistinguishable mass on which the whole social structure rested. It was as though the very soil moved, rising in mountains or yawning in chasms about the feet of those who had so long securely battened on it. The earth shook, the sun and moon were darkened, and the people, the terrible unknown people, had put in the sickle to the harvest.

Italy roused herself at last. The emissaries of the new France were swarming across the Alps, pervading the peninsula as the Jesuits had once pervaded Europe; and in the mind of a young general of the republican army visions of Italian conquest were already forming. In Pianura the revolutionary agents found a strong republican party headed by Gamba and his friends, and a government weakened by debt and dissensions. The air was thick with intrigue. The little army could no longer be counted on, and a prolonged bread-riot had driven Trescorre out of the ministry and compelled the Duke to appoint Andreoni in his place. Behind Andreoni stood Gamba and the radicals. There could be no doubt which way the fortunes of the duchy tended. The Duke's would-be protectors, Austria and the Holy See, were too busy organising the hasty coalition of the powers to come to his aid, had he cared to call on them. But to do so would have been but another way of annihilation. To preserve the individuality of his state, or to merge it in the vision of a United Italy, seemed to him the only alternatives worth fighting for. The former was a futile dream, the latter seemed for a brief moment possible. Piedmont, ever loyal to the monarchical principle, was calling on her sister states to arm themselves against the French invasion. But the response was reluctant and uncertain. Private ambitions and petty jealousies hampered every attempt at union. Austria, the Bourbons and the Holy See held the Italian principalities in a network of conflicting interests and obligations that rendered free action impossible. Sadly Victor Amadeus armed himself alone against the enemy.

Under such conditions Odo could do little to direct the course of events. They had passed into more powerful hands than his. But he could at least declare himself for or against the mighty impulse which was behind them. The ideas he had striven for had triumphed at last, and his surest hold on authority was to share openly in their triumph. A profound horror dragged him back. The new principles were not those for which he had striven. The goddess of the new worship was but a bloody Maenad who had borrowed the attributes of freedom. He could not bow the knee in such a charnel-house. Tranquilly, resolutely, he took up the policy of repression. He knew the attempt was foredoomed to failure, but that made no difference now: he was simply acting out the inevitable.

The last act came with unexpected suddenness. The Duke woke one morning to find the citadel in the possession of the people. The impregnable stronghold of Bracciaforte was in the hands of the serfs whose fathers had toiled to build it, and the last descendant of Bracciaforte was virtually a prisoner in his palace. The revolution took place quietly, without violence or bloodshed. Andreoni waited on the Duke, and a cabinet-council was summoned. The ministers affected to have yielded reluctantly to popular pressure. All they asked was a constitution and the assurance that no resistance would be offered to the French.

The Duke requested a few hours for deliberation. Left alone, he summoned the Duchess's chamberlain. The ducal pair no longer met save on occasions of state: they had not exchanged a word since the death of Fulvia Vivaldi. Odo sent word to her Highness that he could no longer answer for her security while she remained in the duchy, and that he begged her to leave immediately for Vienna. She replied that she was obliged for his warning, but that while he remained in Pianura her place was at his side. It was the answer he had expected—he had never doubted her courage—but it was essential to his course that she should leave the duchy without delay, and after a moment's reflection he wrote a letter in which he informed her that he must insist on her obedience. No answer was returned, but he learned that she had turned white, and tearing the letter in shreds had called for her travelling-carriage within the hour. He sent to enquire when he might take leave of her, but she excused herself on the plea of indisposition, and before nightfall he heard the departing rattle of her wheels.

He immediately summoned Andreoni and announced his unconditional refusal of the terms proposed to him. He would not give a constitution or promise allegiance to the French. The minister withdrew, and Odo was left alone. He had dismissed his gentlemen, and as he sat in his closet a sense of deathlike isolation came over him. Never had the palace seemed so silent or so vast. He had not a friend to turn to. De Crucis was in Germany, and Trescorre, it was reported, had privately attended the Duchess in her flight. The waves of destiny seemed closing over Odo, and the circumstances of his past rose, poignant and vivid, before his drowning sight.

And suddenly, in that moment of failure and abandonment, it seemed to him again that life was worth the living. His indifference fell from him like a garment. The old passion of action awoke and he felt a new warmth in his breast. After all, the struggle was not yet over: though Piedmont had called in vain on the Italian states, an Italian sword might still be drawn in her service. If his people would not follow him against France he could still march against her alone. Old memories hummed in him at the thought. He recalled how his Piedmontese ancestors had gone forth against the same foe, and the stout Donnaz blood began to bubble in his veins.

A knock roused him and Gamba entered by the private way. His appearance was not unexpected to Odo, and served only to reinforce his new-found energy. He felt that the issue was at hand. As he expected, Gamba had been sent to put before him more forcibly and unceremoniously the veiled threat of the ministers. But the hunchback had come also to plead with his master in his own name, and in the name of the ideas for which they had once laboured together. He could not believe that the Duke's reaction was more than momentary. He could not calculate the strength of the old associations which, now that the tide had set the other way, were dragging Odo back to the beliefs and traditions of his caste.

The Duke listened in silence; then he said: "Discussion is idle. I have no answer to give but that which I have already given." He rose from his seat in token of dismissal.

The moment was painful to both men. Gamba drew nearer and fell at the Duke's feet.

"Your Highness," he said, "consider what this means. We hold the state in our hands. If you are against us you are powerless. If you are with us we can promise you more power than you ever dreamed of possessing."

The Duke looked at him with a musing smile. "It is as though you offered me gold in a desert island," he said. "Do not waste such poor bribes on me. I care for no power but the power to wipe out the work of these last years. Failing that, I want nothing that you or any other man can give."

Gamba was silent a moment. He turned aside into the embrasure of the window, and when he spoke again it was in a voice broken with grief.

"Your Highness," he said, "if your choice is made, ours is made also. It is a hard choice, but these are fratricidal hours. We have come to the parting of the ways."

The Duke made no sign, and Gamba went on with gathering anguish: "We would have gone to the world's end with your Highness for our leader!"

"With a leader whom you could lead," Odo interposed. He went up to Gamba and laid a hand on his shoulder. "Speak out, man," he said. "Say what you were sent to say. Am I a prisoner?"

The hunchback burst into tears. Odo, with his arms crossed, stood leaning against the window. The other's anguish seemed to deepen his detachment.

"Your Highness—your Highness—" Gamba stammered.

The Duke made an impatient gesture. "Come, make an end," he said.

Gamba fell back with a profound bow.

"We do not ask the surrender of your Highness's person," he said.

"Not even that?" Odo returned with a faint sneer.

Gamba flushed to the temples, but the retort died on his lips.

"Your Highness," he said, scarce above a whisper, "the gates are guarded; but the word for tonight is 'Humilitas.'" He knelt and kissed Odo's hand. Then he rose and passed out of the room...

Before dawn the Duke left the palace. The high emotions of the night had ebbed. He saw himself now, in the ironic light of morning, as a fugitive too harmless to be worth pursuing. His enemies had let him keep his sword because they had no cause to fear it. Alone he passed through the gardens of the palace, and out into the desert darkness of the streets. Skirting the wall of the Benedictine convent where Fulvia had lodged, he gained a street leading to the marketplace. In the pallor of the waning night the ancient monuments of his race stood up mournful and deserted as a line of tombs. The city seemed a grave-yard and he the ineffectual ghost of its dead past. He reached the gates and gave the watchword. The gates were guarded, as he had been advised; but the captain of the watch let him pass without show of hesitation or curiosity. Though he made no effort at disguise he went forth unrecognised, and the city closed her doors on him as carelessly as on any passing wanderer.

Beyond the gates a lad from the ducal stables waited with a horse. Odo sprang into the saddle and rode on toward Pontesordo. The darkness was growing thinner, and the meagre details of the landscape, with its huddled farm-houses and mulberry-orchards, began to define themselves as he advanced. To his left the field stretched, grey and sodden; ahead, on his right, hung the dark woods of the ducal chase. Presently a bend of the road brought him within sight of the keep of Pontesordo. His way led past it, toward Valsecca; but some obscure instinct laid a detaining hand on him, and at the cross-roads he bent to the right and rode across the marshland to the old manor-house.

The farmyard lay hushed and deserted. The peasants who lived there would soon be afoot; but for the moment Odo had the place to himself. He tethered his horse to a gate-post and walked across the rough cobble-stones to the chapel. Its floor was still heaped with farm-tools and dried vegetables, and in the dimness a heavier veil of dust seemed to obscure the painted walls. Odo advanced, picking his way among broken ploughshares and stacks of maize, till he stood near the old marble altar, with its sea-gods and acanthus volutes. The place laid its tranquillising hush on him, and he knelt on the step beneath the altar. Something stirred in him as he knelt there—a prayer, yet not a prayer—a reaching out, obscure and inarticulate, toward all that had survived of his early hopes and faiths, a loosening of old founts of pity, a longing to be somehow, somewhere reunited to his old belief in life.

How long he knelt he knew not; but when he looked up the chapel was full of a pale light, and in the first shaft of the sunrise the face of Saint Francis shone out on him...He went forth into the daybreak and rode away toward Piedmont.

Milton Keynes UK
Ingram Content Group UK Ltd.
UKHW040832071024
449371UK00007B/749

9 789362 095299